A
History
of
the
Wife

Also by Marilyn Yalom

A History of the Breast

Blood Sisters: The French Revolution in Women's Memory

Maternity, Mortality and the Literature of Madness

Le Temps des Oranges: Aristocrates, Bourgeoises, et Paysannes Racontent

A
History
of
the
Wife

Marilyn Yalom

HarperCollins*Publishers*

HarperCollins books may be purchased for educational, business, or sales promotional use. For information please write: Special Markets Department, HarperCollins Publishers Inc., 10 East 53rd Street, New York, NY 10022.

FIRST EDITION
Designed by Joseph Rutt

Library of Congress Cataloging-in-Publication Data

Yalom, Marilyn.
    A history of the wife / Marilyn Yalom.
        p. cm.
    ISBN 0-06-019338-7
    1. Married women—History. 2. Housewives—History. 3. Marriage—History. 4. Women—History. I. Title.

HQ1206.Y35 2001
306.872—dc21

                                                            00-058153

00 01 02 03 04 QW/F 10 9 8 7 6 5 4 3 2 1

For my girlfriends—all wives, at one time or another.
Carole, Cathy, Cynthia, Diane, Helen, Jean, Lia, Margi, Mary,
Minerva, Myra, Phyllis, Stina, Sue B., Sue G., Vida

CONTENTS

ACKNOWLEDGMENTS
ix

INTRODUCTION
Is the Wife an Endangered Species?
xi

ONE
Wives in the Ancient World: Biblical, Greek, and Roman Models
1

TWO
Wives in Medieval Europe, 1100–1500
45

THREE
Protestant Wives in Germany, England, and America, 1500–1700
97

FOUR
Republican Wives in America and France
146

FIVE
Victorian Wives on Both Sides of the Atlantic
175

SIX

Victorian Wives on the American Frontier

226

SEVEN

The Woman Question and the New Woman

263

EIGHT

Sex, Contraception, and Abortion in the United States, 1840–1940

294

NINE

Wives, War, and Work, 1940–1950

317

TEN

Toward the New Wife, 1950–2000

352

NOTES

401

CREDITS AND PERMISSIONS

427

INDEX

431

ACKNOWLEDGMENTS

This book could not have been written without the scholarship of hundreds, perhaps thousands, of individuals working in the fields of women's history and family history. The numerous works I cite in the endnotes represent only a part of the vast primary and secondary literature from which I have constructed *A History of the Wife*. Fellow and sister travelers, named and unnamed, I salute you all!

Many colleagues known to me personally have contributed mightily to this book. First and foremost, I wish to thank the scholars and staff at the Stanford Institute for Research on Women and Gender, my intellectual home for the past quarter century. Among them, I have depended heavily on the critical reading of Senior Scholar Susan Groag Bell and the unflagging support of Professor Laura Carstensen, the current Institute Director. Senior Scholars Edith Gelles and Karen Offen also offered substantial comments on the manuscript, especially on chapter 4.

Various Stanford faculty members have given me valuable advice: Professor Barbara Gelpi of the English department, Professor Jean-Marie Apostolides of the French department, and Professors Keith Baker, Aaron Rodrigue, and Paul Seaver of the History department. A special word of thanks to Myra Strober, Professor of Education, for her contributions to the last chapter and her influential presence in my professional life.

Professor Shulamith Magnus of Oberlin College provided useful comments on the biblical material and Emeritus Professor Ira Lapidus of the University of California/Berkeley, enlightened me on Muslim practices. Professor Monique Canto-Sperber, the French translator of Plato, was a critical reader of the Greco-Roman section. Professor

Samuel Rosenberg of the University of Indiana commented generously on the medieval chapter. Professor William Tuttle of the University of Kansas was similarly helpful concerning World War II. Cynthia Fuchs Epstein, Distinguished Professor of Sociology at the Graduate Center, CUNY, encouraged me from the start and provided insightful observations along the way. Novelist Beth Gutcheon added considerably to my knowledge of nineteenth-century quilt making.

Margaret Pirnie and Kate Bedford were indefatigable research assistants. I benefited from their strong arms carrying piles of books to and from the library, and from their youthful reactions to the oddities of marriage throughout the ages.

I am grateful to Basic Books editor Joanne Miller, whom I have known for many years, for suggesting that I focus on the wife, rather than on the couple, as originally intended. My literary agent and friend, Sandra Dijkstra, never faltered in her enthusiasm for this project and procured good American and British publishers. Joelle Delbourgo generously supported this book during her tenure at HarperCollins, and Julia Serebrinsky magnificently carried the editorial process to completion.

As always, I counted on my husband, Irvin Yalom, Emeritus Professor of the Stanford psychiatry department, for a close reading of the text and spirited discussions when we disagreed. Married to him for forty-six years, I have come to know the plethora of meanings hidden in the little word "wife."

INTRODUCTION

Is the Wife an Endangered Species?

DEAR ABBY: I have been engaged to a wonderful man for more than two years and cannot seem to set a wedding date. He loves me and my 9-year-old daughter. He does all of the laundry, the dishes and the cleaning, and he accepts my daughter as his own. He works two jobs so we don't go without anything.

Sounds perfect, right?

The problem is, I don't think I love him. I say that I do, but I don't feel it. He is all a woman could ask for in a husband, but is that enough to replace love? Or have I read too many romance novels?

He wants to get married as soon as possible. I am 29, have never been married and I feel my daughter needs a father. I am also afraid I won't find a man who will ever love me as much as he does.

Can I find a man whom I love, who accepts my daughter as his own—or should I marry a man I don't love but who would be a wonderful husband and father?

FOR BETTER OR WORSE

DEAR FOR BETTER: If you marry this man, knowing in your heart that you do not love him, you will be doing yourself and him a great disservice. Marriage is supposed to last forever. And forever is a long time to live with yourself, feeling that you sold out because you were afraid you wouldn't find a man you can love. Let him go.

July 3, 1998, *San Francisco Chronicle*

*F*or most of human history, such a letter could not have been written. Not only were most women unable to write, but most had little say in the choice of their husbands. If they had sexual relations outside of marriage and especially if they had a child out of wedlock, they would have been disgraced, and even executed in some societies. In early Puritan America, those judged guilty of "fornication"—sexual acts between persons not married to each other—were usually fined and publicly whipped. The stigma surrounding the unwed mother was so severe that she did everything possible, including infanticide, to keep the newborn hidden. If a single mother could not bear the thought of being parted from her baby, the only socially acceptable response was to find a husband.

Today, a single mother no longer faces the public censure of the past. She can, like the mother in this letter, reject the offer of a man eager to marry her. It is not enough for him to love her, accept a child who is not his own, work two jobs to support them, and do the laundry, dishes, and cleaning. The author of the letter is holding out for something more—she wants to find a man *she* can love. And in this decision, she is supported by that popular moral arbiter, Abigail Van Buren.

Do you believe that Dear Abby gave the woman good advice? Should this mother leave a man who has taken on the roles of partner, provider, and de facto father? Is Abby correct in believing that reciprocal romantic love is the only basis for a lasting marriage?

This letter tells us a great deal about women's attitudes toward marriage at the present moment. It tells us that the single mother, no longer forced to wed, wants to be able to marry in the name of *love*—that intoxicating mix of sex and sentiment that most adults have experienced and no one can define. Once upon a time, women married for other reasons: for economic support, to cement family alliances, to have children, to counter loneliness, to be like all the other women. Once upon a time, women wore the title "wife" like a badge of honor. To be a parson's wife, a baker's wife, a doctor's wife told the world loudly and clearly that one had fulfilled one's "natural" destiny. It spoke for legitimacy and protection in a world that was proverbially unkind to spinsters. Whether one was happily married or not, the wedding ring, in and of itself, was a measure of female worth.

Today, the word "wife" does not convey the same unambiguous message. It no longer implies, as it once did in middle- and upper-class homes, that one will be provided for by one's husband. It is no longer the sole gateway to sexual and domestic pleasures, since nonwives and nonhusbands now live together openly as never before. It is not even the indispensable passage to motherhood—as many as 40 percent of American babies are now being born out of wedlock.

For business and professional women, wifedom today can be a mixed blessing. Some wives are able to make use of their husbands' contacts; others find it expedient to underplay their conjugal status, especially in the face of colleagues and bosses who demand primary loyalty to the firm. An increasing number of married women choose to keep their maiden names. With divorce on the horizon for approximately half of all American spouses marrying today, why bother changing your name when you may have to take it back again? Why bother marrying at all when you don't need a husband to have sex, economic support, shared residence, and even children?

In this book I ask how we have come to such a problematic moment in the history of the wife. I argue that the transformation of wifehood in the past fifty years is, in many ways, the distillation of changes that have been going on for a long time—changes that have not been uniform across nations, religions, races, ethnic groups, and social classes, yet tend to cluster around certain common issues. Starting with the ancient Hebrews, Greeks, and Romans, I focus on issues that persist into our own era, even as they change and give way to new, more pressing concerns. Some of the concerns that are particularly relevant to our own time have roots reaching back hundreds and even thousands of years.

For example, in classical Greece, a father would betroth his daughter to a bridegroom with the words: "I pledge [daughter's name] for the purpose of producing legitimate children." Throughout the ancient world, the primary obligation of a wife was to produce offspring. Woe to the barren wife of biblical times—not only would she be enveloped in shame, but often replaced by a second (or third) wife. Well into modern times, wives could be disposed of for not producing children—especially among royalty and the aristocracy, where the necessity for a male heir placed even greater pressure on the wife. And the pressure to produce offspring has by no means disappeared from all parts of the world. In certain Islamic lands, for example, marriage contracts written at the behest of the bride forbid the husband to take a second wife, except when she, the first wife, proves to be childless.

Many women and men still marry for the express purpose of having children. I recall a perceptive comment by one of my sons in the mid-1970s when he heard that his baby-sitter was getting married. "Why is she getting married? She doesn't have a baby." True, this was California in the throes of a sexual revolution that had not escaped the notice of my five-year-old. People were already cohabiting openly, as they would continue to do throughout all parts of the United States during the next decades. And oddly enough, my son's words were prescient: today it is common for heterosexuals who have been living together for months or years to choose marriage only if they choose to have a child or know that a baby is already on the way. So the issue of children in the decision to marry is by no means outdated. Some marriages never occur or do not survive because the woman wants to have a child and the man does not . . . and vice versa.

The "wife" and the "mother" share a fuzzy boundary. Their responsibilities often overlap and sometimes conflict. Any woman who has been both wife and mother knows that the time, care, energy, and material resources she gives to her children may be resented by her husband. And this same woman also knows that children can create a permanent bond between spouses, one that projects the couple into the future through the very product of their lovemaking. Even if spouses don't always love each other, they usually share with one another a love for their children.

In the past, most marriages were affairs of the pocketbook rather than affairs of the heart. Men wed women who had dowries; women wed men who could support them. From biblical days to the 1950s, it was a husband's duty to provide for his wife. She, in turn, was expected to provide sex, children, and housekeeping. It was a quid pro quo that was not just tacitly understood by the two parties but written into religious and civil law.

Today, whatever the initial monetary considerations of the prospective spouses—such as the bride or groom's earning power or family assets—there is no longer the assumption that the husband will be the sole provider for his wife. Most couples now marry with the expectation that both parties will contribute to the family economy. Indeed, since it is increasingly difficult for a family to survive on a single paycheck, the dual-career family has become the norm. More than three out of five American wives are employed full- or part-time. Today a wife cannot count on complete economic support within the marriage, nor on alimony if the marriage ends in divorce. In fact, it is no longer rare for a wife to earn more than her husband, or to be sued for alimony in the event of divorce.

Yet the wife is still expected to provide many of the same services she has always provided, such as childcare and housekeeping. Men, too, one may argue, are expected to share some domestic responsibilities, and they are clearly doing more, but they have not yet become full partners as caretakers and homemakers, while most women are working as hard as the men in the workplace and slowly narrowing the gender gap in earning power; women as a group now earn 75 percent of what men earn in the same jobs as compared to 59 percent in the 1970s. With wives sharing the role of provider—a role that used to be exclusively or predominantly male—and men wondering how to reconceptualize masculinity, the malaise between the sexes may have reached an all-time high. The old quid pro quo has broken down, and the new conjugal model of equal sharing at home and at work has not yet been fully realized.

Love, as we have seen from the letter at the beginning of this chapter, has become synonymous with marriage in the Western world. Scholars are fond of trying to pinpoint the moment in history when love began to take priority over all the other considerations. Some point to the early Middle Ages, when romantic love emerged from troubadour poetry and court life in Southern France. While it is true that the medieval cult of love honored woman as she had never been before, the honored woman was always someone else's wife. Courtly love required a minimum of three players: husband, wife, and the wife's lover. The raptures experienced by the nonmarried pair were considered unlikely within the quotidian boundaries of conjugal life.

I'm of the school that believes love began to take priority in marital arrangements as early as the sixteenth century, especially in England; that it came to America with the Puritans in the seventeenth century; and that it slowly began to dominate the scene by the late eighteenth century among the middle class. In aristocratic and upper-class families, considerations of wealth, lineage, and status continued to influence the choice of a wife or husband well into the twentieth century. This is not to say that love was absent from earlier unions. We find isolated records of passionate love experienced by spouses among the ancient Hebrews, Greeks, and Romans. But since arranged marriages, rather than love marriages, were the norm in premodern times, brides and grooms did not enter marriage with the expectation of "loving" each other as we understand the term.

Most wives would probably have settled for harmony. A wife who fulfilled her part of the bargain by providing sex, children, childcare, cooking, and housekeeping—not to mention the care of the vegetable garden and, in rural settings, the barnyard animals—probably considered herself fortunate if she were treated respectfully by her spouse, without physical abuse. The common law "rule of thumb" that allowed a man to beat his wife with a switch as long as it was not as large as a man's thumb lasted in many parts of England and America into the nineteenth century.

Unfortunately, the notion that a wife is there to serve and obey her husband and that he has the right to beat and bully her has not entirely disappeared. We find remnants of these old beliefs not only in traditionalist societies, but also in our own. In the United States today, all too many wives are forced to seek shelter in battered women's homes— that is, if they are lucky enough to find their way out of an abusive relationship. Today, few mainstream American or European men would admit to the belief, held among certain fundamentalist Christians, Muslims, and Jews, that wives should be subservient to their husbands, and even fewer would agree that men should be able to beat their wives. Yet old ideas die hard, and some people of both sexes secretly think of wives as lesser beings than their husbands. For some, the wife is still the "little woman," a "weaker vessel," the daughter of Eve, who, according to biblical, medieval, and Reformation theology, *should* be ruled by her husband. Dependence of the wife upon her husband in moral as well as economic matters was the rule for most of Western history, and is still the norm in many parts of the world.

At the same time, the notion of the wife as the equal of her husband has been gaining ascendancy. Since the eighteenth century, when ideas of companionate marriage began to have currency among the middle and upper classes, the trend has been toward more egalitarian partnerships. From the nineteenth century onward, when American women fought for and won the right to attend public and private schools, female seminaries, and colleges, they have been increasingly able to share the intellectual, economic, social, and political concerns that once were the exclusive purview of men. Today, the disparity between the sphere of the husband and the sphere of the wife may be smaller than it ever has been, with wives bringing home paychecks and husbands diapering their babies.

Law and education have certainly played major roles in this transformation. It is no longer legal for a man to beat his wife, even with a rod thinner than a thumb. It is no longer unusual for a married woman to have a separate bank account in her own name. And with access to education in every discipline, it is now possible for a woman to enter marriage with the same job opportunities as her husband. Today, men look for wives who can provide not only sex, love, children, and housekeeping services, but also wages and participation in community life. The requirements for today's wife give added meaning to the biblical proverb "Whosoever findeth a wife findeth a good thing."

I write this book with the belief that it is still "a good thing" to have a wife and to be a wife—under certain conditions. Those conditions involve relative equality between the spouses, mutual respect, and affection. They also include sufficient means—both personal and societal—to provide for one's ongoing material needs, including education and medical services. To be a wife still offers the challenging option of going through life as a member of a pair. In the best of circumstances, we are validated and strengthened through a long-term, loving union. We learn to compromise and to develop a sense of humor about our own peculiarities and those of our mates. We find comfort and support in facing the inevitable ordeals that life puts us through. We are able to share our thoughts, hopes, joys, fears, sorrows, experiences, and memories with an intimate witness of our life. In the worst of circumstances, we are diminished and undermined by the relationship and forced to consider divorce as a way out—which doesn't prevent us from marrying again.

To be a wife may no longer be a badge of honor, but it is far from a badge of woe. The employed wife may not want to be identified as "the wife of so-and-so," and the full-time homemaker is wise to eschew the self-denigrating label "just a housewife." They may both prefer to use the gender-neutral terms "spouse" or "partner." Whatever the particular sexual, economic, and domestic arrangements between a husband and a wife, one cannot be a spouse of either gender for very long without giving up some of one's independence. This means accommodation and compromise, deep commitment and dogged perseverance. The woman or man who cannot envision living with such constraints would do well to reconsider *before* the wedding day. Being a wife, or husband, is not for everyone, though about 90 percent of Americans do marry at least once in their lives. And even those who divorce marry again in three out of four cases.

Many still marry using the wedding service of the 1552 Church of England Prayer Book (whose roots go back in Latin, French, and English to the Middle Ages.) The vows taken by the spouses still sound uncommonly beautiful: "I take thee to be my wedded wife (or husband), to have and to hold from this day forward, for better for worse, for richer for poorer, in sickness and in health, to love and to cherish, till death us do part." Originally, the wife also promised "to obey," but for some time now, those words have been omitted. With this single change, a woman in the twenty-first century can make the same vows as her medieval and Renaissance foremothers. It is a small but significant difference, and one that will shape the future of the wife for years to come.

The interdependence of spouses offers a more likely paradigm today than the earlier dependence of wife on husband. As world leaders, Americans and Europeans are creating a model of shared conjugal authority, which may seem foreign to much of the globe, but that much of the globe will probably come to emulate.

And if I may venture into even more uncertain territory, I believe we shall see in the twenty-first century a further development in the history of the wife: American states will legalize same-sex partnerships, following the Vermont model of "civil unions," which provide gay couples with numerous benefits including inheritance rights, tax breaks, and the power to make medical decisions for a partner. Across the border, Canada has erased virtually all legal distinctions between heterosexual marriages and same-sex unions. In Europe, many Western nations (for example, Denmark, Sweden, Switzerland, Belgium, and France) offer the option of civil unions, regardless of one's gender, and Holland has converted its registered same-sex partnerships into full-fledged marriages, complete with adoption, social security, and tax rights. Who will be the "wife" in a gay or lesbian marriage? Can the term "wife" have meaning in a union where there is no sexual difference between the partners? Or will the "wife" survive as a social and psychological construct implying traditional feminine qualities, such as softness, deference, nurturance, and emotionality?

At this particular moment of history, when the word "wife" has become problematic and could become obsolete, it makes sense to take stock of her inheritance. Where did Western ideas about the wife begin? How were laws and practices affecting wives passed on from generation to generation? What major patterns of wifehood have been woven into the present scene? Which threads have persisted and which have been broken?

From this interface of past and present scripts, we may be able to glimpse future images of the married woman.

*A
History
of
the
Wife*

ONE

Wives in the Ancient World

Biblical, Greek, and Roman Models

Why should we begin with biblical, Greek, and Roman wives? Because the religious, legal, and social practices of those ancient civilizations provided the template for the future treatment of married women in the West. The wife as a man's chattel, as his dependent, as his means for acquiring legal offspring, as the caretaker of his children, as his cook and housekeeper are roles that many women now find abhorrent; yet certain aspects of those antiquated obligations still linger on in the collective unconscious. Many men still expect their wives to provide some or all of these services, and many wives still intend to perform them. Those women today who rebel against such expectations are, after all, rebelling against patterns that have been around for more than two millennia. It's important to understand what they are rebelling against, and what some of their antagonists—for example, certain conservative religious groups—are trying to preserve.

BIBLICAL WIVES

The charter myth for the Judeo-Christian wife is the story of Adam and Eve. Ever since their story was written into the Bible (around the tenth century B.C.E.), Adam and Eve have been designated, first by

Hebrews and later by Christians and Muslims, as the progenitors of the human race. From the start, Eve has been honored as the foremother of humanity and simultaneously reviled as the spouse who first disobeyed God.

Eve listens to the serpent while Adam scratches his head in puzzlement. Adam and Eve *by Lucas Cranach, the Elder, circa 1530. (Norton Simon Art Foundation, Pasadena, California).*

Initially, as related in Chapter One of Genesis, God created man and woman at the same time. "And God created the human in his image, in the image of God He created him; male and female He created them."[1] But by Chapter Two, a new version of human creation had found its way into Scripture, which suggested that Eve was something of an afterthought. In this version, God created Adam first, from the dust of the ground. Then, reflecting on His handiwork, He declared: "It is not good for the human to be alone. I shall make him a sustainer beside him."

The subsequent account of Eve's creation from Adam's rib has fueled the age-old argument that woman is intrinsically inferior to man and dependent on him for her very existence. Even the Hebrew word *icha,* or "woman"—from man—suggests this one-down position.

Eve's story then goes from bad to worse. She follows the serpent's advice to eat from the Tree of Good and Evil, contrary to God's commandment, and then tempts Adam to eat of it as well. These acts have permanent consequences for both sexes: God punishes Eve by inflicting the pangs of childbirth on all mothers and the burden of sweat-producing labor on all men. In addition, it is decreed that the female will be in a subordinate position to her husband for eternity. As God tells Eve after the Fall, "Your urge shall be for your husband and he shall rule over you." Like most myths, this one sought to explain a cultural phenomenon that had been entrenched for so long it seemed to be the will of God.

But there are other ways of looking at this story, which put Eve in a more favorable light. Some feminists have suggested that Eve was not just an afterthought, but an improvement over Adam. And even conservative commentators recognize that she represented more than a biological necessity. The notion of the wife as a man's companion, "sustainer" or "helpmeet" (from the Hebrew word *'ezer*) has had a long and meaningful history among Jews and Christians. Indeed, one later commentary in the Talmud (the code of Jewish religious and civil law) sees the *'ezer* as providing a moral check on her husband: "When he is good, she supports him, when he is bad, she rises up against him."[2] And most of all, those arguing for the equal partnership of husband and wife can cite the moving last words of Chapter Two of Genesis: "Therefore does a man leave his father and his mother and cling to his wife and they become one flesh."

In biblical days, a Hebrew husband was allowed to have more than one wife. For each, he had to give his father-in-law a sum of money, the *mohar* of fifty silver shekels (Deut. 22:28–29) and then he had to provide for her upkeep. This probably meant that only the affluent could afford more than one.[3] In addition, the groom or his family was expected to give gifts to the bride and her family. Once the *mohar* had been paid and the gifts accepted, the marriage was legally binding and the bride effectively belonged to her husband, even if they did not yet live together.

A bride's father would generally give her a *chiluhim,* or dowry. The dowry consisted of material goods to be used in the future household, including servants and livestock, and even land, as well as a portion of the *mohar* that reverted to the girl "as payment for the price of her virginity."[4] The specific sum of the dowry would be written down in the marriage contract, or *ketubah,* as well as the sum of money that would revert to the wife in the event of divorce or widowhood. Jewish marriage contracts going back to the eighth century B.C.E. usually contained a ritual formula pronounced by the groom to the bride in the presence of witnesses: "She is my wife and I am her husband from this day forth and forever."

The last stage of the marriage was the banquet that preceded the wedding night. These festivities could go on for as long as a week, though the marriage was consummated the first night. If, however, the husband found that his bride was no longer a virgin, he could have her killed according to the words of the Torah: "then they shall bring out the damsel to the door of her father's house, and the men of the city shall stone her with stones that she die" (Deut. 22:21).

Once married, a bride was obliged by law and custom to obey her husband—a requirement so fundamental to the biblical idea of a wife that it remained in most Jewish and Christian wedding vows until the late twentieth century. After all, wives were considered a husband's "property," alongside his cattle and his slaves. And above all, a wife would have been consumed by the need to produce a son. For only as the mother of a son would she have been fully honored in her new family.

And even then, if a husband wanted to get rid of his wife, he had only to write out a bill of divorce, hand it to her in the presence of two witnesses, and send her away. The wife's agreement was not required.

The Ketubah, or Jewish marriage contract established in Biblical times, stipulated the size of the bride's dowry and her rights if she were divorced or widowed. This Italian Ketubah from 1752 joining "Nathan, the son of Eliah Molho, and Gracia, the daughter of Israel Ha-Levi," was witnessed by two rabbis' sons. (Musée de l'Art et de l'Histoire Judaïque, Paris)

The Hebrew law allowed that a husband can cast off his wife if "she finds no favor in his eyes" because he has discovered something shameful in her (Deut. 24:1). What was shameful in those days? Adultery, for sure, even the suspicion of adultery, but also immodesty, disobedience, and barrenness. Rabbinical commentaries from later centuries all insisted on the husband's right to initiate divorce and the wife's need to avoid any behavior that might lead a husband to seek to divorce her.[3]

Even today, among Orthodox Jews, it is the husband who plays the determining role in a divorce. If a wife wants a divorce, the husband must consent to it and give her a document called a *get*. If he refuses—because he thinks she will eventually come back to him or because he hopes to exchange the *get* for reduced support payments or custody rights—the wife cannot be freed from the religious marriage bond and remarry. There are hundreds of Orthodox Jewish women in the United States and Israel today in this state of marital limbo. But a husband can divorce his wife without her consent, as long as he is able to hand the document to her.

The notion that a wife cannot initiate divorce has biblical precedent, yet even in biblical times, there was one peculiar circumstance that allowed a wife to take action. If a wife was widowed and had no children, her dead husband's brother was expected to marry her to "give her seed," according to a tradition known as levirate marriage. But if the brother refused to marry her, or to have sex with her after their enforced marriage, the wife was permitted to go to the elders at the town gate and lay her claim against him. There, in front of the whole populace, she was allowed to humiliate him for not fulfilling his obligations: "She shall pull his sandal off his foot and spit in his face and declare: 'Thus we requite the man who will not build up his brother's family' " (Deut. 25:9–10). The overriding Hebrew concern with progeny allowed for this rare display of officially sanctioned female revenge.

It is true that this dismal wifely scenario is based upon prescriptive texts, which did not always correspond to everyday life. There are certainly many indications in the Bible suggesting behaviors different from the prescribed norm. For example, despite the great pressure on wives to produce children, a husband might continue to love his barren wife, and even to favor her over a first or second wife who had given him a son. This was the case of Elkanah, who preferred his childless wife,

Hannah, to his other wife, Peninnah, the mother of his children. Once finding Hannah weeping over her childless state, Elkanah tried to soothe her by saying: "Hannah, why are you crying and eating nothing? Why are you so miserable? Am I not more to you than ten sons?" (I Samuel 1:8). Even with all the societal honor bestowed upon a mother and the humiliation heaped upon a childless wife, there was then, as now, no way to legislate an individual's feelings.

Married couples were held in high esteem among the ancient Hebrews, as evidenced by the many stories about them. This contrasts with the New Testament, where couples do not play significant roles. In time, Jews and Christians alike looked to the older Hebrew examples for positive (and negative) conjugal models.

Among the positive examples of what one might hope for in a wife, Sarah, the wife of Abraham, comes first to mind. Hers was a careful balancing act of wifely strength and submission. As a good Israelite spouse, she was obliged to follow even the most morally questionable of her husband's commands. Twice at his behest she passed herself off as his sister, rather than his wife, so that he could gain favor first with the Egyptian pharaoh, then with the Semitic King Abimelech. Though these acts entailed sleeping with foreign monarchs, Sarah followed her husband's orders; in the end, this strategy proved beneficial, since they came away from each incident with increased riches.

Because Sarah had passed the childbearing age without producing offspring, she encouraged Abraham to take her Egyptian slave girl, Hagar, as a second wife. But later, when Sarah felt humiliated by Hagar's pregnancy, Abraham found himself in the awkward situation of having to decide between the two women. Though he decided in favor of the first wife and sent Hagar into exile, God Himself intervened by sending the servant back with the assurance that she would bear a son to Abraham and become the ancestor of a great people. Thus Abraham once again had two wives in residence and a firstborn son, named Ishmael. Centuries later Ishmael would be claimed by the Muslims as the forefather of the Arab people. In their old age, Abraham and Sarah miraculously produced a son of their own, Isaac—an event that Sarah greeted with astonishment and perhaps some sense of embarrassment.[5] As was the custom, she nursed her baby, probably for two to three years, and a great feast was celebrated when the baby was weaned.

Abraham and Sarah may be no more than mythical characters representing the ancestors of the Hebrew people, but in the course of their narrative, they emerge as a real couple living together in biblical times: they wander as nomads to villages and cities, moving with their kinsmen, animals, servants, slaves, and goods; they set up their tent among peoples who cannot be counted on for kindness; they show hospitality to strangers in the form of curds and milk and freshly made loaves of bread; they exchange opinions, complaints, laughter. And when Sarah dies before her husband, we are not surprised to read that "Abraham came to mourn Sarah and to keen for her" (Gen. 23:2). Not ashamed of publicly mourning a wife like Sarah, Abraham went to great trouble to provide her with an appropriate burial site, in the cave of Machpelah near Hebron, which he purchased at an exhorbitant price from the Hittites.

The marriages of Sarah and Abraham's son Isaac to Rebekah and their grandson Jacob to Rachel (and Leah) give us further insights into the status of wives in ancient Israel. In the case of Isaac and Rebekah, a servant was sent to the land of Abraham's birth to contract a marriage for Isaac. The servant made the marriage agreement not with Rebekah herself, but with Rebekah's brother Laban. (Brothers often stood in for fathers and had the right to dispose of their sisters.) The marriage was contracted without the bride or groom ever seeing each other. Still, Rebekah had some say in the matter. After Laban had given his acquiescence, he said: " 'Let us call the young woman and ask for her answer.' And they called Rebekah and said to her, 'Will you go with this man?' And she said, 'I will' " (Gen.24:58–59). This is one of the few indications that a nubile Hebrew woman sometimes had the right to accept or refuse a prospective groom.

The actual meeting of Rebekah and Isaac did not take place until she had journeyed with his servant back to Canaan. The story ends with Isaac's favorable reaction to his bride: "And Isaac brought her into the tent of Sarah his mother and took Rebekah as wife. And he loved her, and Isaac was consoled after his mother's death" (Gen. 24:67). The last sentence is particularly moving, for Isaac not only loves the wife who had been chosen for him, but finds an emotional replacement for his mother. We can imagine Freud nodding in agreement.

The story of the marriage of Isaac and Rebekah's son, Jacob, to Rachel is more complicated. Rebekah sent Jacob (rather than a servant) back to her brother Laban to seek a wife. Laban received his nephew Jacob hospitably, but not without making him work for his keep. After a month, they reached an agreement on the wages Jacob would receive if he remained in Laban's service. The wages were in effect a bride-price for Rachel. Rachel, however, had an older sister, Leah, who, by tradition, should have been married first. The two young women are described in the following manner: "Laban had two daughters. The name of the elder was Leah and the name of the younger Rachel. And Leah's eyes were tender, but Rachel was comely in features and comely to look at, and Jacob loved Rachel" (Gen. 29: 16–18). Jacob contracted to serve seven years for Rachel. In the eloquent words of the biblical narrator: "And Jacob served seven years for Rachel, and they seemed in his eyes but a few days in his love for her" (Gen. 29:21).

But when the time came for Jacob to reap the fruits of his labors, he was cruelly deceived by his uncle. In the dark of night, he was given Leah rather than Rachel, and bedded the wrong woman. In the morning, seeing that it was Leah, Jacob said to Laban: "What is this you have done to me? Was it not for Rachel that I served you?" Laban replied that it was not the custom in his land "to give the younger girl before the firstborn," and proposed that Jacob serve another seven years to acquire Rachel as well.

All in all, Jacob spent twenty years serving his crafty uncle Laban, acquiring two wives and their slave girls and quite a number of children. Since sons represented the ultimate good in biblical households, the wives competed with each other in producing male offspring. First Leah, the least loved, was compensated by the birth of three sons, and Rachel, who remained barren, became jealous of her sister. So she said to Jacob: "Here is my slavegirl Bilhah. Come to bed with her, that she may give birth on my knees, so that I, too, shall be built up through her" (Gen. 30:3). Placing the baby on her knees after its birth indicated adoption.

The competition between wives was intensified by the use of mandrakes, plants thought to have magical aphrodisiac and fertility-promoting properties. With the help of these plants, Leah continued to produce more sons and a daughter, and Rachel, finally, gave birth to a son. Jacob was now the father of a miniature tribe. This story illustrates the fierce rivalries between wives living in a society that valued married women primarily as the mothers of sons. And like the story of Sarah,

Abraham, and Hagar, it illuminates the role of female "outsiders" within Hebrew households—Egyptian slave girls, for example, whose bodies facilitated the very existence of Hebrew families.

The Hebrew Bible has a rich cast of spouses performing many variations on marital themes. One of my favorites is the terse interchange between Job and his wife, after Job had been laid low by God. Having lost all his sons and daughters, his servants and animals, then afflicted with boils from head to toe, Job sat down among the ashes and accepted the will of God. But not his wife, as the following verses show.

> *"Then said his wife unto him. Dost thou still retain thine integrity? Curse God, and die."*
>
> *But he said unto her, "Thou speakest as one of the foolish women speaketh. What? shall we receive good at the hand of God, and shall we not receive evil?" In all this did not Job sin with his lips (Job 2:9).*

We hear the bitter voice of the wife and mother, overwhelmed by sorrow and unforgiving of a God deemed responsible for the death of her children. In the Bible, she is described as "one of the foolish women" who cannot bear up to suffering. Job, on the other hand, resists despair—at least initially. Their interchange draws from an antique Mediterranean tradition in which wives were often seen as foolish: caught up in the grief of their losses, insolent to indifferent gods, they were presumably unable to see the "larger picture," be it political or metaphysical. Like the Greek queen Clytemnestra who never stopped blaming Agamemnon for the sacrifice of their daughter Iphigenia, Job's wife had no compunctions about cursing the God who had taken away her children. Whatever the prescriptions about wifely obedience, wives obviously opposed their husbands in the privacy of their homes, and even opposed the supreme patriarch—God Himself.

Men are supposed to be more steadfast. Though Job experiences grave psychological anguish and questions God's justice, he never succumbs to blasphemy. In the end God rewards him with "twice as much as he had before" (Job 42:10). At this point the narrator does not deign to mention Job's wife.

In contrast to Job's wife and certain other negative models, a picture of the ideal wife is presented in the final section of Proverbs. It is clearly written from the male point of view, beginning misogynistically with the notion that a good woman is hard to find and rising to a wifely encomium unique in all the Bible.

> *Who can find a virtuous woman? for her price is far above rubies.*
> *The heart of her husband doth safely trust in her . . .*
> *She will do him good and not evil all the days of her life.*
> *She seeketh wool, and flax, and worketh willingly with her hands.*
> *She is like the merchants' ships; she bringeth her food from afar.*
> *She riseth also while it is yet night, and giveth meat to her house-*
>   *hold, and a portion to her maidens. . . .*
> *She stretcheth out her hand to the poor. . . .*
> *Her children arise up, and call her blessed; her husband also, and he*
>   *praiseth her.*

Such is the dutiful, hardworking, charitable woman who brings honor to her husband and children. Any man in any age might dream of such a wife.

Husbands and wives as couples are, as I have mentioned, notably absent from the Gospels, except for the miraculous story of Mary and Joseph, briefly told in Matthew and Luke. Mary was probably twelve or thirteen when she and Joseph were committed to one another. Our term "engagement" does not carry the weight of their commitment: although they were not yet living together when Joseph discovered that Mary was pregnant, she was legally his wife. Fortunately for her, given the death sentence that could be inflicted on Jewish brides who were not virgins, "Joseph was a just man, and not willing to make her a public example." Instead, "he was minded to put her away privately." But before he did so, "the angel of the Lord appeared unto him in a dream," and convinced him that Mary had become impregnated by the Holy Ghost. Joseph and Mary did not consummate their marriage "till she had brought forth her firstborn son" (Matt. 1:18–25).

Aside from Mary and Joseph, there are no New Testament couples of any significance. Instead, the accent in the Gospels is on the individual and personal salvation. How we behave on earth, as individuals responsible for our actions, will determine whether we inherit the Kingdom of Heaven or whether we shall spend eternity in Gehenna, the Hebrew equivalent of Hell. In any event, in the afterlife, there is no marriage, as

Jesus makes explicit. "When they rise from the dead, they neither marry, nor are given in marriage, but are as the angels" (Mark 12:25). The strong apocalyptic bent in Jesus' message seems to have made marriage irrelevant.

What did Jesus think about marriage on earth? His thoughts were expressed in a commentary on divorce, a practice he explicitly condemned. Citing the creation story when God made both male and female and they became one flesh, Jesus declared: "What God hath joined together, let not man put asunder" (Mark 10:9). Then he went on to specify that "Whosoever shall put away his wife . . . and shall marry another, committeth adultery" (Mark 10:11). It is important to remember that the ancient Hebrew law proscribing adultery applied exclusively to married women, requiring them to limit their sexual activity to only one man. There was no such requirement for married men, who were allowed to have sex with unattached women, such as widows, concubines, and servants, as well as their wives. A convicted adulteress could be put to death by stoning, along with her illicit sexual partner. But Jesus, in opposition to Hebrew practice, equated the male prerogatives of divorce and remarriage with adultery. Whoever wanted to be a Christian and married—male or female—would have to be permanently monogamous.

Jesus also challenged the excessive punishment meted out to the adulteress. In a by now famous incident, he was asked whether a woman "taken in adultery, in the very act," should be stoned, according to Mosaic law. His response has become proverbial: "He that is without sin among you, let him first cast a stone at her" (John 8:7). Jesus' emphasis upon compassion rather than revenge, and upon the equality of all men and women in sin, struck a new chord in religious history. Nonetheless, Christian society continued to mete out strong punishment to adulterers for centuries to come. Both parties to the act were paraded through the streets nude in thirteenth-century France, and, worse yet, subject to being buried alive and impaled in fourteenth-century Germany.[6] The Kingdom of Sicily under the emperor Frederick II in 1231 adopted a series of laws intended to soften the penalty against adulterers; instead of the sword, confiscation of property was decreed for the man who had fornicated with a married woman, and the slitting of her nose was deemed sufficient for the condemned wife.[7] In seventeenth-century Puritan New England, the usual punishment was a whipping or a fine, combined with a symbolic execution: the adulterer stood in public for an hour with a rope around his or her neck.

In biblical times, adultery was but one of several "abominations" that carried a death penalty among the ancient Hebrews. Anther was homosexuality. The condemnation of homosexual acts reads: "Thou shalt not lie with mankind, as with womankind: it is abomination" (Leviticus 18:22).

The prohibition against lying "with mankind, as with womankind" is addressed to men and to be taken literally. That is, it applies exclusively to male homosexuality. There is no similar injunction against female homosexuality in the Hebrew Bible. Perhaps female homosexuality was disregarded because the male writers of the Bible either ignored or trivialized it. Or perhaps it was seen as less heinous because lesbian practices are not party to the "spilling of seed" that male homosexuality entails.[8]

Why homosexual acts were so reviled by the biblical Hebrews has been the subject of endless debate. One answer has to do with the ancient focus on procreation: any sexual act, such as masturbation, coitus interruptus, and bestiality, that did not contribute to progeny was vehemently condemned. Whereas other inhabitants of the ancient Mediterranean world, most notably the Greeks, but also the Romans, tolerated same-sex couples, Judaism was consistently antihomosexual.[9]

As for Christianity, Jesus said nothing on the subject of homosexuality—and this in contrast to numerous condemnations of adultery. Saint Paul, however, explicitly condemned both male and female homosexuality (Romans 1:26–27, I Corinthians 6:9, and I Timothy 1:10). His negative view of same-sex eroticism was rooted in a widespread system of thought that took heterosexual relations as natural and all other forms of sexuality as unnatural. God had established the natural order of things in Genesis, and any deviation from heterosexual coupling was seen as a rejection of God's design.

When I think about ancient Judaism and early Christianity, I am struck by certain basic differences in their conceptions of marriage—differences that have persisted in some form to this very day. Judaism taught that marriage was connected to the *mitzvah* of procreation—a divine commandment and a blessing.[10] Because marriage was seen as the only sanctioned way Jews could fulfill their obligation to reproduce, men and women were literally obliged to marry. Numerous rabbinical sayings found in the Torah and Talmud reaffirm this sentiment: for example, "Whoso findeth a wife findeth a good thing, and obtaineth favor of the Lord" (Proverbs 18:22).

Christianity, on the other hand, took an early deviation from this position. Following the models of Jesus and Saint Paul, early Christianity valued celibacy above marriage. In the words of Saint Paul, "The unmarried man cares for the Lord's business; his aim is to please the Lord. But the married man cares for wordly things; his aim is to please his wife; and he has a divided mind. . . . The married woman cares for wordly things; her aim is to please her husband" (I Corinthians 7:32–34). Acquiring a wife or husband was seen as interfering with the more primary business of forming a union with the Lord. If, for the Jew, the only way to obey God's commandment was to marry and produce offspring, for the Pauline Christian, the best way to fulfill God's commandment was to abstain from sex altogether.

While a wife was considered "a good thing" for Hebrews but a potential obstacle to salvation for Christians, both Judaism and Christianity took it for granted that females were inferior to males and needed the lifelong tutelage of men. At the time of Jesus, Jewish women were strictly confined to the home, especially if they were wealthy and lived in cities. They rarely went out, except to the temple, and when they did, they had to cover their heads and faces, with only their eyes showing. Pamela Norris, in her engrossing book *Eve,* argues that even with only *one* eye left uncovered, Jewish women knew how to call attention to themselves by using eye makeup and wearing colorful clothes and jewelry that jingled as they walked.[11] Such adornments had been condemned in Scripture (most notably Isaiah 3:19–23) and continued to evoke the wrath of rabbis, convinced that male surveillance was required to control women from their innate bent toward seduction and troublemaking.

In this vein, the words of Saint Paul would be cited endlessly by patriarchal advocates for the next two thousand years. "Wives, be subject to your husbands, as to the Lord. For the husband is the head of the wife as Christ is the head of the church" (Ephesians 5:22). Wifely obedience was to be conspicuously manifested in church, where, according to Paul, "women should keep silence. . . . If there is anything they desire to know, let them ask their husbands at home" (I Corinthians 14:34–35).

Early patristic thinkers, most notably Tertullian, Saint Jerome, and Saint Augustine, argued that the Fall, initiated by Eve, had conferred a moral taint on all carnal union, even that within marriage. There were, however, gradations of difference in the repugnance toward marital sex expressed by the church fathers. Augustine justified coitus according to the rationale of the three goods of marriage: procreation, social stability, and the safeguard it provided against fornication. He declared that married couples should engage in sex only to beget children, and should scrupulously avoid copulating merely for pleasure.[12]

Saint Jerome went even further. He considered sex, even in marriage, as intrinsically evil. He rejected sexual pleasure as filthy, loathsome, degrading, and ultimately corrupting. This linkage of sex and sin, with blame attributed primarily to the daughters of Eve, became increasingly entrenched within the church, and by the fifth century was common currency among ecclesiastical authorities. It was also related to the rise of monasticism, which, by the sixth century, offered an alternative to marriage for Christian men and women. (Institutionalized celibacy has not been a part of Jewish or Muslim practice.)

Yet a few Christian theologians took a counterposition in praise of marriage. They pointed to the words of Jesus when he defended it as a God-given, indissoluble bond and to the wedding at Cana, where he miraculously provided wine for the wedding guests (Mark 10:6–9; John 2). They could even point to Saint Paul, who, having conceded the necessity of marriage for the purpose of procreation, endeavored to endow it with deep spiritual meaning by comparing it to the union between Christ and the church. They could also cite Paul's prescription for spouses to love each other, with specific focus on the marital bed: "The husband must give the wife what is due to her, and the wife equally must give the husband his due. . . . Do not deny yourselves to one another" (I Corinthians: 7:3–5). Paul may have derived this concept from the Hebrew Bible, for in Exodus (21:10) a husband is ordered to provide his wife, even a slave wife, with "meat, clothes, and conjugal rights." This recognition of a couple's affective and sexual needs will be picked up later, during the Reformation, as the basis for a more positive view of marriage than that of the early church.

Both Judaism and Christianity supplied enduring models of good and bad wives. Since all women were the daughters of Eve, they were, according to both Jewish and Christian lore, capable of leading men astray. But there were also the examples of the Old Testament matriarchs—Sarah, Rebekah, Rachel, and Leah—and the "virtuous woman" of Proverb 31, who brought nothing but blessings to her husband. Throughout the ages Jewish women have been reminded of their industrious, fruitful foremothers.

And Christians could look to the supreme model of the Virgin Mary for virtues that were touted above all others: obedience and chastity. Although the marriage of Mary to Joseph was merely an artifact of her mission to produce the son of God, she was held up as the image of ideal wifehood. Christian women, for centuries to come, would sense the tension between Mary's miraculous purity and their own carnality.

WIVES IN ANCIENT GREECE

We know a great deal about wives in ancient Greece, and we know very little. All the great Greek literature, with the exception of Sappho's poetry, was authored by men and reflects a male view of women. The voices of the wives—and there are many in Greek literature—have emerged from the mouths of men. It's as if we could only know the lives of twentieth-century American women from the writings of Ernest Hemingway, John Updike, and Philip Roth. What we learn from Greek texts concerning the social and legal condition of married women tells us virtually nothing about *their* hopes, fears, and disappointments.

What did a Greek wife feel toward the goddess Hera, patron of marriage, protector of women, and sister-wife of Zeus? Did she pray to Hera as Christian women would later pray to the Virgin Mary? Dignified images of Hera adorned Greek shrines and temples, but oral and written tales depicted her as a fiercely jealous wife, given to plots against the other women Zeus favored and his illegitimate offspring. The disparity between these two images—the rancorous wife and the sacred matron—suggests that Greek wives may have felt both awe and empathy for Hera, as they called upon her for protection against their own husbands, whose license with other females was always a potential source of discord.

During the Homeric era (eighth century B.C.E.), the ideal wife was Penelope in *The Odyssey*—a mature, clever, and faithful woman. While Odysseus, the hero of the Trojan War, wandered for nineteen years,

Grave stela from Athens, circa 400 B.C.E., erected to honor a husband and wife. (J. Paul Getty Museum, Los Angeles)

Penelope managed their kingdom in Ithaca, raised their son Telemachus, and warded off the many suitors who vied to replace her husband. She procrastinated by saying she would make her choice only after she had completed weaving her father-in-law's shroud, which she did by day and then unraveled at night. By the time this strategy was discovered, Odysseus was already on his way home and arrived in time to recover his wife.

The scene of their reunion is surely one of the best loved in all literature. Penelope, having given up hope of ever seeing Odysseus alive, was reluctant to accept a disguised beggar as her husband. In receiving him coldly and putting him to an identity test, she proved to be as crafty as her proverbially wily husband. The test Penelope had devised centered around the marriage bed. When she instructed the old nurse to move the bed outside the bedroom, Odysseus flared up with exasperation and reminded Penelope that their marital bed—the one he had crafted as a young man—could not be moved, for its bedpost was made from an olive tree around which he had constructed their entire bedroom.

With this proof, Penelope "ran up to Odysseus, threw her arms round his neck and kissed his head. . . . Penelope's surrender melted Odysseus' heart, and he wept as he held his dear wife in his arms, so loyal and so true."[13] Loyal and true, prudent and faithful, these are the words that describe Penelope, the ideal wife. His was the wider world of war and wandering, adventure in distant lands and foreign beds, while she waited and wove and remained loyal to her spouse.

At the moment of their reunion, they do not forget that other woman—Helen—the source of all their woes. Helen of Argive, better known as Helen of Troy, was the antithesis of the faithful Penelope. The wife of Menelaus, she allowed herself to be carried off to Troy by Paris, thus causing the Trojan War. Helen the beautiful, Helen the frivolous, "the face that launch'd a thousand ships" in the stirring words of Christopher Marlowe, was the most famous femme fatale of antiquity, one of those dangerous women men fear for their voluptuous beauty. In the Greco-Roman world, Helen and Penelope represented the bad and the good wife, an opposition that Christians would later attribute to Eve and the Virgin Mary.

Yet it is hardly for their stereotypical qualities that Penelope and Odysseus have enchanted readers for generations. Even if she represents the home-bound wife and he the wandering hero in accordance with the sex roles meted out to the two genders, what rings especially true for modern readers is their playful gamesmanship and deep intimacy, their sense of a shared history unattenuated by their long separation, their reunion in bed with the pleasures of lovemaking and "the fresh delights of talk." This pillow talk (did the Greeks have pillows?) is the special province of spouses in all ages. "He heard his noble wife tell of all she had put up with in his home. . . . And in his turn, royal Odysseus told her of all the discomfiture he had inflicted on his foes." Which couple has not delighted in this kind of verbal interchange before or after lovemaking? Such a scene of harmonious domestic intimacy is indeed rare in the pages of antique literature. It provides literary evidence for the belief, current among many classicists, that marriage at the time of Homer was more egalitarian than it would become three centuries later in Athens, and that Homeric women enjoyed a respect and freedom unknown to Greek women of the classical period.[14]

When we turn from the Homeric period to the classical age in fifth-century Athens, the source of information about wives is considerably larger, if still confined to male-authored documents. The great tragedians of this later period—Aeschylus, Sophocles, and Euripides—confront us with terrible domestic violence inflicted by willful husbands and wives. Oedipus and Jocasta, Agamemnon and Clytemnestra, Jason and Medea are destined to destroy one another. Clytemnestra kills her husband Agamemnon on his return from the Trojan War (with the help of her lover) on the grounds that Agamemnon had sacrificed their daughter Iphigenia when he set out for Troy. Medea kills the two children she had with Jason as revenge upon him for renouncing her in favor of a new wife. And what of Oedipus, who unwittingly killed his father, Laius, and married his mother, Jocasta, only to discover the truth years later—a discovery that caused Oedipus to blind himself and Jocasta to commit suicide. These stories reveal a deep-seated fear of vengeful wives, such as Clytemnestra and Medea, and the pollution that could issue, however unwittingly, from an incestuous widow like Jocasta. A good Greek widow would not have remarried in the first place. The dark truths embodied in these dramas suggest the smoldering tensions that existed, and continue to exist, between many spouses. Wives do indeed nurture murderous thoughts towards the husbands who replace them with other women or harm their children, though they rarely act out their revenge in such spectacular fashion.

Greek comedy, on the other hand, probably came closer to the daily reality of conjugal life, even when grossly exaggerated. In *Lysistrata,* first presented in 411 B.C.E., Aristophanes seized upon the timeless idea of a wife refusing her husband sex and expanded it into an outlandish political comedy. When Lysistrata and her sister conspirators decide to oppose the warlike ways of men by simply denying them sexual satisfaction, Greek society comes to a standstill. At least in this instance, the power of the bed proved stronger than the power of the sword. With its ribald props and comments, the play seems as fresh today as the sixties slogan "Make Love, Not War."

Daily life in classical Athens was ordered according to a set of prescribed conventions for adults of both genders. Marriage seems to have been largely a matter of property arrangements—financial deals, with little regard for the sentiments of the bride and groom. A family with a marriageable son would look for a daughter-in-law with a sufficient dowry that could be used to support the young couple. While this was especially true of upper- and middle-class families, even lower-class unions, those of shopkeepers and fishermen, were concerned with property of one kind or another.

Another concern was citizenship. In fifth-century Athens, citizenship was hereditary, but only if both parents were Athenians and of the citizen class. As of 451–450 B.C.E. under laws instituted by Pericles, male citizens had to marry females whose parents had been citizens, if they wanted their children to have the same coveted status.[15]

While such facts concerning the "public" nature of marriage are not difficult to find, it is much more difficult to find out anything about private sentiments. What did a young girl of fourteen of fifteen—the traditional age for marriage in classical Greece—feel when informed that her marriage was imminent? The prospective groom would have discussed the matter with her father, but the girl herself was probably never consulted, and probably had little, if any, contact with her future husband. There is reason to believe that marriage was often "a traumatic affair for the bride."[16] At a still tender age, she was obliged to leave her own *oikos* (household) and enter into the *oikos* of her husband, where her treatment would depend upon the kindness, or ill will, of her husband and his mother. A classic Greek lament recognizing the pain of separation puts these words into the mouth of the bride leaving her family of origin:

> *Everyone is driving me away.*
>   *everyone is telling me to leave.*
>
> . . . .
>
> *I am leaving with tears and with a*
>   *heavy heart.*[17]

The marriage betrothal (the *eggue,* or "promise") would have taken place long before the marriage ceremony. It was essentially an oral contract, made between the man who gave the woman in marriage—usually her father—and the bridegroom. The father would say "I pledge [woman's name] for the purpose of producing legitimate children." The groom replied: "I accept." The bride was not present. Betrothal was, in and of itself, a binding commitment with both legal and financial penalties if the marriage was not concluded. This is a far cry from the lack of ceremony today when lovers move in with one another without asking their parents, and with little fear of reprisal if they separate.

Marriage for a Greek man and for a Greek woman was the defining fact of their lives. For both of them, it was a rite of passage marking the transition from childhood into adulthood. The marriage ceremony was usually celebrated in winter and lasted for two or three days. On the first day, the father of the bride made offerings to the gods of marriage, Zeus and Hera. The bride sacrificed her toys to Artemis, who was the goddess of chastity and childbirth as well as nature and the hunt. On the second day, there was a wedding feast at the bride's home. The bride, wearing a veil, was then transported in a cart or carriage by her husband and his best friend to her husband's home, where she would live. A crowd of people preceded them singing the wedding chant (called the *Hymen*) and lighting the way with candles or torches.

The wedding procession was a very old custom, as can be inferred from the description of such a scene on the shield of Achilles in *The Iliad.*

> *. . . under glowing torches they brought forth the brides*
> *from the women's chambers, marching through the streets*

while choir on choir the wedding song rose high
and the young men came dancing, whirling round in rings
and among them the flutes and harps kept up their stirring call—
women rushed to the doors and each stood moved with wonder.

Like the women spectators along the route, we get to glimpse some of the festivities lavished on a wedding.[18]

Once the bride had been ushered into her new home, the attendants stood outside and sang the epithalamium, or song for the wedding chamber. The newlyweds enclosed in the bridal chamber were expected to consummate their union, an act by which the husband took full possession of his wife. From this point on, the bride's husband would replace her father as her *kyrios* (guardian and master). Aristotle (384–322 B.C.E.) distinguished between the "statesman-like" rule of the husband over his wife and the "royal" rule of a father over his child, but whatever the gradations of difference in authority, he upheld the conventional view that "the male is more fitted to rule than the female" (*Politics* I:12).

Despite the conventions, laws, and ceremonies that propped up ancient Greek marriage, it was by no means an irreversible affair. In Athenian society, a wife did not enter definitively into her husband's family until she had given him a child. Until that moment, her father could terminate the marriage at any time, usually for reasons that had to do with family property; then the father would become, once again, his daughter's *kyrios*. Moreover, a husband could repudiate a wife at will, without justification, but only if he were willing to give back the dowry.

Although heterosexual marriage was the only legally recognized form of couplehood in classical Greece, husbands were by no means limited to sexual relations with their wives. They could find supplemental sex beyond the marriage bed with concubines, male and female slaves, male and female prostitutes, and male and female lovers. The only officially forbidden fruit was the wife of another citizen. The orator Apollodorus is often quoted as saying that the Athenian man could have three women: his wife for producing heirs and watching over his property, his concubine for daily attention to his body (meaning sexual relations), and *hetaeras* (courtesans) for pleasure.[19]

Wives, on the other hand, were segregated from men other than their husbands, and severely punished if caught with a lover. At the least, a woman's husband would divorce her and send her back to her family of origin. In one notorious instance, an incensed Athenian husband named Euphiletos killed his wife's lover, Eratosthenes, and then won his case in court as justifiable homicide. Having caught the adulterous pair sleeping together, Euphiletos had thrown his wife's naked lover to the ground, tied his hands, refused his offer of a compensatory sum of money, and killed him on the spot. When brought to trial for murder, the husband successfully defended himself with a speech prepared by a well-known man of letters, Lysias, who subsequently recorded the incident for posterity. Apparently the tribunal was convinced that Euphiletos had acted not only in his own self-interest, but also in the interest of the Athenian city-state, since adultery, were it to go unpunished, could undermine the whole social order. Such was the rationale for a husband's murderous revenge in 400 B.C.E.[20]

At the same time, the law offered few recourses for injured wives. Even the most horrendous marriages could not be terminated at the behest of the wife, especially after the birth of a child. Her only recourse to an abusive husband was to abandon the conjugal roof—a process requiring authorization from the archon (one of the nine chief magistrates)—and to return to the custody of her father or another appointed *kyrios*. A special law looked out for the interests of the woman who had been married only for her money and then ignored by her husband after she had produced an heir; she could compel him by law to have sexual relations with her at least three times a month. (Try to imagine how the wife was able to enforce such a decree!)

In ancient Greece, wives were generally younger than their husbands—by ten to twenty years. Since they were strictly excluded from almost all activities outside the house, they could hardly be full companions to their husbands, who spent most of their waking hours away from home in the agora (forum), marketplace, gymnasium, and brothel. Marriage was respected as an institution that provided progeny and good housekeeping; it was not expected to fulfill one's longing for a soul mate.

Instead, the ideal union, at least among the cultured elite, was homosexual. In direct contrast to the Judeo-Christian mentality, the homosexual union between a man and a boy was presented as both natural and laudable. Plato (427–348 B.C.E.) extolled boys who enjoyed physical contact with men and believed that when these boys become adults, "they're sexually attracted to boys and would have nothing to do with marriage and procreation if convention didn't override their natural inclinations." Like heterosexual couples, homosexuals joined by "affection, warmth, and love" were deemed to be suited for "lifelong relationships."[21]

In addition to Plato, such diverse Greek writers as Xenophon, Aristotle, Aristophanes, and Plutarch, covering a span of five centuries, did not consider homosexual relations unusual. When we consider the large body of textual evidence, it is hard to disagree with the view that homosexuality in ancient Greece, at least among the upper classes, "was not only a widespread practice but perhaps a universal one and one that was certainly considered to have high cultural value."[22] But it would be wrong to assume that it was unproblematic. As several classicists keep reminding us, even the most enthusiastic proponents of homosexuality limited it to the man-boy relationship.[23] Pederasty was a sanctioned social institution designed to initiate young men into a virile fraternity, with a prescribed set of conventions for the adult male, who was usually under forty, and his boy lover, aged twelve to eighteen. It was not viewed as a replacement for marriage.

Since women in Athens were generally restricted to female company in their homes, and since affection between husbands and wives was not particularly stressed, some married women may have found solace with other women, though we know virtually nothing about lesbian practices in classical Greek society. What little we know comes from an earlier source, from the poetry of Sappho, who was born on the island of Lesbos around 612 B.C.E. and who is believed to have headed an association (thiasos) of young women. In these female communities, women learned music, singing, poetry, and dance. The belief that Sappho loved several women is based on the fragments of her poems that have come down to us, and the references to her found in the works of subsequent Greek writers.

The one extant song that still exists in its entirety is Sappho's "Hymn to Aphrodite." In it, Sappho petitions the Goddess of Love to transform her unrequited passion for a young woman into reciprocal love. Aphrodite gives an encouraging response:

Who,
O Sappho, does you injustice?
For if indeed she flees, soon will she pursue,
*   and though she receives not your gifts,*
*   she will give them,*
and if she loves not now, soon she will
*   love,*
even against her will.[24]

Sappho's poetry would have been unknown to almost all Greek wives, since most could not read, and all but courtesans were excluded from the male banquets where her poetry might have been recited. Some women, like Sappho, undoubtedly found pleasure in the arms of other women, as they do today, but then it would have been a very dangerous liaison indeed. The Greek wife was not her own property. Given by her father to her husband "for the purpose of producing legitimate offspring," she spent the greater part of her adult life being pregnant, nursing and tending children, preparing food, and producing cloth. She did not record for posterity the pleasures she might have derived from a lover.

ROMAN WIVES

During the next few centuries, when the center of the Mediterranean world shifted from Athens to Rome, there was a corresponding shift in ideas about the nature of marriage. Under the early Roman republic, from the fifth to the second century B.C.E., marriage resembled the Greek model: control over women passed "naturally" from fathers to husbands. Married women were expected to behave according to the dictates of *pudicitia*—a code word for strict morality, including its literal meaning "chastity." The mythical heroines of this early period were celebrated for their uncompromising fidelity to their one and only husband, even after they had become widows. The legendary Lucretia went so far as to commit suicide after she had been raped by Sextus Tarquinius; in Livy's account from his *History of Rome*, written around 25 B.C.E., she summoned her father, husband, and friends, and dramatically stabbed herself before them.[25] Married couples assumed the duty

Portrait of a husband and wife. Wall painting from Pompei, before 79 C.E. (Museo Archeologico Nazionale, Naples)

of perpetuating the husband's family name and of providing sons for the young republic, which depended on soldiers for its very existence. Men who reigned on the battlefield and in the Senate were expected to be the rulers of their homes. But in time, during the late republic and the empire, a more egalitarian ideal took root—one that emphasized the partnership of husband and wife.

These two different ideals were spelled out in Roman law as marriage *cum manu* and marriage *sine manu* (literally "with hand" and "without hand"). The gradual shift from marriage "with hand" to marriage "without hand" meant that a woman, even after her marriage, remained under the nominal tutelage of her father instead of becoming the "ward" of her husband.

Roman fathers were responsible for finding suitable matches for their daughters, while mothers, aunts, married older sisters, and matronly friends could also become involved in the search. The young girl herself was not encouraged to take the initiative in any way and was expected to accept her parents' choice. The father negotiated the *sponsalia* (betrothal), often when his daughter was quite young, in early Rome as young as six or seven. This was something of a preliminary business arrangement that might or might not result in a marriage.

After the austere years of the early republic, when such basic concerns as physical health and family name determined the choice of a spouse, more venal considerations such as money and political connections came to the fore. Pliny the Younger, writing around 100 C.E. to a friend who had asked him to find a husband for his brother's daughter, described a suitable candidate in terms of his public service, his appearance, and his family's fortune: "He has held the offices of quaestor, tribune and praetor with great distinction. . . . He has a frank expression, and his complexion is fresh and high-coloured; his general good looks have a natural nobility and the dignified bearing of a senator. (I personally think these points should be mentioned, as a sort of just return for a bride's virginity.)" Then with a show of reluctance, he wrote, "I am wondering whether to add that his father has ample means. . . . In view of the prevailing habits of the day and the laws of the country which judge a man's income to be of primary importance."[26] For all Pliny's high-minded manner, money was the conclusive remark.

But if money was primary, personal qualities such as good looks and character added weight to the suit. Women were expected to be virgins, and in return, men were expected to be well mannered, dependable, and energetic, especially in the gentry class to which Pliny belonged. No one expected the bridegroom to be a virgin.

The marriage betrothal itself was sometimes negotiated by professional intermediaries, such as marriage brokers, who ran a thriving business in Rome. Two fathers might agree on the marriage of their children or a prospective bridegroom could negotiate on his own behalf. Once the men had settled matters between them, the groom would give the bride (*sponsa*) a ring to wear on the third finger of her left hand—a custom we have preserved in the form of the traditional engagement ring. The young woman's father was expected to throw an engagement party. Along with weddings and coming-of-age celebrations, betrothals helped fill up the busy social calendars of upper-class Romans.

We know very little about the relationship of the engaged couple.[27] Did fiancés spend time together, with or without a chaperone? Was it unusual for a well-bred maiden to speak to her future husband before the wedding day? Ovid (43 B.C.E.–18 C.E.) claims that his erotic poems, the *Amores,* should be read by "the maid not cold at the sight of her promised lover's face," which suggests that *sponsi* (fiancés) during the early empire at least knew what the other person looked like.[28] But given the licentious nature of Ovid's writing, I do not think parents would have put it in their daughters' hands.

Roman marriage laws required the father's consent (but not the mother's), and also that of the bride and groom. Provided they were above the official age of puberty—twelve for a girl, fourteen for a boy— a male and female could enter into marriage by a declaration of what the lawyers called *maritalis affectio* (marital affection and intent) and by bringing the bride to the bridegroom's house. Such marriage was legally binding even without further ceremony. Emphasizing consent as the primary determinant of a valid union, Roman authorities spread this notion throughout the empire, and eventually throughout the whole Western world. It is the requirement of mutual consent that, during the course of many centuries, helped to change a wife's position. She could no longer be given by her father to her husband like a piece of property.

Weddings were generally planned for the second half of June. It was considered unlucky to marry in May or before June 15, when the temple of Vesta, goddess of the hearth, had its annual cleaning. On the day before the wedding, the bride dedicated her toys to the household gods of her childhood and put away the clothing she had worn as a child. For the wedding, her hair was parted into six locks held together by ribbons, producing a cone-shaped effect, and then covered by a red-orange veil known as a *flammeum.* She wore a full-length white tunic woven from a single piece of cloth, and tied with a belt with a complicated knot that only the husband was supposed to untie.

The wedding took place in the bride's house in the presence of friends and relatives. In fact, it was a duty (*officium*) to accept a wedding invitation, since the guests were considered part of the official formalities. A priest or friend of the family who bore the title of *auspex* presided over the ceremony, during which the matron of honor (*pronuba*) joined the spouses' right hands, and they kissed. Then the marriage contract, if there was one, was signed and witnessed.

Presents were given to the new couple by family members, friends, and even slaves. After a wedding banquet as luxurious as the bride's parents could afford, a peculiar mini-drama would take place. The bride pretended to cling to her mother, while the groom's friends dragged her away amid cries, songs, and obscene jokes. This ritual reminder of rape is still practiced by certain cultures today, including the Gypsies. The bride was then taken in a public procession to her husband's home, followed on the road by two servants carrying a distaff and a spindle—traditional symbols of wifely duties. At the entrance of her new residence, she was offered fire and water by the bridegroom—the elements essential to the running of a household. As in Greece, the members of the procession sang an epithalamium outside the bridal chamber while the newlyweds were expected to consummate their union.

The famous epithalamium written by the Latin poet Catullus (84?–54 B.C.E.) describes a wedding procession that does not seem to have changed significantly from the time of Homer. Catullus first addresses the bride and then the boys who light the way to her new home.

> *Come forth, fair bride! Delay no more!*
> *Come forth and hear the hymn we pour*
> *To Hymen, mighty god, for thee!*
> . . . .
> *Raise, boys, your torches! Raise them high!*
> *I see the scarf of crimson nigh.*
> *On! To her home the bride to bring,*
> *And, as ye move, in measure sing*
> *Hail, Hymen! Hymenaeus . . .* [29]

At the end of this high-spirited poem, Catullus urges the bridegroom to receive his wife amorously in the hope of producing progeny.

Progeny was always a major reason for a man to take a wife. Like the Hebrews and Greeks before them, the Romans thought of marriage as an institution designed to give a man legitimate children. Moreover, Roman citizens were encouraged to procreate as part of their civic duty. During the last century of the republic and the beginning of the empire, when it seemed that the old patrician families were dying out because of the many wars, legislation was introduced to stimulate marriage and offspring. Augustus (emperor from 27 B.C.E. to 14 C.E.) decreed that men between the ages of twenty-five and sixty and women between twenty-five and fifty were obliged to marry or remarry. Rewards were given to those who produced many children, and especially to the parents of three children, which constituted the Augustan ideal of a successful family. But the upper classes did not necessarily heed or need these benefits, and found ways to limit the size of their families. Children entailed expense and attention, which sophisticated Roman men and women were not always willing to provide.

Rudimentary forms of contraception were in use by this time, such as vaginal suppositories made from wool saturated with various substances believed to prevent fertilization; among the most commonly mentioned were honey, cedar gum, alum, and lead or sulphates mixed with oil. Abortion was a common practice and one that the law did not condemn until the end of the second century. And there was no law to prevent the abandonment and exposure of infants, disproportionately utilized for females. This practice resulted in the survival of more boys than girls, which gave the latter an edge in the marriage market. Finding a wife to bear children and perpetuate the family name was the civic duty of every bachelor. While procreation was never the exclusive justification for contracting a marriage for the Romans as it had been for ancient Hebrews and Greeks, the lack of children could be used as grounds for divorce. Tradition has it that the first Roman divorce, that of Spurius Carvilius, surnamed Ruga, in 230 or 231 B.C.E., was occasioned by the childlessness of his wife.

Divorce was so common a feature in Roman life among members of the elite from the late republican period onward that few persons of any note seem to have been married to only one spouse. Men divorced not only to acquire a childbearing wife, but, more commonly, for social or political advancement. Major political players like the generals Pompey and Mark Antony had no less than five wives apiece. However perfunctory these divorces, they often took an emotional toll on the family and particularly on the children—as in our own time. The great orator and statesman Cicero (106–43 B.C.E.) observed how "astonishingly upset" his nephew Quintus was when he heard that his parents were contemplating divorce. The divorce did not take place, yet Quintus nonetheless became embroiled in the conflict between his parents, taking his mother's side, for the next five years.[30]

Cicero, himself, chose divorce after he had been married for some thirty years. Although his wife Terentia had been very generous to him by lending him money from her personal fortune to finance his electoral campaigns and had been very dear to him when he was in political exile, he later decided to leave her because he felt she was no longer providing adequately for him, nor for their daughter, Tullia.[31] But Terentia had another view of the matter: Cicero left her for a younger, richer woman. According to Plutarch, Cicero married his pupil because "the young woman was very rich . . . he was persuaded by friends and relations to marry her, notwithstanding his disparity of age, and to use her money to satisfy his creditors." This second marriage was destined to be short-lived. When Cicero's daughter, Tullia (who had been married three times), died in childbirth, he divorced his second wife because she did not show sufficient grief at his daughter's death. Cicero's expedient treatment of his two wives is indicative of the ease with which men could initiate and obtain divorce, without public condemnation. At this period of Roman history, women also began to have access to divorce, as long as they had their father's approval.

Adultery, too, during the late republic and early empire seems to have been on the rise for members of the ruling class. Some married women became as famous for their affairs as other Roman wives for their virtue. Clodia, the wife of the consul Metellus, was known to have had many lovers, including Catullus, who called her Lesbia in his poems. The emperor Augustus's daughter Julia was exceptionally flamboyant in her affairs, so much so that Augustus felt compelled to banish her to an island. Four of her lovers were sent into exile and the fifth was executed.

Attempts to correct this moral laxity were codified in 18 B.C.E. in the *Lex Julia* promulgated by the emperor Augustus. Henceforth, a husband was required to prosecute an adulterous wife within sixty days of his discovery of the act. The law took a different view of what was appropriate action for an injured wife, since it explicitly stated "that wives have no right to bring criminal accusations for adultery against their husbands, even though they may desire to complain of the violation of the marriage vow, for while the law grants this privilege to men it does not concede it to women."[32] When a wife was convicted of adultery, the husband was required to divorce her, and she had to forfeit half her dowry and a third of her property, and be banished to an island. Pliny the Younger, obliged to officiate at a divorce trial under this law, gives us an eyewitness account of the proceedings:

> *The case heard on the following day was that of Gallitta, charged with adultery. She was the wife of a military tribune who was just about to stand for civil office, and had brought disgrace on her own and her husband's position by an affair with a centurion. Her husband had reported it to the governor, and he had informed the Emperor. After sifting the evidence the Emperor cashiered the centurion and banished him. There still remained the second half of the sentence . . . but here the husband held back out of affection for his wife and was censured for condoning her conduct. Even after he had reported his wife's adultery he had kept her in his house, apparently satisfied once he had got rid of his rival. When summoned to complete his accusation he did so with reluctance. . . . She was duly found guilty and sentenced under the Julian law.*[33]

The way that class and gender issues play out in this case is quite striking. In the first place, the husband and wife are of senatorian rank and the centurion is not, which makes the affair a "disgrace" on the social level—an insult to the husband's superior position. The centurion is easily disposed of. Once his rival was out of the way, the husband would have been content to take his wife back, but the law said otherwise. The wife had to be disposed of as well. It is noteworthy that the husband held back "out of affection for his wife." His wife's adultery had not destroyed his feelings for her, no matter what the law decreed.

Mutual affection in Roman marriages was considered highly desirable. The ideal of close ties between spouses, even to the point of joint exile or joint suicide, were part of a Roman Stoic tradition. But *public* displays of affection were frowned upon. In one notable case, a senator was expelled from the Senate for kissing his wife in front of their daughter. While considering this punishment "perhaps somewhat extreme," Plutarch, who recorded the incident, hastened to add that "it is disgraceful . . . to kiss and embrace in the presence of others."[34]

Any excessive emotion was suspect. Older men deemed too indulgent toward their younger wives could become objects of ridicule. Pompey (106–48 B.C.E.) was famous for what was considered exaggerated sentiment toward his last two wives. He married his fourth wife, Julia, Julius Caesar's daughter, to advance his career, which did not prevent him from falling in love with her—he at forty-six and she exactly half his age. In the reproachful words of Plutarch: "he let his fondness for his young wife seduce him into effeminate habits."[35] She, too, it appears, was enamored of him, but their mutual rapture was cut short by her early death in childbirth. Inconsolable as he was, Pompey soon made another political marriage, this time with the widow Cornelia. It did not take him long to become thoroughly captivated by that highly cultured lady, whose attractions beside those of youth and beauty included her knowledge of geometry, philosophy, and the lute.

When Cornelia and Pompey were married in 52 B.C.E., wives of the Roman aristocracy enjoyed responsibilities and pleasures that would have been unthinkable in ancient Greece. They could hold on to property received from their original families and become very wealthy in their own right. Their dowries, administered by their husbands, would be returned to them in the event of divorce. They had access to private education and could attend public events, such as banquets, salons, and spectacles. Whether these events consisted of readings by poets, dances by naked girls, or sexual orgies, marriage did not prevent women from being present and participating fully.[36]

Wives from the upper class moved about outside their homes with considerable independence since their domestic duties, including breast-feeding, could be turned over to nurses, servants, and slaves. It was so uncommon for upper-class women to nurse their babies during this period that Tacitus (56–120 C.E.), among others, chided the wives of imperial Rome for no longer suckling their offspring, and attributed the lack of civic virtue among the young to their lack of mother's milk.[37]

Roman wives were full mistresses of their homes and "keepers of the keys," with one notable exception. Husbands held the keys to the wine cellar, since their wives were not allowed to drink wine. That interdiction was founded in age-old fears that an intoxicated wife would not be able to remain "pure."

If a husband was sent into battle or exile, a Roman wife had to be ready to take over his affairs. Then she usually stayed behind in Rome and looked after the family property.[38] She was expected to share her husband's public glory and his personal misfortunes. In her short, four-year marriage to Pompey, Cornelia had an equal measure of both. In the end, during the civil war, she followed Pompey's flight away from Rome and was witness to his murder when he landed in Egypt after a major military defeat.

Fragment of a Roman sarcophagus showing a breast-feeding mother and attentive father. (Louvre, Paris)

The most famous couple of this era was Antony and Cleopatra. Their story, already legendary in their lifetime, has fed the Western imagination for over two millennia. Shakespeare, Shaw, and Cecil B. DeMille are among the many later-day interpreters who have revised the story, but the historical facts alone can stand by themselves as testimony to romance on an epic scale. And however legendary, their story sheds light on the status of wives in the Roman empire.

Cleopatra, queen of Egypt, had had a short affair with Julius Caesar, which had produced a son named Caesarion. Later, in 41 B.C.E., after Caesar's death, when Antony was part of the second Roman Triumvirate (shared with Octavius and Lepidus), he summoned Cleopatra to Southern Turkey, where they began their fateful liaison. Antony had already been married three times before he met the Egyptian queen, but he was still ripe for falling passionately, madly, and irrevocably in love.

While Antony's third wife, Fulvia, maintained his home in Rome and acted as a deputy husband on his behalf in his quarrels against Octavius (who would later become emperor under the name of Augustus), Antony spent the winter of 40–41 B.C.E. with Cleopatra in Alexandria. All the Roman accounts of their union depict Cleopatra as the seductive foreigner, whose "Oriental" ways played havoc with Antony's upright warrior mentality. But what do we really know of the give-and-take between them? Only, that their bodies comingled sufficiently to produce twins, a boy and a girl named Alexander and Cleopatra.

In the meantime, Fulvia was forced to flee Rome for political reasons, and as she was coming to meet her husband, she fell sick and died. Obliged to return to Rome to set his affairs in order, Antony managed to reconcile himself with Octavius. To seal the arrangement that would divide up the empire into three regions, Antony was expected to marry Octavius's sister, Octavia. Since both Octavia and Antony had recently lost their spouses, they were considered perfect for one another. Octavia was expected to take over the care of Antony's two young sons. This, as a good Roman spouse, she was quite prepared to do, but did she know that Antony also had two more children, the twins recently born to Cleopatra? In any event, both parties agreed to celebrate their nuptials in Rome, after receiving from the Senate a dispensation of the law by which a widow was not permitted to marry until ten months after the death of her husband. (Then, as now, annulments and dispensations are the purview of the powerful.) Antony struck a coinage to celebrate his wedding to Octavia. It was the first time that a living woman's portrait appeared on a Roman coin—an honor bestowed upon her as Antony's wife.

For several years Antony managed his two marriages, the official one in Rome, the unofficial one in Egypt. He and Octavia produced two daughters. But the balance was tipping in favor of Cleopatra, as could be sensed from the coins Antony issued in 37 B.C.E. with his portrait on the one side and Cleopatra's on the reverse.[39] A year later, in Italy, Octavia received the startling news that her husband and the Egyptian queen were married. The lawyers assured her that, since Cleopatra was a foreigner and since Romans of the citizen class were legally bound to marry other Romans, this was not a binding marriage. Prepared to forgive all, Octavia traveled East in 35 B.C.E. bringing the troops and gold her husband so desperately needed. At Athens she found a letter, ordering her to send on the provisions, and to return, herself, to Rome. Three years later, Antony sent her a formal notice of divorce. According to Plutarch writing a century after the events, "Antony sent orders to Rome to have Octavia removed out of his house. She left it, we are told, accompanied by all his children, except the eldest by Fulvia, who was then with his father, weeping and grieving. . . ."[40] Hence she lived under the wing of her brother, Octavius, who would soon become sole ruler of the Roman empire.

Octavius had every reason to be displeased with Antony's treatment of his sister, divorced so cavalierly for the Egyptian queen. He was particularly enraged by Antony's will, which ordered that even if he died in Rome, his body, after being carried in state through the forum, should be sent to Cleopatra at Alexandria. Octavius charged Antony with many offenses, among them the gift to Cleopatra of the library at Pergamon with its 200,000 volumes. Equally telling was the charge that "at a great banquet, in the presence of many guests, he had risen up and rubbed her feet" and that he left a public trial at a crucial moment, when Cleopatra happened to pass by in her chair, so as "to follow at her side and attend her home." Was this the conduct of a true Roman, for whom any public display of affection was considered inappropriate?

The war declared by Octavius ended in the shattering defeat of Antony and Cleopatra at Actium in 31 B.C.E. Fleeing to Alexandria, where they awaited the imminent arrival of Octavius, Antony and

Cleopatra anticipated payment with their lives. Painful as it would be to die at the respective ages of fifty-two and thirty-nine, they did not want to be left to the mercy of Octavius. No, in true Roman fashion, Antony would commit suicide, and Cleopatra, no less conscious of her honor, would do the same. The story that has come down to us of their last moments, which may or may not be true, seeks to portray them not only as lovers to the end, but also as exemplary Roman spouses united in joint suicide.

Antony is said to have committed suicide when he heard, mistakenly, that Cleopatra was dead. In Plutarch's account, he pierced his belly with his sword and lay down to die, but when he was told that the Queen was still alive, he asked to be taken to her. Cleopatra "laid him on the bed, tearing all her clothes, which she spread upon him; and, beating her breast with her hands, lacerating herself, and disfiguring her own face with the blood from his wounds, she called him her lord, her husband, her emperor. . . ."

Cleopatra's death was reported to be equally spectacular. Though she suffered the visit of Octavius and allowed him to believe she intended to go on living in the interest of her children, she, too, took her own life. According to the legend, she had an asp brought in hidden among a pile of figs. Then she provoked the asp to bite her. But even Plutarch wrote that "what really took place is known to no one." Octavius, it appears, gave credit to the account of the asp bite, and "though much disappointed by her death, yet could not but admire the greatness of her spirit and gave order that her body should be buried by Antony with royal splendour and magnificence."

After their death, it was, ironically, Octavia who raised Antony's children—not only the two daughters she had had with him, but also one of Antony's sons from his marriage to Fulvia and the children of his union with Cleopatra! Octavia raised them all alongside her own three children from her prior marriages. When we look today at the complexities of "recombined" families, we do well to remember Octavia's household and her responsibilities to the many orphans under her roof.

The life of Mark Antony's antagonist—Octavius/Augustus—provides another look at marriage at the highest level. His first marriage to Scribonia, who had already been married twice, was a political union that lasted only two years. After she gave birth to a daughter, Octavius divorced her because she couldn't tolerate one of his favorite mistresses. At the same time, he fell so blindly in love with Livia that he brought her to his bed even while she was pregnant with her first husband's child. Then he forced Livia's husband to divorce her, and married her himself in 38 B.C.E., three days after the child's birth. During the rest of his rule—a full fifty-one years—Augustus remained married to Livia, despite the fact that they never produced a living child and heir together. And when he died in 14 C.E., at the age of seventy-five, his last words were spoken to his wife urging her not to forget the happiness of their married life.[41]

Livia was apparently more indulgent toward her husband's extramarital affairs than her predecessor. She not only accepted his mistresses, but was even said to have procured them for him. But this was not all that was said about Livia. Indeed, judged by the venomous accounts of such historians as Tacitus, she was an infamous intriguing shrew who secured the succession of her son Tiberius (from her first marriage) by removing those who stood in his way. Other historians have been more generous, Valerius Maximus and Seneca among them. And in the opinion of most scholars today, Livia's contribution to Augustus's success was considerable, and their devotion to each other exemplary. As the first empress of Rome, with her personal dignity and harmonious marriage, she set the standard for all successive empresses.[42]

For pictures of Roman marriage among the gentry, there are the letters written by the younger Pliny to his beloved third wife, Calpurnia. Here is a sample:

> Never have I complained so much about my public duties as I do now. They would not let me come with you to Campania in search of better health, and they still prevent me from following hard on your heels. This is a time when I particularly want to be with you, to see with my own eyes whether you are gaining in strength and weight. . . .

> You say that you are feeling my absence very much, and your only comfort when I am not there is to hold my writings in your hand. . . . You cannot believe how much I miss you. I love you so much, and we are not used to separations.[43]

Pliny's letters, even if they were intended for publication, are testimonies to a very great love. Most wives undoubtedly did not receive such adulation.

But many enjoyed conjugal affection if we are to believe the numerous tombstones erected in their honor by grieving husbands. Funeral inscriptions praised them for being dear, holy, excellent, sweet, dutiful, obedient, chaste, loyal, thrifty, delightful, graceful, beautiful, and loving wives. The famous memorial tablet dedicated by her husband to a woman known as Turia in the first century B.C.E. presented the picture of a fully appreciated wife. Her funeral inscription began: "Rare are marriages as durable as this one, uninterrupted by divorce." It told the story of a wife who, after her husband's political disgrace, made superhuman efforts to have him rehabilitated. Managing to bring him covertly back to Rome and then hiding him in the crawl space under her roof, she badgered the city magistrates with countless supplications—not without risk to her personal safety—and was ultimately crowned with success: the spouses were granted the right to live together again. The only cloud on their happiness was the absence of a child. When Turia offered to divorce her husband so that he could marry another, he refused. In the end, he mourned an exemplary woman, "a faithful and submissive wife, good and gracious towards others, sociable and kind."[44]

Preserved in the Louvre, the funerary altar erected around 180 C.E. by Julius Secundus to his wife, Cornelia Tyche, and their daughter, Julia Secundina, after a shipwreck that took both their lives reads: "With an incomparable attachment and fidelity to her husband, and an extraordinary devotion to her children, she lived 38 years, 4 months and 7 days, of which twelve years [were spent] with me." The eleven-year-old daughter was remembered as "remarkable for her goodness, very pure in her conduct, and learned beyond the ordinary station of her sex."

Wives, too, erected monuments to their lost spouses, often described with the same terms of endearment used for the women. It is probable that the same words meant slightly different things when applied to each gender. "Obedient" implied that a woman was compliant toward her husband, whereas it was never acceptable for a husband to be subordinate to his wife.[45] "Chaste" for a husband may have merely meant that he conducted himself discreetly, whereas for a woman *pudicitia* was to be taken literally.

Fidelity to a dead spouse was praised on the part of a widow, despite the laws that penalized women under fifty who refused to remarry. There was even a special honorific term—*univera*—for the woman who married only once. No one expected the same of a widower. A widower might marry immediately upon the death of his wife, but a widow was expected, out of respect for her late husband, to wait ten months—a period later increased to twelve months and then to two years.

Before leaving the ancient world, we shall take a brief look at homosexuality among the Romans, who were almost as tolerant as the Greeks, especially during the late empire. According to historian John Boswell, there were "many same-sex couples in the Roman world who lived together permanently, forming unions neither more nor less exclusive than those of the heterosexual couples around them."[46] Nero, the flamboyant Roman emperor who ruled from 54 to 68 C.E., went so far as to marry two men, sequentially, in public ceremonies. Suetonius wrote of Nero's first homosexual marriage: "Having tried to turn the boy Sporus into a girl by castration, he went through a wedding ceremony with him—dowry, bridal veil and all—which the whole Court attended; then brought him home, and treated him as a wife. He dressed Sporus in the fine clothes normally worn by an Empress and took him in his own litter . . . through the Street of Images at Rome, kissing him amorously now and then."[47] He later also married his freedman Doryphorus. Nero forced the Imperial Court to treat his male brides with the same courtesy bestowed upon his three heterosexual wives (first Octavia, whom he divorced on a trumped-up adultery charge and then put to death; then Poppaea, who died three years later; and finally Statilia Messallina.)

Homosexual weddings seem to have increased during the first and second centuries, but were outlawed in 342. Some of the reactions to these ceremonies sound very much like those voiced today by conservatives facing gay and lesbian commitment ceremonies, domestic partnerships, and the possibility of legalized marriage. For example, Juvenal, in his mordant Satire 2, exclaimed: "Look—a man of family and fortune—being wed to a man!" And in that mocking tone for which he became famous, he spoke of having to attend a friend's wedding, still "a small affair," but one he feared would prefigure a groundswell of increasingly public same-sex weddings.

> . . . . *Such things, before we're very much older, will be done in public—in* public, *and will want to appear in the papers! These brides, however, are racked by one intractable problem: they cannot conceive, and hold their husbands by having a baby.*[48]

For all his mockery of male/male relations, Juvenal painted an even worse picture of heterosexual marriage in his Satire 6 aimed at Roman wives. Indeed, between the perils of matrimony and the pleasures of a male lover, Juvenal asked: "don't you think it better to sleep with a little boy-friend?/ A boy-friend doesn't argue all night or ask you for presents as he lies beside you. . . ."[49] With Roman wives guilty of every form of treachery and debauchery, according to Juvenal, marriage was nothing more than a "noose" for a man to stick his "stupid head" into.

As for same-sex unions between women, there is no longer any doubt that Roman writers were familiar with lesbianism and invariably condemned it as "monstrous, lawless, licentious, unnatural, and shameful."[50] While Roman culture was relatively tolerant of eros between men, it was consistently hostile to love between *tribades*—the Latin term for lesbians. Nonetheless, female homosexuality may have been as much a part of Roman society as male homosexuality, if we are to believe the many disparaging remarks of such first- and second-century writers as Seneca the Younger, Martial, and Juvenal.

Physicians during the Roman period tended to view female homoeroticism as a "disease" that manifested itself in masculine symptoms. Soranus, the noted Greek doctor who practiced in Rome in the second century C.E., believed that the cause of these symptoms was the physical condition of an enlarged clitoris. Because an enlarged clitoris was the most obvious part of the female genital organs that could be compared to a male penis, it was thought that women so endowed took on the "active" attributes of men, instead of the "passive" attributes considered natural for women. To "correct" this condition, Soranos and others counseled a surgical procedure known as clitorodectomy. It is still performed today as an Islamic practice in Egypt, the Sudan, and the surrounding region, despite protests from health professionals and feminist activists against genital mutilation.

It should not surprise us to discover that male homosexual practices were generally tolerated and the female equivalent was uniformly censured in ancient Rome. Men in antiquity simply had greater freedom than women in all respects, including behaviors that have subsequently been called "sinful," "deviant," or "abnormal" by Christians, moralists, and psychiatrists. For at least five hundred years, from Plato to Plutarch, while lesbianism called forth the invective of male writers, men continued to discuss the relative merits of male homosexuality and heterosexual love. Plutarch's *Eroticus* offers a good summary of the debate.

A defender of homosexuality argues that "true love has nothing whatever to do with the women's quarters. . . . There is only one genuine love, that of boys." He associates the love of boys with the virile virtues of philosophy and wrestling, and denigrates "love that dwells in women's laps and beds, always pursuing comfort and softened by pleasures." This attitude expressed during the Roman empire hearkens back to classical Greece, when misogynist contempt for women was standard fare.

But when we listen to the apologists for marital love in Plutarch's dialogue, we know that something has changed since the heyday of the Greeks. A more positive view of heterosexual intimacy, promoted by the Romans, has crept into the discourse. Instead of dismissing conjugal pleasure as an inferior form of love, its spokesman states categorically that "for married couples, sexual relations are a foundation of affection, a communion, as it were, in a great mystery." He speaks of the "mutual love and trust" and the "loving friendship" (*philotes*) that develops between spouses. And defying five centuries of high-culture preference for the love of boys, the apologist for marriage insists there is no greater unity than that which "Eros sets up within a conjugal union."[51] It is significant that the *Eroticus* ends with a heterosexual wedding, to which all are invited.

FROM OWNERSHIP TO LIMITED PARTNERSHIP

During the thousand years of Greco-Roman civilization that extended from Homer to Nero, the idea of the wife underwent formidable changes. One of the most notable concerned her "ownership." In ancient Greece, a young woman was her father's possession until she married. Then she was "given" by her father to her husband. Remnants of this idea still exist in the Western marriage ceremony when the minister asks, "Who gives this woman?" and the bride's father responds, "I do." A marriageable woman was a human commodity, to be transferred from her father's home to her husband's, where she assumed the latter's name and was subject to his control. Husbands had no reason to question this arrangement, and wives accepted it, though some undoubtedly chafed at the bit.

But over time, in the Roman world, the notion of the bride's consent gained legal and social weight. Theoretically, she could "give" herself of her own free will, if she had her father's approval. In practice, this probably meant that fathers consulted daughters on the choice of a husband and that it was difficult to marry them against their will.

Similarly, divorce possibilities opened up for Roman women under the empire that did not exist for their Greek predecessors. A wealthy Roman wife of this period enjoyed a remarkable degree of emancipation. Indeed, if we are to believe only a fraction of Juvenal's satirical picture of Roman society, an imperial wife took for granted her freedom of mobility and sexuality. Juvenal put into the mouth of a Roman matron addressing her spouse the following very modern credo: "Long ago we agreed . . . that you could do as you liked, and that I should be able/to please myself."[52]

In many ways, Roman marriage was conceived of as a reciprocal partnership, with aspects foreshadowing our own idea of marriage. Yet it would be naive to assume that Romans were motivated by the marital values we now espouse. Remember that marriage throughout the ancient world was largely a family affair arranged for economic, social, or political reasons. No one expected the bride and groom to be "in love"—in all probability, they had scarcely seen each other's face. In this respect, I am reminded of Indian arranged marriages today where parents still make choices for their children and give them spouses "to love." How different from our own idea of choosing a mate for oneself because one has fallen in love! Both for traditional Indian families and for classical Romans, it was normal for love to come after marriage. If not, marital harmony was quite enough.

In both ancient Greece and Rome, the job of husband and wife was to contribute to a stable social order. Two principal assumptions were at work here: the Greek ideal that one should 'avoid excess" and the Roman ideal that one should "be true," which meant loyal to one's family, one's friends, and one's homeland. As the ideal of loyalty between spouses began to take precedence over the other loyalties, the stock of the wife began to rise. Roman respect for the monogamous union of husband and wife permeated the empire, and subsequently, in ways that we shall see, worked its way into the Judeo-Christi n morality that we claim today.

TWO

Wives in Medieval Europe, 1100–1500

". . . it is impossible/ that any clerk wol speke good of wyves"
Chaucer, *The Wife of Bath's Prologue*

What do a noble lady in her feudal castle, a city-dwelling burgher's wife, a poor woman working for wages, and a country peasant have in common? How can we group together women from such different social categories, different countries, and different centuries? One approach is to look at the legal and religious statutes that affected medieval wives. Another is to examine prevailing ideas about marriage from the advice literature of the period. As for the daily activities of wives, there are manuscript miniatures, woodblocks, engravings, and even portrait paintings that show them in a variety of occupations. But nothing is more valuable, to my mind, than the few precious documents that preserve a particular wife's view of her own situation. From these different sources, it is possible to construct a mosaic of married women's lives, which, however unfamiliar, still share some traits in common with our own.[1]

LEGAL AND RELIGIOUS CONSIDERATIONS

During the early Middle Ages, the Catholic church gradually took over the jurisdiction of marriage. Previously, much of Europe had followed the Roman model that required the consent of the bride, groom, and their fathers. But from the mid-twelfth century onward, church law known as canon law made two changes that were to have long-term effects. First, the church pressured individuals to marry in the presence not only of witnesses, but also of a priest, and to perform this ceremony "at church." Second, it downplayed the need for parental consent, and foregrounded the mutual will of the intended spouses as the major criterion in the making of a valid marriage. This revolutionary doctrine would endure and flourish over the centuries.[2]

Moreover, once marriage was declared a sacrament (a ceremony through which one obtained God's grace), it could not be undone. The sacramental nature of marriage was accepted broadly from the eighth century onward, although it was not made canon law until 1563 at the Council of Trent. Medieval men and women entered marriage with the knowledge that there was no way out of it, even if it proved to be disastrous for one or both parties. On the whole, the indissolubility of marriage was probably favorable to women, since most divorces had traditionally been initiated by men.[3] It provided wives with a sense of security unknown to single women, except for those in religious orders.

Medieval society was essentially hierarchical: serfs and peasants served their masters, while their masters served yet greater lords and ladies, and everyone served the king. Within this feudal system, the wife—no matter what her social station—was subservient to her husband. As the thirteenth-century English jurist Henry de Bracton formulated it, a woman was obliged to obey her husband in everything, as long as he did not order her to do something in violation of Divine Law. He related a case in which a wife and husband forged a royal writ, and though the husband was hanged, the wife was acquitted on the grounds that she had been ruled by her husband.[4] Both French and English law went so far as to declare that a woman who killed her husband be tried for treason, rather than than the lesser crime of felony, since she had taken the life of her lord and master.

In the German-speaking world, the rights of a husband over his wife were clearly outlined in the *Sachsenspiegel* and the *Schwabenspiegel*— two books that provided the basis for the laws of many German towns. These rights extended to a wife's assets, as well as her person. A husband could dispose of his wife's property, her clothes, her jewelry, even her bed linens. And he had the legal right to beat her, if she did not accede to his wishes. In most countries, husbands could punish their wives however they saw fit, short of murder.

Battering was an accepted practice, sanctioned by law and custom, that allowed husbands to enforce authority over their wives. It was a staple of folk wisdom and literature, and provided comic caricature in the popular reverse images of wives beating their husbands. But the reality was far from comic, as shown from court records that often condoned the behavior of brutal husbands abusing their wives as a matter of course. Even when concerned family members and neighbors intervened and brought the matter to the attention of the courts, the husband usually got off with only a fine or a pledge to "receive his wife in his house and treat her agreeably."[5] Legal wife beating did not disappear with the Middle Ages. It hung on in many places into the nineteenth century; and even after it was no longer legal, battering has continued to maim countless wives from every ethnic and social sector. Our recent efforts to provide shelters for battered wives and to stamp out this now criminal offense run counter to centuries of practice.

Marriage was thus an institution by which men were confirmed as the masters of their wives on religious and legal grounds. But it was also a union intended to provide for the well-being of both parties and eventually their children. At the peasant level, marriage was largely an economic arrangement that took place when two people were able to put together sufficient resources for joint survival. A bride's dowry consisting of money, goods, animals, or land was essential to the founding of a new household. At the least, she was expected to provide a bed, a cow or household utensils. She was also expected to posses those skills necessary for living on a farm—tending livestock and poultry, milking the cow, making butter, spinning and sewing. The groom was expected to provide shelter and support for his wife. In territories and countries where Roman law still applied, especially south of the Loire, it was understood that if the bride's family did not pay the groom what had been promised, the marriage was essentially null and void.[6]

In areas of Europe that held onto Germanic law, peasant marriage was primarily a contract between two families who came to an agreement about the size of the dowry and the wedding day. The wedding ceremony was essentially a legal transfer of the bride to the groom, presided over by her father or another elder within a circle of family members. A thirteenth-century poem in Middle-High German describes such a scene.

Peasant women milking cows, churning butter, and leading the cows to graze. Miniature by the Flemish illuminator Simon Bening from the Da Costa Book of Hours, the month of April. Bruges, circa 1515. (Pierpoint Morgan Library, New York)

Now we must give young Gotelind
As wife to youthful Lämmerslint
And we must give young Lämmerslint
As man, in turn, to Gotelind.
A grey-haired man now did arise
Who in the use of words was wise;
Well versed he was in marrying.
He stood both parties in a ring.
Then first he spoke to Lämmerslint:
"And will you take this Gotelind
To be your wife? If so, say 'aye.'"
"Gladly," the young man did reply.

. . . . .

The man then spoke to Gotelind:
"And do you, too, take Lämmerslint
Willingly, your man to be?"
"I do, sir, if God grants him me."[7]

Still, we should not assume that peasant marriage was *only* a legal and economic affair. Mutual attraction could also play its part. Country youth found opportunity in forests, fields, and haystacks for pre-marital dalliance. Numerous couples did not bother to marry until the female had proved her fertility by becoming pregnant. Childbirth soon after marriage carried little shame, and even the stigma of illegitimate birth does not seem to have been very strong in peasant society, at least not in England.

At the other end of the social ladder, members of the nobility were guided by property concerns on a grand scale. Marriage was the means by which the powerful made alliances and transmitted inheritances. Fathers had the responsibility of finding the best partners for their sons and daughters so as to ensure proper unions and maintain their status into the next generation. Therefore, daughters were carefully super-vised and allowed little opportunity to lose their precious virginity before they married, usually at an early age.

Sons, on the other hand, were allowed the freedom of "youth" in the form of liaisons with girls of lower station, concubines, and prostitutes. With the institution of primogeniture, whereby title and estate passed to the eldest son, younger sons generally had nothing to offer a

Marriage in medieval Europe was a major means of transmitting property. In this Spanish manuscript from the late twelfth century, a lord transmits feudal rights by giving his daughter in marriage to his new son-in-law, with his wife's approval. Liber Feudorum Maior. (Donación de Bernat Ató a Gausfred III. Archivo Corona Aragón, Barcelona)

prospective bride and were unable to marry. This situation made for an imbalance in the number of unmarried men available to prospective brides. Since it was understood from the start that a daughter's marriage was to be made in the interest of her family's economic and social well-being, as well as her own, only a truly recalcitrant young woman would have opposed the wishes of her father or guardian. In general, it seems that the more wealth and status one had, the less say one had in the selection of one's spouse.

Daughters from the merchant class probably had greater latitude in meeting and choosing mates, since they were often their fathers' helpers. Merchants, painters, brewers, doctors, tavern keepers often depended on their daughters, as well as their sons and wives, for assistance, and many of these daughters married men related to their father's business and continued to work after marriage. The rise of towns and cities from the twelfth to the fifteenth century provided what one scholar has called a "window of freedom" for European women.[8] The daughters of burgher families in such places as Paris, Strasbourg, Marseilles, Basel, Venice, London, and the German cities of Lübeck, Frankfurt am Main, Cologne, Nuremberg, and Leipzig had more opportunities than either nobleowomen or peasants to see men from different stations of life and to contract clandestine liaisons, though, in general, they too had their marriages arranged by their elders.

When the financial arrangements between the families of the bride and the groom had been settled, their betrothal was officially contracted. In the early Middle Ages, this settlement was almost as binding as marriage. For example, when Christina of Markyate, member of a noble Anglo-Saxon family in England at the beginning of the twelfth century, delayed her marriage for several years after she had been pressured into an unwanted betrothal by her parents, they were afraid of being seen as "the laughing stock of our neighbours, a mockery and derision to those who are round about." The priest brought in to persuade Christina to wed referred to her betrothal as if she were already married: "We know that you have been betrothed according to ecclesiastical custom. We know that the sacrament of marriage, which has been sanctioned by divine law, cannot be dissolved, because what God has joined together, no man should put asunder." In the end, Christina's case was brought before the bishop, who decided in her favor. She would be allowed to fulfill a childhood vow to remain a virgin and enter the religious life, "to keep herself for God to serve Him freely and for no man besides."[9]

Despite religious decrees during this period pressing for church weddings, they had not yet become mandatory or even customary for the faithful. In Germanic countries, peasants continued to marry under the auspices of a family member, and in Romanized countries like Italy and France, even among the upper classes, marriages continued to be performed in secular settings. In the face of widespread resistance, Pope Alexander III (1159–1181) was forced to abandon his attempts to force Christians to marry in church. The following French nuptial scene, recalling the primitive practice of "bedding" the bride and groom, offers a competing model.

In 1194, Arnoud, the eldest son of the count of Guînes, was married at home. One of the officiating priests left behind this record: "when the husband and wife were united in the same bed, the count called us— another priest, my two sons and me" into the room. Note that the priest himself was married and the father of two sons, both of whom were priests. The count ordered that the newlyweds should be sprinkled with holy water, the bed perfumed with incense, the couple blessed and entrusted to God. Then the count himself invoked God's blessings, asking that the couple "live in His divine love, persevere in harmony, and that their seed multiply with the length of their days." Here the ceremony takes place in the bedroom of the newlyweds, with the father directing the proceedings and presiding alongside the priests.[10] The bride—the only woman present in this assemblage of six people—may have felt frightened in a strange bed, away from her own female enclave. She would certainly have felt the solemnity of the occasion, and especially her obligation to produce an heir for her new family.

Gradually, however, religious pressure to publicize marriages and conduct them in church began to take effect throughout Europe. Thus in 1231, the emperor Frederick II of the kingdom of Sicily (which included much of Southern Italy), promulgated the following law: "we order that all men of our kingdom and especially the nobles who desire to contract marriage must have the marriage celebrated solemnly and publicly, with due solemnity and a priestly blessing, after the betrothal has been solemnized."[11]

The marriage of Saint Godelieve, patroness of Flanders, to the wealthy landowner Bertolf (detail of painting). Not until the end of the Middle Ages did weddings take place commonly inside the church, a practice that became mandatory for Catholics after the Council of Trent in 1563. Master of the Saint Godelieve Legend, fourth quarter of the fifteenth century, Bruges. (Metropolitan Museum of Art, New York)

To celebrate the marriage "publicly," banns were to be read in church during three successive weeks, a period of time considered sufficient for objections to be made. For example, someone might claim that the prospective bride or groom already had a spouse, or a jealous rival might disclose that that the engaged couple were first, second, third, or fourth cousins—degrees of consanguinity prohibited by the church. But barring objections, the wedding would then take place "at church." "At church" commonly meant "at the church's door"—at the entrance or one of the side porches. This is the meaning of the words that describe the Wife of Bath in Chaucer's *Canterbury Tales*: "Husbands at church door she had five." According to Latin liturgies used in England and France, the bride and the groom would stand together before the church door, the man on the right of the woman, and the woman on the left of the man, in the presence of the priest and witnesses.

The service performed at York in England (similar to those performed in Sarnum and Hereford, as well as Rennes in France) gives us the feel of this ancient ceremony.[12] It should take only a slight effort to follow the priest's archaic language as he addresses the people: "Lo, bretheren we are comen here before God and his angels and all his halowes, in the face and presence of our moder holy Chyrche, for to couple and to knyt these two bodyes togyder. . . . If there be any of you that can say any thynge why these two may not lawfully be wedded togyder at this tyme, say it nowe."

Then the priest says to the man: "Wylt thou haue this woman to thy wyfe and loue her and keep her, in sykenes and in helthe, and in all other degrese be to her as a husbande sholde bae to his wyfe, and all other forsake for her, and holde the only to her to thy lyues ende."

The man answers: "I wyll."

The priest then uses similar language for the woman, with the additional words "and to be buxum to hym, serue hym," which means to be obedient to him and serve him.

The woman answers: "I wyll."

At this point the priest asks: "Who gyues me this wyfe?" The woman is usually given away by her father. This part of the marriage ceremony recalls the ancient assumption that a daughter was "gifted" by her father to her husband.

Then the groom takes the bride by the right hand with his right hand—as in the Roman ceremony—and pledges his troth, saying after the priest: "Here I take the [Name] to my wedded wyfe, to haue and to halde, at bedde and at borde, for fayrer for fouler, for better for warse, in sekeness and in hele, tyl dethe us departe." And the woman makes the same vow in the same words.

Now the groom places gold, silver, and a ring upon a shield or a book, and the priest blesses the ring, which the groom then places upon the fourth or middle finger of the bride. Holding his bride by the hand, he says after the priest: "With this rynge I wedde the, and with this golde and siluer I honoure the, and with this gyft I dowe thee." The priest next asks about the bride's dowry—the money or property she brings to the husband.

The ceremony ends with prayer and a benediction, followed by entrance into the church for celebration of the bridal mass. The mass itself, however inspiring, did not add to the validity of the nuptial ceremony, which was considered complete and binding before the church door.

Church weddings, were, of course, not intended for the scattered Jewish communities living in Europe, who were subject to their own laws and rituals. Yet, however self-contained, these Jews were also influenced by the majority Christian culture. Consider, for example, how the Christian insistence on monogamy influenced the Jewish population. By the end of the first millennium, Askanazi Jews, following the custom of their adopted countries in Eastern and Western Europe, were practicing monogamy, whereas Sephardic Jews in Spain under the Moors and in the Near East were still polygamous. While an official ban on polygamy issued by Rabbi Gershom ben Judah of Worms in 1040 put an end to the practice among German and French Jews, Sephardic Jews maintained the right to polygamy for almost another millennium. An all-inclusive ban was not pronounced until the mid-twentieth century, after the formation of the State of Israel.

A considerably more limited example of Jewish acculturation to European modes is found in a thirteenth-century Hebrew-French wedding song, intended for performance during the marriage festivities of a Jewish couple. The song, written in both Hebrew and Old French and representing the voices of the bride, bridegeroom, and chorus, combines images from traditional Hebrew nuptial poetry and the French feudal warrior world. A line from Isaiah evoking the sun and the moon as symbols of the two lovers is followed by the military command "Surrender your castle"—an order derived from medieval warfare, which establishes the central metaphor of the groom's assault on the bride's fortress.

In the translation by medievalist Samuel Rosenberg, French and Hebrew (the latter indicated in italics), sacred and secular, licentious and dignified allusions playfully vie with one another:

To the Hill of frankincense
Our *hatan* [groom] has come.
Light of the sun, light of the moon!

Surrender your castle,
For in his hand is a blood-red sword.
If you resist his advance,
No one can save you.

. . . .

Gazelle, graceful dancer,
I have come to court you
Or else in a great war
I will come to defy you—

. . . .

My armed and raging passion
Will beat its way along your path.
Let me just die now.

. . . .

The bridegroom's voice came forth
And to his attendants said
Even a beautiful song grows stale.
—Lift *hatan* and *kallah* [bride] up on their thrones![13]

This admixture of Hebrew and local culture was a given in the lives of European Jews, who sought to preserve their religious identity despite the restrictions imposed upon them by Christendom.

From the Middle Ages onward, when priests began to participate more regularly in wedding ceremonies, the church gained greater presence in all aspects of marriage, beginning with the conjugal bed, where consummation was mandatory if the union was to be considered binding. According to Christian doctrine, spouses were supposed to copulate only for the benefit of procreation. This position, taken by the fourth-century church fathers, had become dogma by the Middle Ages. Intercourse, for the sheer sake of pleasure, was vehemently denounced. Wives, especially, were admonished to avoid enjoying themselves; it was sufficient to welcome one's husband as a passive recipient, but to share his ardor was expressly forbidden.[14] Sexual relations were considered a *debitum conjugale*—a solemn duty that each spouse owed the other, but not an approved pleasure in its own right, as we hold today.

For most couples, whether they followed such instructions religiously or not, they would have been made to believe that sex, even in

Jewish wedding ring with pointed roof symbolizing the home and inscribed with the characters Mazel Tov. *Fourteenth-century Alsace (Colmar). (Musée de l'Art et de l'Histoire Judaïque, Paris)*

marriage, carried the taint of original sin. While a few Christian thinkers, like the fourth-century churchmen Jovinian and Saint John Chrysostome, had defended marriage and argued that a wife was not an obstacle but an aid to salvation, and that married life was just as worthy as the celibate one, it was the more sinister view of their younger contemporaries, Saint Jerome and Saint Augustine, that had won out. Medieval theology insisted that flesh was prone to evil, and that marriage was, at best, a necessary evil.

Christian theologians presented married life as a lesser state than either widowhood or virginity, since chaste widows and virgins abstained from sex. Saint Jerome had stated unequivocally: "Let married women take their pride in coming next after virgins."[15] This value judgment was made graphically clear in a twelfth-century German manuscript (Der Jungfrauspiegel, preserved by the Rheinisches Landesmuseum in Bonn) that shows, allegorically, three levels of female worth. At the top are the virgins harvesting numerous sheaves of wheat. In the middle are the widows with lesser crops. And at the bottom are wives with their husbands, reaping minimal rewards.[16]

It is hard for us today to imagine the extent to which the ideal of chastity was glorified and spread among the faithful. Just as we are bombarded by commercial images proclaiming the value of sexual activity, so too medieval Christians were surrounded by model images of famous ascetics. Lives of the saints, sung or recited to illiterate audiences, extolled those who had taken vows of chastity. One of the first examples written in Old French, the Life of Saint Alexius (circa 1050), made this point explicit: the protagonist's ascension to sainthood began when he abandoned his wife on their wedding night and fled to live in poverty.[17] The moral for men was clear: it was better to leave your wife and live ascetically than to be a devoted husband. Similarly, female saints who refused to marry or who abandoned their offspring for the religious life were highly praised. Most female saints were virgins, often martyred for resisting rape despite torture and the threat of death.

The sculptures adorning the many new churches that sprang up after 1100 glorified martyred saints, displaying their wounds or holding their decapitated heads in their hands. Couples were less in evidence, except for the notorious case of Adam and Eve. A medieval girl and boy, looking up at their images, would have been reminded that they, too, even in marriage, were capable of the sins of the first human couple. If they wanted to be more certain of salvation, it was better to enter a convent or monastery.

Members of the clergy, living within the church close or in monasteries, were not supposed to marry or have concubines or engage in any sexual activity. The church had been trying to enforce sexual purity for the clergy ever since the Council of Nicaea in 325. Pope Leo IX condemned clerical marriage in 1049, and further Lateran councils

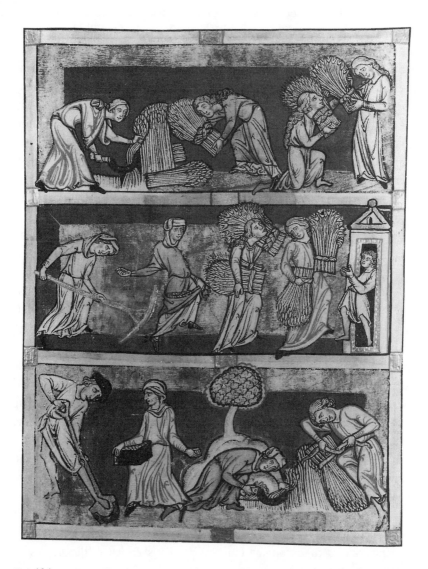

Twelfth-century German manuscript representing the Christian hierarchy of womanhood according to one's level of abstinence: virgins at the top, widows in the middle, wives at the bottom. The less sexual activity, the more sheaves of wheat (heavenly rewards) one could expect. Page from Der Jungfrauspiegel. *(Rheinisches Landesmuseum, Bonn)*

in the early twelfth century pronounced priestly orders an impediment to marriage, and vice versa. But in the early Middle Ages, a significant number of priests still lived with concubines—an arrangement generally accepted by their parishioners—and some priests were even officially married, despite the knowledge that marriage would prevent their rise upward in the hierarchy of the church. We know from the letters of Héloïse and the famous cleric Abelard that they were married in church, in the presence of a canon and several witnesses. While the personnages in question were exceptional in so many ways, their letters written long after their marriage attest to sex and love among the clergy and the pressures brought to bear upon a cleric and his wife.

THE STORY OF HÉLOÏSE AND ABELARD

The history of Héloïse and Abelard, nine hundred years old, still has the shock value of a romance–cum–horror story; yet, according to our best evidence, it is a true story.[18] Abelard was an eldest son who renounced his rights of primogeniture for the sake of study. He soon rivaled all the other peripatetic practioners of philosophy, becoming famous in his twenties both for his public discourses and his good looks. By his early thirties, he was a master of theology. It was during his Parisian residence, when he was thirty-seven years old, that he met Héloïse. She was probably fifteen.

In the letter known as "The Story of My Misfortunes," written in Latin and widely circulated among his contemporaries, Abelard recalled the beginnings of their liaison:

> There was in the city of Paris a very young woman named Héloïse, the niece of a canon named Fulbert. He cherished her to the greatest degree and put all his zeal into pushing her as far as possible in the study of every science. . . . The rarity of literary knowledge among women added even more to the value of this young woman and made her celebrated throughout the kingdom. I saw in her all that usually seduces lovers and judged that it would be feasible for me to share her bed. I thought I could do this very easily: I had such renown at that time, I was so remarkable for my youth and beauty that I did not fear being rejected by any woman whom I judged worthy of my love.

A modern reader will undoubtedly be outraged at the thought of this teacher and cleric plotting the seduction of an adolescent. But instead of imposing our own values on the early twelfth century, let us turn to Héloïse's memories of the same events.

> *What king, what philosopher could equal your renown? What country, what town, what city did not simmer with excitement to see you? Who, I ask, did not hurry to admire you when you appeared in public? . . . What married woman, what unmarried woman did not desire you in your absence, did not burn in your presence? . . . you possessed in particular two gifts that could instantly attract the heart of any woman: you knew how to compose poetry and to sing . . . gifts that were utterly lacking in the other philosophers.*

Abelard was clearly a celebrity, the equivalent of a media star today, capable of drawing oversized crowds and impassioned fans. And despite his attractiveness, he had remained celibate until he became enflamed by his love for Héloïse. In order to gain access to her, he proposed to her uncle that he should lodge in the canon's house in exchange for the private lessons he would give Héloïse.

Before long Abelard had Héloïse completely in thrall. Not only did he approach her with the authority conferred by age, sex, vocation, and fame—he also had the right to chastise her. At that time chastisement was both a verbal and physical affair, allowing Abelard the "opportunity to make her bend more easily through menaces and blows, if seduction failed." Seduction did not fail. But what Abelard had not anticipated was the mutual nature of their passion, the way he too became intoxicated. Both gave themselves to erotic delight with the ardor of first-time lovers.

Yet there was a downside to sexual pleasure: Abelard's work as a philosopher and teacher began to suffer. His students began to complain of his absentmindedness, and rumors began to circulate. Finally, Héloïse's uncle could no longer remain blind to the affair that was going on in his very house, and the lovers were obliged to separate.

Not surprisingly, Héloïse discovered she was pregnant. Abelard decided to send her away to Brittany to his sister, where she spent the rest of her pregnancy. He, however, remained in Paris, and had to confront Héloïse's uncle, Fulbert. Clearly this was an affair between men, and between them they decided that Abelard should marry the woman he had "dishonored." Abelard's only condition was that the marriage take place secretly, so that his reputation and career would not suffer. Because he was only a cleric who had not been ordained, he could, according to canon law, take a wife, but marriage would prevent him from teaching. Interestingly, Héloïse's dishonor would be repaired through marriage, whereas his position as a famous cleric would be tarnished by that same act.

After the birth of their son, named Astrolabe and left in the care of Abelard's sister, the lovers returned secretly to Paris. Abelard intended to marry Héloïse, as he had promised her uncle. The only obstacle to this marriage was Héloïse herself.

True to the prejudices of her age, she believed that philosophy and theology did not belong under the same roof that sheltered wives and babies, or, as Abelard later put it: "What person, absorbed by religious or philosophic meditations, could endure the crying of newborn babies, the songs of their nurses to quiet them, the noisy crowd of servants? What disgust in having to bear the continual filth of little children!" Both Abelard and Héloïse had clearly internalized the old commonplaces used to discourage clerics from marriage.

Héloïse did not want to be the ruin of the man she idolized. She preferred to be called his friend, sister, and lover (*amica*), rather than his wife, and to be joined to him only by her feelings, rather than by the constraints of the conjugal bond. As she wrote later: "And if the name of wife seems more sacred and stronger, the name of 'amica' always seemed sweeter, like the names—without wanting to shock you—of concubine or courtesan." Preferring "love to marriage, liberty to bondage," she sounds more like a liberated woman of the twentieth century than a medieval mother raised by a canon within the church close.

But Héloïse's protests were of no avail; Abelard decided to honor his promise to her uncle. The lovers were secretly married in church at the break of day in the presence of Fulbert and a few witnesses. In order to keep the marriage secret, Abelard and Héloïse then went their separate ways, meeting only occasionally and with the greatest discretion. The story might have ended there, were it not for the horrible incident masterminded by Héloïse's uncle. What happened next wreaked havoc on the couple's union and made their history famous for posterity.

Shortly after the marriage ceremony, while the two spouses were living apart, Fulbert began to speak publicly of the marriage, contrary to
the promise of secrecy he had made. He was not satisfied with the turn
of events, and wanted further compensation for the family honor.
When Fulbert began to beat Héloïse, Abelard decided to abduct her
and place her in an abbey, the very same one where, as a girl, she had
been raised and educated. He had religious garments made for her that
were appropriate to her new life in the monastery. She dressed like a
nun, except for the veil, which was reserved for those who took lifelong
vows. Believing that Abelard had sent Héloïse to the abbey so as to gain
his freedom, Fulbert punished him with a cruel act of revenge. While
he was asleep, servants acting under Fulbert's orders entered Abelard's
room and cut off his testicles.

Years later, when Abelard remembered this event, he not only spoke
of the pain and shame, but also of God's strange justice. "What righteous decision of God had struck me in that part of my body through
which I had sinned!" Though it was common during the Middle Ages
to punish people by mutilating the part of the body associated with a
criminal act, one doubts if this was Abelard's first reaction. Confused
and ashamed, he took refuge in a cloister.

And what of Héloïse? Once again, her fate was decided by Abelard,
and this time, irrevocably. He ordered that she take the veil permanently, and both of them donned the habit the same day, he in the
abbey of Saint-Denis and she in the monastery of Argenteuil. Héloïse
was, at the most, seventeen; Abelard, thirty-nine.

Could this dramatic tale have ended differently? What was there to
prevent Abelard and Héloïse from living together as man and wife? In
truth, there was no outside obstacle. Having been married within the
church, Héloïse and Abelard were legal spouses in every sense of the
word. Even the fact of castration would not have constituted an obstacle, since the church granted annulment only when the marriage had
not been consummated; also, men who have had their testicles
removed could still be capable of sexual activity. But living together as
spouses did not seem to interest Abelard. After all that had happened,
he decided to return to his earlier vocation as a celibate cleric. He lived
out the rest of his life—another twenty-four years—as a monk, writer,
teacher, and founder of the abbey of Paraclet, in which, by a strange
twist of fate, Héloïse would rise to the rank of abbess.

Let us return to her version of their story as told in the two letters she wrote to Abelard from Paraclet. The salutation of her first letter speaks worlds about the difference in their stations: "To her seigneur, or rather her father; to her husband, or rather her brother; [from] his servant, or rather his daughter; his spouse, or rather his sister." Fifteen years after the events which had caused their separation, Héloïse, the abbess of Paraclet, spoke to Abelard with the voice of a mistress and wife. "I am yours," she wrote, "in a unique way. . . . You are linked to me by the greatest of obligations . . . by the nuptial sacrament, and even more strongly because I have always loved you . . . with a limitless love."

Héloïse reproached her husband for having abandoned her after she had followed his commandments in every way. "Give me a single reason, if you can, which explains why, after our mutual entry into religious life, for which you alone made the decision, you have so competely deserted and forgotten me that I have neither your presence nor your words to give me courage, nor even a letter to console me in your absence." She reminded him more than once that she had accepted his decision to take up "the hardship of the monastic life not through devotion," but because Abelard had ordered her to do so. Clearly Héloïse felt that her primary allegiance was to her former teacher, lover, and master, who was still her husband.

Héloïse's passionate feelings for Abelard are expressed even more openly in her second letter. She admits that she cannot chase from her memory the "voluptuous pleasures" they had tasted together: "Wherever I turn, they force themselves into my eyes." Unlike Abelard, who viewed his former actions as sinful and expressed an absence of sexual longing, Héloïse confessed that she still sighed for lost pleasures. "Not only the acts realized, but also the places and the moments where I experienced them with you are so fixed in my mind that I relive everything with you in the same circumstances, and even in my sleep, they give me no peace."

The differences in Abelard's and Héloïse's reactions to their separation have called forth endless commentary over the centuries. Misogynist critics have attributed Héloïse's lust to the lascivious nature of all women, or to women's proclivity to make love the exclusive focus of their lives. Some have praised Abelard for his virtuous retirement into chastity and greater devotion to God. Few have emphasized the difference in their ages—after all, Héloïse was thirty-two at the time of the correspondence and Abelard fifty-four, which may have accounted somewhat for the difference in their sexual appetites, without taking into consideration the effect of his castration. Moreover, as Héloïse honestly confessed, she did not choose the religious life; it was chosen for her. She admitted that she was more afraid of offending Abelard and more eager to please him than God Himself. Hardly the words one expects to hear from the mouth of an abbess!

Ten years after these letters were written, Abelard died and was buried at Paraclet. Héloïse lived on another twenty years, and when she died in 1164, she was buried beside her husband.

This remarkable story, unique in both the quality of the players and the macabre nature of the events, bears witness to the hazards that marriage might entail for a clergymen. A woman living with or married to a priest (alternately called a "priest's wife" or a "priest's whore") may have been tolerated by medieval society, but she, more than he, was usually blamed for *his* lapsed celibacy. While he was allowed to continue his public vocation, the priest's wife was well advised to keep a low profile. Héloïse was sequestered in a convent for most of her married life—a fate usually reserved for single women or widows. Her story, however unique, gives us an account of sexual passion from the perspective of a wife in twelfth-century France, a century famous for the rapid rise of magnificent religious edifices and for a new vision of heterosexual love.

THE BIRTH OF ROMANTIC LOVE

It has been argued that the French "invented" romantic love in the twelfth century.[19] Its model was the perfect knight and the inaccessible lady, usually the wife of a king. Romantic love existed primarily outside marriage in an atmosphere of secrecy, which intensified the experience, as in the myth of Tristan and Iseut, the legendary Celtic couple who drank a love potion by accident and from that point on could not live without each other, even though Iseut was destined to be the wife of King Mark of Cornwall, Tristan's lord. When King Mark began to suspect he was being cuckolded, Tristan was ultimately forced to flee. Nonetheless, he and Iseut carried their love for each other into the grave. As opposed to "ordinary love" that changes according to the circumstances of daily life, the story of Tristan and Iseut represents the power of an irresistible and inexhaustible passion, a "fatal love" that overcomes suffering and even death. Their watchword is the motto of all true lovers: "Neither you without me, nor I without you."

This vision of love, which originated in the courts of Southern France and then spread to the North, offered a new way of conceptualizing gender relations. It reversed traditional masculine and feminine roles, granting the woman power over the man. She was there to command him, he to serve her. True, this vision was limited to a miniscule portion of the feudal world and was designed as a counter-reality to prevailing norms, but for the first time, woman was placed in a position of superiority.

In literature, the true knight would serve his lady selflessly and exclusively, with the same dedication that a vassal owed his lord or a wife owed her husband. She would effect a total transformation in him, leading him toward spiritual perfection, while she remained unattainable. Much ink has been shed trying to determine if the lady really was unattainable. Since she was invariably married, usually to the knight's lord, there was no question of marriage between the lovers. Were they required to be chaste? Theoretically they were, but in practice often they were not.

Consider the example of Lancelot, immortalized in the verse narrative written by Chrétien de Troyes around 1180. Lancelot is both the perfect knight and the perfect lover. Indeed, his extraordinary strength in battle stems from his intense love for Queen Guinevere, the wife of King Arthur. Nothing can stop him when it is a question of saving Guinevere from the evil prince who holds her in captivity, and when the time comes to reward him, she does so in the flesh, as in the following passage from Chrétien's *Lancelot*.

> *Then the Queen stretched out her arms and wrapped them around him, and then drew him tightly to her chest. Thus she drew him into her bed. . . . Now Lancelot has everything he wants because the queen welcomes his company and his caresses with favor, because he holds her in his arms just as she holds him in hers. This play is so sweet and so good, this play of kisses, this play of the senses. . . . Lancelot had much joy and pleasure the whole night long.*[20]

Adulterous love, however forbidden, however immoral, however detrimental to social harmony, was an exceptionally hardy strain. From the Middle Ages on, adultery was one of the constant themes of literature. Other variations of the Arthurian legend focused more directly on the spiritual nature of the knight's quest, but almost always, his prowess was inspired by a great lady.

This elevated position of the beloved probably did not reflect the lives of real wives, and, as one historian has pointed out, "it was the reality of only a narrow stratum of the female population, namely noblewomen."[21] For these women, usually married to older men for social, economic, and political reasons, the vision of the youthful knight in shining armor offered an outlet for their erotic imagination. Eventually, this fantasy vision trickled down from the nobility to the general population, where it has remained to the present day. The Harlequin romance, with its plebian version of savior heroes, continues to feed the imagination of today's disgruntled wives.

In the twelfth and thirteenth centuries, an advice literature sprang up to teach men and women how to conduct themselves in the art of love. This "new" love called for sentiment and sighs, refined speech and noble gestures, with rewards that might be spiritual rather than sensual. Indeed, the highly influential Latin *Treatise on Love* (*De arte honeste amandi*) written by Andreas Capellanus at the court of Marie de Champagne around 1170 argued that "pure love" was preferable to the baser sort. Yet the underlying message points to the expectation of sexual fulfillment.

Flattery was considered an essential part of the art of seduction, with praise directed to a lady's eyes, nose, lips, teeth, chin, neck, hands, and feet. After flattery, the man was urged to take action: "Press her with many a burning kiss," and if she resists, "Well, hug and kiss her anyway."[22] The common wisdom among men was that "every woman can be won."[23]

Another author goes so far as to suggest that even rape is acceptable. "With one hand lift her gown, then place the other square/ Upon her sex. . . . Let her shout and shriek. . . . Press your bare bodies close, and do your will with her."[24] Brute strength was not seen as inconsistent with deeper feelings; indeed, the author advises the rapist to marry the woman if she is faithful to him. In all probability, a young woman who lost her virginity in such a manner was well advised to marry her seducer, especially if she became pregnant.

What about advice books for young women? These, too, became popular in the Middle Ages, though in fewer numbers than the guidebooks for men. Richard de Fournival, physician to the King of France in the thirteenth century, wrote an *Advice on Love* in the form of a letter to his sister. Inspired by the Latin poets, he spoke of love as a "folly of the mind, an unquenchable fire, a hunger without surfeit, an agreeable illness, a sweet delight, a pleasing madness" that could be experienced first by either man or woman.[25] Yet following the ancient bias that saw the man as "active" and woman as "passive," it was never proper for her to be the pursuer and for him to be the pursued. What then was a woman to do?

Richard advised his sister that she must affect "artful guises to disclose her love" to the man in question. She might speak to him of some vague concern, give him long affectionate glances, "in short, anything but a frank and open entreaty."[26] So women were advised to play the coquette, as long as they didn't usurp male initiative. It was unthinkable for a woman to make the first declaration of love or to force the first kiss.

Another thirteenth-century author, Robert de Blois, addressed his *Advice to Ladies* to married women. While he enjoined them to be faithful to their marriage vows, he, too, offered an art of coquetry designed to inflame, rather than suppress, desire. Wives were told to avoid drunkenness and gluttony, to sweeten their breath with some kind of spice, to avoid kissing when overheated, for "the more you sweat, the more you smell."[27] Some women were rebuked for wearing the revealing décolletage that became fashionable about this time. And they were told explicitly to keep roving hands off their chests. "Take care not to allow your breast/ To be felt, fondled, or caressed/ By any hands save those that ought."[28] Only the husband was supposed to be able to touch his wife's breasts.

All in all, treatises on love were probably read or heard only by the elite. Yet they tell us that Love with a capital "L" had set up shop at the center of the literate discourse—which represented a small segment of the population, to be sure, but an influential one.

Among the illiterate members of society—that is, most of the population—love was no less the subject of speech and song. One type of song popular with people of lower social strata—the lament of the "mal mar-iée" (the unhappy wife)—repeatedly explored the triangle of wife, hus-band, and lover. According to Ria Lemaire, who has studied these songs extensively, they were sung by women while dancing with other women or with mixed-gender groups.[29] These songs expressed a woman's complaints about her husband and her desire to take a younger, more attractive lover. The husband is invariably "bad, violent, ugly, avaricious, stinking and old" and often beats his wife. The lover is "young, handsome, kind and gallant," as in the following:

> *Fat lot I care, husband, about your love*
> *Now that I have a friend!*
> *He looks handsome and noble*
> *Fat lot I care, husband, about your love.*
> *He serves me day and night*
> *That is why I love him so.*[30]

The woman presents herself as youthful and merry, and names her-self *amie* (friend, sister) rather than "wife." She calls her lover *ami*, indi-cating that she and he are bound together through affinity, rather than legal and religious ties. It was this way of thinking that led Héloïse to say she preferred to be called *amica* by Abelard, though she could claim the title of wife.

The unhappily married wives of the popular songs seem unaffected by feelings of guilt for cheating on their husbands. They speak out defi-antly: "My husband cannot satisfy me/ As a compensation I will take a lover."[31] In one ballad, the speaker complains of being beaten by her husband because she had kissed her *ami*. She knows what she will do for revenge: "I'll make a cuckold of him . . . I'll go and sleep completely naked with my friend."[32] Yet the thrice-repeated refrain—"Why does my husband beat me?"—is probably closer to the reality of her life. It's hard to know whether these ballads of sexual revenge reflect married women's behavior, or merely their hopes and dreams.

These cultural artifacts suggest that some wives, at different levels of society, were subverting the message of an ascetically oriented church and taking pleasure in such "vices" as disobedience and adultery. Inci-dentally, from the mid-eleventh century onward women and men of the upper classes also defied the church by playing chess, a game recently introduced into Europe by the Arabs. Europeans created the chess Queen as a replacement for the Arabic Vizier (chief minister), and by the end of the Middle Ages, she became the most powerful player on the board. The chess King and Queen represented the fundamental pair: though the King was the most important piece, the Queen became more powerful than the mate she served. This chess hierarchy may provide an interesting gloss on the complexity of marital relations in late-medieval Europe.

MOTHERS AND OTHER WORKERS

Most medieval wives eventually became mothers, many within the first year of marriage. Motherhood was generally a desired state, seen as the fulfillment of a woman's God-given role. Wives who had a hard time conceiving turned to midwives and healers, went on pilgrimages, bought potions and amulets, and prayed to the Virgin Mary and saints of both genders. They desired sons as heirs for the family estate or, at a lower level, as workers on the farm. They needed daughters to effect alliances with their peers or help with the daily chores. For economic, social, religious, and emotional reasons, children were perceived as a blessing.

The church took a hard line on any practice that prevented conception, as it still does today. The common contraceptive method of coitus interruptus was regarded primarily as a male sin, whereas abortion was considered a female sin. Infanticide, too, was considered a female crime, whether the baby was done away with for economic reasons or because the mother wanted to conceal the product of fornication or adultery.[33] But church and secular courts heard very few cases of infanticide during the Middle Ages; only later, in the sixteenth century, when infanticide was legally equated with murder and carried a death penalty, did the number of court cases increase significantly.[34]

With no means of birth control available beyond coitus interruptus and the natural contraception resulting from lactation, it was common for women to have a large number of children. Seven or eight would have been considered "normal," though some women, like Margery Kempe (1373–1431), had as many as fourteen, and some even more. Kempe's successive experience of parturition and her responsibility for bringing up so many children may have played into her decision to renounce sexual activity while her husband was still alive—a subject to which we will return.

The experience of childbirth was fraught with hazard. Women with means were assisted by midwives, whereas poor women would depend upon female relatives and neighbors. Husbands were excluded from the birthing scene—indeed, it was considered unlucky for them to be there—and surgeons were a rarity, brought in only to remove a fetus from the body when all other means had failed. Since the possibility of maternal mortality was always present, parish priests made sure that pregnant women would confess and receive holy communion before their lying-in.

A special mass on behalf of pregnant women and those in labor entered the liturgy. The Virgin was invoked as the "benign assister of women in travail," with power to succor "poor women, labouring with child" and "deliver them from all dangers." God the Father, too, was entreated to "bring matters to a speedy and successful issue."[35]

The lying-in after a delivery was a special time for the new mother. In well-to-do families, she rested in bed, received visitors, and was the object of considerable attention. Game boards were sometimes given to mothers in affluent Italian families to help them enjoy their time of confinement. Especially if the child were a boy, a husband might commission a birth salver or tray with a game board on one side and a painting on the other. One at the Fogg Museum at Harvard University, from the first decade of the fifteenth century, has a chess board on one side, and a birth scene on the other. The new mother is sitting up in a high bed, while attendants bring her a meal. Lower down, her baby has just been bathed and is being swaddled. Typical of such paintings, guests are coming and going on each side. Of course, poorer women in Italy and elsewhere were usually up and about as soon as they could stand.

For six weeks after childbirth, a mother was prohibited from attending church, in accordance with the Old Testament decree that a woman was impure during this period. The "churching" of a woman was the ritual that allowed her back into society. The service began outside the church, with a blessing of the woman who had recently given birth. She would be sprinkled with holy water by the priest and then led, by her right hand, inside.

On the whole, both rich and poor mothers nursed their babies, sometimes with supplemental milk from a cow, especially among the

A Birth Scene. *Painted on one side of an Italian game board, made for a mother to use during her lying-in period, circa 1410. (Courtesy of the Fogg Museum, Harvard University Art Museums)*

peasantry. But some members of the nobility, most notably in Italy and France, were already employing wet nurses, who were often chosen with care from good families and brought to live within the baby's residence (as opposed to the later practice of sending babies out to live with the wet nurse.)[36]

We get a female perspective on the medical problems women faced from the writings of Trotula, a unique woman physican who practiced in Salerno in the late eleventh or twelfth century, and whose name is associated with several treatises that circulated in Latin and the vernacular throughout the Middle Ages. Trotula wrote of menstruation and childbirth, infertility and abortion (which she condemned), and the way to restore the appearance of virginity. She also gave women numerous recipes for hygiene and beauty, including one that would reduce the size of one's vaginal opening, presumably after childbirth, so as to please one's husband. With the directness of Middle English, this passage begins: "Now it is to touche of some wyman that han thair prive membre [genitals] so large and so eville-smellying, where-thorow [because of which] their hosebondes forsaken hem because of largenes and be [because of] the wykked smel, ne han no wille [desire] to come nere hem."[37] Wives, then as now, had the responsibility of keeping their husbands sexually happy, as well as producing offspring.

Women also had the responsibility of bringing up the children and educating them during their first years. When a boy was about seven, the father was supposed to take charge of his education, while the mother continued to educate the girls—that is, of course, if the family was sufficiently well-off to educate their children at all.

Public education, with a focus on reading, writing, and arithmetic, was available by the end of the thirteenth century to upper-class girls in Flanders and Paris, and a few decades later in Italy.[38] By the turn of the fifteenth century, girls' schools were established in Germany and Switzerland. In England, public schools were attended exclusively by boys. On the whole, girls from wealthy families and the nobility were taught at home by tutors. Peasants, for the most part, were uneducated.

How did the city girls spend their days, once they were married? The German medievalist Erika Uitz has shown that many burgher wives worked outside as well as inside the home.[39] They not only acted as deputies for their husbands when the men were ill or away, but many formed partnerships with their husbands in such enterprises as trading, finance, the textile industry, inn and tavern keeping, bakeries, breweries, bathhouses, and various crafts.

In many German towns and cities, one of the requirements for full mastership in a guild was to have a wife, under the assumption that a workshop could not be properly run without her presence.[40] In some cities, women themselves were admitted to guilds as their husbands' partners. Thus the city of Basel in Switzerland in 1271 allowed women to join the guild for builders provided that their husbands were alive. In London, women with small businesses could also be guild members, and a few Parisian craft guilds allowed for "mistresses" as well as "masters." Generally speaking, widows were allowed to continue their husbands' crafts, but if they remarried a man who was not a member of the same guild, they had to abandon the craft.

Some women worked independently of their husbands, most notably in textile work and beer production. We know from a German business document dating from 1420 that one female brewer contracted to teach two men her skill. The enlightening document reads:

> *I, the aforementioned Fygin with the knowledge, approval and permission of my aforementioned husband have agreed with the honourable wise gentlemen mayors and town council of Cologne . . . that I shall loyally and industriously and to the best of my ability teach two men to make good grut. . . . With this document I have obliged and committed myself to do this for the aforementioned gentlemen and the town of Cologne for eight consecutive years, beginning with the date of this document. And whenever they let me know that they need me for their grutmaking I shall, unless I am ill, come to their town of Cologne to instruct and teach . . . for this reason they shall give me one mark of the Cologne currency to cover my labour and my upkeep.*[41]

Apparently the husband in question felt this was a welcome addition to the family income, even if it entailed his wife's overnight absence for a number of days.

Many married women were midwives, and a few practiced as doctors—that is, until the fourteenth and fifteenth centuries, when the faculty of such prestigious centers as the University of Paris disallowed the term "physician" for any but university graduates (all men) and enforced the expulsion of women from the medical profession. The case of the lady Jacoba Felicie, preserved in the records of the University of Paris, demonstrates how one woman practicing as a doctor in Paris and its suburbs, was forced to desist from offering her services.[42] One way of getting around such interdiction was for a doctor and a midwife to be married, a situation that was common in certain Flemish cities.

Outside the cities, peasant wives spent their days preparing meals, cleaning house (a fairly rudimentary occupation, since the houses were small and there was little furniture), milking the cows, feeding the poultry and the swine, tending the vegetable garden, fetching water from the well or stream (if she did not have children to perform that time-consuming task), doing the laundry at the nearest pond or stream, spinning, and sewing. In addition, they nursed and swaddled their babies, supervised children, and cared for the sick and the elderly. They also helped in the fields, hoeing, weeding, harvesting, and gleaning when the harvest was over. And in all of these occupations, peasant wives rarely had any help other than their children.

"Help" was a distinguishing characteristic of households above the level of most peasants and the urban poor. The wives of men in trade and the professions usually had at least one servant, and great households employed many more. The letters of the Paston family in fifteenth-century England suggest some twelve to fifteen servants in an affluent household, under the general supervision of the wife.[43] Keeping an eye on the servants, including provisions for their food and clothing, added heavily to the managerial duties of the Paston wives and their likes. All wives, whatever their station, were deemed responsible for household management, given a gender division of labor that has been with us since time immemorial.

GRISELDA AND THE WIFE OF BATH

Le Mesnagier de Paris and Chaucer's Wife of Bath in The Canterbury Tales, both written around 1400, offer two radically different pictures of wifehood. The Parisian author, a man probably old enough to be the grandfather of his fifteen-year-old spouse, proposed a model of wifely submission based on traditional religious instruction and the figure of Griselda widely known from popular fable. Griselda is the obedient wife par excellence. Taken from a humble family by a powerful nobleman, she promises him, as her sole dowry, that she will obey him in all things. Little does she know that this will entail enduring episodes of extreme cruelty and humiliation. But at each ordeal—giving up her children to presumed execution, returning to her father's home barefooted when her husband announces he is taking a second wife—she obeys him without the slightest reproach. Of course, the story ultimately ends happily, like the story of Job, for Griselda passes all the tests of unconditional obedience with flying colors. However unreal Griselda may seem to us today, the Parisian husband assumed his wife would take her model seriously.

While half of Le Mesnagier de Paris addressed the religious and moral duties of a wife, especially to her husband, the other half concerned more practical domestic matters: the care of the garden, the supervision of servants, and, in detailed recipes, the preparation of food. The latter was probably the main reason this work has survived for so many centuries.

We know absolutely nothing about the fate of the young wife for whom this book was written—whether she ultimately became a good cook and housekeeper, whether she remained chaste and obedient, whether she shared with her husband the affection he obviously had for her. In all probability, she outlived him and married again, as her husband had anticipated in the Prologue to his book, when he opined that her acquisition of "virtue, honor, and duty" would serve not only him, but "if the case arises, another husband" in the future.[44]

For an antithetical portrait of a wife where the "case" did arise and who married no less than five times, let us look at Chaucer's Wife of Bath—Griselda's opposite in every way. Though the Wife of Bath confirms every stereotypical flaw men have attributed to women since antiquity, she stands convincingly for an archetypal powerful woman who must have existed in the Middle Ages and who exists in every age.

She is bossy and manipulative, gossipy and argumentative, loving and lusty. In defiance of the prevalent ascetic ideal, she makes a case for sexual enjoyment. She asks "To what end/ were reproductive organs made?" And she replies: "for necessary business and for pleasure." For her part, she will use her "flower . . . in the acts and fruits of marriage."[45]

As a paragon of female lust and dominance, the Wife of Bath confronts the Griselda myth head-on. She fights with her husbands, lies and remonstrates, suffers blows and returns them in kind, and is not satisfied until her last husband—the one she loves best—cedes control and declares, "My own true wife, do as you wish the rest of your life." This, she says, put an end to argument and brought perfect harmony into their home.

Griselda and the Wife of Bath exemplify the two extreme poles of a debate about married women that went on throughout the Middle Ages. Men idealized the selfless devotion represented by Griselda. Women belied that ideal, leaving men disappointed and resentful. Frenchmen who wrote books such as *The Book of the Knight of La Tour-Landry* and the *Fifteen Joys of Marriage,* and the English authors of *Why*

Not to Take a Wife and *The Purgatory of Married Men* dragged misogynist resentment across the centuries, seeking to prove that the only good wife is one who is beaten regularly and kept underfoot.

THE STORY OF MARGERY KEMPE

The unique autobiographical text known as *The Book of Margery Kempe* provides a very different picture of the late-medieval wife. Her experience as a quirky mystic contradicts the fictive female prototypes of that period. Margery Kempe was born in 1373 into a well-to-do middle-class family from King's Lynn, Norfolk. At the age of twenty, she married John Kempe, a man of lesser social status. After the birth of her first child (the first of fourteen), she suffered some form of postpartum psychosis, from which she was rescued eight months later through a vision of Christ. Henceforth, her life would follow a turbulent path marked by frequent sobbing and mystical conversations with the Lord. It is this religious trajectory that she, an illiterate woman, decided to set down through dictation when she was about sixty. Despite the intermediary of a scribe and Margery's third-person style, her own voice comes through vividly. Here is how she speaks of herself during the period that followed her breakdown and redemptive vision.

> And presently the creature grew as calm in her wits and her reason as she ever was before, and asked her husband, as soon as he came to her, if she could have the keys of the buttery to get her food and drink as she had done before. Her maids and her keepers advised him that he should not deliver up any keys to her. . . . Nevertheless, her husband, who always had tenderness and compassion for her, ordered that they should give her the keys. And she took food and drink as her bodily strength would allow her, and she once again recognized her friends and her household, and everybody else who came to her in order to see how our Lord Jesus Christ had worked his grace in her.[46]

It is this mixture of the domestic and the divine that distinguishes Margery Kempe's autobiography from the other spiritual writings of her era, and provides unique insights into marriage from the perspective of a wife. Margery describes her husband as tender and compassionate, willing to trust her with the keys to the larder she had possessed before her illness, and hopeful only of her recovery. Perhaps he was somewhat awed by his wife, especially since she came from a more distinguished family than his own, as she sometimes reminded him. But if Margery was occasionally hard on her husband, she was usually harder on herself. She presented herself as proud and envious, headstrong and snappish, unable to learn from past experience. In the early years of her marriage she took pride in "her showy manner of dressing" and "was enormously envious of her neighbours if they were dressed as well as she was." And then, as she put it, "out of pure covetousness, and in order to maintain her pride, she took up brewing, and was one of the greatest brewers in the town of N. for three or four years until she lost a great deal of money."

After brewing, she took up corn-grinding—another unsuccessful venture. These reversals of fortune were interpreted as "scourges of our Lord that would chastise her for . . . her pride." Her religious bent began to manifest itself in all aspects of her life, and came to a head in the incident recounted as follows.

> One night, as this creature lay in bed with her husband, she heard a melodious sound so sweet and delectable that she thought she had been in paradise. And immediately she jumped out of bed and said, "Alas that ever I sinned!" Afterwards, whenever she heard this same melody, she shed very plentiful and abundant tears of high devotion, with great sobbings and sighings for the bliss of heaven. . . .

However bizarre her weeping and sighing appeared to her neighbors, Margery was convinced that she was in communication with a higher order of reality, known only to mystics like herself. The night she heard the music of paradise was a turning point in her relationship to her husband. She writes:

> And after this time she never had any desire to have sexual intercourse with her husband, for paying the debt of matrimony was so abominable to her that she would rather, she thought, have eaten and drunk the ooze and muck in the gutter than consent to intercourse, except out of obedience.
> And so she said to her husband, "I may not deny you my body, but all the love and affection of my heart is withdrawn from all earthly creatures and set on God alone." But he would have his will with her,

and she obeyed with much weeping and sorrowing. . . . And often this creature advised her husband to live chaste and said that they had often (she well knew) displeased God by their inordinate love, and the great delight each of them had in using the other's body, and now it would be a good thing if by mutual consent they punished and chastised themselves by abstaining from the lust of their bodies.

Admittedly, Margery Kempe was not a "representative" woman. Yet her strange personality does not diminish the value of the record she left behind: it shows how Christian theology expounded from the pulpit worked its way into the marital bed. The medieval emphasis on chastity, with its repugnance for sexuality, ran counter to her husband's personal inclinations, and even her own previous behavior. Now that she had been enlightened by a mystical experience, she began to reconsider the pleasure they both took in sex. In keeping with Christian doctrine, "inordinate lovemaking" was seen as displeasing to God. Intercourse was acceptable only as a procreative function, and Margery, who had already had more children than the norm, was determined to give it up.

Her husband, however, was not yet ready to take the vows of chastity she so ardently desired. In a state of perpetual disquiet, Margery increased her devotions: she attended church two or three times a day, prayed all afternoon, fasted, and wore a hair shirt. If we now tend to think of this garment as a perverse fantasy, we have only to read her account to be convinced of its reality: "She got herself a haircloth from a kiln—the sort that malt is dried on—and put it inside her gown as discreetly and secretly as she could, so that her husband should not notice it. And nor did he, although she lay beside him every night in bed and wore the hair-shirt every day, and bore him children during that time." We may well wonder about a husband who does not notice his wife's hair shirt, even as they continue to have intercourse. But we also have to wonder about the accuracy of an account written by a woman who was, by the standards of any age, wildly eccentric.

Among her many religious practices, Margery began going on pilgrimages to various English shrines, but she could not leave "without the consent of her husband." In this respect, she followed traditional law and custom, since a medieval wife needed her husband's permission to leave the domicile. This her husband freely granted, and sometimes he even accompanied her. It was during their pilgrimage to York that another definitive moment occurred. The two of them had refrained from intercourse for a full eight weeks, and when questioned on the subject, her husband responded "that he was made so afraid when he would have touched her, that he dared do no more." Obviously Margery's conversations with God and her ongoing desire for chastity were having their effect. It took considerable negotiation between them before both agreed on the following arrangement: "Sir, if you please, you shall grant me my desire, and you shall have your desire. Grant me that you will not come into my bed, and I grant you that I will pay your debts before I go to Jerusalem." . . . Then her husband replied to her, "May your body be as freely available to God as it has been to me."

This momentous event occurred around her fortieth year, and was formalized in a vow of chastity before the bishop of Lincoln. It inaugurated a series of pilgrimages that took her as far as the Holy Land, Italy, and Spain. Clearly Margery Kempe had sufficient means to travel, and little worry about her children, some of whom were probably grown up and the others presumably left behind in the care of servants and relatives.

Though Margery Kempe's story stands out in the annals of medieval wives, it is not unique. Other famous holy women were also married.[47]

Among the earliest, Mary of Oignies (who died in 1213) was married off at fourteen by her parents in Brabant, but, persuading her husband to live chastely, she convinced him that they should devote themselves to the care of lepers.

Angelo of Foligno (1249–1309) was a well-to-do wife and mother until the age of forty, whereupon she experienced a conversion and devoted herself to a life of poverty and penance.

Saint Bridget of Sweden (1303–1373) was married at thirteen by her influential parents to a man of comparable station, and they had eight children. Upon her husband's death in 1344, she retired to a Cistertian monastery, where she dictated her revelations to a prior. She went to Rome in 1350 and remained there, founding a new religious order, the Brigittines, which had wide influence throughout Europe, especially in her native Sweden.

The Prussian visionary Dorothea of Montau (1347–1394) was married at sixteen and bore nine children, and all but one died young. Unhappily married, she eventually prevailed upon her husband to take a joint vow of chastity with her. In her late years she went on pilgrimages to Aachen and Rome, and ended her years as a recluse.

The medieval worldview that prized celibacy above marriage and motherhood allowed these wives to convince their husbands to let them embrace a religious vocation, which included vows of chastity and the abandonment of their children. Margery Kempe scarcely mentioned her children in her story. She was primarily interested in leaving behind the record of her spiritual journey. On one of her many pilgrimages, she visited the celebrated anchoress Julian of Norwich, the other medieval Englishwoman responsible for a literary milestone. Julian's *Showings* was the first work written in English by a woman, and *The Book of Margery Kempe* was the first autobiography set down in English by either a man or a woman.

CHRISTINE DE PIZAN

During this same period in France, another "female first" occurred in the case of Christine de Pizan (1363–1429). She was the first woman to earn her living by her pen. A woman of Italian origin, Christine was raised in an atmosphere of cultivated affluence in Paris, where her doctor-astrologer father was brought by Charles V. She learned to read and write, but received no formal education. At the age of fifteen she married a twenty-four-year-old nobleman, Etienne de Castel, a man of scholarly inclinations and great personal charm. As Christine wrote later, "I could not have wished for a better husband."[48] They had three children and lived very happily together for ten years. After his untimely death, she resorted to writing as a means of livelihood to support herself, her children, and her widowed mother. In time she produced some thirty works, the best known of which is her prefeminist utopia, *The City of Women* (*La Cité des Dames*). But as a wife, Christine de Pizan is best remembered for the beautiful lyrics she wrote for the husband she lost too soon. "In Praise of Marriage" is a rare female-authored description of a medieval wife's happiness in bed . . . with her husband.

A sweet thing is marriage,
I can certainly prove it from my own experience.
It's true for anyone with a good and wise husband
Like the husband God helped me find.
. . . .
The first night of our marriage
I saw right away
His great worth, for he did nothing
To give me offense or pain.
But before it was time to arise
He kissed me a hundred times, I'm sure,
Without demanding any base act.
Certainly the dear man loves me well.
. . . .
Prince, he drives me crazy with desire
When he tells me he's entirely mine.
He will make me swoon with sweetness,
Certainly the dear man loves me well.[49]

By contrast, "A Widow's Grief" expresses the devastation of Christine's loss.

I am a widow clad in black, alone.
With saddened face and very simply dressed;
In great distress and manner most aggrieved
I wear the mourning that is killing me.

Whatever the commonplaces of medieval thought—that wives were the bane of men's lives, that both chastity and widowhood were holier states than marriage—Christine de Pizan was one woman who found great joy in the role of the wife and great sorrow when she had been "promoted" to widowhood.

THE DOWRY, ITALIAN-STYLE

A look at Italy in the late Middle Ages confirms the major marital patterns we have seen so far, but with distinctive features unique to Italian culture. Unlike France and England, which had accepted the church's jurisdiction of the marriage ceremony by the thirteenth century, Italy was slow to give up its civil ceremonies in favor of religious ones. Marriage was firmly a family affair, the goal of which was to provide benefits for each of the two families. These could consist of wealth brought in the form of a dowry by the daughter-in-law to her husband, the prestige of association with a noble or powerful name, or simply the network of kin that one could turn to in times of need. Marriage was certainly not something that could be decided by the two young people forced to live together for the rest of their lives. *Quelle idée!*

Parents and matchmakers looked for suitable parties from the same class—nobles with nobles, merchants with merchants, artisans with artisans, peasants with peasants. Sometimes wealthy members of the mercantile class "married up" into the nobility, but marriages that bridged too wide a gap—for example, that of an aristocrat and an artisan—were considered violations of the social code.

As in Roman times, girls from good families had little say in their marriage arrangements, and were carefully protected from chance encounters with potential suitors. The writer Boccaccio (1313–1375) went so far as to say that some girls and even wives could not go to church or weddings, for fear of being approached by inappropriate men, and that in extreme cases, they could not stand next to a window or so much as glance outside.[50] The window was, in fact, a likely venue for temptation, for here young women watched the men pass by. In most Italian cities, it was common practice for young men to stroll up and down in front of the windows, trying to catch the eye of the young woman sitting on the other side of the open shutters.

Different regions of Italy had somewhat different customs, but on the whole, marriage usually consisted of three separate events: 1) the betrothal sealed by the prospective groom and the father of the prospective bride; 2) the exchange of consent between the bride and groom, often referred to as the "ring day"; and 3) the move to the husband's home.

The betrothal was, in its own way, taken as seriously as the marriage vows. To break a betrothal in fourteenth- or fifteenth-century Florence could entail catastrophic consequences—long-term enmity between families and the loss of future marriage possibilities for the defecting party. Both Catholics and Jews were subject to a heavy fine if the betrothal contract was broken.[51]

In the following journal entry, the Tuscan merchant Gregorio Dati recorded the marital rituals that took place over a period of three months: "On 31 March 1393 I consented and pledged myself under oath to take Isabetta for my wife. On 7 April, Easter Monday, I gave her the ring in the presence of Ser Luca, notary. On 22 June, a Sunday, after nones, she moved into my house, the home of her husband, in the name of God and good fortune."[52] There is no mention of a priest. Marriages at the bride's home or in the notary's office, without the presence of a priest and without a church ceremony, seem to have been the rule. Like most marriages, this one took place on a Sunday—the day on which the greatest number of people could witness the spousal procession and escort the bride to the groom's house.

In Italy, marriage was mandatory for almost everyone, male and female. Unmarried women were either nuns, sent into cloisters at an early age—sometimes as early as seven, though they did not pronounce their vows until twelve or thirteen—or servants trying to amass a sufficient sum for a dowry. In the later case, the employer frequently pledged to pay the dowry when the young woman came of age after years of service without remuneration beyond room and board.

Tuscan women usually married at eighteen or younger, while men married at thirty in the city and twenty-six in the country. The large age gap between spouses—eight years on the average, but as much as fifteen among the rich—encouraged husbands to expect submission from their wives, and for wives to expect protection and tutelage from their husbands. It is hard to know whether our modern ideas of "reciprocity" and "compromise" had much meaning within a family predicated on so great a difference in age and authority.

As in ancient Rome, a wife always married into her husband's family and moved to his home, thus perpetuating the patrilineal and patrilocal system. A Tuscan home might contain two or even three generations, and various kin related to the husband. An Italian husband never moved into his father-in-law's home, as occurred sometimes in French families whose sole heir was a daughter. This unusual arrangement was called "son-in-law marriage" (*marriage à gendre*). In Jewish families, it was also common for a well-dowered bride to bring her new husband into her parents' home, especially when a rich merchant's daughter had the honor of marrying a poor rabbi's son. But in Catholic Italy, a wife always lived on foreign territory, so to speak.

The dowry system provided the foundation for marriage at every level of society. In Florence, after 1430, there was even a dowry fund (*Monte delle Doti*) under municipal management: a girl's father started making deposits when she was a child (not unlike our contemporary college funds) and the accrued sum would be paid to the husband at the time of the wedding.[53]

Fathers were obliged by law to "dower" their daughter with a share of the family patrimony. This meant that each daughter was given a sum to take with her into the marriage, while sons would inherit the rest of the father's property. The dowry was more than a sum of money enabling the couple to start off with some capital: it was the symbol of what the bride, her family, and the new couple were worth. A young woman's dowry was public knowledge—it was registered with the notary and noised about among the neighbors.[54]

The dowry, subsequently administered by the husband, was supposed to take care of household needs and, if the husband died first, provide for the widow. The general provision throughout Europe was that the widow would receive one-third of the total estate. Ultimately, whatever remained would pass on to the descendants of the union. Determined at the time of the betrothal, the dowry was often paid in installments, each of which was duly notarized. The first payment was usually made before the bride moved into her husband's house, and the other payments might continue over years. These subsequent installments could be the source of conflict in a marriage, if the wife's family was unable or unwilling to keep up the payments. Another part of the wife's contribution to the marriage was the trousseau consisting of linens and personal effects.

The husband's material contributions to the household—in addition to the house itself—came in the form of "gifts." He usually paid for the clothes worn by the bride on her wedding day, which, among display-conscious Florentines, could add up to a tidy sum. He was also expected to furnish the bridal chamber, a special feature of which were the "wedding chests." These could be quite elaborate, carved to represent mythological subjects meant to edify the bride and groom, such as conjugal duty, fidelity, and the danger of passions. Often these chests were displayed in the procession to the house of the new couple and then placed at the foot of the marital bed.

While upper-class husbands were prepared to lay out large amounts as a kind of "counterdowry," even humbler folk were not immune to such practices. The sons of peasants offered gifts in the form of the bride's clothing, which they sometimes paid for with the first install-ment of the dowry—a practice that became increasingly common at all levels of society during the fifteenth century.

At the highest level, these gifts were subject to a set of byzantine arrangements. A Florentine husband retained legal ownership of the gifts he gave his bride, all of which would revert to him if the marriage were annulled. Often husbands wrote in their wills exactly what the wife was entitled to, were he to die, especially in the event that she should marry again. It was not unusual for a widow to leave her hus-band's home, without the clothes and jewelry given her at the time of her wedding, or her dowry and trousseau, which her children were sometimes slow to return to her. Florentine archives are filled with suits of widows against offspring who refused to restore dowries to their mothers or stepmothers.

Sometimes the gifts were taken back soon after the marriage. The husband may have just borrowed them from friends and relatives for the wedding period, to be returned within a year. Or he might be obliged to sell them to professional lenders, so they could be passed on to other husbands—for a fee.

An even more complicated set of rules prevailed over the giving of rings. On the wedding day, the husband gave his wife two or three rings. In addition, in Florence, either on the day of the wedding or the next morning, the husband's father and some members of his family presented the bride with several rings, as many as as fifteen or twenty in wealthy noble families. Many of the rings were given by the married women of the family to welcome the new bride into the female fold. But these gifts, too, had only ritual value; they were no more the pos-session of the bride than the clothes and jewels offered by her husband. In time, they would be passed on to future brides entering the kinship circle.

During the course of the fourteenth and fifteenth centuries, the sums laid out for dowries, gifts, and weddings increased considerably throughout Italy. It became more and more difficult for families to dower all their daughters, and many young women chose the convent instead of marriage as a cheaper alternative. (To place a girl in a convent rather than in marriage cost about half as much.) In the Veneto, the region around Venice, by the sixteenth century dowries had reached such size that the recent decline in Venetian commerce was blamed on the willingness of patrician husbands to live off their wives' dowries.

We tend to think of the dowry as a disadvantage for women, and it certainly was for those who had difficulty acquiring one. It was undoubtedly the most obvious indicator of a woman's marriageability and the most crucial factor in determining who would marry whom. But for a woman with a handsome dowry, it was a permanent status symbol persisting long after the marriage had taken place.[55]

For all the information about the artifacts of marriage—dowries, rings, contracts, and the like—they tell us little about the interpersonal relations between husband and wife, which are always difficult to ferret out. The family memoirs (*ricordanze*) written by men were generally circumspect in expressing emotions, and similar documents written by women were extremely rare. There was, however, one moment when circumspection sometimes broke down: when a wife died. Then a husband sometimes permitted himself the words of affection the wife may, or may not, have heard while she was alive.

Such words as *dulcissima* (sweetest), *dilectissima consors* (most delightful partner), and *dilectio* (fondness) are found in the journals of several memorialists regarding their recently deceased wives, suggesting an affection that went beyond merely conventional praise. A writer from Bologna burst forth with an extravagant lament: "I loved her more than seemed possible, because I don't believe there is or has ever been a woman better than she."[56]

Negative feelings were expressed and recorded at another end point—when a marriage broke down. Then husbands and wives had every reason to express their grievances before the ecclesiastical authorities who were charged with granting annulment and divorce. The curious story of Giovanni and Lusanna, discovered and presented by historian Gene Brucker, allows us to enter into the personal space of a Florentine couple.[57] Based on the records of a court notary, it is a story of sex, passion, adultery, clandestine marriage, and annulment. In its own peculiar way, it tells us about the circumstances under which fifteenth-century Florentine women did—and did not—contract legal marriages.

THE STORY OF LUSANNA AND GIOVANNI

Lusanna and Giovanni were born in 1420 in Florentine homes that were separated by a five-minute walk. And there the similarities in their origins end, for Lusanna was the daughter of an artisan and Giovanni the son of a high-ranking notary. The Della Casa family, of which he was a member, belonged to the upper echelons of Florentine society, whereas Lusanna's family consisted of petit-bourgeois artisans and tradesmen. In the highly stratified Florentine world of the early Renaissance, a match between these two families would have been unthinkable.

And, indeed, when it came time for Lusanna to marry at the age of seventeen, her father arranged a marriage for her to Andrea Nucci, a twenty-nine-year-old linen-maker and the son of a prosperous baker, living only a few hundred meters away. Lusanna's sizeable dowry of 250 florins was duly noted in the marriage contract drawn up by the local notary.

Five years later, while visiting one of the neighborhood churches, Giovanni saw Lusanna. Lusanna, it appears, was extremely beautiful, and though married, she would not have been out of bounds for a wealthy Florentine merchant sniffing about for an affair. Still in his early twenties, he was not yet of an age to marry, but certainly of an age and position to entertain an irregular liaison. For the next decade, Lusanna and Giovanni were lovers. As a member of the artisan community, she seems to have moved about freely and unchaperoned, something that would have been impossible for her upper-class counterparts. In addition, she was unencumbered by children.

As for her legal husband, we know next to nothing about him, except that he died in 1453, making a marriage between Lusanna and Giovanni not only possible, but, from her point of view, highly desirable. When Giovanni finally consented to a wedding ceremony, Lusanna's brother, Antonio—now the guardian of his sister's honor—argued for the presence of a notary, who usually officiated at Florentine weddings and drew up the nuptial contract. But at this point, Giovanni, demurred, insisting that the marriage must be kept secret for fear of alienating his father, who would disinherit him. Giovanni suggested instead that his friend, the Franciscan friar Fra Felice Asini, officiate at the wedding.

Did this wedding actually take place? This is the question that had to be determined by the archbishop of Florence in 1455. The case had gone up all the way to the Pope, who had sent a letter to the archbishop with the following concerns: "Our beloved daughter in Christ, Lusanna di Benedetto, a Florentine woman, has informed us that, despite a marriage legally contracted between herself and a certain Giovanni di Lodovico della Casa, he has married another Florentine woman in a public ceremony with an exchange of vows and rings and with other customary solemnities." The Pope's letter instructed the archbishop to investigate the case and, if Lusanna's allegations proved true, to dissolve Giovanni's second marriage, and impose penalties upon him for contracting a bigamous union.

Testifying on behalf of Lusanna were twenty witnesses, including three members of her family and Giovanni's erstwhile friend, Fra Felice Asini. According to their collective memory, the wedding party had consisted of Giovanni and Lusanna, her brother Antonio and his wife, his stepmother, and two friends. Fra Felice testified that after supper Giovanni stated that he wanted to take Lusanna as his wife, and that the members of the wedding party formed a circle around him and the couple. First the friar asked the bride and groom, in that order, whether they wanted to be married to each other. When each had responded affirmatively, Giovanni took a ring from his left hand and placed it on Lusanna's finger. The bridegroom exchanged kisses with the members of Lusanna's family, and presented them with gifts. Giovanni and Lusanna then went into a bedroom to consummate their marriage. Such was the improvisational event that Lusanna judged to be a valid marriage.

After the wedding, Giovanni did not live continuously with Lusanna, though he spent occasional nights with her. When she appeared in public, Lusanna continued to wear her widow's garb, but at home she dressed as a married woman. In the city, Giovanni and Lusanna kept their marriage secret, but in the country, they enjoyed the rustic life of married lovers. Five local peasants testified that they saw Giovanni and Lusanna together, and considered them husband and wife.

Eight months later, Lusanna discovered that Giovanni had contracted a marriage with Marietta, the fifteen-year-old daughter of a distinguished family. This had occurred shortly after the death of Giovanni's father, which, according to Lusanna's supporters, should have been the occasion for him to publicly acknowledge his marriage to her. On several occasions she pleaded with him to do so and abandon his second union, but he refused. At this point there was nothing for her to do but appeal to the ecclesiastical authorities.

Giovanni denied that the two had ever been married. He admitted to having had sexual relations with her since 1443, and tried to blacken her name by presenting an image of her as a promiscuous woman with several lovers. In the words of his procurators: "Motivated by lust, Lusanna desired to have carnal relations with him [Giovanni], for he was young and well endowed. . . ." Giovanni's witnesses vouched for his good reputation, and some of Lusanna's neighbors pictured her as a woman of low moral character. A wife who stared openly at men when she walked in the street, instead of lowering her eyes as good women should; a wife who was known to have had a lover while her husband was alive, and maybe more than one—how could one believe her word?

The case dragged on for several months, with Giovanni contending that Lusanna had never been more than his concubine, and Lusanna insisting that she was his legitimate wife. Giovanni played upon the sense of improbability for one of his rank and youth to marry a socially inferior "old" woman (remember that they had been born in the same year). Lusanna's procurator retorted that beautiful women of lowly origins were known to have married men of a higher class. In the end the archbishop decided in favor of Lusanna. Even a clandestine marriage such as this one—something the church had tried to abolish through its insistence on the publication of banns three weeks before a wedding and the celebration of weddings in church—had to be recognized, if both parties had pledged, in the presence of witnesses, to become husband and wife. Giovanni's second marriage was declared bigamous, and he was ordered to acknowledge Lusanna as his lawful wife and treat her with "marital affection," under penalty of excommunication. For once, it seems, justice had been meted out to the lowly.

But this is not the end of the story. Giovanni appealed the arch-bishop's verdict. Because he was rich and well connected, he was able to effect a reversal of the earlier judgment. Somewhere between 1456 and 1458, the marriage between Giovanni and Lusanna was declared null and void. Giovanni would go on to found a legitimate family with Marietta, a partner from his own class and one capable of bearing children so as to continue the Della Casa family line. No trace of Lusanna has been found after 1456.

In the end, money, power, social convention, and the desire for legitimate heirs prevailed. Giovanni and Lusanna's story is a testimony to two contradictory realities that seem to be prevalent in every age. On the one hand, sexual love is a force that strains to fulfill itself, no matter what the obstacles. The barriers of class (and race or religion) or the vows of fidelity spouses swear to one another may be swept aside by the sheer force of sexual passion. Lovers who have known that kind of intensity will say to themselves, "Ah, yes."

On the other hand, most people tend to respect the laws and customs honored by their families, communities, and nations, and among them, none ranks higher than the belief that sexual love belongs, first and foremost and perhaps exclusively, within marriage. Men and women, even those predisposed to multiple sexual partners, usually pay public homage to the ideal of monogamy.

In the case of Giovanni, in his "youth" he had allowed himself an adulterous affair with a married woman. But when the time came for him to fulfill the marital expectations of his family and social milieu, he was not about to legalize his union with Lusanna—a woman of a lower station and "barren" to boot. He did what was expected of him. He married a much younger woman from his same background, one who enhanced his family's reputation and gave him children. From the point of view of the social order, he "did the right thing." But from the point of view of the moral order, his actions are more questionable.

And what should we think of Lusanna's story? She was certainly not a representative Italian wife by any means. Like Héloïse 250 years earlier, she was headstrong and passionate, willing to take risks for her lover despite the censure her behavior was bound to incur. Although her liaison did not result in the enduring second marriage she had hoped for, it did not lead to any of the severe forms of pun-

ishment that had been standard for proven adultery during the earlier
Middle Ages.

Members of the Jewish community in Italy during this period were,
of course, not subject to canon law; they had their own authorities
who determined whether a marriage was valid or not, and what to do
if it became dysfunctional. The following incident recorded in 1470
opens a window into a Jewish marriage during the late Middle
Ages.[58]

Hakkym ben Jehiel Cohen Falcon, a Jewish innkeeper from Pavia,
appealed to Jewish authorities for permission to take back his wife after
she had fled the conjugal home. For months she had been pressing
him to give up his livelihood as an innkeeper. "You've got to leave this
business," she complained, but the husband, by his own admission,
paid her no heed. Finally, as he tells the story, "my wife picked herself
up right at noon, took all the silver vessels and her jewelry, and
repaired to the house of a Gentile woman, a neighbor, to whom my
wife went frequently."

When the husband tracked his wife down at the neighbor's home, he
found her in the company of two Gentile women, two male citizens,
the auxiliary bishop, and the bishop's chaplain. The bishops had come
to encourage her to become a Christian. When the husband managed
to speak to his wife privately in German, this is the conversation that
ensued.

> He: "Why have you come here and why don't you return home?"
> She: "I'm going to stay here and I don't care to return, for I don't
> want to be the mistress of a tavern."
> He: "You can do whatever your heart desires in this matter."
> She: "You can't fool me again. . . . You've lied to me ten times and I
> don't trust you."

The bishops assured the husband that nothing would be done
hastily, and that she would have forty days to make up her mind. While
the husband went home weeping, the wife was taken to a convent "in
which a very rigorous Christian discipline prevailed." She stayed there
all day and all night, but by the next day she had a change of heart. She
sent word to the bishop that she wanted to return home, saying "I am

the wife of a *cohen,* and if I stay here a day or two more I can no more return to the shelter of his home, for he must divorce me." Cohens, descendants of the priestly caste, were apparently held to a higher standard than other Jews, who were not obliged to divorce if their wives went astray. With his wife restored to his home, "weeping for her sin" and asking for forgiveness, the husband put his case to the rabbis: was he permitted to take her back? Whatever their decision, he was resigned to follow their instruction.

This tantalizing document, like those concerned with the story of Giovanni and Lusanna, does not tell us how the woman fared in the end. Did the authorities allow her to resume her role as a wife? Was she obliged to live with ongoing reproaches from her husband and the Jewish community? Did he give up innkeeping and find another business? Running away from home is something that many wives have resorted to, and that most have probably contemplated at one time or another. Sometimes it *does* take extreme behavior to change an intolerable situation.

In medieval Europe, where marriage was the norm for almost all adults, wives and husbands were generally bound together until the death of a spouse. Of course, married life then, given the disparity in age between husband and wife and the shorter longevity for both sexes (the average life expectancy was around thirty), usually meant that spouses were rarely together for more than ten or fifteen years.[59] The remarriage of widows and of widowers was a common phenomenon— in some ways comparable to the frequent remarriages that occur today after divorce. A marriage of ten or fifteen years? Well, perhaps we should consider that time enough and not expect marriage to endure for the rest of one's life, which today averages almost seventy-four years for an American man and almost eighty for a woman. Perhaps the institution of lifelong marriage made more sense when one didn't expect to live so long.

And it certainly was easier to stay married when the institution was propped up by the combined force of religion, family, and community. In comparison, marriage today seems sadly lacking in such supports. But in comparison with our era, premodern marriages usually lacked the very qualities we treasure most highly: love, personal choice, and equality between husband and wife.

The medieval wife was not unaware of love. Popular songs and ballads, courtly poems, and narratives attest to the visibility of romantic
love at every social level. But marriage was too serious a business to be
dictated exclusively, and even predominantly, by love. After all, most
marriages depended on the combined resources of the two spouses. It
was openly acknowledged that a farmer's wife was indispensable to the
running of the farm, that a burgher's wife was a valuable asset to her
husband in the practice of his business, craft, or profession, and that a
great lady was needed to preside over a castle or manor.

By the end of the Middle Ages, there are signs that the status of some
wives was on the rise. Many upper-class women in such cities as Venice
and Paris, English wives from the landed gentry, and burgher wives
throughout Europe were beginning to enjoy a higher level of material
comfort and increased authority. An indication of the wife's enhanced
position can be found in the portraits of married couples, either on separate panels or together in the same painting, that began to appear from
the fifteenth century onward. Paintings of couples in the side panels of
religious tryptichs, such as the "Donors Engelbrechts and his wife"
(circa 1425–1430) in the Merode Altarpiece at the Cloisters in New
York, had been around for some time, but many other fifteenth-century
portraits were frankly secular and celebrated conjugal life.

One of the earliest in this new spirit is the portrait of Lysbeth van Du
vendoorde (1430, Rijksmuseum). From information written on the
back of the painting, we know that she married Symon van Adrichem, a
Rhineland bailiff, on March 19, 1430, and that she died in 1472. In the
painting she speaks lovingly of her husband through a scroll carrying
these words: "Long have I yearned for the one who opens up his heart."
He, in turn, in a portrait that has been lost, says of her: "I have been anxious to know who it is that would honor me with love." These courtly
expressions of reciprocal love do honor to both husband and wife.

A self-portrait of the German painter known as the Master of Frankfurt with his wife at his side shows the spouses at the respective ages of
thirty-six and twenty-seven (1491, Royal Museum of Fine Arts,
Antwerp). She wears a wedding ring on the third finger of her right
hand, holds a flower, and is accompanied by such suggestive objects as
cherries, bread, and a knife—domestic symbols of the good life.

The famous early-fifteenth-century painting, *Arnolfini and His Wife*,
by Jan van Eyck, the equally famous double portrait of *The Money*

Lender and His Wife by Quentin Metsys from around 1514, the less famous *Alltagsleben* engravings executed by Israhel Van Meckenem between 1490 and 1503, and other Flemish, Dutch, German, and Italian works seem to imply increased respect for the married couple—especially as compared to earlier medieval attitudes, when the ideal of marriage ran a poor third to virginity and widowhood.[60] This more favorable view of marriage, and concurrently of the wife, would work its way into the religious and social upheavals of the following century.

The Organ Player and His Wife *by Israhel van Meckenem, circa 1495–1503.
Spouses making music together, with their marriage bed in the
background. (National Gallery of Art, Washington, D.C.)*

THREE

Protestant Wives in Germany, England, and America, 1500–1700

A wise husband and one that seeketh to live in quiet with his wife, must observe these three rules. Often to admonish: seldome to reproove and never to smite her.

A Godly Form of Household Government,
London, 1614

It should not surprise us that the history of the wife has been so intricately linked to the history of religion. Even today, in many parts of the world, married women's destinies are determined by religious systems. To take an extreme case, think of such countries as Iran, Pakistan, and Afghanistan, where Islamic law requires all adult women to be covered from head to toe in public and can still punish the adulteress by stoning or execution. Western secular laws on marriage, relatively more favorable to women, are rooted in a canon that is essentially Judeo-Christian. We tend to forget that early New England was a theocracy formed by Puritans whose religious beliefs shaped the conduct of every inhabitant. Although many of their beliefs can be traced back to the Bible, others were formed during the tumultuous period of the Protestant Reformation.

This chapter will examine the mutations of marriage that arose from the religious upheavals of the sixteenth century and spread to North America via Germany, Switzerland, and England. It asks three basic questions: How did Martin Luther's pronouncements on marriage and his own marriage affect his generation and subsequent generations to come? How did the changes initiated by Henry VIII and refined under Elizabeth I help shape the Anglican vision of holy matrimony? How did English Protestants and especially Puritans create a model of appropriate behavior for American wives?

MARRIAGE IN LUTHER'S GERMANY

Few people influenced the institution of marriage more than the Augustinian monk Martin Luther. When he posted his ninety-five theses on the church door in Wittenberg in 1517, his immediate objective was to question the church practice of selling indulgences (papal dispensations that reduced or eliminated the need for penance). He subsequently raised a host of other stormy subjects, including the question of whether priests needed to be celibate. Today, while indulgences are seen as a quaint anachronism, the celibacy of priests is still controversial. On this matter, the Catholic church continues to be as intransigent as it was in 1525 when Luther married the former nun Katherina von Bora.

Luther's opposition to the tenet that priests could not marry was grounded in Scripture. He couldn't find any statements by Jesus in the New Testament condemning the marriage of the apostles—indeed, the Apostle Peter had been married, and it was possible, Luther thought, that Saint Paul and Jesus himself might have been married as very young men. Saint Paul had allowed for a priest to have a wedded wife (1 Timothy 3:2 and Titus 1:6), and that was good enough authority for Luther. Moreover, since numerous clergymen lived with concubines, many of whom bore children, he deemed it better for them to be married than to live in sin. He expounded these ideas in his 1520 "Open Letter to the Christian Nobility of the German Nation," concluding with three characteristically blunt assertions:

"*First,* Not every priest can do without a woman, not only on account of the weakness of the flesh, much more because of the necessities of the household. . . ." (Note that women were seen as necessary for the satisfaction of men's sexual and housekeeping needs.)

"*Second,* The pope has as little power to command this, as he has to forbid eating, drinking, the natural movement of the bowels or growing fat. . . ." (Here sex was seen as "natural" alongside other bodily activities.)

"*Third,* Although the law of the pope is against it, nevertheless, when the estate of matrimony has been entered against the pope's law, then his law is at an end, and is no longer valid; for the commandment of God, which decrees that no one shall put man and wife asunder, takes precedence of the law of the pope. . . ."[1] (Divine law overrides papal law.)

That same year, in his "Prelude on the Babylonian Captivity of the Church," Luther argued that marriage is not a sacrament—a religious ceremony of sacred significance. He and like-minded reformers reduced the seven Catholic sacraments to three; only baptism, penance, and the Eucharist remained, since they were mentioned in the Bible and considered necessary for salvation. But this did not mean that marriage was to be any less significant in the life of a Christian. On the basis of Scripture—always his ultimate test in matters of faith—Luther recommended it to everyone, both priest and layman. He also expressed his personal abhorrence for divorce, though he allowed that "it is still a question for debate."[2]

While Luther departed from orthodoxy in his unequivocal support of marriage, even for priests, he did not depart from the Catholic church's view of women as inferior beings, valid primarily for reproduction. For Luther, as for most of his predecessors and contemporaries, women had been "created for no other purpose than to serve men and be their helpers."[3]

Family relationships were therefore intrinsically hierarchical, with the husband at the head of the household, the wife second in rank, and children duty-bound to obey their parents. Luther's writings, and especially his *Small Catechism,* which was standard reading in Lutheran homes for centuries to come, articulated his view of the family. The obligations of the spouses to one another followed gender-specific lines, with the husband required to give "honor unto the wife, as unto the weaker vessel" and the wife to submit herself to her husband "as unto the Lord." Yet, following the words of Saint Paul, Luther also insisted that mutual love between husband and wife was a God-given mandate.[4]

Lutherans throughout the world, in America as in Germany and the Scandinavian lands, have integrated into their faith this lesson of reci-

procity in conjugal love and inequality in matters of authority. They
also have abided by Luther's view that a fully realized Christian vocation included conjugal, as well as religious, responsibilities.

In 1525 at the age of forty-two, Luther was willing to practice what
he preached. By marrying Katherina von Bora, aged twenty-five, he
joined the growing ranks of Reformation clerics who had taken a wife.
His was by no means the first marriage of a former Catholic priest, but
it was probably the most influential.

And who was this woman, Katherina von Bora, who has come down
in history as Luther's wife? What we know of her derives exclusively
from Luther and some of his contemporaries, since virtually none of
her own writings, not even her letters to Luther, have survived. What a
pity we cannot know her better! The energetic personality that emerges
even through the filter of male observers is unforgettable.

Katherina came from a noble family of modest means. Her mother
died when she was a baby, and when her father remarried, he placed
her in a cloister school. At nine, she was designated for the religious life
in the Cistercian convent of Nimbschen in Saxony, where her cousin
was the abbess. At sixteen she took the veil and would have lived permanently as the bride of Christ, had not Reformation history caught up
with her.

In 1522 her kinsman, the prior of an Augustinian monastery near
Nimbschen, renounced his vows and joined the Lutherans with a number of his brethren. Katherina and her sister nuns were profoundly
affected by his decision. They sent out letters to their families, asking to
be able to renounce their vows as well. But their families had no interest in restoring these young women to secular life—after all, most of
them had been sent into the convent so as to avoid paying a marital
dowry, and many had already paid some form of dowry to the convent.
Why should their families want to take these women back?

With no response from their families, the nuns took matters into
their own hands. They wrote directly to the Reformation leader, Dr.
Martin Luther, explaining that their newly enlightened consciousness
did not permit them to live as nuns any longer. But how were they to
escape from a nunnery in a land divided by fierce religious factions,
and where were they to go?

A daredevil plan was improvised with a fish merchant. On Easter
Eve, 1523, Katherina and eight other nuns were hidden in a wagon

*Katherina von Bora (1499–1552), wife of Martin
Luther, by Lucas Cranach, the Elder.
(Nationalmuseum med Prins Eugens
Waldemarsudde, Stockholm)*

among herring barrels, and three days later they were delivered to the
Augustinian monastery at Wittenberg, where Luther was still a monk
and professor of biblical theology. He undertook to place these women
in good homes and some in marriages. News of their whereabouts
quickly spread, as in the letter from a Wittenberg student to one of his
friends announcing that "a few days ago a wagonload of vestal virgins

came to town, more eager for wedlock than for life. God grant them husbands before they fare worse!"[5]

Katherina spent two years in Wittenberg, learning domestic economy and keeping her eye open for a suitable match. One learned young man from a patrician family in Nürnberg was attracted to her, as she was to him, but he was forced to bow to the objections of his parents to marriage with a portionless ex-nun.

Luther, taking up her cause, suggested the parson Kaspar Glatz. Katherina found Dr. Glatz unacceptable, but let it be known that she would consider Luther's friend, Dr. Amsdorf, or Luther himself. Clearly she was no shrinking violet. Despite her lack of a dowry, Katherina was conscious of her origins in a family from the minor nobility and her irreproachable convent background.

While not every man would have wanted to take an ex-nun as a wife, Luther began to think she might be right for him. With the approval of his father, a man of simple origins who had prospered as a copper miner, Luther married Katherina and embarked upon a very successful union. What began as a match of convenience for both of them eventually turned into a marriage of love.

Their betrothal, considered the official marriage, took place in the presence of four witnesses and was followed two weeks later by a public celebration attended by Luther's father and mother. For all Luther's public fame, he had to depend upon the largesse of his patrons to finance the wedding banquet. This was the first of many economic constraints the new bride was to encounter.

What was it like for her to move into the monastery at Wittenberg, with its dirty straw mattresses and years of neglect? What did she feel in bed next to a middle-aged man with a paunch, neither handsome nor refined? Later she would criticize his coarse expressions and peasant manners, but early in the marriage, she probably held her tongue. Indeed, recognizing the gap in their age and stature, she addressed him deferentially as *Herr Doktor* throughout their married life.

Katherina was not one to sit about and complain. From the start, she took over the management of her home with a determined will. The Augustinian monastery, first loaned to Luther by the Elektor Frederick and then given to him as a wedding present by the new Elektor, had forty rooms on the first floor with cells above. In time it would house Katherina and Luther's six children (one of whom died in infancy), six or seven orphaned nephews and nieces, the four children of one of Luthor's widowed friends, Katherina's aunt Magdalene, tutors for the children, male and female servants, student boarders, guests, and refugees. Katherina was not just a good *Hausfrau;* she became a remarkable manager of an oversized boardinghouse.

For the sake of cleanliness, she installed an indoor bathroom, which probably also served as a laundry. For the sake of economy, she created a brewery, planted a vegetable garden, and developed an orchard that produced apples, pears, grapes, peaches, and nuts. She herded, milked, slaughtered, and sold the cows, and made butter and cheese. No one has ever accused Katherina of laziness, though her critics—and there have been many—found her bossy and overbearing. Luther sometimes referred to her as *Dominus* ("My Lord"), and occasionally punned on her name *Kethe* ("Katie") with the word *Kette* ("chains"). Yet for all his theories about the hierarchy of men and women in marriage, he seems to have accepted her yoke with good grace. "In domestic affairs," he said, "I defer to Katie. Otherwise I am led by the Holy Ghost."[6]

As a wife, Katherina ministered to all aspects of her husband's physical and emotional needs—his diet, his illness, his bouts of depression. There was a long tradition behind her that expected the wife to be a healer, or, at the least, to oversee her husband's health. One of the duties of a wife, as set out in a 1467 German manual, was to accompany her husband when he had a tooth pulled. It contains a drawing of a husband sitting in a chair, one hand held by his wife, while the surgeon-dentist performs the extraction.[7]

Katherina knew the secrets of herbs and poultices. She monitored Luther's diet and gave him massages. When he fell into fits of depression—which he interpreted as the work of the devil—she was there to see that they ended, sometimes by dramatic means, such as having the door removed to the room in which he had locked himself. Katherina may have shown deference in public, but in private she knew when to intervene and override his decisions.

And in economic matters, she took the reins firmly in hand. Luther's generosity to students, needy relatives, friends, and hangers-on had to be curbed, if the household was to survive. One senses that some of Katherina's detractors resented the restrictions she placed on Luther's munificence, as well as her acute business sense. Like so many women married to men of the mind—the wives of absentminded professors

One of the duties of a wife was to accompany her husband for a tooth extraction. Pen drawing from a chess manual, 1467. (Württembergische Landesbibliothek, Stuttgart)

and Jewish rabbis, for example—the distaff half of the couple attended to material issues by default, though in Katherina's case, inclination also played its part.

As parents, Katherina and Martin Luther seem to have been of one mind: they welcomed their six children joyously, observed their weaning and teething with the attentiveness of "modern" parents, took pride in their achievements, and deeply mourned the loss of two daughters, one dead at less than a year and the other at fourteen. Certainly there were differences in the kinds of care the two parents gave to their children. Katherina had carried them in her body, given birth in pain, and breast-fed them. She probably cleaned up after the son who, according to Luther, relieved himself in every corner of the house. Would she have cried out to one of the children, as Luther did: "Child what have you done that I should love you so? What with your befouling the corners and bawling through the whole house?"[8] In comparison to Abelard's disgust at the bawling and filth of children, which both he and Héloïse saw as incompatible with intellectual pursuits, Luther's acceptance of children as the core of his rejuvenated life speaks for one of the Reformation's most dramatic shifts. Henceforth the pastor's home, replete with managerial wife and children underfoot, would offer a new model for Protestant couples throughout the world.

Other women in Switzerland and Strasbourg (a "free city" under the control of Austria) followed in the footsteps of the Germans by marrying Protestant reformers, most of whom were former priests. They shared their husbands' zeal for the Reformation, as well as the hardships and dangers occasioned by religious strife. Like Katherina von Bora, these wives provided companionship and comfort to embattled theologians, and shelter for Protestant refugees. Sometimes they, too, were forced to flee when Reformation politics became too heated.

Wibrandis Rosenblatt (1504–1564) married no less than three Protestant reformers in Basel and Strasbourg, bearing children to all of them; and prior to those unions, she had been the wife of the Basel humanist Ludwig Keller, who died in 1526 after only two years of marriage. With a daughter from Keller to raise, Wibranbis then married the minister of Saint Martin's church in Basel known as Oecolampadius, a learned theologian and professor. She was twenty-four and he forty-five, causing some of his contemporaries, including Erasmus, to comment mockingly on the difference in their age. Oecolampadius seems to have been thoroughly satisfied with his choice. In 1529 he wrote to a fellow reformer, Wolfgang Fabricius Capito: "My wife is what I always wanted and I wish for no other. She is not contentious, garrulous, or a gadabout, but looks after the household."[9] What Wibrandis thought of him we do not know, but she bore him a son and two daughters in a three-year period, entertained Protestant ministers and their families, exchanged letters with the wives of other reformers, shared her husband's victories in the religious battles of Basel, and mourned his death in 1531.

Wibrandis was widowed in the same month as Wolfgang Capito, to whom her second husband had written so glowingly of his marital choice just two years earlier. It took less than a year for Capito, encouraged by his matchmaking friends, to settle upon Wibrandis and for her to accept him as her third husband. With the children from her first two unions, she moved to Strasbourg, where Capito was a well-known pastor and professor. Once again, Wibrandis fulfilled her multiple duties as wife, housekeeper, and mother, producing no less than five children in her ten-year marriage to Capito. Her nine children all survived until the great plague of 1541, which carried away three of them . . . and Capito as well.

At the very same moment, Elisabeth Butzer, the wife of the reformer Nathanael Butzer, was stricken. Knowing that she was about to die and hearing of Wibrandis's loss Elisabeth had her summoned to her bedside. Wibrandis came at night (ashamed to be seen in public during the day, since she had been so recently widowed) and listened to Elisabeth's appeal. Would she marry the soon-to-be-widowed Butzer? This deathbed appeal from one woman to another says something about the kind of people they must have been: a wife concerned for the future well-being of her husband, a widow whose reputation for goodness and hard work had preceded her. Wibrandis married Butzer the following year.

While Butzer mourned his deceased wife, he was simultaneously learning to appreciate his new one. He expressed both of these sentiments in a letter to a friend: "There is nothing that I could desire in my new wife save that she is too attentive and solicitous. . . . I only hope I can be as kind to my new wife as she to me. But oh, the pangs for the one I have lost!"[10] The new household consisted of the married couple,

Wibrandis's mother, and Wibrandis's five surviving children; it was augmented by the birth of two more children (one dying at an early age) and an adopted niece. In toto, Wibrandis gave birth to eleven children from four different beds.

The Butzer home in Strasbourg, like the Luther home in Wittenberg, offered refuge to embattled Protestants, such as the Italian Vermigli, who wrote of his stay with them in 1542: "For 17 days after my arrival I was entertained in Butzer's home. It is like a hostel, receiving refugees for the cause of Christ."[11] No mention is made of Wibrandis, the person responsible for seeing that he and the others were properly cared for. Indeed, for an entire year, Wibrandis was left alone in Strasbourg to manage the household, while her husband was assisting the archbishop of Cologne. And on several occasions, while Butzer was away on business, she held down the fort, caring for her sick mother, sick children, and a continuing stream of refugees.

Nathanael Butzer left for England in 1548 at the invitation of the archbishop of Cranmer to work on biblical translations and to teach at Cambridge. Meanwhile in Strasbourg, Wibrandis was not amused to hear from one of her husband's colleagues that "she had better come to care for Butzer else he might marry some one else. The Duchess of Suffolk would have him. She is a widow."[12]

Eventually Wibrandis came to England with the whole family, but Butzer, exhausted by his labors, died in February 1551. It was then the responsibility of Wibrandis to return with her family to Strasbourg. Her surviving letters from this period, some in German, some in Latin, attest to her ability to manage financial matters on her own. One letter was to Archbishop Cranmer, asking him subtly for help. It brought in a grant of one hundred marks.

After the family returned to Strasbourg, Wibrandis and her children moved back to her home city of Basel. It was here that she died during the plague of 1564, and here that she was buried beside her second husband, Oecolampadius.

The German-speaking Protestant wives of Basel, Strasbourg, and Wittenberg added significantly to the Reformation: they made it possible for their husbands to survive and prosper. They helped create a new model of familial relations, one in which the wife—however subservient to her husband's needs—was nonetheless his acknowledged partner in molding the moral character of their children and in creating a Christian community around them. Encouraged to read the Bible available to them in Luther's vernacular translation, they began a tradition of mixed-gender discourse on Scriptural matters that has lasted for four centuries. The word *Hausfrau* does not begin to suggest the varied nature of their activities within the house, nor those other activities, such as letter-writing and traveling for family and business reasons, that brought them into the wider sphere of religious and social reform.

MARRIAGE IN TUDOR AND STUART ENGLAND

In Germany and Switzerland, the Reformation moved very quickly. By the second quarter of the sixteenth century, the right of the clergy to marry and the nonsacramental status of marriage became common Protestant doctrine. This was not the case in England, where both issues took longer to be resolved. Henry VIII, whose desire to divorce his first wife, Catherine of Aragon, would eventually lead to a rupture with the papacy and to the establishment of the Church of England, initially attacked Luther. He called for a bonfire of Luther's books in May 1521, and then wrote his own work in defense of the sacrament of marriage *(Assertio Septum Sacramentorum.)* Henry's conservative theology contrasted sharply with his subsequent personal behavior. While he got rid of his wives by means more foul than fair and successively married a half dozen, he and his spokesmen continued to delay the religio-legal transformations of marriage that had already been effected by Protestants in Germany and Switzerland.

Nonetheless, eventually following the lead of continental Protestants, matrimony was dropped from the list of sacraments in 1536.[13] Paradoxically, once marriage had been desacralized, the Church of England made every effort to emphasize its worth and dignity. Anglican sermons reminded the faithful that "marriage is a thing that pleaseth God" and waxed poetic on the joys of "nuptial love." The new Prayer Book of 1552 included a marriage service similar to the one from York (described in the last chapter) that had been in use since the Middle Ages, with a few significant changes. It continued to hold that marriage was ordained for procreation and the avoidance of fornication, but the emphasis on "mutual society, help, and comfort" was louder and clearer than before. In comparison with the medieval view that placed marriage behind chastity and widowhood in a hierarchy of holiness, the

The Wives of Henry VIII. *Catherine of Aragon, Jane Seymour, Catherine Howard, Ann Boleyn, Ann of Cleves, Catherine Parr. British engraving, 1796. (Courtesy of the Achenbach Foundation, Fine Arts Museums of San Francisco)*

new pronouncements championed marriage above the other two estates. In time marriage would become the "ethical norm" as well as the numerical norm for Christians.[14] Moreover, with the disappearance of monastic life in Britain as well as northern Europe and Switzerland, there was no longer an institutional alternative for the nonmarried.

One aspect of the Prayer Book service that did not change was the authority of husband over wife. Wives took the exact same vows as their husbands "to have and to hold from this day forward, for better for worse, for richer for poorer, in sickness and in health, to love and to cherish," but only the wife pledged "to obey." The bride's vow to obey, adapted into English from the medieval Latin service, inspired endless discussion, since it seemed to contradict the new emphasis on mutual love and spiritual equality.

Conduct books giving advice on marriage offered something of a double message. On the one hand, they supported male dominance as a God-given mandate whose pedigree went back to Genesis; on the other, they promoted the notion of mutuality in marriage whose source was Saint Paul (especially Colossians 3:18–20, and Ephesians 5:21–33).[15] Numerous Puritan ministers tried to address this contradiction in their weekly sermons, which were often published subsequently in book form.

William Gouge, an influential Puritan divine, struggled mightily to reconcile the new emphasis on mutuality with time-honored patriarchal practices, especially after a few of the wealthy wives in his congregation objected to some of his pronouncements—for example, that wives should not dispose of family goods without their husbands' assent. They also objected to the forms of reverence they were expected to show their husbands when rising from the table or parting, and the admonition to be humble and cheerful at all times, even when the husband had made an unjust reproof.[16]

In his 1622 treatise, *Domestical Duties,* Gouge tried to accommodate these objections. Himself a married man, he wrote of the give and take that marriage requires, and went so far as to recommend that the husband make of his wife "a joint governor of the family with himself."[17] Following a traditional metaphoric division of roles, he compared the man to the head and the woman to the heart, both necessary for survival. Yet while acknowledging "the small inequality which is betwixt the husband and the wife," Gouge concluded that "even in those things wherein there is a common equity, there is not an equality, for the husband hath ever even in all things a superiority."[18] Like all the other clergymen of his day, strict Puritan or moderate Anglican, Gouge believed that the order of patriarchy was no less immutable than the order of the stars.

Yet Gouge and most of his Puritan colleagues showed an advance over past patriarchal practices when they disallowed wife beating as a form of punishment. Wife beating was by the late sixteenth century regularly prosecuted in the church courts, but without much effect, according to surviving court and medical records. The astrologer/physician Robert Napier, practicing in Great Linford in the first decades of the seventeenth century, recorded cases of wife beating as a matter of course. For example, the distraught wife of Stephan Rawlins complained that she had to endure beatings and abuse every time her husband went on a drinking spree. Elizabeth Easton's husband was abetted by his family when he slapped his wife "like a dog."[19] Unfortunate wives could do very little to escape this kind of abuse, since divorce in the form of "separation from bed and board" was very costly and difficult to obtain. The new spirit of the age promoted by progressive Anglicans and Puritans alike opposed the physical chastisement of wives and permitted corporal punishment only for children and servants. Husbands were admonished to treat even unruly wives with understanding, to rebuke them verbally when necessary, and, above all, to love them. As William Gouge put it, love was "a distinct duty in itself peculiarly appertaining to a husband" and must be "mixed with everything wherein he hath to do with his wife."[20]

We can date the nascent primacy of love in marriage arrangements to this era. Historian Eric Carlson, who has studied marital practices among country folk in Tudor towns and villages, states unambiguously, "The most important consideration was love."[21] While it is true that monetary and social matters weighed in heavily among the nobility and gentry, this high-status group accounted for only about 10 percent of the population, and even here love marriages were on the rise. At the least, an upper-class woman usually had veto power over the prospective husbands paraded before her, and could single out the one she was most likely to love.

Young people of the popular classes living in rural areas enjoyed considerable freedom and opportunity to meet each other in both public and private venues—in fields, forests, parks, and barns, at streams, and along country roads. They met at markets, fairs, and church, and at the alehouse after church. Many worked side by side as servants or apprentices in the houses of their employers. Since most left home by their mid-teens to enter apprenticeships or employment, they were forced to become more mature and more independent than today's youth, who often enjoy parental support into their twenties and beyond.

Four hundred years ago in England, most young people in their early twenties were preoccupied with the business of acquiring the necessary resources for setting up an independent household. Men married between twenty-four and thirty, women between twenty-two and twenty-seven—and around 10 percent of the population did not marry at all.[22] The average age for brides was twenty-four, with bridegrooms about three years older. Upper-class women married earlier, between sixteen and twenty-four, with an average age of twenty. Members of the gentry and nobility were anxious to establish advantageous alliances for their daughters while they were still young.

Courtship was proverbially the most carefree time in a woman's life. She was generally free to entertain several suitors simultaneously. This is not to say that her parents automatically gave their goodwill. They had many ways of expressing disapproval for an unwelcome suitor, ranging from silence and coldness to direct prohibition and, in extreme cases, beating or locking up a daughter. Sometimes a father stated in his will that a daughter's marriage portion would be determined by her willingness to marry the man of his choice.[23] Since most parents cared about the well-being of their children, and little was more important than the choice of a spouse, it was necessary for them to intervene before a commitment between a nubile woman and her suitor had been made. In England, unlike most continental countries, parental consent was not a legal requirement for marriage, though in practice clergymen usually required it for children under twenty-one.

Engagement had long centered around the ancient ritual of joining hands and vowing to wed known as "handfasting." It was a popular practice that did not disappear with the religious innovations of the Reformation and Counter-Reformation. Indeed, it lasted in England into the mid-eighteenth century, and in Scotland into the twentieth. Handfasting was essentially a solemn, binding contract, and for many people the equivalent of marriage. Whether it occurred in the presence of two or three witnesses, as the church courts insisted it should for the sake of verification, and by a clergyman, as the church strongly recommended, or whether it took place with no human witnesses, the handfasting betrothal could not escape the eye of God. Englishmen and -women did not take their vows lightly, because they believed that God was witness to their words. It is hard for us to imagine today—in a time when promises are made and broken with the ease of throwing away disposable items—that people took them so seriously.

There was no set formula for the betrothal vows. It was enough to promise, in words of the present, to take the other person as one's "handfast" or "wedded" wife or husband. The Prayer Book offered a version of betrothal that some couples began to use, though many continued to invent their own ceremonies, sometimes impulsively and without witnesses, which could cause trouble later, if one of the parties tried to back out of the commitment.

More prudent women asked their fathers, kinsmen, friends, employers, or clergymen to act as intermediaries in public handfasting ceremonies that were often held in homes and inns, where numerous witnesses could attest to the act. And there was often a ring or coin given as a sign of betrothal. Sometimes a couple consummated their union immediately after the betrothal ceremony, as in the case of Elizabeth Cawnt and Robert Hubbard in 1598, who claimed that such was the custom of their county.[24] It was relatively common for country folk to consider themselves as married from the moment of betrothal, and to begin living together.

Communities tended to be tolerant of post-betrothal sexual activities, as long as the couple wed before the baby's birth. Perhaps for this reason a couple was expected to solemnize their nuptials not more than six months after betrothal. But some didn't bother with a church wedding until a baby was on the way; handfasting may have been sufficient to bind the couple but only a religious service could make the baby legitimate. It has been estimated that between 20 and 30 percent of brides arrived at the altar pregnant.[25]

For families of higher status and stricter scruples, betrothal had to be followed by a church wedding before the couple could engage in sex and set up joint residence. The engaged couple simply entered a special category "betwixt single persons and married persons," enjoying more liberties than the celibate and less responsibilities than husband and wife.[26] Different ministers had different ideas about the proper length of an engagement. Some suggested a short period—between three and four months—so the partners would not be tempted "into sin" before the church wedding.

Weddings were expected to take place in the parish church of one of the two parties. Since the mid-sixteenth century, "at church" no longer meant at the church door, but inside the church, where the bride and groom first received communion and then publicly recited their vows. The ceremony orchestrated by the Anglican priest had many of the words and symbols that are still in use today, most notably the wedding ring, which reflected the unending bond of matrimony. One symbol that has been lost was the priest's traditional "kiss of peace" to the bride—a practice that Protestant ministers in the United States continued well into the nineteenth century. In the sixteenth century, the Anglican priest's kiss was the signal for the wedding party to claim their kisses from the bride and to seize her garters, as well as those of the groom.[27]

After the ceremony, the marriage was duly recorded in the parish book registry. If the couple later moved away from their parish, a copy of the registry entry provided proof that they had been properly married and that any children born of the union were legitimate. The church wedding was surrounded by all sorts of festivities—parading the couple to and from church, eating and drinking, music and dancing—at home, in the tavern, or on the village green.

Puritans, on the other hand, eschewed church weddings and all revelry that seemed to be either pagan or popish. They distinguished themselves from Anglicans by doing away with all ritual that was not specifically mentioned in Scripture, such as the minister's blessing the ring and the groom's placing coins on the service book, not to mention the more outlandish holdovers of popular culture, like outdoor parades and hazing the bride and groom. Puritans married at home in intimate, unostentatious ceremonies that stressed the couple's reciprocal obligations to each other under the watchful eye of God. The most scrupulous even did away with wedding rings.

Puritans were the most consistent supporters of traditional biblical authority—that of parents over children and husbands over wives. Their ministers exhorted children to honor their parents in all matters, including the choice of a spouse. Parental authority was by no means a new subject of discourse, but it reached something of a crescendo in the late sixteenth century. While many moralists came down on the side of the parents, deploring the tendency of young people to "follow their own will and let out the reins unto their own . . . unsettled lusts," the general tide was beginning to turn in favor of the young.[28] Parents who forced their children into marriage for the sake of monetary considerations were increasingly condemned. The clergyman Thomas Becon's observation in 1560 that some parents abused their authority by marrying off their children "for worldly gain and lucre" was echoed over and over again for the next hundred years.[29] Puritans in particular, despite their universal agreement that children should submit to the will of their parents, disliked marriages contracted solely for material gain; instead, they emphasized spiritual compatability and affection as the basis for a lasting union.

The English, on the whole, seem to have allowed for love matches to a greater extent than continental Europeans. By the turn of the seventeenth century, English conduct books assumed that a man would choose a wife "according to his own heart," and that a woman, though not so free as a man, had the right to respond to male initiative.[30] Montesquieu in the eighteenth century and Engels in the nineteenth contrasted the freedom of English daughters to marry "according to their own fancy, without consulting their parents" with the situation of Europeans, who were required by law to obtain their parents' consent.[31] This greater freedom was connected to the generally uncloistered lives that British women enjoyed, as opposed to their European and especially their Mediterranean counterparts. It also reflected the later age of English marriage for both men and women, and the narrower age gap between brides and grooms.

Still, it would be wrong to assume that England under the Tudors and Stuarts renounced its patriarchal inheritance. Ministers continued to remind their parishioners that children should honor their parents and that wives should obey their husbands. Both of these forms of submission inspired not only sermons and tracts, but also stories, poems, and plays, including those of the best known Elizabethan playwright, William Shakespeare.

* * *

Over and over again, Shakespeare's plays turn upon the conflict of parental authority and the opposing will of youthful lovers. Reading *Romeo and Juliet, The Taming of the Shrew,* or *The Winter's Tale,* we hear the echoes of contemporary questions: What should parents do to arrange the best matches for their children? Should a daughter be able to refuse a match proposed by her parents? Should young people be able to follow the inclinations of their hearts, even when parents object? Whether the story was set in a mythical Sicily or Bohemia, Shakespeare put a theatrical gloss over the changing attitudes toward marriage that evolved during his lifetime (1564–1616), and among these, none was more vocal than the growing belief that young people should wed according to mutual attraction, rather than by parental decree.

There is a scene in *The Winter's Tale* that articulates this debate. The young prince Florizel woos a shepherd's daughter named Perdita (who is, of course, a princess abandoned at birth). In the presence of Perdita, the shepherd who had adopted her, and two unknown travelers in disguise, Florizel asks everyone to witness his vows, and the shepherd asks his daughter if she gives her assent. Then the shepherd father betrothes Perdita and Florizel with these words:

> *Take hands; a bargain;*
> *And, friends unknown, you shall bear witness to 't:*
> *I give my daughter to him, and will make*
> *Her portion equal to his.*

We recognize several of the elements we have seen elsewhere in the betrothal ceremony: the bride and groom join hands as in handfasting, the father gives his daughter to the groom, witnesses attest to the vows, and the father promises a dowry. By virtue of the young people's consent in the presence of witnesses, this makes for a binding betrothal.

At this point one of the travelers—who is none other than Florizel's father in disguise—initiates a probing dialogue with his son.

> POLIXENES: *Soft, swain, . . . Have you a father?*
> FLORIZEL: *I have; but what of him?*
> POLIXENES: *Knows he of this?*
> FLORIZEL: *He neither does nor shall.*

POLIXENES: Methinks a father
Is, at the nuptial of his son, a guest
That best becomes the table . . .

Florizel agrees in principle that a father should usually be consulted in his son's marital choice, yet demurs in his own case: "for some other reasons, my grave sir,/ Which t'is not fit you know, I'll not acquaint/ My father of this business." So here we have a clear-cut picture of a son who selects a bride without his father's knowledge because the latter would probably object to her lowly station; the son simply follows the dictates of his heart. Of course, in this comedy—Shakespeare's last—everything works out for the best.

In *Romeo and Juliet,* Shakespeare had made the theme of youthful love and parental opposition the stuff of great tragedy. The quintessential lovers must oppose not only their respective parents, but their two clans—the Montagues and the Capulets. Despite the Italian setting, the story certainly reflected problems that were current in Shakespeare's England—namely, feuds among gentry families and the practice of clandestine love marriages. Indeed, the clandestine marriage of two well-born sixteen-year-olds, Thomas Thynne and Maria Marvin, whose families were staunch enemies, may have inspired Shakespeare to write *Romeo and Juliet;* both the real marriage and the writing of the play occurred in 1595. Six years afterward, the elder Thynnes were still not reconciled to their son's marriage, as evidenced by a surviving letter from Maria to her mother-in-law hoping that God would be instrumental in the "turning of your heart towards me."[32]

Romeo and Juliet, however imaginative, sheds light on the marital practices of Elizabethan gentry. For example, Juliet was not yet fourteen when the suitor Paris asked for her hand. At first Juliet's father responded "Let two more summers wither in their pride/ Ere we may think her ripe to be a bride." So initially he considered her too young, and preferred to see her married at fifteen or sixteen. Yet he did not think her too young to be wooed, and advised Paris to "get her heart." The father's consent was dependent on the daughter's willingness. Later—for reasons that are never made clear—the father goes back on this position, and assumes that he alone has the right to give his daughter away, even without her consent. He and his wife order Juliet to prepare for imminent marriage with Paris. The father becomes angry when Juliet says, "I'll not wed, I cannot love,/ I am too young." As far as he is concerned, a father has the right to say, "I'll give you to my friend."

But as the audience knows, Juliet cannot, under any circumstance, marry Paris because she and Romeo have already been secretly married by Friar Laurence. Since the friar knows this, he comes up with the plan that will ultimately lead to Juliet's death, as well as Romeo's. The implication is that the friar is an unreliable, meddling soul. He should not have married them clandestinely in the first place, and he should not have tried to cover up the marriage with his harebrained, dangerous scheme of having Juliet fake death. But even worse is the hard-nosed position taken by the Capulet father. His intransigence precipitated the disaster. Moral: one cannot force a person to marry someone she doesn't love. And second moral: no parental (religious, ethnic, national) barrier should interfere with the natural inclinations of youthful lovers.

The Taming of the Shrew presents another marriage contracted without the consent of the son's father in the case of Lucentio and Bianca. But the real meat of the play concerns Petruchio and Kate and the proper relationship between a husband and his wife. A husband—so the play suggests—must command absolute obedience from his wife, at least in public.

In Shakespeare's England, a disobedient wife was one of the stock characters of comedy. Popular literature told husbands how to subdue shrewish wives or, conversely, made fun of the man who did not know how to enforce his authority. The wife who wore the breeches and the henpecked husband appeared in numerous comic treatises, broadsides, and woodcuts throughout England and Northern Europe.[33] Some sharp-tongued women were not only reviled in text and image, but actually brought before the courts as "common scolds," often by neighbors complaining of behavior that disturbed the peace.[34]

Now, it is true that there is often a discrepancy between prescription and practice: what is prescribed is not always the way one behaves. *The Taming of the Shrew* is a good example of one woman's attempt to subvert this prescription, and one man's attempt to restore it. Petruchio believes that good marriages are based on a wife's total submission to her spouse. And his job is to bring Kate—a notorious shrew—around to this point of view. Does he succeed?

A New Yeare's Gift for Shrewes *by Thomas Cecil, circa 1625–1640. English broadside that reads:* Who marrieth a Wife uppon a Moneday. If she will not be good uppon a Tuesday. Let him go to ye wood uppon a Wensday/ And cutt him a cudgell upon the Thursday. And pay her soundly uppon a Fryday. And She mend not, ye Divil take her a Saterday./ Then may he eate his meate in peace on the Sunday. (British Museum, London)

In the final scene of the play, Kate appears to have been tamed by Petruchio. She wins the wager he had made with two other husbands by showing herself more willing to obey than their wives. Adopting the selfless "Griselda" model, she goes so far as to make the following declaration to the two other women.

> *Thy husband is thy lord, thy life, thy keeper,*
> *Thy head, thy sovereign—one that cares for thee.*
> *. . .*
> *I am ashamed that women are so simple*

To offer war where they should kneel for peace,
Or seek for rule, supremacy, and sway,
When they are bound to serve, love, and obey.

And she advises her sister wives to "place your hands below your husband's foot," which she does as a sign of complete submission to Petruchio.

The question, of course, is whether Kate really means it—does she really agree with Petruchio that a wife's subservience to her husband bodes "peace, love, and quiet home"? Or is she merely a clever woman paying lip service to her spouse in public, and following her own will in private? Or is it possible that she and Petruchio are both acting out roles they will laugh about in bed?

A young woman living at the time of Shakespeare, who attended such plays, listened to her minister's sermons on Sundays, and bantered in the alehouse with her friends, would have absorbed conflicting views on her obligations as a daughter and wife. The minister told her to obey her parents and her future husband. The plays she saw, songs she sang, and books she read (if she could read), told her to obey the impulses of her heart. Looking around her, she saw married couples, like her own parents, whose union bespoke stability, if not always harmony. She also saw women jilted by suitors or deserted by husbands—unlucky women who had chosen unwisely. And even worse, reprehensible women whose sexual freedom had become known and led to public whippings for fornication. Why even the rumor of sexual promiscuity could ruin a woman's chances for marriage! And what of unmarried women with babies, forced not only to bear the humiliation but the burden of lifelong support? There was little sympathy for single mothers, who were viewed as an affront to public morality and, worse yet, a potential drain on public charity.

Anything that insulted the dignity of marriage could not be tolerated. Adultery, however common, was vigorously denounced by clerics of every stripe. Puritans vehemently condemned it for both men and women, and even attempted to change the double standard that had prevailed for centuries.[35] Generally speaking, a wife's adultery was grounds for marital separation (while men's adultery was not), and for a short period, beginning in 1650, female adultery was made a capital offense, though it was enforced only two or three times.[36] Even nonadulterous couples living apart from one another were not allowed to remain separated for long. The case of Helen Dixon is illustrative: having refused to follow her husband to "a strange place where she had no acquaintance," she was called up before the church court and ultimately forced to join him.[37] With all these cautionary tales before her, a young Englishwoman of any sense would think long and hard before making a marital commitment.

Marriage would normally give her status and protection. In the best of circumstances, she would have an economic provider and an affectionate companion. She and her husband would become, according to the words of one inspired pastor, "yoke-fellows . . . fixing their hearts in the good liking of each other."[38] She would be able to engage in sexual relations without the fear of sin. She could have legitimate children to love and care for, who would in turn care for her in her declining years. By entering the estate of holy matrimony (an estate now championed above celibacy), she would be fulfilling her Christian vocation. Conversely, if she did not marry, she could count only on being consigned to the end of the table with the "spinsters." (The term "spinster" derived from "spinning," a wage-earning occupation for many unmarried women.)

Still, marriage was by no means an unqualified blessing for a woman. Marriage meant giving up one's freedom and becoming the subject of one's husband. It meant accepting his authority, his whims, and sometimes his fists. It meant running the risk of conjugal disharmony and the ongoing mental strain that women experienced in such unions. Records of the early seventeenth-century physician Robert Napier concerning more than a thousand female patients treated for mental illness conclude that they were especially troubled by the oppression they experienced as daughters and wives.[39]

Marriage was also the fearful gateway to pregnancy and the travails of labor, which pre-nineteenth-century women endured without the benefits of anesthesia or antisepsis. It entailed the possibility of dying in childbirth, the frequent loss of children, and probable widowhood. In the end, most English daughters did marry, though they married later and in fewer numbers than their continental counterparts.

Perhaps what distinguishes English marriage from continental marriage of this period is the belief that marriage was, at its best, essentially a form of companionship. Returning to the words of Genesis, English Protestants took very seriously God's statement, "It is not good for the man to be alone" and that a wife was to be "a sustainer beside him."

Hand in hand, two Christian souls were encouraged to share the pleasures and duties of this earth as they simultaneously made their way, step by step, to eternal life.

And among the pleasures that Protestants recognized and condoned were the pleasures of marital sex. Puritans in particular, contrary to the now popular view of them as inhibited hypocrites, saw regular sexual intercourse as necessary for a lasting marriage. Husbands and wives were expected to try to please each other, and abstinence was generally frowned upon, especially when one partner would unilaterally abstain by his or her choice. In the words of William Whateley's conduct book (*A Bride's Bush,* 1623), "mutual dalliances for pleasure's sake" were to be encouraged in bed, where wives had the same rights to sexual satisfaction as their husbands.[40] Indeed, if we take Puritan writers seriously, gender distinctions regarding dominance and submission were to be abandoned in the bedchamber: "the wife (as well as the husband) is therein both a servant and mistress, a servant to yield her body, a mistress to have the power of his."[41]

The Anglican priest and poet John Donne (1571–1631) devoted one of his ten Marriage Songs (Epithalamiums) to the "Equality of Persons." He not only put the wife on a par with the husband in sexual matters, but blurred conventional gender boundaries in such lines as "her heart loves as well as his," "The bridegroome is a maid, and not a man," and "then the bride/ Becomes a man." Lovemaking was not a matter of rigid sex roles, but of uninhibited mutual pleasure, where women could sometimes act with the boldness of men, and men might sometimes take on the passive qualities attributed to women. As the husband of a woman who bore him twelve children, Donne envisioned domestic bliss as a total union of body and soul. Consider this wedding-night scene from "The Bridegroomes Comming":

> *Their soules, though long acquainted they had beene,*
> *These clothes, their bodies never yet had seene;*
> *Therefore at first shee modestly might start,*
> *But must forthwith surrender every part,*
> *As freely, as each to each before, gave either eye or heart.*[42]

This is a far cry from the medieval distrust of the body and prior religious instruction to engage in sex only for the benefit of procreation. It reflects a new appreciation of physical love in marriage, not only as a deterrent to "fornication" but also as a good in its own right.

Reading the poems and sermons written by Tudor and Stuart men allows us to understand the religious and cultural ambiance that surrounded women's lives. But from the turn of the seventeenth century onward, we can do better: we can read the many surviving letters, diaries, memoirs, and poems penned by women themselves. From this point onward, it will be somewhat easier to enter into the subjective experience of married women. While this body of writing gives voice to only the most privileged, and tends to be guarded on many issues, it brings us closer to the wife of the past.

The letters from the Thynne family, mentioned earlier in connection with *Romeo and Juliet,* constitute a rich source of information about two generations of women from the landed gentry. The marriage between John Thynne and Joan Haywire in 1575 was an arranged marriage between a sixteen-year-old girl from a wealthy merchant family and John Thynne, heir to the Longleaf estate. Her letters to him throughout twenty-nine years of marriage show the growth of a young, deferential woman into an efficient and knowledgeable mistress, both at Longleaf and at her own dowry castle in Trashier. Her complaints that her husband was spending too much time in their London home, while she was left to manage affairs in the country, was repeated in similar letters by other women from the landed gentry.[43]

The second Thynne marriage, that of Thomas Thynne and Marie Marvin, began as a love match in 1595 and remained one until Marie's death in childbirth eighteen years later, when she was only thirty-four. Despite the fact that Thomas's parents were never reconciled to the marriage, he inherited Longleaf upon the death of his father in 1604, and lived there with his wife, who took over the role of managing the estate. The move to Longleaf did, however, occasion some discord between the couple. Marie's letters show how hurt she was when he did not trust her judgment in running his affairs and held "such a contempt of my poor wits." She complained that he left her "like an innocent fool here" while he was in London—echoing her mother-in-law's earlier complaint. Nonetheless, Marie insisted she would not be inferior to any of her neighbors "in playing the good housewife," and continued to think lovingly of her spouse as "an admirable good husband."

* * *

Personal diaries, which began to be written around this time, provide an excellent record of the historical period and prevailing mentalities. One of the first and most important penned by an Englishwoman is the diary of the Puritan Lady Margaret Hoby (1571–1633).

Margaret Dakins Hoby was the only daughter of a large landowner in Yorkshire.[44] According to the custom for women of her class and religion, she was taken into the household of a strict Puritan from the landed nobility, the Countess of Huntingdon. Under her protection, Margaret learned to supervise a large estate, and was married at age eighteen to another protégé of the household. Widowed two years later without progeny, she quickly remarried, and then was once again widowed. At the age of twenty-five, she took as her third husband Sir Thomas Hoby, a man she had rejected earlier, perhaps because of his short stature and unprepossessing appearance.

Lady Hoby started her diary in 1599 as a record of her religious life. She began each day with family prayer and Bible reading, then prayed again in private, attended the public prayer and lecture given by the chaplain of the manor, and took part in the singing of Psalms that was usual in Puritan households. Before retiring, she also prayed once again in private. On Sundays she went to church twice. As the spiritual mentor of her household, she read to the women and discussed the Sunday sermon with them.

Her diary also records her numerous activities as a busy manor wife concerned with every aspect of the management of their estate at Hackness, which had been a part of her dowry. Her time was spent supervising the servants, paying wages and other bills, doctoring the sick, and lending a hand in domestic tasks, such as washing linen, weighing and spinning wool, dying cloth, making wax lights and oil, distilling aqua vitae, overseeing the beehives, and preserving food. She kept an eye on the workmen who sowed rye and planted corn. She bought sheep and had trees planted. She seems to have enjoyed working in the garden, taking especial pride in her roses. She and her servants made most of the clothing for the family, and Margaret herself took care of the health of her household by administering medicine and performing simple surgery.

When neighbors came to call, their conversations were dutifully sober: On March 13, 1600, they spoke "of diuers nedfull dutes to be known"—duties such as choosing marriage partners for their children and becoming godparents to the children of their friends and relatives. Families of her station also took children into their homes, as she herself had been taken in by the Countess of Huntingdon. Her diary entry of March 1603 reads: "my Cossine Gates brought his daughter, Iane, beinge of the age of 13 years auld, to me, who, as he saied, he freely gaue to me." Since she had no children of her own, the presence of a thirteen-year-old girl may have been very welcome.

Her husband seems to have been away much of the time. As a member of Parliament and numerous commissions, a justice of the peace and self-appointed judge of those who did not attend church regularly, he functioned largely in the public sphere, while she ran the estate and looked after their private interests. Their principal joint activities when he was home were dining, attending church, taking walks, and discussing business matters. Theirs was an ordered Puritan existence—a stable partnership, if not a union of soul mates.

Concerning her inner spiritual life, Lady Hoby was given to rigorous self-examination. She accepted God's punishment for the smallest of sins, and often fasted as a form of penance. Here are some of her self-recriminations.

September 10, 1599: "[I] neclected my custom of praier, for which, as for many other sinnes, it pleased the Lord to punishe me with an Inward assalte."

September 14, 1599: "Lord, for Christs sack, pardone my drouseness which, with a neclegent mind, caused me to ommitt that medetation . . . which I ought to haue had."

July 1600: "I please the lord to touch my hart with such sorrow, for some offence Cometted, that I hope the lord, for his sonne sake, hath pardoned it according to his promise. . . . I read a paper that wrought a farther humiliation in me. I thanke god."

Margaret Hoby, a devout Christian, was far removed from the hair shirt and histrionics of Margery Kempe two centuries earlier. Her brand of Puritan introspection was quieter, less public, yet no less aware of personal failings, no less fearful of God's punishment, no less hopeful for forgiveness and salvation. This is the Puritan conscience that would be transported to America.

THE PURITANS' BAGGAGE

Our knowledge of married women's lives in seventeenth-century New England is considerably enriched by another "first"—Anne Bradstreet (c. 1612–1672), the first American poet of either sex. Her history was both typical and atypical of the lives of colonial wives. On the one hand, following the norms of her time, she married a man of her social rank and religious sect, gave birth to eight children, and remained primarily at home while her husband was active in business and public life. On the other, Bradstreet was exceptionally well educated, especially for a female, and became a renowned poet on both sides of the Atlantic. We look to her work, as to that of Héloïse, Margery Kempe, and Christine de Pizan, for an example of what was possible for a remarkable woman within the tight gender constraints of the past.

Anne Dudley Bradstreet was born in either 1612 or 1613 in Northampton, England. Her father was a lawyer and estate manager, and her mother a gentlewoman. As scrupulous Puritans, they experienced religious discrimination under King James I, who was notoriously unfriendly to any deviation from the rites of the established Anglican church. The family was closely connected to the Puritan minister John Dod, coauthor of the influential treatise *A Godlie Forme of Household Government: For the Ordering of Private Families, according to the direction of God's Word*. In it, Dod echoed the hierarchy that had existed in Christianity for centuries—the wife was to be subservient to her husband, just as children were to be subservient to parents, and servants subservient to their masters. Since this order was believed to be ordained by God, it was only by maintaining it and respecting one's superiors that an individual had any chance of salvation. But Dod also echoed more recent Protestant theology in his vision of spouses as spiritual equals, the wife seen as her husband's Christian "sister" and "inheritor with him of the Kingdom of heaven."[45]

Anne Dudley met her future husband, Simon Bradstreet, when she was only nine. At that time he was assistant estate manager to her father, then steward to the earl of Lincoln. Eleven years her senior, Simon had studied at Emmanuel College, Cambridge, a center for nonconformist religious views to which the Dudleys had also sent Anne's brother. Unlike her brother, Anne received a nonsystematic education at home.

Anne married in 1628 when she was only fifteen or sixteen, considerably earlier than the average English bride of twenty-four or twenty-five. Within two years of their wedding, Simon and Anne Bradstreet and the Dudley family emigrated from England to Massachusetts. They crossed the Atlantic in 1630 on the *Arbella,* named for Anne's childhood friend, Lady Arbella Johnson, who also emigrated with her husband. The *Arbella* was one of eleven ships carrying seven hundred passengers to the Massachusetts shores.

The reasons for immigration were religious. The Dudleys and Bradstreets were increasingly uncomfortable in the anti-Puritan climate that existed under James I and Charles I. Like the Pilgrims a few years earlier, they looked to the New World as a haven where they could practice their religious beliefs more freely and create a society closer to their understanding of the will of God.

The ten-week crossing on the *Arbella,* with its malodorous, tightly packed quarters, must have been especially hard on gentry folk like the Dudleys and Bradstreets. The women and children slept in compartments between the main deck and the roof of the hold, and the men slept in hammocks. Their diet consisted of saltmeat or fish and hard biscuits, and the only heat came from a cooking stove. Cold winds, rough waters, and seasickness plagued most of the passengers, but the only casualty on the *Arbella* was the birth of a stillborn child. When they arrived in Salem in June, they encountered a frontier community that was bleaker than anything they had anticipated.[46] Many of the settlers, like Lady Arbella and her husband, died within the first months. Before the winter had set in, the Dudleys and Bradstreets moved to nearby Charleston, and, in 1631, to Cambridge (then called Newtowne), where Harvard College would be founded by the end of the decade.

Like many other immigrant wives coming to America since the seventeenth century, Anne Bradstreet experienced both a difficult journey and a sense of shock upon arrival. She must have wondered if this land of sparse shelter and bad manners could provide a suitable home for her and her family. As she later wrote: "I fovnd a new World and new manners at wch my heart rose," meaning manners that disgusted her.[47] Yet Anne was arriving with many more resources than most immigrants, namely her relatively affluent parents, her siblings, and a husband, who, like her father, was to become influential in the governance of the Massachusetts Bay Colony.

Her initial afflictions were compounded by "a lingering sicknes like a consvmption together wth a lamenesse," a condition which she interpreted as a "correction" sent by the Lord to humble her and do her good.[48] It was common for Christians, and especially for Puritans, to interpret illness as a trial sent by God. Anne was to have many such trials throughout her lifetime.

Equally unsettling was the fact that she did not, for the first five years of her marriage, produce a child. As she remembered: "It pleased God to keep me a long time wthout a child wch was a great greif to me, and cost me many prayers + tears before I obtained one. . . ."[49] American wives, like their European counterparts, could think of few curses worse than barrenness. Children were considered a blessing from the Lord, especially in a country where the injunction to "be fuitful and multiply" had no geographical limits and where children supplied much of the farm and household labor. Most married women desired children and had frequent pregnancies, limited only by the natural contraception that occurs from breast-feeding. Anne could have bought fertility medicines from the midwife Jane Hawkins, who practiced in Boston in the 1630s, or she could have taken a common potion made of dried beaver testicles grated and mixed with wine, believed to facilitate conception.[50] But on such matters, she left no record.

With the birth of her son Simon in 1633, Anne embarked upon the demanding role of mother in a frontier community. Between 1633 and 1652, she give birth to a total of eight children, the "eight birds hatcht in one nest" evoked in one of her poems.[51] Her four sons and four daughters all survived into adulthood. At a time when one could expect to lose a quarter or half of one's children before they became adults, Anne's good fortune with her children was a further reason for her to praise the Lord.

Like other Puritan mothers, Anne Bradstreet breast-fed her babies. In England during the early seventeenth century, when upper-class women commonly took in wet nurses, Protestants condemned wet-nursing as unhealthy and unnatural. Puritans and other strict Protestants considered it a mother's religious duty to nurse her babies. Contrary to our "puritanical" ideas today, mothers breast-fed in the presence of visitors and spoke about the process with "unpuritanical" ease. Here are Anne Bradstreet's graphic words on the subject: "Some

American oak cradle, 1625–1675. (Metropolitan Museum of Art, New York)

children are hardly weaned although the teat be rub'd wth wormwood or mustard, they wil either wipe it off, or else suck down sweet and bitter together. . . ."[52] She used the weaning process as a metaphor for the lives of certain Christians who are "so childishly sottish that they are still huging and sucking those empty breasts," and remain unable to move on to "more substantiall food"—i.e., a higher sphere of existence— without the bitterness God forces into their lives. Anne Bradstreet's breast imagery sprang from her personal experience as a mother and from her conception of God's cosmic order.

While Anne Bradstreet welcomed her pregnancies, she was by no means immune to the fears that parturition represented for a colonial mother, since one-fifth of adult women's deaths occurred in childbirth.[53] One of the poems Anne addressed to her husband, "Before the birth of one of her Children," makes these fears explicit.

How soon, my Dear, death may my steps attend,
How soon't may be thy Lot to lose thy friend,
We both are ignorant, yet love bids me
These farewell lines to recommend to thee,
That when that knot's unty'd that made us one,
I may seem thine, who in effect am none.[54]

We glimpse Anne's premonition, fortunately unfounded, that she would die in childbirth. We also get a sense of her loving relation to the "friend" she found in her husband.

Her five marriage poems attest to a profound love, the kind that any wife in any age might hope to experience. "To my Dear and loving Husband" expresses those feelings in a charming, straightforward manner.

If ever two were one, then surely we.
If ever man were lov'd by wife, then thee;
If ever wife was happy in a man,
Compare with me ye women if you can.[55]

From Ipswich, where they had moved in 1635, she wrote "A Letter to her Husband, absent upon Publick employment," evoking a union of mind and body that transcended separation.

My head, my heart, mine Eyes, my life, nay more,
My joy, my Magazine of earthly store,
If two be one, as surely thou and I,
How stayest thou there, whilst I at Ipswich lye?
. . . . .
Flesh of thy flesh, bone of thy bone,
I here, thou there, yet both but one.[56]

And in another poem to her husband, she playfully imaged their union in creaturely pairs—two deer, two turtles, two fish—who, browse "together at one Tree," "roost within one house," and "in one River glide."[57] This passionate wife is far removed from the sexually repressed Puritan stereotype formed on the basis of fire-and-brimstone sermons rather than a handful of conjugal love poems.

It was by no means common in the seventeenth century for women to write poetry, either in England or the New World. About half of Puritan women could not read and even more could not write.[58] And many colonists were of the mind of John Winthrop, the first governor of the Massachusetts Bay Colony, that women should not "meddle in such things as are proper for men, whose minds are stronger." Here he was referring to the case of Anne Yale Hopkins, the wife of Governor Edward Hopkins of Connecticut, whose mental instability—according to Winthrop—was caused by "giving herself wholly to reading and writing." His diagnosis reflected age-old beliefs about the proper sphere for wives: "For if she had attended her household affairs, and such things as belong to women, . . . she had kept her wits, and might have improved them usefully and honourably in the place God had set her."[59]

Anne Bradstreet was well aware of this common attitude, which she confronted in one of her shorter poems, "The Prologue," by imagining herself in the minds of her detractors: "I am obnoxious to each carping tongue/ Who sayes my hand a needle better fits." And then, with a bow to men's presumed superiority, she simply asked that women be granted "some small acknowledgement" of their poetic ability, however limited, dubbing her own verse "unrefined stuffe" in contrast to the "glistering gold" of men.[60] It not hard to understand why Anne Bradstreet felt the need to defend herself against the tight community of Puritans for whom lofty poetic expression was deemed an exclusively male purview.

Puritans had many ways of differentiating between what was proper for men and what was proper for women. Women and men entered church by separate doors and were seated according to their sex and rank: men with men, women with women, maidens with maidens, children with children.[61] The most prominent men sat in the foremost pews. Only men were expected to speak publicly.

Most Puritan women were content to attend church services without drawing attention to themselves. Their major concern was getting there in the first place. A weekly walk to a church two or three or even five miles away was no small matter for mothers with small children, not to mention sick and elderly charges. The Bradstreets' and Dudleys' move to Ipswich may have been occasioned by the distance they had to travel from Cambridge to Boston in order to attend services. Given her frequent illnesses and the demands of motherhood, Anne Bradstreet was not always able to trek across the Charles River and devote an entire day to the logistics of church attendance.

Puritan men throughout the seventeenth and eighteenth centuries often petitioned their governing officials for new churches on the grounds that their wives and children needed one closer to home. And pressure was brought to bear by the women themselves in more personal ways. Thus Hannah Gallop wrote to her uncle John Winthrop, Jr. (son of the first governor of Massachusetts and himself the Governor of Connecticut), to support the establishment of a church in Mistick, Connecticut, because mothers "that have young children sucking" obliged to travel long distances "manie times are brought exeding faint & much weakened, & divers are not able to goe al winter."[62]

Ultimately the Bradstreets moved in 1645 or 1646 from Ipswich to Andover, where they hoped to create a new community. The town records note that Simon Bradstreet's house lot consisted of twenty acres. Once again Anne had to pack and unpack the family's belongings, set up housekeeping in a frontier settlement where foxes and wolves in the adjacent forests posed a constant threat, and reorganize the lives of her children and servants. Her eldest son, Samuel, was being prepared to enter Harvard College, and her youngest son, Simon, was sent to Ipswich for his grammar school education. In Andover Anne gave birth to her last three children and somehow continued the literary work that was integral to her life.[63] It was there that Simon thrived as the owner of a sawmill and became a public figure with activities that took him to various parts of New England. The Bradstreets prospered in Andover, which held on to its social homogeneity and agrarian charm right into the twentieth century.

The minister of their congregation was John Woodbridge, married to Anne's sister, Mercy. When the Woodbridges traveled to England in 1647, they took with them Anne Bradstreet's poems, which were published in London in 1650 under the title *The Tenth Muse,* apparently to the surprise of the author. In his preface to this volume of some two hundred pages, John Woodbridge described Anne Bradstreet as a "Woman, honoured, and esteemed where she lives, for her gracious demeanour, her eminent parts, her pious conversation, her courteous disposition, her exact diligence in her place, and discreet managing of her family occasions." And in keeping with this flawless portrait of an industrious, well-bred wife thoroughly committed to her family and community, he hastened to add that "these Poems are the fruit but of some few houres, curtailed from her sleep, and other refreshments."[64] In no way did Woodbridge want to present Bradstreet's literary work as a rival to her primary domestic responsibilities. To get some sense of the negative attitude toward women writers at that time, one has only to read the public letter addressed by Thomas Parker to his sister, which appeared in London in 1650. He condemned her literary achievements in no uncertain terms: "your printing of a Book, beyond the custom of your Sex, doth rankly smell."[65]

The Tenth Muse was Bradstreet's only publication during her lifetime, though she continued to write until her death in 1672. Her *Several Poems Compiled with Great Variety of Wit and Learning*, posthumously published in 1678, was one of only four books authored by women in seventeenth-century New England, as compared with 907 authored by men.[66]

This is not the place to examine Bradstreet's long metaphysical poems or her biblical commentaries or her scientific and alchemical treatises. But it is the place to argue that whatever restrictions Puritan society placed upon girls and women—and there were many—they were at least expected to use their minds for religious instruction. Both men and women were encouraged to read the Bible, especially the "Geneva Bible" prepared under the auspices of John Calvin and translated in 1560 by English Protestant exiles living in Switzerland. In 1642, Massachussets passed a law requiring parents to teach their children and apprentices to read so they could become familiar with Scripture.[67] Women were also encouraged to discuss the weekly sermon in female groups, a common practice in England that was brought to the New World by the generation of Anne Bradstreet's parents.

Anne Bradstreet's mother, Dorothy Dudley, offered a stellar example of the Puritan wife devoted to both public and private worship. In the eulogy she wrote for her mother, Anne specifically named these activities: "The publick meetings ever did frequent,/ And in her Closet constant hours she spent." Mrs. Dudley was praised as "A worthy Matron of unspotted life,/ A loving Mother and obedient wife,/ A friendly Neighbor, pitiful to poor,/ . . . A true Instructer of her Family."[68] For

Anne, her mother had provided a model of selfless devotion to a strong-willed husband and to the children who still counted on her for counsel and support in the New World.

Anne's father, Thomas Dudley, confirmed this vision of a loving, obedient, friendly, compassionate spirit in the letter he wrote to Anne's sister, Mercy, at the time of his wife's death, though considering the circumstances, it would have been bad form to say anything less. He could probably have added many of the other virtues so prized in Christian wives: humility, meekness, modesty, submissiveness, and patience. It may be hard for us today to imagine that these were the main qualities lauded in women. In private, colonial women had to be physically and emotionally robust just to sustain themselves and their families during an unforgiving New England winter, but in public they were obliged to conform to the appearance of the weaker vessel. And many women, like Dorothy Dudley, had so internalized the Puritan ethos that they undoubtedly believed the creed of female frailty and wifely dependence. It was less common to speak of men's dependence on their wives; yet observers of marriage throughout the centuries have noted that husbands often fall to pieces, and even die, after the death of a wife . . . or they quickly marry again. The latter was the case for Thomas Dudley, who, despite his devotion to a wife of forty years, remarried barely four months after her death.

Anne Bradstreet was in her own way no less exemplary than her mother. To her mother's conjugal and maternal strengths, she added the gifts of the writer, inaugurating a tradition of American women poets that would, in time, embrace Emily Dickinson and Adrienne Rich.

Yet we would be wrong to generalize on the basis of Anne Bradstreet's marital happiness. Others were not so lucky. Anne's younger sister, Sarah, for instance, made a disastrous marriage that ended in scandal and divorce. After a trip to London with her husband, Benjamin Keayne, in 1646, Sarah returned to Massachusetts alone amid charges that she had preached in mixed assemblies and performed acts unbecoming to a wife. Her husband accused her of having infected him with syphilis, presumably acquired through adultery.

While her father, then the governor of Massachusetts, was able to push her divorce through the General Court, she was nonetheless excommunicated from Boston's First Church for "Irregular prophecying" and "odious, lewd & scandalous uncleane behavior with . . . an Excommunicate person."[69] She seems to have gotten off easily since the penalty for proven adultery was whipping or a fine, or both. It was common in both New England and the South for adulterous offenders to be required to stand in public with a rope around their necks as a form of mock execution, or to appear in church draped in a white sheet, holding a white wand, and, one way or the other, to apologize to the community. Laws had even been passed to punish adultery with death, as early as 1612 in Virginia and 1631 in Massachusetts, but that penalty was almost never exacted.[70] (Capital punishment for adultery in Massachusetts, Connecticut, and New Haven seems to have been enforced only three times.) Sarah was permitted to marry again, in spite of the fact that her first husband was still living, but she did lose custody of her daughter.

Divorce, if rare, was more available to New Englanders of both sexes and all classes than it had ever been in England, where it was the prerogative of the rich. Since marriage was not a sacrament for Puritans, but merely a civil contract between two people, it could be undone like any other contract. Puritans granted divorce as a last resort, under the assumption that the aggrieved party, usually the woman, would then marry again and be safe from the temptations of either adultery or fornication. In seventeenth-century Massachusetts, divorce was most commonly granted for adultery, desertion, long absence, failure to provide, bigamy, and cruelty. Over half the divorce cases in New England cited adultery as the cause. One woman filed for divorce when her husband admitted "that he had Rog[e]red other women and meant to Roger Every Likely Woman He Could and as many as would Let Him."[71] New England women initiated divorce more often than men, which suggests that, unlike Benjamin and Sarah Keayne, wives were more desperate than their husbands to terminate an unhappy marriage.

The charges against Sarah Keayne leveled by her husband in the First Church records indicate that it was not only her sexual behavior that was in question, but also her "prophecying." Traditionally, a Christian wife was expected to remain silent in church, following an injunction initiated by Saint Paul and reaffirmed by Governor John Winthrop.

Despite these expectations, some Puritan wives did speak out, among them Anne Hutchinson, whose pronouncements on religious matters led to what was known as the "Antinomian controversy" (a term of reproach rather than a reference to her ideas). The daughter of a nonconformist clergyman who had been removed from his pulpit, she emigrated from England to Boston in 1634 with her husband and children (she was to bear fifteen during her lifetime). In the New World, on the half-acre lot assigned to the Hutchinsons, Anne continued to fulfill the domestic and social obligations expected from the wife of a successful merchant. She also commanded respect as an experienced nurse and healer, who delivered babies and administered medicines made from her own herbal recipes.

But soon Anne took on another role: that of religious dissenter. Following the lead of John Cotton, who preached a theory of total dependence on God's grace (rather than on good works), Anne began to organize women's meetings to discuss the Sunday sermon and expound her own unorthodox views. Here the women who had to sit silently in church were able to speak out and express themselves in the supportive company of other women. Soon the women-only sessions were expanded to include men, and Anne's spacious parlor was harboring sixty to eighty people.[72]

Before long the church authorities, threatened by Hutchinson's growing influence, accused her of departing from accepted Puritan beliefs. Refusing to be silenced, she traveled to neighboring communities, gathering supporters as well as detractors. Governor Winthrop, convinced that wives were meant to obey husbands and had no business questioning the established order, sided with the faction against her. She was charged with trying to play the part *"of a Husband [rather] than a Wife, and a preacher [rather] than a Hearer."*[73] Ultimately excommunicated and banished, she then moved out of Massachusetts with a small group including her husband and became one of the founders of Rhode Island. Four years later, after her husband's death, she settled on Long Island Sound and was killed by Indians in August 1643.

Of course, few Puritan wives were either religious leaders or poets. Most were occupied with the endless chores of housekeeping and mothering. They married earlier than their English counterparts, usually between twenty and twenty-three, and gave birth to an average of six or seven children. Under the best of circumstances, as in the case of Anne Bradstreet, they lived long enough to see their children into adulthood and died at a venerable age, but the premodern pattern of a wife's early death, as well as the death of some of her offspring in child-hood, was probably more common. And it was certainly common for widowed husbands and wives to remarry, forming new families consist-ing of children from prior marriages. When we think of today's "recom-bined" families occasioned by divorce, they pale in comparison with the number of recombined families occasioned by death in early Amer-ica. Sisters and brothers shared beds with half-siblings (sometimes three and four to a bed), as well as bedrooms with their parents.

Most New England families lived in homes consisting of only one or two rooms, with an outside wash house and dairy. Wives were respon-sible for keeping these spaces clean, for cooking meals, washing and mending clothes, spinning wool, churning butter, making bread, pre-serving foods, taking care of the children, and passing on all these skills to their daughters. They also taught them to make soap, wax, candles, and brooms. Most wives planted vegetable gardens, fed the hens and pigs, and milked the cows.

There was a clear-cut division of labor between men and women. Most men obtained food from hunting, fishing, and tillage. They con-structed their homes, made the necessary tools, raised and sheared sheep, were active in the making of leather goods, and engaged in flax culture and lumbering.[74] Some were shopkeepers, craftsmen, doctors, or lawyers. If a husband ran a business or practiced a craft, often his wife assisted him. Indeed, the keeping of a tavern and selling of spirits were so predicated on the cooperation of a wife that some authorities refused a license to the man without one. A man from Taunton, Massa-chusetts, was denied a renewal of his license after his wife's death on the grounds that he was "not being soe capable of keeping a publicke house."[75]

Husbands and wives counted on their children for help, and also on indentured or "covenant servants" aged eighteen to twenty-five, who committed to several years of labor in return for transportation to the New World and maintenance during their term of service. As many as one-third of colonial households included indentured servants; yet there never seemed to be enough servants to go around.[76] Often, these servants had close relations with the mistress of the house, who took an interest in the young woman's future and even helped her find a hus-band when her servitude came to an end. Indentured servants were prohibited from marrying beforehand, though some did, when an obliging bridegroom was willing to pay off the servant's remaining time.

The relations between employers and the domestic servants living under their roof always had the potential for discord, as in the case of Anne Bradstreet's sister-in-law Mary Winthrop Dudley, who described her insolent servant to her stepmother as a "great affliction." "If I should write to you of all the reviling speeches, and filthie language shee hath used towards me I should but greive you."[77]

Many servants had equally negative pictures of their mistresses, especially if the latter were given to administering blows—a right they and their husbands possessed as "superiors." Some female servants were sexually harassed by their masters, as was Elizabeth Dickerman, who complained to the Middlesex County Court that her master John Harris had forced her to be with him, and that "if she tould her dame . . . shee had as good be hanged." The court accepted Elizabeth's charge and ordered John Harris to be whipped twenty stripes.[78] When a servant became pregnant, by her master or any other man, she not only risked public ignominy, but also an extra year of service to make up for the time lost in pregnancy, childbirth, and lying-in. A Virginia statute of 1672, recognizing the unfairness of this requirement when the master himself was the father of his servant's bastard, decreed that he could not claim any extra service from her.[79] One wonders how many mistresses looked the other way so as to accommodate their husband's extramarital urges.

Being a good housekeeper, with or without servants, was the sine qua non of a good wife. American women, of necessity, identified themselves with housekeeping and often took pride in their ability to cook, preserve, spin, weave, knit, sew, and embroider. The story of colonial, republican, and frontier wives, from the seventeenth to the twentieth century, is savored with apple pies and colored with hand-patched quilts. These homey objects, however sentimentalized in our time, were nonetheless true markers of a wife's accomplishments. In her remarkable book, *Good Wives,* Laurel Ulrich notes that a cook might be known for such specialties as "roast pork or goose with apples, . . . eel pie flavored with parsley and winter savory, . . . leek soup or gooseberry cream," though for ordinary meals the most common dishes were boiled meat and beans, parsnips, turnips, onions, or cabbage.[80] In most homes, where everything was cooked on a single blaze within a cavernous fireplace, the one-pot meal was the norm.

Then there were "seasonal specialities"—cheese making in the spring, gardening in the summer, and cider-making in the fall. Anyone who has ever picked apples and smelled them fermenting has had a whiff of the pungent, time-consuming process undertaken to produce the gallons of cider that would be enjoyed throughout the year.

A woman like Beatrice Plummer of Newbury, "who took pride in huswifery," was appreciated by her first two husbands, before she had the misfortune to marry a man more interested in her financial worth than her ability to make bacon and bread.[81] Though he had signed a prenuptial agreement allowing her to retain ownership of the estate she had inherited from her previous husband, the new husband changed his mind and tried to force her to tear it up. Ultimately their marital discord ended up in court, leaving behind testimony to one housewife's pride as a cook and homemaker and one husband's rapacious concern for her property. Because she had not torn up the prenuptial document, she was able to hold on to her estate. It is not clear whether she held on to the husband, who was fined for his abusive conduct.

Prenuptial agreements allowing women to control the property they possessed prior to marriage were rare, but less rare than in England, where they had been used only by the rich. The contract signed by one Plymouth, Massachusetts, woman and her husband in 1667 stated that she was entitled "to enjoy all her house and lands, goods and cattle, that she is now possessed of, to dispose of them at her own free will."[82]

Upon marriage, a husband automatically gained control of his wife's property unless a prenuptial agreement stipulated otherwise. The male appropriation of female property followed the English common law principle that treated the husband and wife as a "unity," with her worldly possessions "merging" into his. He had the right to rule over her entire estate, except for personal items, such as her clothes, bedding, and other "paraphernalia."

Legally, a husband was his wife's guardian, and as such, liable for her conduct, including her debts. If she committed a minor crime, the court ordered the husband to pay the fine, though the wife often had to endure some form of public humiliation. For example, "scolds" convicted of defaming others by their gossip and abusive tongues were placed in a "ducking" stool and submerged in water.

If a wife wanted to sue someone for wrongs done her, it was usually her husband who brought the suit, though she could file suit herself if she had her husband's permission. Single, divorced, or widowed women—*feme sole,* to use the common law term—could sue on their own behalf and enter into other legal and business transactions, but married women could not engage in business ventures, except as assistants to their husbands.

One right a woman did have was to be named as executor of her husband's will. By law, a widow was entitled to a third of her husband's estate; in practice, husbands often specified that a larger portion be set aside for their widows or that they be allowed to continue living in the family dwelling.[83] Some women inherited a husband's farm or trade, which, as widows, they were allowed to run. Others took the widow's portion to start new enterprises, such as innkeeping and the sale of liquor—businesses that were overwhelmingly associated with widows in early New England.

Many women—then as now—could expect to end their lives in widowhood. This was not the result of greater longevity for women, as it is today, since seventeenth-century men and women had roughly the same life expectancy. But wives were generally younger than their husbands, if only by a few years, and thus died somewhat later. While widowhood could entail a certain amount of independence for the rare woman with sizable means, most widows were dependent on their children, particularly their sons, for a room in the family dwelling or a monetary allotment. In the worst-case scenarios, poor widows fell back upon the generosity of the church or public charity.

The study of early American history has, until recently, lacked attention to women. Attempts to rectify this neglect during the past thirty years have produced excellent results, yet these studies are by no means abundant, and they are by no means consistent in the pictures they offer of colonial wives.

Some (for example, Lyle Koehler's) tend to emphasize the negative aspects of women's subordinate position, reminding us that whatever new freedoms were enjoyed in the New World, these did not include greater freedom for daughters and wives. Nancy Woloch argues that the ideology of female subordination, prevalent in England as elsewhere in Europe, "was transported intact and easily replanted in colonial soil," and that as a result, women in the colonies were excluded from positions of power and authority and only entered public history "by catastrophe or deviance—such as Indian captivity or witchcraft charges."[84] Other historians, (for example, Laurel Ulrich) without denying the submissiveness demanded of women, underscore the many ways wives commanded authority as mothers, deputy husbands, neighbors, midwives, philanthropists, and even frontier heroines.

One factor that probably did play out to the advantage of American women was the large proportion of males to females throughout the seventeenth century in both the North and South. The Pilgrims aboard the Mayflower arriving at Plymouth in 1620 included only 28 women among 102 passengers. The first settlers of Jamestown, Virginia, in 1607 had no women at all, but the group arriving in the fall of 1608 included Mistress Forrest, the wife of Thomas Forrest, and her maid, Anne Burras. Although the mistress soon died, the maid quickly found a mate, and their marriage was the first to be performed in Virginia.

There were so few females during the early years that the Virginia Company, which oversaw colonization, took the unusual step of importing shiploads of single women, 140 between 1620 and 1622. A wife could be "bought" for between 120 and 150 pounds of tobacco as reimbursement for her passage.[85] In the Chesapeake (Maryland and Virginia) men outnumbered women 6 to 1 during the early decades, and 3 to 1 as late as the 1680s.[86] This imbalance was true, too, of the slave population transported to Virginia from 1619 onward at a ratio of 3 men to every 2 women. Whereas in England there was a *surplus* of women—roughly 9 males to 10 females—in the New World a potential wife was much in demand regardless of her social class or the portion she could bring to a marriage. Indentured servants as well as wealthy widows could all find husbands if they wanted to—and almost all did.

The state of Maryland promoted itself as a paradise for female servants in search of a husband: "The Women that go over into this Province as Servants have the best luck here as in any place of the world besides; for they are no sooner on shoar but they are courted into a Copulative matrimony. . . ."[87] Following the successful importation of females to Virginia and Maryland, Carolina publicized its own glowing prospects: "If any Maid or single Woman have a desire to go over, they will think themselves in the Golden Age, when Men paid a Dowry for their Wives; for if they be but civil, and under 50 years of Age, some honest Man or other, will purchase them for their Wives."[88]

The paucity of marriageable women seems to have given them

greater choice in selecting a husband, a situation that some women took full advantage of. Mrs. Cecily Jordan, for example, widowed in 1623 in Virginia, became immediately engaged to Rev. Greville Pooley on the condition that he keep the engagement secret for the sake of decency, as behooved her recent widowhood. But Pooley made the engagement known, and so displeased his fiancée that she linked herself to another suitor, causing Pooley to institute a breach of promise suit. This celebrated case was won by Mrs. Jordan.[89]

Another Virginia woman with two fiancés, Eleanor Spragg, was punished in 1624 by her congregation for "her offence in contracting herself to two several men at one time." While her punishment consisted only of public repentance, the clergy announced that similar offenses would be punished with whippings or fines.

At least one Virginia woman had such a strong sense of her value in the marriage market that she refused the traditional vow of obedience. At her wedding in 1687, Sarah Harrison Blair was asked the usual question: did she promise to obey her husband? "No obey," she replied. The minister repeated the question two more times, but she continued to repeat "No obey." In the end, the ceremony was concluded on her terms, in defiance of standard liturgical practice.[90]

With such a scarcity of Anglo-American women, one wonders why there were not more intermarriages between either Indian and black women and the male settlers. The French in New France, where there was a similar shortage of women, were known to have contracted numerous intermarriages. In the early Jamestown settlement, John Rolfe did not consider it beneath him to marry Pocahontas, the daughter of the Indian chieftain Powhatan. Whether she was, or was not, his savior according to the legend, the marriage was considered a good thing not only for Rolfe and his Christianized bride, but also for peaceful relations with Native Americans.

After the introduction of slave workers in the Virginia tobacco fields, there was a time when they, too, sometimes married whites—several documented cases of this have survived.[91] It seems that in the early days of colonization, when the status of slaves was uncertain (after all, there were no slaves in England), Africans were treated somewhat like indentured servants, and there was little social distance between white servants and black slaves. But as the institution of slavery evolved and slaves became increasingly dehumanized, a taboo against sexual rela-

Pocahontas (1599–1617), daughter of the Indian chief Powhatan and wife of the Virginia settler John Rolfe. In 1616, she went with her husband to England and was lionized by London society. She died on the return voyage to America at the age of eighteen. Engraving by Simon van de Passe, 1616. (National Portrait Gallery, Washington, D.C.)

tions and marriage with blacks, as with Indians, took root. As early as 1630 in Jamestown, a certain Hugh Davis was ordered to "be soundly whipped before an assemblage of Negroes and others for abusing himself to the dishonor of God and the shame of Christians by defiling his body in lying with a Negro, which fault he is to acknowledge next Sabbath day."[92]

In 1661, Maryland passed the first antimiscegenation law, directed at prohibiting white female and black male marriages.[93] In 1691, Virginia declared that a white person could not marry a black or an Indian, and any white who did would be banished from the colony.[94] In 1705, Massachusetts passed a law against intermarriage between the races. That same year, an observer of American mores claimed that the example of John Rolfe "might well have been followed by other settlers for the vast improvement of the country," were it not for fear that the women "shou'd conspire with those of their own Nation, to destroy their husbands." By 1717, Governor Alexander Spotswood of Virginia wrote to a correspondent in London: "I cannot find one Englishman that has an Indian wife."[95] He could probably have said the same for the union of an English colonist and a black woman, since between 1705 and 1750 Pennsylvania, Massachusetts, Delaware, and all the southern colonies passed laws prohibiting interracial marriages.[96]

In the American colonies, there was no intermediate status assigned to the children of nonwhites and whites, as in other New World settlements—for example, the *metis* in Canada or the *mestizos* of Latin America. However, in Florida and Louisiana where Spanish or French rule prevailed, mulattos were recognized as forming a class of their own, with many of the rights of whites, at least until the nineteenth century, when almost all the United States passed laws prohibiting marriages between white persons and blacks or mulattos.[97]

Without competition from Native Americans and blacks, seventeenth-century white women enjoyed the advantages of scarcity. The facts of life in a frontier society made them indispensable to the survival of their families and communities. As early as July 31, 1619, the gentlemen of the Virginia House of Burgesses acknowledged that "in a newe plantation it is not knowen whether man or woman be the most necessary."[98] The Puritan minister John Cotton, "teacher" of the First Church of Boston from 1633 to his death in 1652, expressed what was probably a commonly accepted view: "Women are Creatures without which there is no comfortable Living for man: it is true of them what is wont to be said of governments, *That bad ones are better than none.*"[99] Such a backhand compliment reflected a considerable change from the medieval religious stance that no wife was better than a good one.

As we look back on this period from the vantage of the year 2000, it can be argued that sixteenth- and seventeenth-century Protestants prepared the soil for modern marriage. The American historian Edmund Morgan reminds us of the high value placed on mutual love in Puritan marriage: "If husband and wife failed to love each other above all the world, they not only wronged each other they disobeyed God." But Morgan hastens to add that love did not have the very same meaning in the seventeenth century that it has today. It should not be confused with romantic passion, and was never meant to rival the love of God. Rather, marital love was conceptualized, in the words of one minister, as "the Sugar to sweeten every addition to married life, but not an essential part of it." It was, at best, affection in harmony with duty and reason.[100]

Another historian, John Gillis, is convinced that Puritan conjugality "came closest to the modern norm of companionate marriage, even to the extent of proclaiming the equality (albeit limited) of partners."[101] In all probability, the Puritan wife did not ask for so much. She was generally content to fulfill her role as the "heart" of the family, leaving the role of "head" to her husband. She sat in her assigned pew in church, and retired to her closet to pray. But in bed, if Anne Bradstreet is in any way indicative of more general practices, some of them knew a thing or two that might surprise us.

FOUR

Republican Wives in America and France

Something new was added to the identity of Western women in the eighteenth century: a political consciousness. Forged in the crucible of revolution when both America and France threw off the rule of monarchy, the political awareness of women on both sides of the Atlantic took on new dimensions. Whether they were patriots or loyalists, women felt they were as implicated in national events as their husbands, fathers, brothers, and sons. While very few made history in the public sense of the word, women were cocreators of the new republican societies that emerged from the Revolutionary struggle. In this context, "women" should be understood as wives, since almost all adult females were married in colonial America, as well as the majority of eighteenth-century Frenchwomen.

THE COMPLEAT WIFE IN COLONIAL AMERICA

During the eighteenth century, American wifehood was still constructed around three basic identities. A wife was, first and foremost, her husband's sexual and emotional partner, albeit a "junior partner." She became, in most cases, a mother, with parental obligations shared with her husband. And in all cases, she was a housekeeper, with daily duties that consumed most of her energy.

Almost all women allotted time to religious activities, such as prayer, Bible reading, church attendance, and discussion of the sermon in all-women groups. Most women in cities and towns visited with each other, not only to socialize but also to lend a hand when a neighbor was sick or lying in after childbirth. Women with means enjoyed elaborate entertainment with their peers—dinners and parties and trips that might last several days or weeks. They set aside time for letter writing and the arts, most notably the harpsichord or pianoforte, needlework, and poetry. As in all periods of history, economic advantages made some women's days considerably easier than others, but so did geographical differences; for example, city dwellers had less arduous lives than their country cousins, and residents of the North had educational opportunities for their daughters that were not yet available in the South.

A wife's status was determined by her husband's occupation. She was known publicly as the blacksmith's wife, the governor's wife, the minister's wife, the merchant's wife, and not by any rank of her own—except in a few unusual cases where a married woman acquired renown as an exceptional midwife or an inspired religious leader.

Once married, a woman became, in the eyes of the common law inherited from England, a *feme covert,* one whose legal person was subsumed or "covered" by that of her husband. Only he could sue or be sued, draft wills, make contracts, and buy or sell property, including property that had originally belonged to his wife. With virtually no legal rights and with divorce very difficult to obtain, brides put themselves under the protection, or at the mercy, of their husbands.

English, French, and American treaties from this period echoed the same tune: that woman was the "weaker vessel," the "softer" sex, inferior in reason to man, created to serve a husband and nurture children. When, in the eighteenth century, Enlightenment thinking began to rival strictly religious interpretations of human history, Nature was invoked rather than God as the final authority, but with no less certainty of woman's subordinate destiny. In the words of Jean-Jacques Rousseau, whose book on education, *Émile,* was influential on both sides of the Atlantic: "The man should be strong and active; the woman should be weak and passive. . . . What is most wanted in a woman is gentleness . . . she should early learn to submit to injustice and suffer the wrongs inflicted on her by her husband without complaint."[1]

Popular British and American writers rearticulated age-old arguments supporting the inequality of husband and wife. Whether one attributed women's inferior status to a defect in reason or to God's decree, the result was the same: colonial women and men were expected to believe that wives were weaker than their husbands and were destined to be dependent on them. Clergymen, physicians, and moralists agreed, "Providence designed women for a state of dependence, and consequently of submission."[2] Some advice books, like John Gregory's *A Father's Legacy to his Daughter* (1774), nuanced their vocabulary so as to recommend that wives strive to "please" their husbands rather than "serve" them, without changing the essential message: female deference was necessary to gain male protection and support.

If a wife did not show proper deference or was frankly disobedient, there were ways for a husband to enforce his authority, namely "moderate physical correction" as allowed in Anglo-English law. This could take the form of wife beating or locking a wife in her room, but was not supposed to entail permanent injury or loss of life. Violent husbands were looked upon with disfavor by the law, and some were even brought to court by their wives, with the aid of concerned family members and neighbors. In this way, a few mistreated women managed to escape abusive relationships. Most of them probably suffered in silence.

The common assertions about women's "natural" inferiority and need for male dominance, and the laws that enforced such assertions, must have influenced the way women saw themselves. Historian Mary Beth Norton's assessment of numerous women's diaries and letters led her to believe that most women did indeed think of themselves as inferior to men and had what we would today call low self-esteem. Norton's documentation of women's statements to that effect is impressive . . . and appalling. Terms such as "poor helpless woman," "vacant brain," "imbecility," "small talent," "poor judgment," "insipid," "stupid," "strange," "inconsistent," "disconsolate," "distressed," "dull," and "liable to errors" represent a minuscule fraction of the language women consistently used to deprecate themselves and other members of their gender.[3]

The only arena where a women was expected to shine was within the home, which was considered her "natural" domain. Here a wife could take pride in her efficient management of a household that still depended largely on homemade goods. The middle-class woman with one or two servants still produced most of the family food from the adjacent farm, vegetable garden, and dairy; she still worked at the spinning wheel and the loom, even if city women were increasingly able to purchase ready-made cloth; and most wives still made clothes for all the members of the household, including the servants, though more affluent women were able to hire the services of a seamstress. If freed from certain basic demands of housewifery, some privileged women turned to more artistic forms of creation: bed rugs and curtains embroidered in intricate crewel patterns, or lace caps and sleeve ruffings. Heaven forbid their fingers should be idle, since as one moralist put it, "Idle afternoons . . . make bad wives."[4] When we see these beautiful artifacts of the American past in museums and special collections, we do well to remember that only a sprinkling of women had the leisure to follow their creative bent.

Northern urban women with means rose before eight, spent their mornings in housework, dined around two, and visited friends or pursued some form of leisure, such as riding, reading, or music, in the afternoon.[5] Well-to-do women in the South also divided their time between housewifery and entertainment. All the southern colonies had a reputation for hospitality, and it was not uncommon for friends and relatives to descend unannounced upon a city or rural matron, expecting food and lodging.[6]

But most wives of the middling and poorer sort were never free from an endless round of drudgery. Without the means to hire servants, even at the relatively low rates found in cities, these wives—who may themselves have served terms as maids, cooks, or laundresses before their marriages—merely continued the life-sustaining work that had always devolved upon women. A good number of wives assisted in their husbands' trades and crafts, and often took over the business if they became widows. In rural areas, work was incessant, since one had to produce everything oneself, without the nearby markets and stores that made life easier for city women.

Wives who moved with their husbands to sparsely settled communities in search of land and greater opportunity often found themselves isolated and lonely. A judge on circuit in North Carolina in 1778 wrote to his wife that he had stopped at the home of a married couple, who lived so far from everyone that the young wife did not have a single woman she could associate with nearer than eighteen miles away.[7] Many of these frontier women wrote home to their relatives, venting their dissatisfactions and deploring the hardships they had to bear,

though others thrived in adverse situations, just as some of their immigrant ancestors had done before them.

Until recently, many historians tended to idealize the lives of colonial
women in comparison with their twentieth-century descendants. How
could wives today complain about the pains of childbirth and child-
rearing, when they have only two or three offspring as compared with
the brood of six or eight that was common in the past? How could they,
with their electric ovens and washing machines, bemoan the demands
of housework, when their American ancestors made everything from
scratch, including the soap? Those "noncomplaining" women, noted
for their industry and piety, were held up as models to "decadent" modern women, much as Roman women of the republic were glorified during the empire.

But neither the imperial Romans nor hagiographic American historians bothered to ask what those "exemplary" women of the past might
have thought of their own situations. They never asked whether those
women were happy. It is one thing to judge a society by its public face
on the friezes of temples or the pages of government documents, all
created by men; it is quite another to look at the expressions of
women's subjective experiences in their poems, letters, diaries, and
memoirs, or wherever else one can find them.

One indication that eighteenth-century American women were not
always so exemplary can be found in the newspaper announcements
placed by husbands, stating that a wife had "eloped from his bed and
board" or "clandestinely left his home."[8] Alongside notices of stray
horses, fugitive slaves, and runaway servants, these announcements
testify to domestic friction at every level of society. Why did a husband
place such a notice? Ostensibly, he wanted to absolve himself of any
debts that his wife might incur, but it was often obvious that he primarily wanted to expose her to public shame. Subscribers placing advertisements might accuse a departing wife of carrying off valuables that
did not legally belong to her, such as silver plate, money, or jewelry, or
she might be charged with flagrant infidelity, as in the following:

> CATHERINE TREEN, the wife of the subscriber, having, in violation
> of her solemn vow, behaved herself in the most disgraceful manner, by
> leaving her own place of abode, and living in a criminal state with a
> certain William Collins, a plaisterer, under whose bed she was last

night, discovered, endeavoring to conceal herself, her much injured hus-
band, therefore, in justice to himself, thinks it absolutely necessary to
forewarn all persons from trusting her on his account, being deter-
mined, after such flagrant proof of her prostitution, to pay no debts of
her contracting.[9]

Occasionally, a wife fought back and defended her conduct, as in this announcement placed by Sarah Cantwell:

John Cantwell has the impudence to advertise me in the Papers, cau-
tioning all Persons against crediting me; he never had any Credit till he
married me: As for his Bed and Board mention'd, he had neither Bed
nor Board when he married me; I never eloped, I went away before his
Face when he beat me.[10]

The untold story behind any one of these announcements could be the starting point for a wildly imaginative novel.

ABIGAIL ADAMS, WIFE AND PATRIOT

The history of Abigail Adams, wife of the second president of the United States, John Adams, is perhaps the one known example of eighteenth-century wifehood that lives up to the ideal. Her treasure-trove of letters evoke what her biographer, Edith Gelles, has called, an "exemplary wife, mother, sister, daughter, friend, and patriot of early America."[11] Yet her life story, however unique, also contains many common features shared by colonial women in general.

One of Abigail's best-known remarks touched upon the future of marriage. When she wrote to her husband, then a member of the 1776 committee drafting the Declaration of Independence, to "Remember the Ladies," she had in mind the one-sided relationship between spouses. The letter continues: "Do not put such unlimited power into the hands of the Husbands. Remember all Men would be tyrants if they could." Then she suggested a new mode of marital interaction, one in which men such as her husband would "willingly give up the harsh title of Master for the more tender and endearing one of Friend." And she closed with a heartfelt plea for the promotion of female happiness: "Regard us then as Beings placed by providence under your protection

Pastel portrait of Abigail Adams as a young woman by Benjamin Blyth, circa 1766. (Courtesy of the Massachusetts Historical Society)

and in immitation of the Supreem Being make use of that power only for our happiness."[12]

While "happiness" had not yet become the major criterion for judging a life that it has become in our own era, it was beginning to enter the vocabulary of self-assessment, edging out such terms as "piety" and "virtue." It entered the Declaration of Independence in the revolution-ary statement that all men (sic) were entitled to "Life, Liberty, and the pursuit of Happiness," an entitlement that quickly took root in the female, as well as the male, psyche. Abigail's conception of happiness was inextricably linked to the long-standing biblical belief that a man's protection of his wife was divinely ordained, and mirrored the domin-ion of God over his people. What was radical, however, was the notion that the happiness of women, as a distinct group, had to be protected by the laws of the land. Without specific laws restricting the power of men over their wives, some husbands would continue to generate mar-ital discord and cause female misery with impunity.

Surely Abigail's sudden outburst of bold ideas and inflammatory rhet-oric were inspired by the general revolutionary discourse of the times. An analogy between the "tyrant" British king, whose American subjects were clamoring for political voice, and the "tyrant" husband long accus-tomed to abusing his voiceless wife is made explicit in one playful sen-tence: "If perticuliar care and attention is not paid to the Laidies we are determined to foment a Rebellion, and will not hold ourselves bound by any Laws in which we have no voice, or Representation."[13]

John's response to Abigail was patronizing and dismissive. "As to your extraordinary Code of Laws, I cannot but laugh." Acknowledging the ripple effect of the cry for independence among various groups, such as children, apprentices, Indians, and Negroes, he saw in her let-ter "the first Intimation that another Tribe more numerous and power-full than all the rest were grown discontented." Then falling back on a well-worn justification for male dominance, he assured her that "the Despotism of the peticoat" was every bit the match for "the Name of Masters" that husbands enjoyed.[14] So much for serious attention to Abigail's proposal.

In the opinion of Edith Gelles, it was "remarkable in early American history" for a woman to make such a critique of masculine power.[15] Like the Englishwoman Mary Wollstonecraft sixteen years later in her *Vindication of the Rights of Women,* written during the turmoil of the French Revolution, Abigail argued that women, too, should benefit from the democratic aspirations of a fledgling nation. And if, unlike Wollstonecraft, Abigail's plea was a private one, she had every reason to believe she could exert some influence on public policy through the intermediary of her husband.

Despite John's cavalier treatment of his wife's request, he was indeed more "friend" than "master" in their private relationship. Abigail consistently addressed him as "Dearest Friend" in the thousands of letters written during the years of his absence from Massachusetts, where she continued to reside while he was away on national business in Philadelphia, New York, Washington, Paris, and England. It was she who took over the direction of their property in Braintree, Massachusetts, exercising the administrative and legal responsibilities that were usually the purview of men. In this respect, Abigail Adams was not unique during the Revolutionary period. Many wives were called upon to assume the role of "deputy husband" when their spouses went off to fight in the Continental army or in the militia. They had to make business and family decisions that previously would have been made by the menfolk. They had to confront on their own the dangers of enemy troops, and sometimes endure the horrors of warfare—homes destroyed over their heads, children lost in the havoc, physical injury and rape. Sometimes they had to quarter either enemy or patriot soldiers in their homes, with all the disruption such uninvited guests entailed. They had to negotiate food shortages, forced moves, and grave family illnesses caused by dysentery and smallpox. Yes, these women often had to be resilient and brave just to stay alive.

Few had the resources at their disposal that Abigail Smith Adams enjoyed. In the first place, she came from a well-to-do family. Her father, the Reverend William Smith, was established in Weymouth, Massachusetts, and her mother was a member of the highly respected Quincy clan. Like most other New England girls from this period, Abigail did not have a formal education, as did the boys of her social class, but she did have access to her father's large library. She was fifteen when she met John Adams in 1759; he was twenty-three, a graduate of Harvard, and a lawyer in the village of Braintree.

The surviving letters documenting their courtship give little trace of the future president of the United States known for his severity and frequent ill humor. He is playful and affectionate, addressing Abigail as "Miss Adorable" and requesting "as many Kisses, and as many Hours of your Company after 9 O'Clock as he shall please to Demand" (October 4, 1762). She addresses him as "My Friend" and signs "Diana" (August 11, 1763) following the popular mode of adopting a pen name from ancient history or classical mythology. Later she will settle on the name of "Portia," doubly inspired by the virtuous Roman matron and the nimble-minded jurist in *The Merchant of Venice*.

Formally recognized as Abigail's future husband in 1763, John wrote tenderly to "the dear Partner of all my Joys and sorrows" and expressed the hope that he would soon "be bound to your Ladyship in the soft Ligaments of Matrimony" (April, 1764). Abigail's letters to him are somewhat more subdued concerning her romantic sentiments, though she is characteristically spontaneous, as in the letter of April 12, 1764, that begins: "My Dearest Friend, Here am I all alone, in my Chamber, a mere Nun I assure you." There is often an undertone of reverence for the superior male, her senior by eight years, that sometimes borders on the obsequious. "E'er long May I be connected with a Friend from whose Example I may form a more faultless conduct, and whose benevolent mind will lead him to pardon, what he cannot amend."

John continues with expressions of praise for Abigail and the members of her sex noted for their "Kindness," "softness," and "Tenderness" (April 14, 1764). He also playfully makes a catalog of Abigail's defects (May 7, 1764). The charming list includes an indifference to playing cards and learning to sing, "Walking, with the Toes bending inward," "sitting with the Leggs across," and hanging her head "like a Bulrush." Though Abigail received this list "with as much pleasure, as an other person would have read their perfections," she did take exception to his comment on her legs: "I think that a gentleman has no business to concern himself about the Leggs of a Lady" (May 9, 1764). We have not yet arrived at the Victorian era when human legs were referred to as limbs and the prudish hid even their piano legs with coverlets.

If, in these early letters, Abigail showed the deference to John that was considered fitting for someone of her age and gender, she was by no means self-effacing, and it is clear that they related to each other with the ease and reciprocity of loving friends. Indeed, the hallmark of their correspondence—a hallmark that became more vivid with time— is the mutuality of their affection and respect for one another. A few weeks before their wedding, John expressed to Abigail his belief (and one that was typical of the eighteenth century) that she would have a beneficent influence on his character: "You shall polish and refine my sentiments of Life and Manners, banish all the unsocial and ill natured Particles in my Composition, and form me to that happy Temper, that can reconcile a quick Discernment with a perfect Candour" (September 30, 1764).

Perhaps these sentiments strike the reader today as quaintly old-fashioned. Do we still expect spouses to exert a moral influence upon each other? The notion that husband and wife should make each other better people does not resonate with the most visible goals of contemporary American society. How many young people marry with the conscious expectation that they will become kinder and wiser by virtue of choosing a decent, generous mate? Happier, richer, more successful. Yes! But better human beings?

Abigail and John's hopes for one another were completely realized in a partnership that endured for over fifty years. John went on to become a founding father of the new Republic, minister to France and England, vice president to George Washington, and second president of the United States. And Abigail was, without a doubt, "the wife of." But she was also the woman who survived many years on her own, running the property in Braintree and raising the children without their father when John was away—four years when he was across the ocean, and long months when he was later called to Philadelphia and Washington.

Abigail and John were exceptional human begins, to be sure, yet their story should not be lost on us. For it is a story of lasting love, painful separation, and dogged perseverance. Abigail claimed toward the end of her life that separation from her husband during the Revolutionary period had been the greatest of her personal trials. The Revolution had forced her to spend years apart from the one she still called "My protecter, the friend of my youth, my companion and husband of my choice."[16] At the time of her death in 1818, John (who was to live eight more years) eulogized her as "The dear Partner of my Life for fifty four Years as a Wife and for many years more as a Lover."[17] "Lover" in those days could refer to the chaste young woman he courted as well as the woman he married.

Abigail and John represented all that was new and best in eighteenth-century marriage. While patriarchal structures still prevailed on both sides of the Atlantic, a new ideal of companionate marriage was taking root. Imported from the propertied class of England by the colonial elite, it would blossom and spread on a fertile shore.[18] Companionate marriage meant that one had the right to choose one's mate in the name of love. It meant that spouses were bound primarily by affection, friendship, respect, shared values, and interests. It implied that the newly formed couple would have a separate identity from that of their parents, and that the "horizontal" relation between husband and wife would supersede the "vertical" relation between parents and children. As early as the seventeenth century in the Netherlands, and throughout the eighteenth century in England, France, Northern Europe, and America, double portraits of husbands and wives gave graphic substance to this new ideal.

Portrait of Chief Justice and Mrs. Oliver Ellsworth by Ralph Earl (1751–1801). Ellsworth, chief author of the American federal court system, shares the stage with his wife, the mother of eight children. With his hand resting on the symbols of his accomplishments and their country estate pictured in the background, Ellsworth represents the consummate eighteenth-century gentleman at ease in his clothes and rank, while his wife, wearing an oversized muslin headpiece and neck-to toe apparel, appears stiff and constrained. (Wadsworth Atheneum, Hartford, Connecticut)

COMPANIONATE MARRIAGE MEETS
THE AMERICAN REVOLUTION

The Revolution probably hastened the spread of companionate marriage in America. While gender hierarchy certainly did not disappear, husbands and wives were expected to share the same political loyalties and to demonstrate many of the same civic virtues. Thus Abigail Adams considered herself no less a patriot than her husband, even if he was the one to act in the public domain and she remained at home. Her exertions on the home front to replace her absent husband were seen as necessary sacrifices for the good of the nation.

Before the late 1760s in the American colonies, it was not considered appropriate for women to be privy to political discussions. But as discontent with the mother country became more and more vociferous, women participated more frequently in the political discourse. The Philadelphia poet Hannah Griffitts expressed the new female consciousness in a letter to General Anthony Wayne dated July 13, 1777: "There was a time that I knew nor thought no more of politics than I did of grasping a sceptre but now the scene is changed and I believe every woman is desirous of being acquainted with what interests her country."[19] In 1776, Samuel Adams wrote to his wife, Betsy, the news of recent military and political events, even as he acknowledged that "it has not been usual for me to write to you of War or Politicks." Four years later he wrote even less defensively: "I see no Reason why a Man may not communicate his political opinions to his wife, if he pleases."[20]

During the Revolutionary years, wives became as active in following the political turmoil as their husbands. They read newspapers and pamphlets, kept informed of military operations, and discussed politics with both women and men. The change in women's political awareness and participation was, according to historian Mary Beth Norton, "truly momentous."[21]

The women of Boston have left a rich record of their involvement in revolutionary activities.[22] Although they could not participate directly in government—they could not hold office or vote in town meetings—they found ways of entering the political arena. During the decade that led up to the Revolution of 1776, they appeared not only as spectators, but also as rioters, boycotters, and military supporters in such historic events as the Boston Massacre, the Boston Tea Party, and the Siege of Boston.

They were crucial to the success of the boycott of imports from Great Britain. As early as 1767, a group of women pledged not to use ribbons and other imported fabrics. In order to make this boycott work, it was necessary for them to produce their own textiles, especially in the cities, where women had become used to buying cloth produced abroad. Spinning bees became a popular form of female patriotism, with the sale of the wool given to charity.

In 1770, collective action coalesced around the boycott of tea. In February of that year, the *Boston Evening Post* reported that "upwards of 300 mistresses of Families, in which Number the Ladies of the highest rank and influence" signed a petition to abstain from buying tea.[23] As mistresses of households, married women were able to put consumerist pressure on the British several years before the Boston Tea Party of December 1773, when their menfolk boarded three English ships and dumped chests of tea into the harbor.

In the wake of the Boston Tea Party, when the British closed the port of Boston and established military rule, women joined the men in defying the enemy. Housewives were part of the crowds that prevented British soldiers from carrying out certain operations, such as searching for hidden arms. And when war broke out in nearby Lexington in April 1775, and Boston became a city under siege, patriot women and their families left Boston en masse, leaving behind the loyalists.

The women forced to abandon Boston in the spring of 1775 found support throughout Massachusetts among other patriot women. Abigail Adams did her best to aid the refugees who swarmed through Braintree, and her literary friend, Mercy Otis Warren, sent out letters, poems, and plays from her home in Plymouth, encouraging other women to think and act as patriots.

If Boston was the first city to arouse a new female political consciousness, it was by no means the last. Wives in Connecticut, for example, confronted merchants suspected of hoarding items in order to drive up their price. In one instance, a crowd of twenty-two women in East Hartford demanded entry into a merchant's home, discovered a cache of sugar, and, with their own scales, weighed the sugar and paid what they deemed a fair price—much less than the four dollars a pound suggested by the merchant's wife.

Consider also the women of Philadelphia. In 1780, they went so far as to found an all-women's organization destined to help the war effort. A broadside composed by Esther deBerdt Reed proposed that patriotic women renounce extravagant clothing and ornaments and donate the money they saved to the revolutionary troops. Her proposal, known as "the offering of the Ladies," met with immediate success. Within three days, a group of thirty-six Philadelphia women suggested that other women throughout the colonies organize, county by county under the leadership of the wife of each state governor, and send their offerings to Martha Washington for distribution among the troops. While the positions of honor were assigned to the wives of male officials, contributions were to be solicited by and from all women.

The Philadelphia organizers divided their city into ten districts to be canvassed by pairs of women. Some of the noted canvassers were Sally McKean, wife of the Pennsylvania chief justice; Julia Stockton Rush, wife of Benjamin Rush; and Mrs. Robert Morris (Rush and Morris were both signers of the Declaration of Independence). These ladies did not think it beneath them to solicit contributions from females of all stations, including servants. Within a month, they had collected $300,000 Continental dollars (an inflated sum worth about $7,500 in coin money) from over 1,600 persons.

That same month newspapers throughout the country reprinted Esther Reed's original proposal. The women of New Jersey, Maryland, and Virginia joined the Ladies' Association and organized similar campaigns, raising enough money to purchase sufficient linen and make over two thousand shirts for the soldiers. With General Washington's public praise for this show of "female patriotism," many wives began to feel that they, too, were partners in the war effort.

Wives whose husbands were loyalists had less exhilarating experiences. They found themselves under attack from their patriot neighbors, often verbally and even physically. In 1775, when a Massachusetts wife expressed her politics by naming her newborn son in honor of a British commander, a crowd of women attacked her house, stopping short of tarring and feathering both mother and child. Disruptions in friendships were inevitable, as wives lined up on either side of the revolutionary divide. Even some marriages were riven by conflicting political views. Elizabeth Graeme, a wealthy Philadelphian, split with her Scottish husband, Henry Fergusson—which did not prevent the government of Pennsylvania from confiscating her property because of *his* loyalty to the Crown.

Another socially prominent loyalist wife, Grace Growden Galloway, remained in Philadelphia after the departure of her husband and daughter for British-occupied New York. Seeking to separate her fate from that of her husband and to protect the legacy inherited from her wealthy father so as to pass it on to her daughter, she took on the legal system—but to no avail. Ultimately she lost her Philadelphia mansion and all the other family holdings, and died in 1781, embittered by the discovery that the deed to her father's property carried only her husband's name.[24]

Some loyalist wives actively supported the British war effort. They carried letters through the lines to the redcoats, served as spies, and aided British prisoners. But most, it appears, merely tried to survive and keep their families alive. Like their patriot counterparts, most loyalist wives and mothers put their families first. They would have agreed with the position of Helena Kortwright Brasher, who, despite her revolutionary sentiments, condemned her husband's words: "My country first and then my family."[25]

REPUBLICANS AND ROYALISTS: THE VIEW FROM FRANCE

A decade after the American Revolution, it was the turn of the French to experience their own bloody upheaval. The conflict pitted republicans against royalists, the underclass against the affluent, the "people" against the nobility. Wives from both sides of the political spectrum, but especially aristocrats, saw their husbands lose their heads at the guillotine, and sometimes lost their own heads as well. The foreign wars in defense of the Revolution also took their toll of men, leaving behind thousands of families headed by widows.

Before the Revolution, wives from the upper echelons of society (the "haute bourgeoisie" and the nobility) led lives that were relatively separate from the lives of their husbands. With marriages arranged on the basis of money, rank, and family name, spouses were not expected to share an intimate rapport and common interests. Indeed, it was not considered chic for aristocratic husbands and wives to appear too attached to one another. If a married man was of an amorous disposition (and what self-respecting Frenchman was not!), he would establish a liaison outside the marriage. His wife, too, if she were so inclined and her husband willing to look the other way, could take a lover without fear of disgrace.

A small number of upper-class wives devoted themselves to cultural and intellectual pursuits. Most of the literary salons were run by married women, with or without the attendance of their husbands. Among the best-known female luminaries, Madame du Châtelet, the translator of Newton, was considered the equal of the great scholars of her day, and Madame d'Épinay was also a learned lady known for her pedagogical writing. It is true that these two "wives" were associated more with their famous lovers—Voltaire and Grimm, respectively—than with their husbands, which says tomes about the differences in French and American society.

Later in the century, in the period leading up to the Revolution, some wives collaborated extensively in their husbands' careers, for example, Madame Condorcet, Madame Roland, and Madame Lavoisier. In the famous portrait of Monsieur and Madame Antoine Lavoisier painted by Jacques David in 1788, Lavoisier the chemist sits at his desk, his hand poised with a pen and his eyes staring up at the beautiful face of his wife, Anne, while she stares out of the frame at the viewer. This quite remarkable painting contrasts with many other representations of married couples, where the wife stares adoringly at her husband and the husband looks away into the public world. The Lavoisier double portrait speaks for the new ideal of companionate marriage, which championed mutual affection and respect.

Lavoisier looks to his wife not only for love, but also for inspiration. It is her face that will make his pen record the great works of science for which he will be remembered. While she herself was an accomplished painter, she put her art at the service of her husband's scientific studies and would be remembered as his assistant and muse. This is made explicitly clear in a poem written by Jean François Ducis, one of Lavoisier's friends.

Antoine Laurent Lavoisier *[1743–1794]* and His Wife *[Marie Anne Pierrette Paulze, 1758–1836] by Jacques Louis David (1748–1825). Lavoisier, the founder of modern chemistry, looks to his wife for inspiration. (Metropolitan Museum of Art, New York)*

Epouse et cousine à la fois	*Wife and cousin at the same time*
Sûre d'aimer et de plaire	*Assured of loving and of pleasing*
Pour Lavoisier soumis à vos lois	*With Lavoisier subjected to your laws*
Vous remplissez les deux emplois	*You fill the two roles*
Et de muse et de secrétaire.[26]	*Of muse and secretary.*

Many wives will recognize the role of secretary and muse. After Lavoisier's untimely death on the guillotine in 1794, his widow continued to be involved in the publication and illustration of his works. The role of wife as helpmeet to the "great man," if not yet his full intellectual equal, is one that a few privileged women began to play more prominently in eighteenth-century Europe.

But however emancipated some wives were at the upper echelons of French society, the sense that women were different from and inferior to men was no less decisive in Revolutionary France than in Revolutionary America. The sexist ideology promoted by Jean-Jacques Rousseau and his followers, which defined women as domestic creatures to be commanded by their husbands and excluded from public life, prevailed in republican politics, in spite of a counter-discourse championing women's equality that had existed even before the Revolution and that intensified between 1789 and 1793. Eighteenth-century Frenchwomen were much more active in clamoring for their rights than American women of this period, and they also had several sympathetic men speaking on their behalf, as historian Karen Offen amply documents in *European Feminisms, 1700–1950*.[27] The Marquis de Condorcet, for example, a celebrated mathematician and *philosophe,* contested the laws that subordinated women in marriage as early as 1787, and spoke out in the National Assembly during the early years of the Revolution for a "a lasting equilibrium between married persons" and even for the citizenship of property-owning women. But women— married, single, or widowed, with or without property—were not meant to be included in "The Declaration of the Rights of Man and the Citizen" proclaimed in 1789. The subversive "Declaration of the Rights of Women and the Female Citizen," written in 1791 by the playwright and pamphleteer Olympe de Gouges, and other petitions addressed to the National Assembly claiming female rights were contemptuously dismissed by radical republicans. The makers of the constitution of 1791 "effectively wrote women out of the new order of citizenship" and consigned them to their roles as wives and mothers.[28] If a wife had influence over her husband's politics, she was wise to keep it well hidden from her neighbors.

Such was the case of that remarkable wife, Madame Roland, hailed by many as the "most noble woman" of the Revolution and the only one, alongside Marie Antoinette, to have exerted an undeniable influence on revolutionary politics.[29] For two years between 1791 and 1793, when the Revolution was at its height, Marie-Jeanne (Manon) Phlipon Roland was her husband's right hand in his important government posts. She was always careful to present herself as a conventional nonassertive wife, and not the meddling harpy her husband's enemies would later vilify. In the memoirs she wrote from her prison cell in 1793, she recalled the political discussions that took place among the deputies from the radical Left who met regularly in the Roland apartment:

> *I knew what role was appropriate for my sex, and I never abandoned it. The meetings took place in my presence without my taking any part in them. Placed outside the circle near a table, I worked with my hands or wrote letters, while they deliberated. But were I to dispatch ten missives—which sometimes happened—I did not lose a word of what was uttered, and sometimes I had to bite my lips so as not to say a word of my own.*[30]

Even at this stage of the Revolution, when her husband was not yet in the limelight, she carefully hid her passionate interest in politics and her role in promoting her husband's career. A year later, when her husband was being considered for the position of minister of the interior, the deputy Brissot turned to her as a mediating influence. In her words: "Brissot came to see me one evening . . . asking if Roland would consent to assume that burden; I responded that . . . his zeal and activity would not be repelled by this nourishment."[31] Sophie Grandchamp, Mme Roland's closest friend in these years, later claimed that Manon Roland was even more eager to assume political power than her husband.

Once he had taken on his new post, Mme Roland played the part of the minister's wife with relish. Twice a week she entertained, once for her husband's colleagues and a second time for other notables in the world of business and administration. She was, however, not given to extravagant shows of luxury, for that would have been out of keeping with republican ideals.

Behind the scenes, however, Mme Roland was a much more vigorous partner. She was the chief force behind the Office of Public Opinion, which her husband ran, and the author of many of its publications. This is how she later described her work as the literary interpreter of Roland's thoughts:

> If it was a question of a circular, of a piece of instruction, of an important public document, we would confer about it according to the trust we had in one another, and impregnated by his ideas, nourished by my own, I took up the pen which I had more time than he to use. Since we both had the same principles and the same mind, we ended by agreeing on the form, and my husband had nothing to lose by passing [his projects] through my hands.[32]

Soon, however, rifts between Roland and the King (who was still nominally in power) became apparent, and Roland was forced to resign. Mme Roland tells us that his letter of resignation was a joint venture between husband and wife ("we drafted between the two of us his famous letter to the King") that they then printed and distributed to all the departments of France.

Yet is was not the monarchy that eventually destroyed the Rolands, but the far Left. After the incarceration of the royal family in August 1792, Roland was once again appointed deputy and minister of the interior, but his (and his wife's) somewhat more moderate political views were not acceptable to the likes of Danton, Marat, and Robespierre. On September 25, 1792, Danton rose in the National Assembly to question Roland's reappointment as minister. He said: "If you extend an invitation to him [Roland], extend it also to Mme Roland, because everyone knows that Roland was not alone in his department. I, I was alone in mine."[33] Danton knew exactly how to cast aspersions on his rival: given the eighteenth-century fear of women's intrusion into the polity, a statesman known to share political power with his wife was an easy target for ridicule. And if we think that such attitudes were restricted to bygone eras, we have only to remember the negative reactions to Hillary Clinton's involvement in health care early in President Clinton's administration, before she was forced to withdraw from visible policy-making and later became a popular wife, because she "stood by her man" in his most abject hours.

Madame Roland was arrested in connection with Robespierre's 1793 purges of a large group of deputies, including her husband. While he fled to the provinces, she remained to confront his enemies, not believing they would annihilate someone who was "only a wife." During her five-month imprisonment, she wrote her memoirs, a work that was to become the most famous eyewitness chronicle of the Revolution. When she was condemned and executed in November 1793, her husband, still in hiding, committed suicide.

Being "only a wife" provided absolutely no protection for women during the Revolution, whether they were the wives of republicans committed to the new nation or aristocrats loyal to the monarchy. The following stories of Elisabeth Le Bas, Marie-Victoire de La Villirouët, and Elisa Fougeret de Ménerville demonstrate how the Revolution forced some married women to assume heroic roles they could never have anticipated in their earlier lives.

Elisabeth Duplay was barely twenty when she met Philippe Le Bas, a deputy to the National Assembly and friend of Maximilien Robespierre, who lodged in her father's house. She had gone to the Assembly with Robespierre's sister, Charlotte, to observe the public session, and was quickly smitten by Le Bas. The attraction was mutual, and within a few months, Le Bas declared himself to Elisabeth, but not without testing her republican principles. He wanted to make sure she would be a fitting wife, willing to give up frivolous pleasures and eager to nurse her children. Then Le Bas approached Elisabeth's family. Since they were strong republicans, he assumed they would be delighted to have him as a son-in-law. Moreover, he was ten years older than Elisabeth, well educated, and well placed. After some hestiation on the part of Elisabeth's mother—after all, there were older sisters to be married before the youngest daughter—she and her husband gave their consent.

The wedding date was set. Elisabeth had twenty days to prepare her trousseau. Her father, the owner of several houses, placed a vacant one at their disposal. But then, national politics intervened: Le Bas was named for a special mission and forced to leave his fiancée the same day. Elisabeth was inconsolable. Despite her friend Robespierre's sober admonitions, she "did not want to be a patriot any longer."[34] Between the needs of the nation and her need for Philippe, there was no contest. Ultimately she succeeded (through Robespierre) in bringing Philippe home long enough for them to be married. And within a few months, she was pregnant.

This love match between ardent republicans was cut short by political catastrophe. When Maximilien Robespierre fell in the coup of Thermidor (July 27, 1794), Le Bas, too, went to meet his death. Elisabeth later wrote that she became "distraught, almost crazy," and, despite the presence of her infant son, lay on the floor for two days. Then, because she was Le Bas's widow and the mother of his child, she was locked up in the Talarue prison with her baby. As she recalled, "I had been a mother for five weeks; I was nursing my son; I was less than twenty-one years old; I had been deprived of almost everything."

Elisabeth and her nursing baby remained in prison for nine months. Each night she would descend to the water trough in the courtyard to wash his diapers, which she dried between her mattresses. She resisted the advances of her prison warders and government agents, who wanted her to marry another deputy and abandon her "infamous" name. Instead, she clung to her married name, and when she finally emerged from prison, she kept it for the rest of her life. Her memories of her one year of wifehood helped her survive sixty-five years of widowhood, during which she never lost faith in her husband, nor in the revolutionary ideals he had died for.

The histories of Mme Roland and Mme Le Bas show the extent to which republican women could be implicated in their husbands' public lives and condemned for their husbands' political activities. The case was even bleaker for aristocratic women, often imprisoned and frequently guillotined for their noble birth. The situation of wives from the aristocracy was, however, extremely varied, depending on the region, the relation of a specific family to its community (which might or might not protect them), and numerous other factors, including the presence or absence of a husband. If the husband had emigrated to join the antirevolutionary armies or simply to save his skin, and the wife was left behind to look after their family and property, her fate was always precarious. She might be thrown into prison because of her noble status, or because it was suspected that she was illegally in contact with a husband who had escaped abroad.

The case of Marie-Victoire de Lambilly, countess of La Villirouët, illustrates many of these issues. This little Breton woman, twenty-six years old and four feet eight inches tall, was imprisoned in October 1793 on the grounds that she was "an ex-noble, and the wife and sister of male émigrés."[35] At the time of her incarceration, she had been separated for twenty months from her husband, who had left France to join the counterrevolutionary forces in Germany and the Lowlands. Before leaving, he had given his wife power of attorney to administer his property. She was also legally in charge of their three small children, one born six weeks after his departure.

Before her imprisonment, Mme de La Villirouët had lived with her children at the home of an aged aunt, but when Robespierre on June 2, 1793, declared all wives, fathers, mothers, children, brothers, and sisters of émigrés to be "suspect," she was arrested and incarcerated.

The difference between Mme de La Villirouët and her coprisoners was that she refused to wait out the Revolution in silence. From her cold, damp, and unheated cell she sent out a volley of missives to local and national representatives, protesting her arrest and the conditions under which the prisoners were forced to live. In October 1794, a year after her incarceration, she wrote a legalistic letter that refuted the words of her denunciation. As for her being an ex-noble: "one does not preside at one's birth." As for being the wife of an émigré: "since the month of July, 1792, I have not received news of my husband. . . . I have every reason to believe he no longer exists."

But what is remarkable in her defense is her assertion that she, a wife, should not be judged by her husband's actions. She wrote: "But suppose that he was an émigré—is that a reason for making me responsible for his conduct and his acts? Always and everywhere a husband is the head [of the family] in law and deed—thus one cannot indict a wife for her husband's conduct." It was unusual for a wife to postulate a separate moral and legal existence from that of her husband and to claim that she could not be blamed for his. Ultimately Mme de Villirouët's epistolary efforts proved successful; in January 1795, as a result of her flood of letters, she and all her her coprisoners were freed.

The Revolution catapulted thousands of French wives into situations where they were required to assume male prerogatives and act aggressively. Mme de La Villirouët, like Mme Roland, recognized that the role of being a "woman writer" would leave her open to ridicule; yet she did not hesitate to use her literary talents to save herself and others in her same situation.

Four years later, in January 1799, she was obliged to go beyond writing. At that time she and her husband had been living quietly in Paris, he under an assumed name. When he was arrested as a former émigré and faced the possibility of a death sentence, she decided to appear at his trial as his defense attorney. Of course, this woman had no training as a lawyer, and it was uncertain that she would be allowed to plead his cause. But such were her persuasive powers that she gained permission to represent her husband and had her day in court, where she convinced seven judges, "all in full dress, sporting mustaches and great sabers," to acquit her beloved spouse. The forty-two-minute defense she presented to the court, recounted in her memoirs for her children, suggests she knew how to counter the charges against her husband in a convincing legal manner and that she also knew how to move the judges "as fathers and husbands." The guards who had brought M. de La Villirouët into the courtroom did not make a move to stop him when he walked over to kiss his wife at the end of her speech, and it took the judges only thirty minutes to announce his acquittal. Mme de La Villirouët had clearly profited from the novelty and pathos of a wife defending her spouse.

Another aristocratic wife propelled by the Revolution into unexpected conduct was Elisa Fougeret de Ménerville. Born into a family of influential magistrates, she was married at eighteen to a man thirteen years older, with a considerable fortune and a good reputation. Typical of women of her class, she accepted her parents' choice without hesitation. For the first five years of their marriage she and her husband were to live with her family, an arrangement she welcomed with joy. But before the five years were up, in October 1791, she, her husband, and two young children left France with a wave of émigrés fleeing the Revolution.

They found temporary shelter in Belgium and Holland, before settling in England. At each move, the news from France was worse—her mother and sisters were imprisoned, her father guillotined. And the farther she and her husband traveled from home, the further their resources dwindled. Finally, in London, Mme de Ménerville, who had started her marriage with gilded carriages and beautiful diamonds, became a working woman. She followed the example of the other émigré wives, many of whom were the sole support of their families. In her words: "I painted many fans for a merchant in the City who sent them to Portugal. I did petit point for another who sent it to Russia. I gave French lessons . . . I embroidered dresses, which was the most lucrative occupation. . . ."[36] While most of the upper-class men found it impossible to earn money in a strange country, their wives were more flexible. They had not been trained for the military or the law. They knew only how to sew, cook, and dabble in the arts, but these skills served them well. Whatever hopes had been dashed by the Revolution, some wives took pride in becoming the family wage earners.

In the decade between the beginning of the Revolution and the advent of Napoleon (1789–1799), Frenchwomen acquired a political consciousness they never had before. It is a consciousness that royalists like Mme de Ménerville would gladly have done without. Most wives of her class would have been content to follow the old ways, to let their fathers and husbands think politically for them. But the Revolution forced them into positions where they had to think and act on their own. While they had no official voice in government, they found numerous ways of negotiating a system designed to exclude them. Whatever their political loyalties, royalist or republican (with the possible exception of Mme Roland), their first concerns were for the survival of their families.

NEW ICONS: THE REPUBLICAN MOTHER AND THE MOTHER-EDUCATOR

What were the effects of the slogan "liberté, égalité, fraternité" on married women after the turmoil had subsided? Did women's new political consciousness and the memory of their patriotism bear any immediate fruit? The short answer is "no." Neither American nor French wives benefited, as female groups, from the revolution that had played havoc with their lives. While their husbands became citizens, they remained "the wives of."

In America, no new legislation fulfilled the hopes of Abigail Adams that wives would be protected from tyrannical husbands. While Americans threw off the shackles of British rule, no new legal system replaced the British common law: a wife was still mandated to serve and obey her husband. Her identity was still submerged, or "covered," by his.[37]

And in France, the situation for married women actually regressed. The progressive spirit that had reigned early in the Revolution of 1789 was washed away in the blood of the Terror. The Civil Code, finalized under Napoleon in 1804, quashed all prior efforts to institute principles of equality between husband and wife; basically, it reinstated and strengthened the old inequities. French wives were made wards of their husbands, to whom they owed absolute "obedience" in exchange for "protection." Most married under the legal regime known as community of property, which did not allow wives to manage or sell their own property, or keep their own income. The husband was formally vested with the administration of all assets belonging to the wife, as well as his own.

Feminist thinkers, articulate and hopeful in the first years of the Revolution, were judiciously silent under Napoleon. The formidable Madame de Staël was sent packing into exile by an emperor who could not tolerate female brilliance. Mary Wollstonecraft's *Vindication of the Rights of Women* (1792), with her call to educate young women so they would not be subject to the "slavery of marriage," was no longer required reading in her native England, or in France and America.[38]

It is true that there was an attempt to establish a new relationship of women to the polis in what historian Linda Kerber has called "republican motherhood."[39] Both American and French women were enjoined to nurture citizens for the republic, and to assume responsibility for their civic education, which gave their domestic responsibilities a political cast.[40] Since girls were educated at home, if they were educated at all, and boys, too, in their early years, the mother was entrusted with the development not only of literacy, but also of piety and patriotism. Patriotic texts, modeled on the Catholic catechism, were made available to French mothers in order to promote republican virtues. One of the dialogues for "The Good Mother and Her Children" begins with the children asking, "Mother, tell us something about the Republic, that we

French mother reading the Declaration of the Rights of Man and Citizen to her son. Engraving by Niquet le Jeune, 1789. (Musée Carnavalet, Paris)

have been hearing so much about." To which the mother responds, "The Republic, my children, is a government based on equality . . ." and so forth.[41]

Long before the flowering of public education, both France and America called upon mothers to instill in their young—and especially in their sons—the social virtues considered necessary for cohesive nations. The valorization of the republican mother, or the mother-educator as she was called in France, would serve as a springboard for some bold French and American women to plunge into social and political activities during the next century.

But another way of looking at republican motherhood—one that is argued by Edith Gelles for the American scene—is to see it as a step backward for women, as an exclusionary device that would keep wives from exercising the new skills they had acquired out of revolutionary necessity.[42] Motherhood would remain an intrinsically domestic profession, no matter how much it was linked to ideas of the public good. Like the women of ancient Greece, French and American mothers were, at best, "passive" citizens by virtue of their ability to transmit citizenship to their sons. "Active" citizenship belonged only to men, and would remain an exclusively male prerogative until the twentieth century.

Civic motherhood was a prescriptive ideal that probably bore little relationship to the lives of real women. How many women, American or French, thought of themselves primarily as the educators of future citizens? At the most, a small minority. Most women were likely to conceptualize their maternal role within the context of the family rather than the state, that is, if they conceptualized their role at all.

The nurturing rhetoric that often follows periods of revolution and war is a form of reassurance, especially for men, that the nightmare of bloodshed is over. To pun upon a popular psychological concept, it can be said that the ideology of republican motherhood was a form of regression in the service of the male ego.[43] I do not see it as a conscious conspiracy to restrict women to maternity and domesticity, but, in the end, the effects were the same. Wives and mothers, republican or otherwise, would be expected to remain at home and leave the public sphere to men.

Yet there is one great European work of art that captures and preserves the vision of the wife as an active, courageous, political figure—Beethoven's opera *Fidelio,* first performed in 1805. Influenced by the original ideals of the French Revolution and by Beethoven's lofty conception of womanhood, it grants to Leonore, rather than to her husband Florestan, the heroic role. She is the savior who descends into prison to free her long-suffering spouse from the hands of a tyrannical captor. The soaring climax of the finale ("O, Gott, welch ein Augenblick!") is as triumphantly transporting as Beethoven's better known "Ode to Joy." And in this case, the triumph has special resonance for wives.

FIVE

Victorian Wives on Both Sides of the Atlantic

But the best of household fairies,
Is the wife whose golden hair is
Drooping o'er her husband's Chair—his
Little Woman.

Theo Gift, "Little Woman"[1]

She rose to his requirement, dropped
The playthings of her life
To take the honorable work
Of woman and of wife.

Emily Dickinson, "The Wife," ca. 1863

"Tis next to a chattel slave, to be a *legal* wife."

Lucy Stone, Letter to Antoinette Brown Blackwell,
June 9, 1850

"I's sho' try dis marrin' business but I ain't gwine try it no
more."

Eliza Holman, thrice-married former slave[2]

Most social historians agree that modern Western marriage emerged in the period between the American Revolution and around 1830. During those fifty years, love became the most celebrated criterion for choosing a spouse, even if property, family, and social status continued to weigh heavily in the decision. A young American woman, Eliza Chaplin, expressed the credo of her generation when she wrote to a friend in 1820: "Never could I give my hand unaccompanied by my heart."[3] In many homes, and especially in America, parents accepted the fact that their children would select a husband or wife on the basis of inclination, leaving their progenitors little more than veto power. While love marriages had certainly existed in prior centuries, now they became the popular ideal and perhaps even the norm.[4]

Many theories have been advanced to explain *why* such a definitive change occurred. Was it a natural evolution of the ideal of companionate marriage, as practiced previously by the enlightened bourgeoisie of Great Britain, Northern Europe, and America? Was it the general spirit of revolution that helped release children from their parents' tutelage and allowed for more independent choices? Was it backlash to the Age of Reason that permitted the passionate torrents of Romanticism to flow among readers of love poetry and fiction? Was it the revival of Christianity by Anglo-American evangelicalism, which spread the belief that "heaven-sent" marriages should have the urgency of divine love? Was it the result of nascent industrialization, which removed many young women from the home and placed them in mills and factories, where they were no longer under the watchful eye of parents? Whatever the reasons, the gradual emancipation of young adults from their parents and the primacy accorded love matches solidified during the nineteenth century.

This chapter considers how the ideal of romantic love meshed with more practical realities in England and America. The letters, diaries, and reminiscences of women who contemplated or experienced wifehood; sentimental poems and romantic novels written by both men and women; and the sober advice offered by self-appointed experts reveal the interplay of idealistic and materialistic aspirations in the making of marital unions. Despite differences in geographical region, social class, race, ethnicity, and religion, a dominant middle-class vision of love-based marriage emerged and then prevailed on both sides of the Atlantic.

LOVE, MARRIAGE, AND MONEY IN GREAT BRITAIN

The Victorian validation of love was by no means construed as license for unbridled physical passion. However intense the attraction and however intimate the courtship, prospective husbands and wives were expected to abide by a set of social conventions that included deferring sexual intercourse until after they were married. Most middle- and upper-class couples did wait, although there is evidence to suggest that many women, especially those from the lower classes, were pregnant by the time they arrived at the altar. Data from selected English parishes for the period 1800–1849 indicate that between one-fifth and two-fifths of first pregnancies were conceived before the wedding day. Women who gave birth out of wedlock could expect public censure and private hardship, which did not prevent a large number of them, and especially domestic servants, from doing so.[5]

While it was generally agreed that mutual attraction was desirable, most people also agreed that love was not, in and of itself, all that was needed for an enduring union. Similar social and religious backgrounds, mutual respect and shared values were also reckoned in the choice of a spouse, not just by society at large, but by the young women themselves. It is instructive for us today to read the letters and diaries of nineteenth-century women as they struggled over proposals and tried to determine if an ardent suitor would make a good husband. Or if they themselves had the capacity—emotional and otherwise—to become a good wife.

The high moral tone so characteristic of middle-class Victorians often colored the exchange of love letters. According to prevailing etiquette, a young man would write the first letter and the young woman could then reply, if her parents approved. Caution was the order of the day, especially for the woman, who was not supposed to indicate her true feelings until the man had declared his. In that spirit, Thomas Trollope wrote to Frances Trollope (the future parents of the novelist, Anthony Trollope) that he did not know if it were more "expedient for a man to make an avowal of his attachment to a lady *viva voce* . . . or by epistolary correspondence." Having chosen the latter, he proceeded to declare "that my future happiness on earth is at your disposal. It is impossible but that I must feel *every* anxiety till I am favoured with your reply to this note." He suspected that Frances was "not entirely unaware" of the delight he found in her company, and that there might be a "degree of mutuality in this delight," but before Frances could express her sentiments candidly they both knew he had to make an official proposal. He considered it proper to explain that his annual income was about 900 pounds. Although he gave Fanny three weeks "for passing a sentence," Fanny replied the very next day. Now that he had made an official proposal, she could be similarly frank: she responded with "pride and gratitude" and the news that she had only 50 pounds a year from her father and 1300 pounds in stock.[6] Despite the fact that Fanny was almost thirty and Thomas almost thirty-five, both conducted themselves strictly according to the rituals devised for young lovers, and Fanny held back from avowing her feelings until she had been asked to speak. Certainly women had more to lose in a society that condemned female forwardness, especially since there were more eligible women than men—estimates run as high as 100 women in their twenties for 90 men of the same age.

Letters were supposed to be held in strict confidence, and to be returned in the event that an engagement was broken off. An engagement of four to eight months was considered long enough for lovers to determine if they suited each other. Long engagements were discouraged because they might lead a couple into physical intimacy.

The letters of John Austin and Sarah Taylor, who were engaged for five years before they married, offer an extreme example of Victorian high-flown rhetoric and moral introspection. Sarah, a lively, flirtatious girl from a fine English family noted for its dissenting (non-Anglican) leadership and civic service, received stilted epistles from John, asking her to examine her past conduct for "slight stains" on her reputation and to consider whether her soul was "really worthy to hold communion" with his.[7] Sarah wrote to one of her cousins that her love for John would "do more for the elevation and improvement of my character than anything in the world could." Love was the path to moral regeneration. During the period of their engagement, while John studied law in London, Sarah remained in Norwich and read from a list of modern and ancient authors suggested by her fiancé. She saw this period as "five years feeding only on love, and severe study, in order to become worthy of being a wife." Eventually she made the grade, and they were married in August 1819.

But what really made the marriage possible at this stage in their lives

The Long
Engagement
*by Arthur
Hughes,
1859.
(Birmingham
City
Museums
and Art
Gallery)*

was not her moral improvement, but John's father's contribution of 300 pounds annually and her father's promise to provide 100 pounds as well. In marriage considerations, the rapture of love, even when combined with moral aspirations, could never be entirely divorced from economic realities. The basic question was whether the husband could provide for his wife. Love and money were not just the themes of great English and American fiction from Jane Austen to Edith Wharton; they were the fundamental underpinnings of nineteenth-century society. While the high-minded poet Elizabeth Barrett Browning condemned marriages of convenience as a form of "*legal* prostitution" that some people conducted "as of setting up in trade" (letters to Miss Mitford, January and February 1846) and the novelist Dickens created thoroughly despicable characters marrying *only* for money (for example, Mr. and Mrs. Lammle in *Our Mutual Friend*), it was generally agreed that marrying *without* any money at all was at the least "imprudent."

Contemporary advice literature warned the young not to marry until they had a reasonable income—300 pounds a year according to a correspondence that appeared in *The Times* in 1858.[8] Without expecting such a relative fortune, working-class members also waited until they could be self-sufficient. This meant that English men and women married at a comparatively late age—around twenty-six years for females and slightly higher for males.

A woman contemplating marriage did not have to be reminded that her material well-being would depend on the financial situation of her husband. She was not allowed to count on her own resources as a worker or as a property holder. Whatever property a wife brought to marriage and whatever income she earned belonged by law to her husband.

Moreover, in middle- and upper-class families, wives were not expected to earn income. The male head of the household had the sole responsibility for providing for his family. Gone were the premodern days when the labor of wives and children entered into the middle-class family economy and a respectable wife could work alongside her husband in his shop. The hallmark of the lady was that she did not have to work for pay. Only members of the working class and small farmers continued to depend on their wives for joint production and supplemental income.

What, then, were the responsibilities of middle-class wives supported by their husbands? These fell into three major categories: 1) obeying and satisfying one's husband, 2) keeping one's children physically and morally sound, and 3) maintaining the household (cleaning, washing, preparing food, etc.). Much of the third category was performed by paid domestics, which meant that the privileged matron had to be what Mrs. Beeton in her popular *Book of Household Management* (1861) called a "commander of an army" of servants. Aristocratic families in their country estates might have as many as twenty or twenty-five, while a middle-class urban wife would make do with one, two, or five, depending on her circumstances.

Outside activities for privileged wives consisted largely of attending church and visiting friends. Another permissible outside activity was philanthropy, which became increasingly diverse as the century progressed. Philanthropic ladies devoted time to such charities as schools, reformatories, and "benevolent" societies for the old, the invalid, and the poor, with special attention to the plight of unwed mothers and prostitutes wanting to reform, some of whom were enabled to emigrate. A few privileged women, like Sarah Taylor Austin, also pursued intellectual, cultural, and even political interests.

If love provided the gateway through which brides and grooms marched together into conjugal life, the aftermath of marriage placed them in what historians have called "separate spheres." Most middle-class women stayed at home, while most men went out to work. Theoretically, these spheres were of equal worth, assigned on the basis of gender to serve family, business, and civic needs. Practically, as later feminists would argue, the ideology of separate spheres kept women from realizing their full potential, whereas men, active in both public and private realms, were able to experience fuller lives. But feminist protest was not the order of the day in the first half of the nineteenth century.

Instead, a burgeoning advice literature began to tell women how they should fulfill their domestic responsibilities. The flood of British and American manuals directed toward wives and mothers that began in the 1830s and 1840s has continued into our own time. Long before *Good Housekeeping*, Dr. Spock, and Dr. Ruth, experts in household and family management were selling women the idea that they, and they alone, were responsible for the well-being of their homes. They, and they alone, were responsible for the moral and physical health of their sons and daughters. They, and they alone, had the power to inspire men in the direction of the greater social good. No longer the daughters of Eve associated with man's undoing, Victorian wives and mothers were elevated to the position of spiritual guides. The dual influence of romanticism and evangelical Protestantism valorized women's "emotional" nature and turned it to the purposes of wifehood and maternity. Yet however elevated they had become, wives were never to forget their dependence on men. Sarah Stickney Ellis called women "relative creatures" in her 1839 book *The Women of England;* it was an appropriate term, as French historian Françoise Basch demonstrated 135 years later in the English title of her own analysis of Victorian women. Women simply did not exist in their own right. The "essentials of a woman's being," according to the Victorian man of letters W. R. Greg, required that "they are supported by, and minister to, men." John Ruskin stated the paradox of women's powerless power without the slightest ironic intent: "A true wife, in her husband's house, is his servant; it is in his heart that she is queen."[9]

One way of serving one's husband was sexually, for men (rather than women) were now considered the more lustful creatures. In keeping with the new view of woman as angel, she was stripped of all physical desire. The distinguished English doctor William Acton opined that "woman seldom desires any sexual gratification for herself. She submits to her husband's embraces, but principally to gratify him."[10]

Even when physicians recognized that women, too, were capable of sexual pleasure, they were advised to please their husbands first and foremost. Listen to the advice of Dr. Auguste Debay, whose marriage manual was one of the best-selling books published in his native France: "O wives! Follow this advice. Submit to your husband's needs . . . force yourself to satisfy him, put on an act and simulate the spasm of pleasure; this innocent deception is permitted when it is a question of keeping a husband."[11] Faking orgasm was just one more way of sacrificing oneself for the good of the family.

More typical British and American manuals focused on the wife's duties outside the bedroom. She was expected to set the standard for goodness in her family, to rise to the level of a "household fairy," to instill within her home an aura of sweetness, good cheer, love of God, and love of country. Advice-givers like Sarah Stickney Ellis and Mrs. Beeton, paralleled in America by Lydia Sigourney (*Letters to Mothers,* 1839) and Lydia Maria Child (*The Mother's Book,* 1844), among others, helped transform the cult of domesticity into something of a secular religion.

Queen Victoria herself embodied for the masses the apotheosis of wife-and-motherhood. With Prince Albert at her side and surrounded by her nine children, Victoria became a regal icon of domesticity throughout Britain and the world. Victoria's youth had coincided with the ascendancy of love in marriage. She must have read some of Jane Austen's six novels, published early in the century, which depicted marriage as the single-minded goal of every unattached woman. While Victoria was never in the predicament faced by Austen's women, whose fate would be determined by whether they did or did not find suitable husbands, Victoria did absorb the discourse of her day. Marital happiness was a necessity for everyone, including the Queen. And to judge by her letters, public statements, and demeanor, she did enjoy an exceptionally felicitous marriage, until her beloved Albert succumbed to an early death and left her a grieving widow for half a century.

Jane Austen's early–nineteenth-century novels depicted the mutual nature of the mating game within the comfortable middle class, where women as well as men endeavored to choose spouses on the basis of love. There was, however, one significant difference between Austen's heroes and her heroines: a woman could not openly express her feelings until the man in question declared himself. The medieval conduct books that warned women against making the first move would not have been out of place in Austen's time.

Even so, Austen's women did have ways of indicating their desires. They tried to be as physically attractive as possible, enhancing their appearance with the latest fashions, walking in a "feminine" manner, and literally putting their best foot forward. They sang and danced so as to present themselves advantageously in the marriage market, and at least in Austen's books, they were allowed to be intelligent. As Mr. Knightley says in *Emma,* "Men of sense do not want silly wives." Even if this were not true of all men (Austen has given us some notably silly wives, such as Mrs. Bennet in *Pride and Prejudice*), polite society was beginning to accept the view that "sense" was not an exclusively male prerogative and that a well-read wife could do no harm. Austen's heroines were all concerned with finding husbands, and most of them did . . . which corresponded to the reality of early-nineteenth-century England. Nevertheless, approximately 10 to 12 percent of British women remained unmarried throughout their lives, including Austen herself.

A generation after Austen's death in 1817, another woman novelist, Charlotte Brontë, also faced middle age as a spinster. In her early years, she had rejected not just one, but two proposals—one from a very suitable clergyman because she did not love him. Her letter to his sister stated her reasons unambiguously: ". . . though I had a kindly leaning towards him because he is an amiable and well-disposed man, yet I had not, and could not have, that intense attachment which would make me willing to die for him; and, if ever I marry, it must be in that light of adoration that I will regard my husband."[12] Granted, Brontë's vision of marriage bears the hallmarks of the overwrought Romantic imagination, but—rhetoric aside—how far is it from the letter to "Dear Abby" cited at the beginning of this book?

The man Brontë eventually did marry at thirty-nine was surely not someone who corresponded to her earlier aspirations. Arthur Bell Nicholls, a clergyman, seems to have been a rather ordinary person, by no means the intellectual equal of the by-then famous author, and hardly a type "to die for." But at thirty-nine Brontë probably felt she could wait no longer. She spent an apparently happy honeymoon in Ireland with Nicholls's family, and may even have come to love him, before she died nine months later from pregnancy-related sickness.

Brontë's literary heroines fared better. Jane Eyre, at the end of her tumultuous story, was able to say:

> *I have now been married ten years. I know what it is to live entirely for and with what I love best on earth. I hold myself supremely blest— blest beyond what language can express: because I am my husband's life as fully as he is mine. No woman was ever nearer to her mate than I am: ever more absolutely bone of his bone and flesh of his flesh.*

Like Anne Bradstreet two hundred years earlier, Brontë's fictive heroine looked to the language of the Bible to express the ideal of love, equality, and oneness in marriage that many women yearned for.

The typical English novel of this period ended in marriage, as if acquiring a spouse would resolve all of life's problems. In one of Frances Trollope's novels, *The Life and Adventures of a Clever Woman* (1864), the thirty-year-old heroine Charlotte Morris writes in her diary on the eve of her marriage: "unless my life be prematurely cut short, my history does not end here, although the event which usually concludes the history of a woman may be said to be reached."[13] Trollope, who by that time was well into her own history as a wife, mother of six children, and author out of economic necessity, had learned the hard way that marriage is rarely the wedded bliss pictured in poetry and fiction.

MARITAL LAWS IN ENGLAND AND AMERICA

To begin with, the law did not see married women as the equals of their husbands. In fact, wives had absolutely no legal existence, in the words of Sir William Blackstone's 1753 *Commentaries on the Laws of England,* which continued to provide the basis for common law in nineteenth-century England and America. "By marriage, the husband and wife are one person in law: that is, the very being, or legal existence of the woman is suspended during the marriage, or at least incorporated and consolidated into that of the husband: under whose wing, protection and cover, she performs everything." Or, as the popular saying went, "husband and wife are one person, and that person is the husband."

The Law still allowed a husband to give his wife "moderate correction" and to beat her with a stick, provided that it be no larger than a finger and not as large as a man's thumb. Although people of the upper classes claimed that corporal punishment was exercised primarily by people of the lower ranks, today's data on wife beating indicate that it exists at all levels of society, which leads us to assume that it was not, in the past, confined to the great unwashed.

Concerning material possessions, the law left no doubt as to ownership: "A woman's personal property, by marriage, becomes absolutely her husband's." This included whatever property his wife owned before her marriage and her earnings as a married woman. The husband had the right to leave this property at the time of his death to whomever he wished, reserving only a third of it for his widow.

Worse yet for an unhappily married woman, she was not allowed to live separately from her husband, if he insisted upon cohabitation. The

1840 English case of Cecilia Maria Cochrane, who had run away from her husband four years earlier to live with her mother in Paris, is illustrative. When the husband got her back by stratagem and locked her up, she managed to obtain a writ of habeas corpus and brought suit against him. The judge decreed, in accordance with the "general dominion which the law of England attributes to the husband over the wife," that Mr. Cochrane was entitled to prevent his wife "from the danger of unrestrained intercourse with the world, by enforcing cohabitation and a common residence." Cecilia Cochrane was sentenced to "perpetual imprisonment."[14]

Insofar as children were concerned, their legal custody belonged to the father. In the case of divorce, even one caused by an abusive or adulterous husband, the divorced wife could be prevented from seeing her own children. During the first half of the nineteenth century, divorce was exceedingly rare in England, since it could be obtained only by an act of Parliament at the exhorbitant price of 800 to 900 pounds—that is, three times what a comfortable middle-class couple needed to live on in a year! Under those conditions, it is not surprising that only 3 percent of divorces were initiated by wives.[15] How even that small percent of women paid such astronomical fees begs the question of where a wife could acquire the means. Perhaps family or wealthy friends came forth in some cases, or some wives may have "stolen" it from family assets.

The widely publicized case of Caroline Sheridan Norton, separated from her husband, the Hon. George Norton, and denied access to their three children, played a major role in helping to change British divorce and child custody laws. When Mrs. Norton and her husband separated in 1836, he refused to pay her an adequate allowance, although much of the property that had come to her from her parents was now in his possession. Thrown on her own resources, Caroline Norton tried her hand at writing and managed to support herself on her earnings, which, by law, belonged to her husband and which he, from time to time, tried to get hold of. Mrs. Norton wrote a polemical pamphlet outlining her grievances and those of other women in her situation, which helped to win passage of the 1839 Act that allowed mothers limited access to their children. When Parliament finally took up the question of divorce reform, Mrs. Norton's *Letter to the Queen on Lord Chancellor*

Cranworth's Marriage and Divorce Bill (1855) contained her personal story and the following eye-opening information:

> *An English wife may not leave her husband's house. Not only can he sue her for restitution of "conjugal rights," but he has a right to enter the house of any friend or relation with whom she may take refuge . . . and carry her away by force . . .*
>
> *If the wife sue for separation for cruelty, it must be "cruelty that endangers life or limb" . . .*
>
> *If her husband take proceedings for a divorce, she is not, in the first instance, allowed to defend herself. . . . She is not represented by attorney, nor permitted to be considered a party to the suit between him and her supposed lover, for "damages."*
>
> *If an English wife be guilty of infidelity, her husband can divorce her so as to marry again; but she cannot divorce the husband, a vinculo, however profligate he may be. No law court can divorce in England. A special Act of Parliament annulling the marriage is passed for each case.*[16]

Another woman who contributed significantly to the marital reform movement was Barbara Leigh Smith Bodichon, the daughter of a wealthy and influential radical member of Parliament. Her 1854 pamphlet, *A Brief Summary, in Plain Language, of the Most Important Laws concerning Women,* became a key document in the midcentury parliamentary debate. It attracted the attention not only of lawmakers, but also of reform-minded women, who organized a committee to gather proof of the hardships wives endured under the existing laws. A petition with 26,000 signatures, including those of such literary luminaries as Elizabeth Barrett Browning, Harriet Martineau, and Elizabeth Gaskell, was presented to Parliament in March 1856. The petition made the point that "modern civilisation, in indefinitely extending the sphere of occupation for women, has in some measure broken down their pecuniary dependence upon men," and that it was time for "legal protection [to] be thrown over the produce of their labour." Married women of the middle and upper classes were entering "the fields of literature and art, in order to increase the family income," while women of the lower ranks were able to find employment in factory work and "other multifarious occupations." The poor woman, in particular, needed legal protection because she "may work from morning till night to see the produce of her labour wrested from her [by her husband], and wasted in a gin-palace."[17] At this time, according to the census of 1861, one-third of the labor force were women, and of these, nearly one-fourth were married.

The Divorce Act or Matrimonial Causes Act of 1857 transferred jurisdiction of matters relating to separation and divorce from ecclesiastical courts to newly established secular courts. The grounds for divorce remained cruelty and adultery, but a wife had to prove adultery aggravated by desertion, cruelty, rape, "buggery," or bestiality. A man could ask for divorce simply on the grounds of adultery. This double standard, based on the popular view that adultery was more reprehensible on the part of a wife than on the part of a husband, remained in British law until 1929, when the grounds for divorce finally became the same for both parties. The most significant change of the 1857 Act was that a woman who succeeded in obtaining either a separation or a divorce was henceforth entitled to all the property rights of an unmarried person. This was decidedly a step in the right direction, though it changed nothing for the married woman, whose husband continued to have full possession of the family property and his wife's income.

While divorce still remained rare and costly, it was initiated somewhat more frequently by women, as in the 1869 case of Mrs. Frances Kelly, who was granted a judicial separation from her husband, the Reverend James Kelly, on the grounds of "Cruelty" and "Undue Exercise of Marital Authority." The judgment in her favor argued that the husband had purposely attempted to make his wife unhappy so as to bend her to his will. While it upheld the principle of the husband's dominant rights, it also set limits to his behavior: "Without disparaging the just and paramount authority of a husband, it may be safely asserted that a wife is not a domestic slave, to be driven at all cost . . . into compliance with her husband's demands."[18] Increasingly, in the years to come, divorce would become an issue of paramount importance for wives from every segment of Western society, but in nineteenth-century England, it remained largely a privilege of the upper classes, and one that left a greater taint on the divorcée than on her ex-husband.

Finally, in 1870, Parliament passed the Married Women's Property Act, which allowed wives to gain control of their personal property and income. Much of the credit for this legislation belonged to the eminent philosopher John Stuart Mill, elected to Parliament in 1865, and his wife, Harriet Taylor Mill. During the heated parliamentary debate that lasted from 1868 to 1870, Mill published his treatise *The Subjection of Women* (1869), which became an overnight classic for proponents of women's rights. Other distinguished men and women, including Mrs. Bodichon, contributed to the defeat of the conservative faction, many of whom expressed the fear that granting married women property rights would lead to female independence and immorality. As parliamentarian Henry Raikes put it, in a conjugal quarrel, the wife could say: "I have my own property, and if you don't like me, I can go and live with somebody who does." The idea of equal property would, in his opinion, "create a factitious, an artificial, and an unnatural equality between man and woman."[19] Equality between the sexes was still seen by the likes of Raikes as "unnatural."

Among the many arguments in favor of reform were the examples drawn from those American states that had amended the common law so as to allow married women control over their property. While Raikes and other conservatives denounced such "Americanization" of English institutions, reform was the order of the day in 1870 and again, in 1882, when the married Women's Property Bill added stronger measures to the earlier law. From that point on, an Englishwoman could not only hold on to whatever she owned at the time of marriage or acquired after marriage, but she could also enter into contracts and sue and be sued, and dispose of her property by sale, gift, or will.

Special provisions had been added for the wife whose husband had been convicted of domestic violence. The wife of such a man could apply for "an order protecting her earnings and property." The husband could be restrained from "going to or visiting the wife without her consent." The wife could be given legal custody of the children up to the age of ten, with the husband mandated to pay the wife "a weekly sum for the maintenance of herself and such children." Although these provisions did not put an end to wife beating and other forms of abuse, the law had at least established procedures for dealing with a violent husband.

On the whole, American marital laws were similar to British laws for the first half of the century, but individual states wrote their own versions, and some were distinctly more favorable to women. In 1848, when feminist reformers under the leadership of Elizabeth Cady Stanton and Lucretia Mott met in Seneca Falls, they drew up a woman's bill of rights that demanded redress for many inequities in the legal code. Their resolutions, known as the "Declaration of Sentiments," included the following diatribe against the all-powerful husband:

> *He has made her, if married, in the eye of the law, civilly dead.*
> *He has taken from her all right in property, even to the wages she earns. . . .*
> *He has so framed the laws of divorce, as to what shall be the proper causes, and in case of separation, to whom the guardianship of the children shall be given, as to be wholly regardless of the happiness of women—the law, in all cases, going upon a false supposition of the supremacy of man, and giving all power into his hands.*[20]

Eliabeth Cady Stanton and Susan B. Anthony, leaders of the feminist movement for the rest of the century, agreed that the question of marriage was "the foundation of all reforms" for women. As Stanton (who was married) wrote in a 1853 letter to Anthony (who was not): "It is in vain to look for the elevation of woman, so long as she is degraded in marriage. . . . I feel that this whole question of woman's rights turns on the point of the marriage relation."[21] And for Stanton, the only acceptable marriage was based on love, sympathy, and equality between the sexes.

Starting in 1839, when Mississippi became the first state to grant wives property rights, the legal status of married women gradually improved, state by state. Between 1869 and 1887, thirty-three states and the District of Columbia gave wives control over their income. A few states—Louisiana, Texas, New Mexico, Arizona, and California—adopted laws of community property whereby family assets were owned equally by husband and wife. Moreover, in some states, like New York in 1860, women were made joint guardians with their husbands of their children; and, more dramatically, in the event of divorce, some states—Iowa as early as 1838—went so far as to grant sole custody of a child to its mother.

Late-nineteenth-century treatises on the law took into account the changes that had taken place during the preceding two generations. As Hendrik Hartog has shown in his masterful book, *Man & Wife in America*, law school casebooks from the 1890s incorporated the new statutes on domestic relations without abandoning older notions of wifely and husbandly responsibilities. A married woman still owed her husband traditional duties, such as housekeeping and sex. A married man still owed his spouse protection and support. Whatever new rights a wife had acquired in terms of her capacity to keep her property, earnings, and children, her identity as a wife still took precedence over any notion of autonomy. The common law idea of coverture, whereby a wife was "covered by" her husband and owed him deference, cast a long shadow over interpretations of the law, even as more recent statutes in the majority of states produced progress in favor of the wife.[22]

WIFEHOOD IN AMERICA

While Americans shared with their English counterparts a common law heritage, numerous differences in the social makeup of the two countries produced notable differences in the conduct of English and American wives. Foreign travelers in the New World, such as Mrs. Trollope around 1830, were surprised at the "freedom of manners" that girls exhibited, which quickly changed into the "burdens of a teeming wife."[23] The English writer, world traveler, and abolitionist, J. S. Buckingham, in his lengthy visit of the South took note of the "the greater liberty" enjoyed by girls at day schools as compared with girls of the same age in England. Although he looked askance at the "great precosity of manners in both sexes" and the frequency of very early marriages, sometimes as early as thirteen for girls and fourteen for boys, Buckingham was forced to concede that "on the whole, married life appears to be quite as happy as in England."[24]

Whereas both English and continental girls of the better sort were subject to strict rules of deportment and dress, American girls tended to be freer from external controls and subject primarily to the psychological pressures produced by their families and religion. But once they were married, most American women put ideas of freedom behind them. Without the plentiful domestic help found in England, wives were obliged to commit themselves to a never-ending chain of housekeeping chores. The vast majority of American wives did most things with their own hands, with the occasional help of hired workers to do the laundry and seasonal housecleaning. Except in the Southern states, where approximately one quarter of families had slaves, only 15 percent of the overall population could afford the servieces of live-in domestic help.

Less affluent Americans counted on the resources of all family members for economic survival. In most farm families, wives hoed and weeded, husbands plowed and reaped, and children as young as six or seven carried wood and water. In the Tennessee back country, Buckingham noted with compassion "the toils and privations which a settler and his family have to undergo in clearing land, and surrounding themselves with even the barest necessaries. Every member of the family must work hard, from daylight to dark, the women as well as the men, and the children as well as the grown people. . . . In general they were very dirty in their persons, the mother being too weary to wash them."[25]

In the cities, households with scant means were grateful for the extra income of an unmarried son or daughter. Immigrant families, in particular, depended not only on the work of husbands and sons, but on the additional labor of wives who took in laundry and boarders, and daughters who went into domestic service. These working families differed from British families to the extent that they were not irrevocably locked into a system of class; the "working class" of one generation was often the middle class and sometimes even the upper class of the next. The economic and social fluidity of American society is one significant factor that must be taken into account when we look at the experiences of American wives.

Another is the great diversity of national and ethnic backgrounds. If Anglo-Americans continued to be statistically dominant, successive waves of immigrants from Ireland, Germany, Scandinavia, Eastern Europe, and Asia would, between the early nineteenth century and World War I, bring millions of new peoples to the United States, each group with its own language and cultural heritage. The wives of these immigrants were often torn between two sets of behaviors, since old-country conjugal models did not necessarily serve them well in their adopted homeland. The Irish mother who had been socialized to accept her husband's alcoholic abuse, the orthodox Jewish wife who wore a wig in the Eastern European shtetl, the Japanese picture bride admonished to keep her eyes down in the presence of men—all confronted a society that subtlely encouraged them to question past prescriptions.

Special consideration must be given to black women. Before emancipation, slaves could not legally marry. As property of their masters, they were allowed, indeed encouraged to breed so as to produce more slaves, but even a religious ceremony did not guarantee that a couple could stay together. It was common for slave owners to sell members of a family—fathers, mothers, children—to the highest bidder. Families could be torn apart at one stroke of the gavel. Only freed blacks both in the North and South were allowed to marry legally. After the Civil War, black men and women were their own property and could become man and wife according to the laws of each state. For a short period, between 1865 and 1880, there were even scores of marriages between whites and blacks in former Confederate states.

But many legacies from the past did not disappear overnight. In the South, schools, public conveyances, hotels, restaurants, and various forms of entertainment continued to perpetuate a system of segregation and white supremacy. Laws against miscegenation, enacted or reenacted in forty-one states, made it a crime for blacks and whites to marry. In fact, South Carolina did not remove the official ban against interracial marriage from its statutes until 1999, and Alabama put off till the year 2000 its referendum to eliminate a similar provision.

It is impossible to speak of American wives without recognizing their enormous geographical diversity. If the first two centuries of North American history were confined primarily to the East, the last two hundred years expanded overland to the Pacific Coast and beyond. Wives in Illinois, Utah, California, and Hawaii have had very different experiences from their sisters in the North and South, under laws that varied from state to state. For example, women in Wyoming were allowed to vote as early as 1869, and three more western states legalized women's suffrage by 1896. One Wyoming wife, anxious to dispel the myth that suffrage had made the women of her state unfeminine, assured the readers of the *Woman's Journal* that Wyoming husbands still returned from their daily work "to a bright fireside and well-ordered dinner, presided over by a home-loving, neatly gowned, womanly wife."[26] Else-where in America, as in England, women were not granted suffrage until after World War I. The issue of geographical diversity will be prominent in the pages that follow, alongside those of ethnic diversity and social class.

Last, it is important to recognize that the legal and sociocultural sta-tus of wives during the Victorian era was subject to change from an incipient women's movement. The women who met at Seneca Falls in 1848 were mostly married women, and their concerns to improve the condition of their sisters would gradually alter the picture of American wifehood. The group led by Elizabeth Cady Stanton and Susan B. Anthony saw the existing institution of marriage as a form of bondage for women similar to the institution of slavery—an analogy that had first been highlighted by the British writer Mary Wollstonecraft in her 1792 *Vindication of the Rights of Women*. By the 1850s the marriage-equals-slavery rhetoric was commonplace among reformers speaking out against the unfair distribution of power in marriage. In 1855, the early feminist Lucy Stone went so far as to enlist the clergyman officiat-ing at her wedding to state in public that he never performed a mar-riage ceremony "without a renewed sense of the inequity of our present system of laws in respect to marriage."[27]

Alongside the Victorian picture of women as "angels," a new vision of American womanhood was in the making. This vision pictured angels with bodies and brains. The lessons of Jane Austen's and Charlottte Brontë's headstrong heroines had crossed the Atlantic and fed into a progressive American stream of thought. Sarah Grimké, who had grown up in the South but moved to the North in order to pursue antislavery activities, critiqued the exclusively domestic orientation of women in her *Letters on the Equability of the Sexes* (1837). She believed that females brought up to think of themselves as "inferior creatures" naturally suf-fered from a lack of "self-respect," which could, however, be corrected through education; and she argued that such an education would also benefit husbands, since they would ultimately have more interesting companions.[28] In this same vein, the American minister George Bur-nap's lectures, published in 1848, spoke of "the beauties of a well stored mind" and the attractiveness of educated women. He assured them that "a sensible and brilliant conversation will attract the notice of the well-educated of the other sex more than a coronet of jewels."[29]

During the nineteenth century, the importance of education became something of a national obsession. State-funded coeducational primary schools spread rapidly from the East during the 1830s and 1840s, special academies and seminaries for women were established by midcentury, and women's colleges sprang up in the antebellum and postbellum years. By 1890, twice as many girls as boys graduated from high school, and numerous colleges—both state coeducational and private women's schools—were available for young women whose families could afford them.[30]

Education for women was nonetheless seen mainly as a pathway to marriage, and valued primarily for the making of good wives and mothers. The Reverend Burnap spoke for the received wisdom of his age when he wrote of the two sexes "that they should move in different spheres. . . . To woman the care of home, the preparation of food, the making of clothing, the nursing and education of children."[31] Other midcentury spokesmen for women, for example Catherine Beecher in her *Treatise on Domestic Economy* (1841) and Sarah Josepha Hale, the influential editor of *Godey's Lady's Book* from the 1830s to the 1870s, all agreed that domestic education was to take precedence over any other form of learning, given the ultimate female vocation as helpmeet and homemaker. Few condoned education as a means whereby women could gain financial and social independence. Especially in the antebellum South, the idea that education might make a woman step out of her "sphere" was greatly to be feared. Even my own alma mater in Massachusetts—Wellesley College, chartered in 1870—had as its logo "Non ministrari, sed ministrare" (Not to be ministered unto, but to minister), which we in the 1950s lampooned as "Not to be a minister, but a minister's wife."

ELIZABETH CADY STANTON: WIFE, MOTHER, ACTIVIST

Most of us know the name of Elizabeth Cady Stanton, but how many know that this radical founder of the women's rights movement was married for almost fifty years and had seven children? How did this wife manage to fulfill her obligations to her family and become, with her spinster friend Susan B. Anthony, the most famous nineteenth-century activist for women's emancipation? Like Margery Kempe in the fourteenth century, Elizabeth Cady Stanton did not allow her brood of children to hold back her calling, and like Kempe, she dramatized her mission in a remarkable autobiography composed at the end of her life. Though neither Margery nor Elizabeth were "representative" wives, both of their stories shed light not only on their own marriages, but also on the conventions of wifehood in their time and place.

Eighty Years and More: Reminiscences 1815–1897 begins with Elizabeth Cady's childhood as the daughter of a distinguished lawyer in the state of New York.[32] Characteristic of Victorian autobiography, Elizabeth speaks sparingly of her mother, except to say that she was "weary with the cares of a large family, having had ten children," of whom only five survived into adulthood. Growing up with four sisters and one much preferred male sibling, who had the misfortune of dying at an early age, Elizabeth set out to rival and then to replace her brother.

She spent much time in her father's office listening to the clients, talking to the students, and reading the laws regarding women. In her Scotch-American neighborhood, "many men still retained the old feudal ideas of women and property. Fathers, at their death, would will the bulk of their property to the eldest son, with the proviso that the mother was to have a home with him. Hence it was not unusual for the mother, who had brought all the property into the family, to be made an unhappy dependent on the bounty of an uncongenial daughter-in law and a dissipated son."

Much moved by the "tears and complaints" of the women who came to her father for legal advice, Elizabeth was perplexed by the "injustice and cruelty of the laws" shown her in his books. One of the law students teased her by saying, "Now . . . if in due time you should be my wife, those ornaments [her jewelry] would be mine; I could take them and lock them up, and you could never wear them except with my permission. I could even exchange them for a box of cigars, and you could watch them evaporate in smoke."

Her father gave her more serious advice. When grown up, she should "go down to Albany and talk to the legislators; tell them all you have seen in this office—the sufferings of these Scotchwomen, robbed of their inheritance and left dependent on their unworthy sons, and, if you can persuade them to pass new laws, the old ones will be a dead letter." Ironically, when Elizabeth was ready to follow this prescribed course of action, her father opposed it as inappropriate for a married woman.

Until the age of sixteen, Elizabeth studied at a coeducational academy. But when the boys of her class went off to Union College in Schenectady, she was mortified to discover that girls were not admitted. She went instead to Mrs. Willard's Seminary at Troy, a fashionable all-girls school that specialized in the feminine "accomplishments" of French, music, and dancing. Separated from the boys she had previously taken for granted, she now took "an intense interest" in their company.

After leaving school, Elizabeth returned to her parents' home, where she enjoyed friendship with many young women and men. Her life was "intensified by the usual number of flirtations," but with the advice of her brother-in-law she and her sisters put off "matrimonial entanglements" as long as possible.

She was twenty-four when she met Henry B. Stanton, "the most eloquent and impassioned orator on the anti-slavery platform." Elizabeth was staying in Peterboro, New York, at the home of her relative Gerrit Smith, whose mansion served as one of the stations on the Underground Railroad for slaves escaping to Canada from the South. It was also the meeting place of "choice society from every part of the country." Each morning, two carriages of ladies and gentlemen drove off to one of the antislavery conventions held in the area. "The enthusiasm of the people in these great meetings, the thrilling oratory, and lucid arguments of the speakers, all conspired to make these days memorable as among the most charming in my life." In this atmosphere of ethical exuberance, Elizabeth and Henry fell in love.

But Cousin Gerrit, aware of the budding romance, warned Elizabeth that her father would never consent to her marriage with an abolitionist. "He felt in duty bound, as my engagement had occurred under his roof, to free himself from all responsibility by giving me a long dissertation on love, friendship, marriage, and all the pitfalls for the unwary."

Events moved very quickly, despite "doubt and conflict" on Elizabeth's part. She doubted "the wisdom of changing a girlhood of freedom and enjoyment" for the uncertainties of a marriage opposed by her family. She even broke off her engagement "after months of anxiety and bewilderment," but since Henry Stanton was leaving for Europe as a delegate to the World Anti-Slavery Convention, and she did not wish to be separated from him by an ocean, she changed her mind again, and they were married on May 10, 1840, after a turbulent seven-month engagement.

The precipitousness of the Stantons' wedding plans caused them to be married on a Friday, "a day commonly supposed to be a most unlucky day." Elizabeth takes pains to assure us that, since she and her husband lived together "without more than the usual matrimonial friction, for nearly a half a century, had seven children, all but one of whom are still living [in 1897], . . . no one need be afraid of going through the marriage ceremony on Friday for fear of bad luck." Nineteenth-century etiquette manuals indicate that Saturday, too, was not considered propitious for a wedding.[33]

What was more unusual than the day of the week chosen for Elizabeth's wedding was her insistence that the marriage vows "leave out the word 'obey'." Despite the clergyman's objections, Elizabeth Cady was married to Henry Stanton without the traditional vow of obedience. (Two weeks later, Amelia Jenks followed suit when she became Mrs. Dexter C. Bloomer, a name that would subsequently become identified with dress reform and the notorious "bloomers.") Elizabeth was married "in a simple white evening dress," in the presence of a few friends and family members. Then the newlyweds traveled to New York and boarded the vessel that would take them to Europe.

It is clear that Elizabeth Cady's history was exceptional in many ways. She came from an affluent, extremely well placed family; she was educated far beyond the norm for girls of her day; and she had a unique propensity for questioning the status quo. But she was to learn, first in England and then in her homeland, that she was not exempt from the laws and prejudices designed to keep wives in their place.

Accompanying her husband to the antislavery convention held in London in 1840, she was part of the female contingent that was not permitted to sit on the main floor of the convention. Shunted upstairs to the balcony, the female delegates were thus deprived of voting rights. Gail Parker, in her introduction to the paperback edition of Stanton's autobiography, signals this humiliation as decisive in Stanton's emerging feminist consciousness.

Yet in 1840, the new bride was enchanted with most aspects of her wedding journey: the remarkable men and women she and her husband met, their sightseeing in London and Paris in the company of friends, and a trip for just the two of them among the Scotch lakes and mountains. Only Ireland, with its dire poverty, constituted a trial to their sensibilities.

Returning to the United States, Henry decided to begin the study of law with Elizabeth's father. This meant that she would once again live under the parental roof and have "two added years of pleasure" with her sisters. In due time the sisters also took husbands and, according to Elizabeth, they were all "peculiarly fortunate in their marriages."

Before long, Elizabeth gave birth to the first of her seven children. She was a progressive mother for her times, refusing to give in to questionable practices, such as the swaddling of infants from hip to armpit. Every day when the temporary nurse bandaged up the baby, Elizabeth took off the bindings. Less enlightened mothers and nurses continued to swaddle babes into the late nineteenth century, despite mounting criticism of this practice coming from the medical profession that found its way into popular publications—for example, the *Bazaar-Book of Decorum* (1870), which argued that swaddling clothes endangered "the health and vigor of whole generations."[34]

Like most American mothers, Elizabeth nursed her baby. Wet nurses were never fashionable in the North, and the bottle, which had been in existence since before 1800, would not become common until the last decades of the century, after Pasteur's germ theory led to the understanding that boiling bottles would make them safe. Elizabeth fed her baby every two hours, and learned to trust her "mother's instinct."

Motherhood was seen as a serious occupation. Indeed, some American historians have argued that it was *the* major occupation for Victorian wives, superseding the earlier colonial role of "helpmeet" to the husband. During the eighteenth and early nineteenth century, authority over children had shifted from the paternal to the maternal, with the new nation calling on its mothers to nurture good citizens. By midcentury, motherhood was seen as the raison d'être and crowning glory of American women. The homes over which they presided were expected to provide a moral bastion for impressionable young children and a domestic sanctuary for weary husbands returning from the harsh elements of the outside world.

In 1843, Henry Stanton was admitted to the bar and began to practice law in Boston. For the first time, Elizabeth was the mistress of her own home. As she later recalled, "A new house, newly furnished with a

Elizabeth Cady Stanton and her daughter, Harriet Stanton (Blatch).

beautiful view of Boston Bay, was all I could desire. Mr. Stanton announced to me, in starting, that I must take entire charge of the housekeeping. So, with two good servants and two babies under my sole supervision, my time was pleasantly occupied."

Like other affluent Victorian women, Elizabeth entered the separate sphere reserved for wives and mothers, and she entered it enthusiastically. In her words: "When first installed as mistress over an establishment, one has the same feeling of pride and satisfaction that a young minister must have in taking charge of his first congregation. It is a proud moment in a woman's life to reign supreme within four walls . . . I studied up everything pertaining to housekeeping, and enjoyed it all."

A third child came along, and Elizabeth complained of only one problem: "the lack of faithful, competent servants." But unlike most women of her class, Stanton did not think that servants were the only answer. Her "hope of co-operative housekeeping" with other families was undoubtedly inspired by the utopian communities that were springing up in America and Europe, especially Fourier's community in France, with which she was familiar.

In 1847, the Stantons moved to Seneca Falls. There they spent the next sixteen years of their married life and produced four more children. Initially, Elizabeth found Seneca Falls somewhat depressing because she no longer had the circle of friends and activities that had sustained her in Boston. Their residence was on the outskirts of town, where roads were muddy and sidewalks nonexistent. Mr. Stanton was frequently away from home, and his wife had more responsibilities than she could handle. Her analysis of her situation at that time sounds very much like the wifely malaise Betty Friedan identified a hundred years later in *The Feminine Mystique*.

> *To keep a house and grounds in good order, purchase every article for daily use, keep the wardrobes of half a dozen human beings in proper trim, take the children to dentists, shoemakers, and different schools, or find teachers at home, altogether made sufficient work to keep one brain busy, as well as all the hands I could impress into the service. Then, too, the novelty of housekeeping had passed away, and much that was once attractive in domestic life was now irksome.*

For the first time in her life, Elizabeth felt overwhelmed by all that faced her—her homebound isolation, her all too numerous duties, her lack of friends, and the absence of stimulating mental activities. She understood, as she never had before, how women could give up in despair. "Housekeeping, under such conditions, was impossible."

Fortunately for Elizabeth, she was able to retreat with her children to her parental home. There she began to work her way out of her despair by relating it to the situation of all women under similar circumstances. As she later realized, "The general discontent I felt with woman's portion as wife, mother, housekeeper, physician, and spiritual guide, the chaotic conditions into which everything fell without her constant supervision, and the wearied, anxious look of the majority of women impressed me with a strong feeling that some active measures should be taken to remedy the wrongs of society in general, and of women in particular." She did what many great thinkers have always done: she raised her particular unhappiness to a universal level and tried to solve not only her personal problem, but a problem shared with many others. It can be argued that the Seneca Falls Convention of 1848 and the subsequent history of the women's rights movement in the second half of the nineteenth century sprang from the dissatisfactions of one American housewife.

From 1850 onward, Stanton worked with Susan B. Anthony to bring before the American public all the major issues that progressive women were clamoring for, including the overriding issue of women's suffrage. Though neither Anthony nor Stanton would live to 1920, when American women got the vote, they had many moments of triumph in their long partnership. Perhaps none was more gratifying to Stanton than the 1860 passage of the Married Women's Property Act by the State of New York, an act that finally granted wives the right to own their own property and earnings. For the rest of the century, almost up to the moment of her death in 1902, Stanton worked tirelessly with Anthony for the full equality of women. Their intense, purposeful friendship was often compared to a marriage. As historian Caroll Smith-Rosenberg has shown, it was not unusual for nineteenth-century female friendships to rival, in depth of affection, the feelings one was supposed to have for one's husband.[35]

Stanton's eloquent address known as "The Solitude of Self," delivered in 1892 to the United States Congressional Committee on the Judiciary, is a remarkable plea for women's rights in education, employment, and political life. And it is more than that. It is an existential cri de coeur springing from the religious belief that each individual is fundamentally alone.

In it, Stanton totally repudiates the theory that women are intrinsically relative creatures. The roles of mother, wife, sister, and daughter are labeled "incidental relations."[36] The true nature of woman, like the true nature of man, is to be found in "the isolation of every human soul and the necessity of self-dependence." Stanton speaks bluntly of her contemporaries: "No matter how much women prefer to lean, to be protected and supported, nor how much men desire to have them do so, they must make the voyage of life alone."

Drawn from her own personal experience of wifehood and motherhood, Stanton lays out a counter-doctrine to the theory of woman's dependence on the male—one that emphasizes female self-reliance.

> *The young wife and mother, at the head of some establishment with a kind husband to shield her from the adverse winds of life, with wealth, fortune, and position, has a certain harbor of safety, secure against the ordinary ills of life. But to manage a household, have a desirable influence in society, keep her friends and the affections of her husband, train her children and servants well, she must have rare common sense, wisdom, diplomacy, and a knowledge of human nature. To do all this she needs the cardinal virtues and the strong points of character that the most successful statesman possesses.*

In the last years of her life, "when the pleasures of youth are passed, children grown up, married and gone, the hurry and bustle of life in a measure over," Stanton knew full well that "men and women alike must fall back on their own resources" and that "he cannot bear her burdens." Like Stanton herself, this speech was far ahead of its time.

WIVES IN THE SOUTH

The midcentury women's rights movement associated with Stanton was primarily a Northern concept, though most Northern men and women either ignored or opposed it. And most Southerners resisted it because it threatened one of their charter beliefs: that women were essentially frail and decorous creatures destined to be dependent on men. The fear of independent, educated, "unsexed" women expressed itself over and over again in the antebellum South. George Fitzhugh, a noted spokesman for women's subordination (as well as for slavery) argued that as long as woman "is nervous, fickle, capricious, delicate, diffident, and dependent, man will worship and adore her. Her weakness is her strength, and her true art is to cultivate and improve that weakness." And he concluded: "We men of the South infinitely prefer to nurse a sickly woman to being led around by a blue stocking."[37] (It is a mark of change that such a statement would seem ridiculous to a man today.)

In general, Southern women accepted their dependence on men. They had learned the lessons imprinted on them by their families, their religions, and the mass media. In 1855, Gertrude Thomas wrote in her journal that she thanked God for her husband's masterliness, which "suits my woman's nature, for true to my sex, I delight *in looking up* and love to feel my woman's weakness protected by man's superior strength." Catherine Edmondston worried that she was stepping out of her sphere by wanting to publish her poems and had to remind herself: "Well obedience is a wife's first duty." Marie Howard Schoolcraft pointed to the State of South Carolina with pride because "all the ladies *there* are brought up to be obedient to their husbands"—unlike Northern women with their concern for women's rights.[38]

Southern girls were educated for the roles of wife, mother, and mistress of the house. Parents, churches, schools, books, and magazines all pointed young ladies in the direction of the altar. Virginia Randolph Cary, who wrote a book of advice for girls in 1828, supported female education, but only insofar as it prepared women for their didactic mission within the home: "I do most ardently desire to see women highly cultivated in mind and morals, and yet content to remain within the retirement of the family circle."[39]

The new seminaries and colleges rarely departed from the kind of education deemed appropriate for a marriageable middle-class girl: grammar, spelling, handwriting, arithmetic, geography, foreign languages (usually French), and such accomplishments as needlework, drawing, and music. In the Southern women's colleges founded in the 1830s and 1840s, education was fashioned to fulfill male expectations for an ideal wife. Young women were constantly reminded of the dangers of "unsexing" themselves by acquiring too much learning and developing aspirations that did not suit their "place." As expressed in a commencement address at a female college in Georgia in 1857: "You are here the beloved and honored co-equal companion of man. You can remain so long as you fill . . . the place which God and nature have allotted you." Another commencement speaker at a different women's institution reminded the young ladies, "A woman ought not to speak what she pleased, because, if common reputation were true, she sometimes spoke too fast, too much, and too strong, and that whatever she said that did not prove true, her husband had to answer for either by fight or by law."[40]

Since Southern couples prior to the Civil War (like Northern couples) were still governed by eighteenth-century English common law, as codified by Blackstone, a husband did indeed have to "answer for" his wife's conduct. If she let her tongue go too far, he might have to defend her against charges of slander—a common legal complaint in seventeenth and eighteenth century America that lingered on in notions of Victorian propriety. While sharp-tongued "scolds" were no longer punished by having to sit in the "ducking stool," a contraption that repeatedly plunged its victims in water until they retracted their accusations, women—or rather their husbands—could be stiffly fined. The wife's person, her property, and her children were all in the custody of her husband and were his responsibility.

A remarkable study of antebellum women in Georgia, written by Eleanor Miot Boatwright in the 1930s and published only recently, provides us with an in-depth picture of courtship, marriage, and many other aspects of Southern womanhood. Marriage was for most Georgia women the only acceptable status. "Old maids" were proverbial objects of mockery and disdain, at best ignored or tolerated in the household of a relative. Few women were bold enough to remain single by choice, and most felt that any husband was better than none. Girls began to accumulate a hope chest at an early age, and it was not uncommon for them to marry as early as fourteen and fifteen. If she were still single at twenty, a young woman was considered a "stale maid." Still, the chances of finding a husband were generally good, since between 1790 and 1860 men outnumbered women both in Georgia and in the entire United States.[41] (The Civil War slaughter of over 600,000 men in the battlefields would tilt that ratio in the opposite direction.)

An antebellum girl was expected to be a coquette, flirtatious and romantic, but without exceeding the limits of decorum. In plantation

and urban middle-class homes, young women were carefully chaper-
oned by concerned mothers and fathers, many of whom sat up late to
make sure that a daughter in the drawing room gave her beau only
verbal encouragement. Romance flourished in parlors, at church, and
under the moonlight. Although Methodist, Baptist, and Presbyterian
churches still seated the sexes separately, "the ladies all sitting together
in the center, and the gentlemen all repairing to the side-pews, where
they sat apart," young people could intermingle when they walked or
rode horseback to and from church.[42] Barbecues, dances, candy
pullings, and singing bees also provided opportunities for romance.

Once a man had gotten sufficient encouragement from the girl he was
courting, it was considered proper for him to ask for the father's consent before he made a proposal. This piece of decorum was probably
breached more often than not, with sweethearts coming to agreements, or disagreements, before the father had been officially consulted. But however the lovers arrived at an understanding between
them, the woman was to wait for the man to declare his love before she
revealed her true feelings.

Maria Bryan, a twenty-two-year-old Georgia woman from a wealthy
family, with holdings of eighteen hundred acres and one hundred
slaves, described in a letter to her older sister how she was approached
by a love-struck suitor in December 1829.

> . . . there stood Major Floyd filling the front door with his august
> person. . . . I let him into the room and motioned him to a seat. . . .
> well, instead of taking a chair, he just looked at me as if he could think
> of nothing but the lovely vision before him, and when he came to him-
> self sufficiently to sit down, it was not long before he commenced the
> engrossing subject. . . . He hopes, he intreats, that a mere whim, as he
> must call it, would not prevent him from devoting his life to the business
> of making me happy. . . . "Oh, accept the attachment of a living feeling
> being who offers you genuine love, warm from his heart."[43]

Despite Maria's adamant rejection, Major Floyd did not give up
hope. Several months later he repeated his proposal in a letter. Maria
complained again to her sister: "Love, heard from most lips, is to me the
most disgusting word in the world, and you may imagine it to be nau-
seous in the extreme in this instance."

Maria Bryan was almost twenty-four when she found a suitor from whose lips the word "love" was presumably more appealing. In 1831, she married a twenty-four-year-old army engineer, apparently without her father's blessings. She wrote to her sister that the greatest trial of leaving her father's home "was the idea of the unhappiness it appeared to occasion him." Like Elizabeth Cady Stanton, Maria Bryan was willing to brave a father's displeasure in order to marry the man of her choice. It is difficult to know how often marriages were made without parental approval, but it seems that in most cases, especially among people of property, great efforts were made to obtain the father's consent.

People of the popular classes—country folk, working-class men and women, and what Southerners referred to as "poor white trash"—were less hampered by decorum. Many managed to meet on their own terms, away from the eyes of watchful parents and meddlesome friends. Whereas chastity was enforced among upper- and middle-class women, those from the lower class were often pregnant at marriage, that is, if they married at all. One Southern doctor expressed the view that among the poor people in his part of the country, children of illegitimate birth were as common as those born in wedlock.[44]

In certain lowly circles, it was even acceptable for men to resort to paid advertisements, such as the following placed by a man from Arkansas: "Any gal what got a bed, calico dress, coffee-pot and skillet, knows how to cut our britches, can make a hunting shirt, and knows how to take care of children, can have my services till death parts both of us."[45]

A marriage proposal, once accepted, was more binding on the male than on the female. The laws of the State of Georgia and public opinion did not permit a man to repudiate an engagement, but a woman was allowed to break it off, perhaps because she was thought to lose more in remaining single than the man. Women's diaries and letters often reflect their excitement and happiness during the engagement period, but also their anxieties and second thoughts. Prospective brides were fully aware that marriage represented the most important decision of their lives. A few days before her Virginia wedding, Sarah Anderson asked herself in her diary: "Will Dr. B. be all that I want in a Husband? In short will he love me as I desire to be loved? I dont look for perfect bliss, but the whole soul of my Husband devoted to love me. . . . I would be foolish to expect perfect happiness, but my heart will demand *perfect* Love."[46] Love was the one indispensable ingredient for Sarah Anderson, as for many Victorian women.

During the engagement period, the making of a quilt by the bride's friends gave official recognition to the betrothal. Whether they lived in the South, the North, Midwest, or West, quilters participated in a utilitarian activity that had become, by the mid-nineteenth century, a communal ritual and a fine art. First they would make certain design decisions together, such as the size and color scheme. Then each woman would make a square or "block" and sign it with her name in ink or embroidery, before all the finished blocks were sewn together to make the quilt top. A quilt backing was stretched out on a frame, covered with cotton batting, which was then covered with the quilt top. Decorative stitching through the three layers held them in place. Referred to as "engagement quilts" or "bride's quilts," they were intended to last a lifetime and to be handed down to one's descendants.

Weddings took place both in church and at home, with the bride usually wearing white—a color traditionally associated with purity— though later in the century more practical colored dresses were sometimes substituted. The bride often wore orange blossoms in her headpiece or bouquet, and a wedding veil, which had become popular after Queen Victoria had been married in one. It was common for the minister to kiss the bride at the end of the ceremony, which was traditionally followed by a celebration with food, drink, music, and dancing. Since family and friends might have to travel great distances to attend the wedding, a large feast was usually forthcoming. But however lavish or modest, the festivities always included wedding cakes, slices of which were meant to be taken home by the guests. Once married, a woman was expected to forgo "wedding white" and the gay colors of youth in favor of more sober tones. As soon as she became a mother, she would begin to wear a lace cap. If widowed, she would don a "widow's cap" and "weeds" (black mourning clothes) for at least a year.

A married woman's duties varied greatly according to her class, wealth, and locale. In Maryland, Virginia, Georgia, and North and South Carolina, a plantation matron oversaw an estate that often housed dozens and even hundreds of slaves. In Kentucky and Ten-

Elaborate wedding dresses, presented on colored plates, enhanced the pages of Godey's Lady's Book, *a highly successful ladies' magazine founded in 1837 and edited for four decades by Mrs. Sarah J. Hale. July, 1850. (Courtesy of Department of Special Collections, Stanford University Libraries)*

Marriage Certificate, Currier lithograph, 1848. The list of "Requirements of the Husband" and "Requirements for the Wife" is made up of passages from the Bible and an occasional comment from the lithographer. Husbands are told to love their wives, provide for them, and not abandon them. If a husband provide not for his own [wife and children] he is worse than an infidel. 1 Tim. 5:8. *Wives are required to be both loving and obedient.* A wife's desire shall be to her husband. Gen 3:16 [i.e. She shall be subject unto him.] *(Achenbach Foundation, Fine Arts Museums of San Francisco)*

nessee, the mistress of a farm was more likely to supervise only seven or eight. In rural areas, a small slaveholder might work alongside his slaves in the field, or, if the family was too poor to have slaves, the wife would work on the farm with her husband. She would also prepare all meals, produce cotton cloth on her loom, make all the clothes, and regularly carry water to the house from the well or nearest stream.

On plantations, white and black women lived out their unequal lives in close proximity to one another. The mistress of the plantation (usually married, sometimes widowed, rarely single) oversaw all domestic aspects of the plantation. She was responsible for meals eaten in the Big

House, for clothes worn by family members and slaves, for entertaining guests, who often stayed overnight or several days, and for nursing the sick. Like a chief medical officer, she was expected to oversee the health of both whites and blacks, including the delivery of babies and the supervision of the infirmary, if there was one. Some mistresses taught slave children religion and basic literacy, although it was officially illegal to teach slaves to read in all Southern states. In her spare moments, she would pick up her needlework or play the piano, but those moments must have been rare indeed. However frail and decorous the ideal Southern woman was in theory, in practice she had to be hardy and efficient as a plantation wife. The sudden transition from carefree girlhood to dutiful wifehood could be traumatic. Over and over, women recorded the shock of the change in their lives. A confident young bride of seventeen who entered marriage without fearing her new duties as a mistress was thoroughly perplexed "when brought into contact with reality." The wife of a South Carolina planter told him in tears that she didn't know what to do with so many slaves. A shy sixteen-year-old bride needed two years before she could take over the direction of her servants.[47]

Marli Weiner, in her book on plantation women in South Carolina from 1830 to 1880, and Eugene D. Genovese in his work on the antebellum South, describe the complex relationships between mistresses and house slaves.[48] Black and white women counted on one another not only for the smooth running of the household, but often for personal emotional needs as well. They shared intimate secrets about their sicknesses and miseries, and established a world of female interdependence in the midst of patriarchal hierarchy. Often it was the black Mammy, rather than the mistress, who supervised the indoor chores performed by house slaves—from cooking, cleaning, and sewing to suckling white babies. Nevertheless, most mistresses worked side by side with their slaves in many tasks.

One of the biggest joint operations performed by mistresses and female slaves was to make clothes every spring and fall for the entire population on the plantation. The mistresses cut the cloth and the slaves did the sewing. Once this process was done—a process that could last several months—the women distributed the clothing in the slave quarters, and then everyone celebrated. Sophia Watson described the festivities on an Alabama plantation in a letter to her absent husband: "That the Negroes might lose as little time as possible we waited until they came to dinner and then proceeded to distribute the clothes—The men were first served, then the women and lastly the children[.] [A]ll looked well and were perfectly delighted with their new clothes."[49]

Not all the slaves were "perfectly delighted." Harriet Jacobs, telling her story in *Incidents in the Life of a Slave Girl* (1861), edited by Lydia Maria Child, remembered the bad feelings she harbored toward the wife of her master, Dr. Flint: "It was her labor that supplied my scanty wardrobe. I have a vivid recollection of the linsey-woolsey dress given me every winter by Mrs. Flint. How I hated it! It was one of the badges of slavery. . . ."[50]

Sometimes, when a husband was absent, sick, or dead, a mistress had to take over all the administrative responsibilities of the plantation. The correspondence of Sophia Watson and her husband, Henry Watson, during the nine months he was away settling his father's estate gives detailed information about plantation management, especially in his answers to her questions. Sophia's letters reveal the lack of confidence she felt giving commands to the slaves, especially in the beginning, but after three months she was able to write: "They are certainly doing much better than I expected when you left."[51]

Other mistresses were less squeamish about giving orders, and some even administered physical punishment, rather than leaving that vicious work to their husbands or overseers. One former slave from Texas recalled a distinct gender division in the whippings. "Master whips de men and missus whips de women. Sometimes she whips wid de nettleweed. When she uses dat, de licks ain't so bad, but de stingin' and de burnin' after am sho' misery."[52] Another former slave could hardly forget the cruel mistress who had beat her with a cowhide: "Then she go and rest and come back and beat me some more."[53] While the whip was usually in the hands of the men, women who took pleasure in beating their slaves were no less sadistic then their male counterparts.

One of the major stresses in the lives of plantation wives came from successive childbearing. Without reliable contraception, they often feared having still another pregnancy after six or eight or even ten children. A member of the Alabama Clay family, who came home to find his wife pregnant with her eleventh child, shared her sense of "grief and regret." A Southern general, writing to his wife during the war years, referred to pregnancy as "nine months of pain and general ill feeling," and, a year later, sympathized with her when she found out she was again pregnant: "Indeed I did sincerely hope that you had escaped this time, but darling it must be the positive and direct will of God that it should be so." One troubled North Carolina planter's wife complained to her husband in 1867: "Willis, I have not seen anything of my monthlies yet . . ." To which he replied, less sympathetically than the general: "I was never hopeful that you would not have more children, you come of a breed too prolific to stop at your age and if it's the Lords will why we must submit to it." Submitting to God's will was the customary answer to all of life's burdens, including that of having too many children, which this wife called "nothing but trouble and sorrow."[54]

Southern women seem to have been the last to show a decline in fertility in comparison to their Northeastern and Western counterparts. During the nineteenth century, the birth rate of all American white children declined by almost 50 percent—statistically speaking, from 7.04 children per married mother in 1800 to 3.56 children in 1900.[55] This must have been due to conscious efforts, such as sexual abstinence, male withdrawal, abortion, and contraceptive devices (see chapter 8). Historians disagree over the extent to which antebellum Southern women practiced any of those methods, some arguing that couples from the planter class did not try to limit fertility, and others that they did. One factor that may have added to the greater fertility of Southern women was their use of slaves to nurse their babies; since many white mothers were not nursing, they could not have profited from the "natural" contraception that breast-feeding affords by delaying the return of menstruation after childbirth. Slave women, on the other hand, began the century with a slightly lower birth rate—an average of six babies per mother, and did not experience a comparable decline in the number of offspring during the next hundred years. This was due to a variety of interconnecting factors, including their earlier age of sexual activity and the expectation on the part of their masters that they would breed new slaves (see below).

However much they were aided by black wet nurses and nannies, Southern ladies were ultimately responsible for the well-being of their sons and daughters. Indeed, over and over again, in private and public discourse, they were reminded of their obligation to raise worthy children not only for the nation and even for their particular state, but also for "the South"—that romanticized region, reputedly inhabited by beautiful women, gallant men, and grateful slaves. This pastoral vision of Christian benevolence clashes with much of the testimony written by observers from the North and abroad, and from accounts left behind by the slaves themselves.

Slave women did every kind of work on plantations. Field slaves plowed, hoed, picked cotton, and even split rails. House servants cooked, sewed, washed and ironed, nursed babies, cared for children, and attended to the personal needs of their mistresses and masters. They also made soap and dye, wove baskets, and ran errands. There was little time or energy left over for their own husbands and children, but somehow they were expected to manage their personal domestic matters whenever they could. Some were given free time on Saturday for cleaning house and washing clothes. Others were less fortunate, as one former slave recounted: "my mammy had to wash clothes on Saturday nights for us to wear on Sundays."[56]

Slave women could be wives of a sort. Though they could not legally marry, since they were officially the property of their masters, they often lived with de facto husbands, given to them by their owners or chosen by themselves. Practices varied according to the master, but there is no doubt that many owners treated their slaves as a kind of livestock, whose offspring warranted careful breeding. One ex-slave from Alabama told an interviewer: "papa and mamy wasn't married like folks now, 'cause dem times de white folks jes' put slave men and women together like hosses or cattle."[57] Sarah Ford, a former slave from Texas, remembered her mother saying that "dey jus' puts a man and breedin' woman together like mules. Iffen the woman don't like the man it don't make no difference, she better go or dey gives her a hidin."[58] Betty Powers, also from Texas, put it this way: "De massa say, 'Jim and Nancy, you go live together,' and when dat order give, it better be done. Dey thinks nothin' on de plantation 'bout de feelin's of de women."[59]

Rose Williams remembered how she had been forced to mate with a slave named Rufus.

. . . de massa come to me and say "You gwine live with Rufus in dat cabin over yonder. Go fix it for livin." I's 'bout sixteen years old and has no larnin', and I's just igno'mus chile. I's thought dat him mean for me to tend de cabin for Rufus and some other niggers. . . .

Now I don't like dat Rufus, 'cause he a bully. He am big and 'cause he so, he think everybody do what him say. We'uns had supper, den I goes here and dere talkin'; till I's redy for sleep and den I gits in de bunk. After I's in, dat nigger come and crawl in de bunk with me 'fore I knows it. I says, "What you means, you fool nigger?" He says for me to hush de mouth. "Dis am my bunk, too," he say.

"You's teched in de head. Git out," I told him, and I puts de feet 'gainst him and give him a shove and out he go on de floor 'fore he know what I's doin. Dat nigger jump up and he mad. He look like de wild bear. He starts for de bunk and I jumps quick for de poker. It am 'bout three foot long and when he comes at me I lets him have it over de head. Did dat nigger stop in he tracks? I's say he did. . . .

. . . . De nex' day I goes to de missy and tells her what Rufus wants and missy say dat am de massa's wishes. She say, 'Yous am de portly gal and Rufus am de portly man. De massa wants you-uns fer to bring forth portly chillen."

. . . . De nex' day de massa call me and tell me, "Woman, I's pay big money for you and I's done dat for de cause I wants yous to raise me chillens. I's put yous to live with Rufus for dat purpose. Now, if you doesn't want whippin' at de stake, you's do what I wants."

I thinks 'bout massa buyin' me offen de bloc and savin' me from bein' sep'rated from my folks and 'bout bein' whipped at de stake. Dere it am. What am I's to do? So I 'cides to do as de massa wish and so I yields.[60]

In the Old South, a master had the right to make and break slave marriages. He decided whether slaves could marry according to their choice or according to his choice or not at all. But a mistress, too, had some say about her house slaves and might intervene in their romantic affairs. She might chide a girl for fancying the wrong man, as one former male slave revealed in a mimicry of his mistress: " 'Who was that young man? How come you with him? Don't you ever let me see you with that ape again. If you cannot pick a mate better than that I'll do the picking for you.' "[61]

Other mistresses were less heavy-handed. One ninety-year-old former slave remembered: "White fo'ks ax us, 'What do yo'al say when ya court? We tell 'em we jest' laff an talk. Dey ax' us ef de boys ever ax us to kiss 'em an' marry dem. We sey, 'No Ma'am.' Dey say 'Yo'al don't know how to court,' den dey tell us how to court."[62]

"Courting" had meaning only for those slaves whose masters and mistresses treated them like human beings rather than livestock. Mandy Hadnot, an ex-slave from Texas, had the exceptional good fortune of belonging to a childless couple who raised her somewhat like their own child. She remembered: "When I's 16 year ole I want to hab courtin'. Mistus 'low me to hab de boy come right to de big house to see me. He come two mile every Sunday and us go to Lugene Baptist Church. Den she have Sunday dinner for both us." Later, when Mandy decided to marry, her mistress helped her fill a hope chest with sheets and a set of Sunday dishes.[63]

Although slave marriages were not legally recognized, weddings were nonetheless common and often conducted by the master of the house. A Mississippi planter described in his diary the ceremony he had employed for the marriage of seven slave couples. He asked each person if he or she agreed publicly to take the other party and to pledge to discharge the duties of husband or wife. Then he announced, "We have now gone through with every form necessary to authorize me to pronounce each of these several couples as man and wife." He then enjoined "according to the good old custom of our fathers and mothers, that each bridegroom now salute the bride."[64]

Historian Carl Degler noted that this ceremony, though influenced by the standard Christian model, did not call upon God to bless the union, nor did it ask the couple to remain faithful to one another forever. Such a vow would have been meaningless in a society where the master had the right to destroy the couple by selling off a husband or a wife.[65]

Virginia Bell, an ex-slave from Louisiana, described the process of marriage on her plantation: "Iffen any of the slave hands wanted to git married, Massa Lewis would git them up to the house after supper time, have the man and woman jine hands and then read to them outen a book. I guess it was the Scriptures. Then he'd tell 'em they was married but to be ready for work in the morning."[66] Another former slave from Louisiana told a similar story, except that her master was a trifle kinder to the new couple: "When a black gal marry, Marse marry her hisself in de big house. He marry 'em Saturday, so dey git Sunday off, too."[67]

In many other instances, a preacher performed the ceremony, sometimes in the big house and sometimes in church. Nancy King, a former slave from Texas, recalled that she had been married in church by a white preacher during the war. "Old Missie give me the cloth and dye for my weddin' dress and my mother spun and dyed the cloth, and I made it. It was homespun but nothin' cheap 'bout it for them days. After the weddin' massa give us a big dinner and we had a time."[68]

Another ex-slave from Texas fondly remembered the religious ceremony that bound her to a man of her own choosing: "My husband's name was David Henderson and we lived on the same place and belonged to the same man. No, suh, Master Hill didn't have nothin' to do with bringin' us together. I guess God done it. We fell in love, and David asked Master Hill for me. We had a weddin' in the house and was married by a colored Baptist preacher. I wore a white cotton dress and Missus Hill give me a pan of flour for a weddin' present. He give us a house of our own. My husband was good to me. He was a careful man and not rowdy."[69]

Although black weddings often followed the pattern of white ceremonies, from the white wedding dress to the reading of Scripture, there was one particular feature handed down from one generation of slaves to the next: the bride and groom jumped or stepped over a broom. The black custom of jumping over the broom—the equivalent of "tying the knot"—was prevalent throughout the South, though its exact origins are uncertain. Mary Reynolds, a former slave from Louisiana, left behind this picture of the broom ceremony. "[M]assa and missy marries us same as all the niggers. They stands inside the house with a broom held crosswise of the door and we stands outside . . . and we steps over the broom. Now that's all they was to the marryin'."[70] Cato Carter, an ex-slave from Alabama, made this wry observation about black marriages. "[M]ostly they jus' jumped over a broom and that made 'em married. Sometimes one the white folks read a li'l out of the Scriptures to 'em and they felt more married."[71]

Once married, a slave couple usually lived together in their own log cabin or shack, that is, if they belonged to the same master. Most spouses were able to share the same dwelling, but if they belonged to different owners, living together could be problematic. One ex-slave from Texas recalled that her father lived on a neighboring plantation and could come to see her mama only on Wednesday and Saturday nights. Another former slave said her husband had to go back to to his owners after the wedding, but was allowed to come to her on Saturday nights and stay overnight till Sunday.[72] Some husbands were allowed to visit only once every two weeks, but as one black woman remembered: "him sees us more often that that, 'cause him sneak off every time him have de chance."[73] Slaves, like free people, considered marriage a binding commitment; when the marriage was not interrupted through the death or sale of a slave, it was not uncommon for it to last twenty or more years, as historian Herbert Gutman has shown in his study of South Carolina plantation life.[74]

It is difficult to know how many slave brides were pregnant or already mothers when they married. Contemporary white witnesses suggested that most slave girls were sexually promiscuous by the time they were fifteen or sixteen, about the time of first menstruation for nineteenth-century American women. But Gutman's work offers a different interpretation of black female sexuality. He distinguishes between promiscuity and prenuptial intercourse leading to marriage when the girl became pregnant, following a common pattern in many premodern agricultural societies. And, based on responses from the American Freedmen's Inquiry Commission of 1863, he has come to the conclusion that "fidelity was expected from slave men and women after marriage."[75] Although we cannot know how many slaves lived up to that expectation, monogamous sexuality was reinforced in black communities by the slaves themselves, by their churches, and often by their masters and mistresses. Frances Butler Leigh, a former slave owner, observed shortly after 1865 that blacks "did not consider it wrong for a girl to have a child before she married, but afterwards were extremely severe upon anything like infidelity on her part."[76] Husbands, too, were expected to be monogamous, but were less stigmatized if they strayed.

The written and oral histories of former slaves suggest that marriage relations varied enormously from one couple to the next, not only because of external structures, but also because of interpersonal dynamics. There were stable unions and unstable unions; spouses bound by affection and spouses split by animosity; good marriages, bad marriages, and indifferent ones. Wives spoke of their former and present husbands with diverse sentiments, from love and gratitude to hatred and revulsion. Children, too, remembered their parents' marriages with a wide variety of emotions, though positive feelings tend to predominate, especially for mothers. In many instances the children simply did not know their fathers: "don't know nothin' bout my paw" was a common refrain in oral histories, often because the father had been sold when the child was small. When a father was present, he was the undisputed head of the family and commanded submission from his wife and children, just as white men did in their families.

Yet on the whole, mothers figure more prominently than fathers in slave narratives, for all the obvious reasons. Mothers were considered the essential parent by most slaves and their masters, and families tended to be matrifocal. In fact, if the Virginia paradigm can be applied to other states, it was common for masters compiling lists of slaves to identify a child by its mother, and rarely to add the name of the father.[77] Certainly during the first years of a baby's life, a mother was essential to its survival; all mothers breast-fed their babies, even when they were nursing white babies at the same time. As one mother memorably put it: "Sometimes I have a white'un pullin' de one side and a black one de other."[78] A nursing mother was dependent on the vagaries of her owner's whim as to whether she even had the time to breast-feed her own baby regularly. One slave assigned to field work sadly remembered: "I'd leave my baby cryin' in de yard."[79] Others like Charlotte Beverley from Texas were more fortunate. She painted the picture of a kindly mistress, with no children of her own, who saw to it that all the babies were properly cared for in a nursery. "Sometimes they's as many as fifty cradles with little nigger babies in 'em and the mistus, she look after them and take care of them, too. She turn them and dry them herself. . . . I'd blow the horn for the mudders of the little babies to come in from the fields and nurse 'em, in morning and afternoon."[80]

Whether they were wives or single women, with or without babies, female slaves were often subject to sexual advances from their masters and overseers. Betty Powers from Texas spoke bluntly on the subject: " 'De overseer and white mens took 'vantage of de women like dey wants to. De woman better not make no fus 'bout sich. If she do, it am de whippin' for her."[81] Anne Clark, a former slave from Mississippi, reported succinctly: "My mama had two white chillen by marster and they were sold as slaves."[82] Auntie Thomas Johns, only two when her mother was freed, heard tales during her childhood of her mother's Texas master, Major Odom, who was unmarried and "had a nigger woman, Aunt Phyllis she was called, that he had some children by." The major had a reputation for being good to his slaves, not only the five "nearly white" sons he had with Aunt Phyllis, but also the "nigger black" child she had with another man. "When she was drunk or mad she'd say she thought more of her black chile than all the others."[83]

Slave women who resisted their masters' sexual coercion could end up suffering even worse punishment than rape, as in the following story told by a former Virginia slave, Fanny Berry, about another slave named Sukie. "Ole Marsa was always tryin' to make Sukie his gal." One day when she was making lye soap and he approached her, "she gave him a shove an' push his hindparts down in de hot pot o' Soap. Soap was near to bilin', an' it burn him near to death. . . . Marsa never did bother slave gals no mo'." But a few days later Sukie was sent to the auction block.[84]

If a slave got up the courage to complain to her mistress, the latter might confront the man in question, but some wives were so intimidated by their husbands that they were too frightened to defend a sexually abused girl. Former slave Virginia Hayes Shepherd reported that when a slave named Diana asked her mistress to protect her from being raped by her husband, the mistress sympathized with the girl, but was afraid to confront him, lest he beat her and "pull her hair out."[85]

Harriet Jacobs, a teenaged slave, was so hounded by her master, Dr. Flint, that Mrs. Flint got whiff of his intentions and called the girl to her room for an inquiry. After making the girl swear on a Bible to tell the truth, Mrs. Flint commanded: "Now take this stool, sit down, look me directly in the face, and tell me all that has passed between your master and you." Harriet's account of the master's repeated attempts to seduce her brought tears and groans to her mistress's eyes. "She felt that her marriage vows were desecrated, her dignity insulted; but she had no compassion for the poor victim of her husband's perfidy."[86] Even though she promised to protect the girl, Mrs. Flint was so enraged and jealous that she ended up turning against the slave girl, as well as her husband.

The worst fear for a slave was that she or her husband or children might be sold separately, and the family broken up. One former slave girl from Maryland was terrified when her relatively decent master took her "to see how de mean slave owners raffles off de fathers and de husban's and de mothers and de wives and de chillen. He takes us 'round to de big platform and a white man git up dere with de slave and start hollerin' for bids, and de slave stands dere jus' pitiful like, and when somebody buy de slave all de folks starts yellin' and a cryin'."[87] Another remembered how her parents had been separated: "One mornin' we is all herded up and mammy am cryin' and say dey gwine to Texas, but can't take papa. He don't 'long to dem. Dat de lastes' time we ever seed papa."[88]

Fanny Kemble, an English actress married to a very wealthy American plantation owner, wrote movingly of her attempt to prevent the breakup of one slave family. She had come south with her two small daughters and her husband, Pierce Mease Butler of Philadelphia, heir to large slaveholding properties on two Georgia islands, in the winter of 1838–1839. From a stay of almost four months, she kept a journal (published in 1863) that included the following incident.

> *We have, as a sort of under nursemaid and assistant . . . a young woman named Psyche. . . . She cannot be much over twenty, has a very pretty figure, a graceful, gentle deportment, and a face which, but for its color (she is a dingy mulatto), would be pretty. . . . She has two nice little children under six years old. . . . [T]his poor woman is the wife of one of Mr. [Butler's] slaves, a fine, intelligent, active, excellent young man.*[89]

It turned out that Psyche and her husband belonged to different masters: while Joe belonged to Mr. Butler, Psyche and her children belonged to the overseer. Fanny Kemble was horrified to learn that her husband, wishing to please a departing administrator, "*had made him a present* of the man Joe," who would then be taken by his new owner to Alabama. Small wonder that Joe was in a state of frenzy, "his voice broken with sobs and almost inarticulate with passion, reiterating his determination never to leave this plantation, never to go to Alabama, never to leave his old father and mother, his poor wife and children."

Fanny appealed to her husband, "for his own soul's sake, not to commit so great a cruelty." Though he appeared unresponsive to her vehement entreaties (remember, she had been a famous actress!), the story ended well enough. Joe was not sent to Alabama, and Mr. Butler bought Psyche and her children from the overseer so the family could stay together. But as Fanny Kemble reflected, the situation would surely have ended differently "on plantations where there is no crazy Englishwoman to weep, and entreat, and implore, and upbraid for them, and no master willing to listen to such appeals."

Despite this incident of spousal reunification on the slave level, and spousal reconciliation on the level of their owners, the marriage of Fanny Kemble and Pierce Butler was not destined to survive. Their irreconcilable differences, not only on the question of slavery but also on the subject of marriage, were widely publicized ten years later in a bitter divorce. Mr. Butler claimed that the failure of his marriage was due to the "peculiar views which were entertained by Mrs. Butler on the subject of marriage . . . she held that marriage should be a companionship on equal terms." And in support of his statement, he published a letter she had written him much earlier in which she had contested the idea that he should have control over her. Mr. Butler's condemnation of the "the error of this principle of equal rights in marriage" merely reflected the received wisdom of his day, especially in the South.[90] When the couple was granted a divorce in 1849, he was awarded custody of the children in accordance with Anglo-American law and custom.

The story of Fanny Kemble belies simplistic interpretations of conjugal life in the South. It shows how one Englishwoman's attempts to subvert the system contributed to the loss of her husband and her children. It shows how white women's lives were intertwined with those of their slaves. And it shows that marriages—then as now—can become battlegrounds for spouses committed to opposing ideologies and different causes.

How many Victorian marriages were riven by such internal wars? Even today, when couples are less reluctant to advertise their discontents, it is very difficult to gauge the general level of marital discord. Anne Firor Scott, in her classic book *The Southern Lady*, listed a number of women's major grievances, including worries over continual childbearing and the oppressive weight of their domestic responsibilities, including the burden of owning and overseeing slaves.[91]

Some Southern women went so far as to publicly oppose the institution of slavery. In a February 1839 petition to the Georgia Legislature published in the *Savannah Telegraph*, 319 women expressed their prayers for the abolition of slavery throughout the state. A committee of the Georgia legislature called the petition "an unwarranted interference in subjects that should more properly belong to their fathers, husbands and brothers," and advised the women that it "would confer more real benefit upon society, if they hereafter confined their attention to matters of a domestic nature, and would be more solicitous to mend the garments of their husbands and children, than to patch the breaches of the laws and Constitution."[92]

Rebuffed in public and rebuked in private, Southern wives undoubtedly lived under conditions of patriarchal rule that would be unbearable today; yet it would be wrong to think that all or even most of these women were unhappily married. Scott's *Southern Lady* contains numerous examples of happy marriages based on the statements women wrote in their diaries, letters, and reminiscences. Fanny Moore Webb Bumpas wrote in her diary on March 9, 1842: "How comfortable! How great a happiness to have a companion, a partner of all joys & woes in whom entire confidence can be placed." Susan Cornwall Shewmake made the following entry on March 1, 1861: "Tomorrow will be thirteen years since my marriage. How swiftly time has flown and how full of happiness have these years been to me." A Georgia planter's wife expressed gratitude for her relatively long marriage: "God bless my precious husband and keep him at my side as long as I live. . . . We grow older but age only brings an increase of affection. We have joyed and sorrowed together for twenty-three years."[93] Of course, marital satisfaction varied, then as now, depending on the nature of the spousal relationship.

First-person accounts of long-term slave marriages, mainly in the form of oral history, are less sentimental, yet occasionally one finds an eloquent statement in the most simple language; for example, Minerva Wendy from Alabama speaking of her husband of fifty-nine years. "I's a June bride 59 years ago when I git married. De old white Baptist preacher name Blacksheer put me and dat nigger over dere, Edgar

Bendy, togedder and us been togedder ever since."[94] And long after slavery had ended, Caroline Wright from Texas was proud to assert: "Will and me has been married 'bout 75 years and is still married. It's disrespectful how de young folks treats marriage nowadays."[95]

Generally speaking, antebellum white wives in the South differed from Northern wives in their greater number of children, their dependence on slave labor, and such touted cultural features as "Southern hospitality." Yet however different the cultures of the South and the North, they had much in common. Both were regulated by English common law, with wives professing obedience to their husbands. Both were almost exclusively Christian and shared a belief in the higher destiny of white Anglo-Saxon Protestants as compared to the new immigrants from Ireland and other Catholic countries. Southern women with means went North to fashionable spas like Saratoga Springs, became friends with their Northern counterparts, and sometimes married their sons and brothers. Until the Civil War, there was no lack of intercourse between Northern and Southern families.

Many Northern and Southern couples lived in long-established settlements—burgeoning cities, towns, and small rural communities that

Elderly black couple in rural Virginia, 1899. Photo by by Frances Benjamin Johnston. (Library of Congress, Washington, D.C.)

were at least connected to each other by passable roads and regular mail. But as Americans migrated westward, they encountered primitive settings that challenged their resources and brought out qualities in women that would not have been called for, or even considered appropriate, in the East. There was no place for a frail and decorous wife on a farm in Indiana, not to mention the Oregon Trail. Physical strength, psychological endurance, courage, ingenuity, even some measure of independence were demanded from female pioneers.

SIX

Victorian Wives on the American Frontier

The story of the pioneers who settled the American Midwest and West is the rightful stuff of legend, so mythologized by survivors that it's often hard to untangle historical fact from stereotype and fiction. Our best records for the experience of married women are diaries, travel journals, letters, and memoirs—multifarious handwritten documents that have found their way into local archives, and which have only recently been systematically studied.[1]

Many aspects of their lives strangely recall the experiences of immigrants to America two hundred years earlier. For one thing, there was a high ratio of men to women. Men from the eastern states, Canada, and Europe often preceded the women, and then found themselves longing for feminine companionship. They sent back for their wives and sweethearts or ostentatiously welcomed any single woman brave enough to venture forth on her own.

A young man who had left his native Switzerland at the age of seventeen to homestead in Minnesota wrote to his family a few years later to send him a wife as soon as possible. She would have to be quite strong to care for the cows, pigs, and chickens, and keep house in the log cabin he had built, while he would be occupied with "man's work." After a two-year correspondence with the woman chosen by his parents, he met his bride for the first time in Saint Paul on June 4, 1858, at the end of her five-thousand-mile journey to America, and they married the very next day.[2]

Thousands of women responded to the call of the lonely frontiers-men, though few were so bold as one eastern woman who placed this advertisement in a Waterloo, Iowa, newspaper in 1860:

> *A young lady residing in one of the small towns of Central New York, is desirous of opening a correspondence with some young man in the West, with a view to a matrimonial engagement. . . . She is about 24 years of age, possesses a good moral character, is not what would be called handsome, has a good disposition, enjoys good health, is tolera-bly well-educated, and thoroughly versed in the mysteries of house-keeping.*[3]

Presumably her skills as a housekeeper would have made up for her deficiencies in looks.

Promotional pamphlets made a special appeal to women. One brochure noted, "Under the laws of Iowa no distinction is now made between husband and wife in the possession and enjoyment of prop-erty. One-third in value of all the real estate of the husband, in case of his death, goes to the wife as her property in fee-simple, if she survives him."[4] This 1870 declaration coincided with the Married Women's Property Act in England and reflected the laws enacted state by state in America that gave husbands and wives equal ownership of family assets, so it would have appealed to women aware of the new legisla-tion. But the old notion that a widow was entitled to only a third of the family property had not yet disappeared.

Most women, whether they settled in prairie or plains states, were initially shocked by the inhospitable conditions they encountered. The negative reaction of one early female settler in Illinois probably echoed that of many others: "When we got to the new purchase, the land of milk and honey, we were disappointed and homesick, but we were there and had to make the best of it."[5] Makeshift housing in cov-ered wagons, tents, lean-tos, shacks, and sod huts; dust storms and torrential rains, cyclones and floods, mud and dirt, grasshoppers, snakes, skunks, coyotes, wolves, and bears; the feared presence of Indians and white ruffians; the absence of churches, schools, and any other vestige of civilization—these were some of the major com-plaints women voiced. Few greeted their new homes with joy. Carrie Lassell Detrick remembered her mother's dismay at seeing their first

Kansas home: "When our covered wagon drew up beside the door of the one-roomed sod house that father had provided, he helped mother down and I remember how her face looked as she gazed about that barren farm, then threw her arms about his neck and gave way to the only fit of weeping I ever remember seeing her indulge in."[6]

Why then had these women been willing to uproot themselves from familiar settings, from family and friends and the comforts of stable communities, to hazard the great unknown? The simplest answer in most cases is that *they* did not make the decision. The decision to leave was made by their husbands. Since the husband was legally entitled to decide where his family would live, it would have been difficult for a wife to refuse to follow him, especially when he argued on the grounds of economic opportunity.

Mary Jane Hayden recalled the excitement about the discovery of gold in California and her husband's unilateral decision to go there with some other New England men. When she asked him what he proposed to do about her and their six-week-old baby, he answered, "Send you to your mother until I return." After an initial period of silence, Mrs. Hayden, "nearly heartbroken at the thought of the separation," could no longer hold her tongue.

> I said, "We were married to live together . . . and I am willing to go with you to any part of God's Foot Stool where you think you can do the best, and under these circumstances you have the right to go where I cannot, and if you do, you never need return for I shall look upon you as dead." He answered, "Well, if that is the way you feel about it I will not go." Mind you—no word of this was said in anger, for we had never differed in our two years of married life, and so it was settled that we should go the next year to the California gold mines.[7]

Mrs. W. B. Caton similarly accepted her husband's unilateral decision to move to Kansas in 1879: "To me it spelled destruction, desperadoes, and cyclones. I could not agree with my husband that any good could come out of such a country, but the characteristic disposition of the male prevailed."[8]

A poem titled "Overland 1852" gives expression to a commonly recognized difference in attitudes between husbands and wives:

He had a notion to go west,
  he was the restless sort
And Lord knows, land was scarce,
  and our money always short
Still I cried the day he told me,
  and I begged for us to stay
He only said we're goin'—
  it's best we don't delay.[9]

Once the journey was over and some form of rudimentary shelter had been established, husbands and wives set about struggling for existence on their new terrain. With no one to count on but themselves, a couple could not narrowly discriminate between "male" and "female" spheres. Wives were often obliged to participate in the traditionally male jobs of planting, harvesting, tending livestock, even hunting, and this shared work may have added to more egalitarian partnerships in a number of marriages. But for the most part, wives devoted themselves

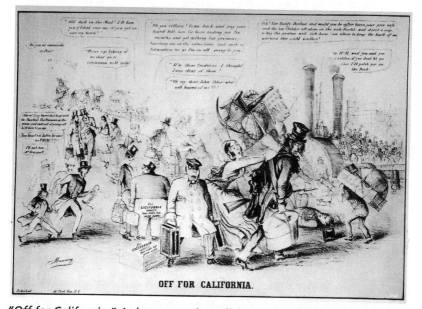

OFF FOR CALIFORNIA.

"Off for California." As her man takes off for California, his wife tries to hold him back, crying "Oh my dear John Peter what will become of me!!!" He responds, "To H-ll wid you and yer Childer, if you dont leg go o'me I'll pitch yer in the Dock." Gold Rush cartoon, circa 1849. (California Historical Society, San Francisco)

to indoor tasks that were similar from one state to the next: preparing food, cooking, sewing, mending, washing, ironing, tidying up, and making the home as attractive as possible with a minimum of articles. Perhaps a prized rocking chair or even a wooden tea caddie was given pride of place. And almost always, there was a baby at the breast or one on the way.

Children were generally welcome as extra labor, and families tended to be large. One study of childbirth in Missouri during this period indicates that the average family had a child every two to three years, and another study estimates an average of ten children per frontier family, though more conservative estimates are only slightly larger than the national norm.[10]

The Swiss couple mentioned earlier—Theodore and Sophie Bost— were pleased to announce the birth of a baby girl in 1859, a year after their marriage. Writing to his parents in Switzerland, the proud new father sent a detailed description of his wife's labor in Minnesota.

> *Dear Parents, thanks to God, Soso has her little girl Julie Adèle next to her, both in good health. She began to be sick Friday, the 19th at 3 o'clock in the morning and gave birth yesterday, the 20th, at 10 o'clock in the morning after very hard labor. She did not want the doctor to come to deliver her, and, against my wishes, we called for the neighborhood mid-wife; but at 2:30 in the morning, I sent for the doctor, who . . . thought it would be best to let nature take its course and didn't arrive till 10 o'clock. After his arrival, nature alone would not have been sufficient, and he had to make Soso suffer quite a bit until the arrival of Mademoiselle a half-hour later.[11]*

Not all wives were so lucky. Beyond the Mississippi, midwives were relatively scarce, and physicians even more so. Birthing mothers could not always count on assistance beyond that of another married woman, a husband, or older daughter. Sometimes, when a husband was detained away from home and a doctor, midwife, or neighbor unavailable, a woman had to give birth alone—surely a terrifying experience for any woman.

It was not just the physical dangers and hardships that oppressed frontier women, but also the psychological privations they endured. They wrote letters and diaries expressing their loneliness, isolation, homesickness, anxiety, despondency, grief, loss, and general misgivings. Mollie Dorsey Sanford (whose story will be told at length later in this chapter) wrote in her diary on October 22, 1860, from Colorado: "I am ashamed to be so homesick. Of course I do not *say* all that I inscribe here . . . I try to be cheerful for By's [her husband's] sake, for fear he might think I wasn't happy with him. He hasn't the family ties that I have and cannot understand."[12] The inability to communicate one's "morbid" feelings to a husband, even one as beloved and loving as Mollie's, made the sense of female isolation even stronger.

Women missed the families they had left behind and bemoaned the lack of female companionship. Whenever possible, they established links with other women, often traveling long miles to participate in a quilting bee, attend a wedding, or lend a hand in childbirth. In her old age, an Oregon woman remembered the female network that early settlers depended upon: "When I was a girl, if a woman got sick she didn't have to hire a trained nurse. Her neighbors came in, did the housework, took her children to their homes to care for till she was well, brought her home-made bread and jellies and other things. . . ."[13] In this respect, we are again reminded of women in colonial America.

But in another respect, nineteenth-century frontier women differed from their earlier forebears: they were not exclusively Anglo-Americans. In addition to immigrants from Canada, Mexico, and other parts of the United States, women traveled to the Midwest and West from most European nations, and later, at the turn of the century, from China and Japan. On the prairies, Scandinavians were the most numerous of the foreigners, and seem to have had an easier adjustment than either Southern or English women, perhaps because most of the Nordic women themselves had come from modest farms. Other immigrants from Ireland, Scotland, Wales, and Germany also seemed to make relatively quick adjustments, but much depended on what one had been used to in the old country. A German wife of the burgher class might well have missed the refinements of her past life, whereas an Irish country girl who had found a husband in America when they were both in service probably rejoiced at the opportunity to homestead, however primitive the conditions.

Because frontier women were ethnically diverse, they spoke different languages, had different customs, and practiced different religions. Protestants, Catholics, and a sprinkling of Jews inhabited the frontier, often in tight communities where women continued to speak their native languages with one another and shore up their particular religious beliefs and rituals. Many groups clung to their old-world traditions of courtship and marriage, even in the face of the freer American modes. European-born women who had crossed the Atlantic to escape the mandated dowries their parents could not afford were often glad to be guided by members of their ethnic communities in America, especially the married women responsible for steering them in the direction of eligible men. Russian immigrants in the Midwest, for example, continued the practice of arranged marriages, with the elder women sizing up a prospective bride by "pinching her strong forearms and noting the shine of her freshly scoured kitchen." Unlike the Russians, Italians quickly abandoned the practice of arranged marriage, and like most other Americans, married "for love," yet they continued to be wed within the Catholic church and to abide by its constraints on conjugal intimacy—no sex on fast days, feast days, or during pregnancy.[14]

Inevitably, the European immigrants were influenced by the predominant Anglo-American culture. Even if they worshiped on Sundays or Saturdays with members of their own faith, during the school season they sent their children to the one-room, coeducational schoolhouses that soon cropped up on prairie and plain, and from their children, if not from other American women, they learned the language and customs of their new homeland.

One type of woman that Euro-Americans rarely got to know were Native Americans. Pioneer wives were more likely to encounter Indian men, who boldly approached them for food, usually when their husbands were away from home. A study of these incidents in women's diaries, letters, memoirs, and novels shows that the Indians were almost always interested in acquiring food—a cooked meal, newly baked bread, or family staples. Contrary to the myth, the Indian men were not generally interested in carrying off scalps or female captives (though there were notorious exceptions), and they inspired virtually no fear of rape.[15] The pioneer women recording these incidents remembered they were frightened, but they managed, nonetheless, to feed the intruder and hold back their rage if he carried away precious provisions. This was considered the prudent thing to do.

Some pioneer women living in close proximity to Indian tribes—for example, the Northern Cheyenne in Montana—showed sympathy with their neighbors, though enduring friendships between women from the two groups were virtually nonexistent. A few accounts penned or told by the Indian women themselves describe tribal life as experienced by the squaws.

Princess Sarah Winnemucca Hopkins spent part of her adolescence in a white school and married two white men (the first marriage ended in divorce). Neither man seems to have had much influence on her adult life, which was devoted primarily to promoting the cause of her people, the Piautes. In 1883 she wrote an autobiography to acquaint Americans with the misfortunes the Piautes had suffered at the hands of the white man.[16] First they had been forced by the arrival of immigrants to move from Nevada to California; later they were herded onto reservations, where they were often swindled by corrupt administrators. She contrasted the present abuse and humiliation of the Piautes with an account of their earlier, idyllic history, including detailed descriptions of the rituals of courtship and marriage.

The girls are not allowed to get married until they have come to womanhood; and that period is recognized as a very sacred thing. . . . The young woman is set apart under the care of two of her friends, somewhat older, and a little wigwam, called a teepee, just big enough for the three, is made for them. . . . She goes through certain labors which are thought to be strengthening. . . . Every day, three times a day, she must gather, and pile up as high as she can, five stacks of wood. This makes fifteen stacks a day. At the end of every five days the attendants take her to a river to bathe. She fasts from all flesh-meat during these twenty-five days, and continues to do this for five days in every month all her life. At the end of the twenty-five days she returns to the family lodge, and gives all her clothing to her attendants in payment for their care. . . .

It is thus publicly known that there is another marriageable woman, and any young man interested in her, or wishing to form an alliance, comes forward, but the courting is very different from the courting of the white people. He never speaks to her, or visits the family, but endeavors to attract her attention by showing his horsemanship etc.

The courtship continues in silence for a year or longer. Even when the Indian brave enters the young woman's tepee, he does not speak to her or her grandmother, at whose side she sleeps. If she confides her interest in the young man to her grandmother, he is summoned by her father, who asks the brave if he really loves his daughter, and asks his daughter the same question. He reminds each of them of their duties as husband and wife. "She is to dress the game, prepare the food, clean the buckskins, make his moccasins, dress his hair, bring all the wood—in short, do all the household work."

Once the couple decides to marry, "a teepee is erected for the presents that pour in from both sides," and they prepare for the wedding ceremony.

> At the wedding feast, all the food is prepared in baskets. The young woman sits by the young man, and hands him the basket of food prepared for him with her own hands. He does not take it with his right hand; but seizes her wrist, and takes it with the left hand. This constitutes the marriage ceremony, and the father pronounces them man and wife. They go to a wigwam of their own, where they live till the first child is born. This event also is celebrated. Both father and mother fast from all flesh, and the father goes through the labor of piling the wood for twenty-five days, and assumes all his wife's household work during that time. . . . The young mothers often get together and exchange their experiences about the attentions of their husbands; and inquire of each other if the fathers did their duty to their children, and were careful of their wives' health.

While we can scarcely generalize about the experiences of other tribes on the basis of this one account, it does point to the importance of rituals marking significant passages in the life cycle, such as puberty, betrothal, marriage, and childbirth. It also points to the gender-specific obligations of husband and wife: Indian women, like their mainstream counterparts, were responsible for "all the household work," except, interestingly enough, during the respite they were granted for twenty-five days after childbirth. And if the husband didn't take over according to ritual, he was sure to be censured, at least by the female population.

*   *   *

The practice of gift giving as a part of the courting ritual was wide-spread among Indian tribes. A young brave might silently sling a deer at the entrance of his sweetheart's tepee. If his courtship found favor, the gifts were accepted. He would also make gifts to the young woman's family—furs, feathers, livestock—and pay a "bride price" amounting to fifty horses or a pile of blankets. Among the Karok Indians, marriage was considered illegal without such payment, and among some coastal tribes, children born to a couple who had wed without abundant gifts would be thought of as bastards.[17]

Native American marital arrangements varied from tribe to tribe. Some allowed for cohabitation before marriage, some did not. Some practiced monogamy and some practiced polygamy. In polygamous tribes, like the Blackfoot, the first wife was honored as the "sits-beside-him" spouse, and reigned over any additional brides. The Fox Indians would bring a couple's younger sister into their sleeping area, where she remained until she was old enough to become the husband's second wife. In matrilineal tribes, a woman could try out one man after another until she chose the one she wanted permanently.

Most tribes expected fidelity and severely punished an unfaithful wife by maiming or expelling her. An adulterous Apache wife was liable to have her nose and her ears cut off. But wife sharing was another matter. This was considered courteous behavior in certain tribes, as in the Pueblo culture, especially during religious rites.

Mixed marriages with white men, while not encouraged, were not taboo. In the early 1800s, trappers and traders often took Indian brides, who were valuable helpmeets in many ways. They could translate between whites and Native Americans, ward off raids, prepare meals on the run, and help with hunting, curing hides, and repairing equipment.

Though many white men did not bother to legalize their mixed-blood relationships, others sought out the services of Protestant ministers or Catholic priests. The legendary trapper Andrew Garcia and his Pend d'Oreille bride were married by a Catholic priest when he was twenty-three and she nineteen.[18] He had slept apart from her until the day when, to the amazement of his fellow trappers, he put a ring on her finger and promised to be a model husband. These early mixed-blood marriages remind us that American history has been, since the arrival of the white man, a story of multiple cultures coexisting and intermingling.

In the annals of American history, no legend is greater than that of the women and men who traveled across the prairies, plains, and mountains to reach the far west. It has been estimated that around 350,000 pioneers traveled on the Oregon and California Trails from 1841 to 1867.[19] The Oregon Trail was known as the "family trail," since it was favored by married men with wives and children, whereas single men were more likely to take the southern route to California, lured by the promise of gold and adventure.

ON TO OREGON

The first American families to travel west to Oregon were four missionary couples in 1838, and among them Elkanah Walker and Mary Richardson Walker. From Mary's diaries and letters, we are able to piece together a remarkable story.[20] In the first place, Mary's union with Elkanah was orchestrated by the Missionary Board after her request to become a missionary on her own had been turned down. Mary had studied at the Maine Wesleyan Seminary for three years beginning in 1830 when she was nineteen, but since no unmarried women were sent to foreign missions, it was only as the wife of a missionary that she would be able to accomplish her goal. Enter Elkanah Walker, a six-foot-four, shy, awkward seminarian in need of a wife. Though Mary had had several other suitors (one in particular to whom she was greatly attracted but rejected because he was an "infidel"), she quickly came to an agreement with Elkanah and waited for him to finish his studies before they married and were sent from her native Maine to Missouri and from there through Indian lands all the way to Oregon. Such a journey into alien territory required a passport issued by the War Department.

In Missouri, they gathered together with three other honeymoon couples and joined a caravan with twenty-five horses and mules. Their provisions included flour, rice, sugar, pepper and salt, which was expected to last until they reached buffalo country and could live largely on fresh buffalo meat. By the time they reached that part of the journey, Mary was worn-out and discouraged. One diary entry reads: "I have a great deal I wish to write. But I am so tired. We have two tents about eight feet by twelve. Have a curtain to separate the families. . . . Mr. and Mrs. Smith are sleeping loudly in the other part of this tent. Mr. Walker lies by my side telling me I have written enough."

In addition to the sheer physical fatigue and lack of privacy, Mary had to put up with her husband's difficult nature. She complained to her diary: "Should feel so much better if Mr. W. would only treat me with some cordiality. It is so hard to please him I almost despair of ever being able to. If I stir, it is forwardness; if I am still, it is inactivity. I keep trying to please, but sometimes I feel it is no use." Shortly thereafter, she "had a long bawl," which seems to have made some impression on Elkanah, for she noted: "Today he has been very kind."

The strains of a three-thousand-mile trip that lasted over six months were both external and internal, some probably engendered by Mary's pregnancy, though, out of Victorian discretion, she never mentioned that fact. In Oregon, a few months after their arrival, she gave birth to the first of seven sons, and like most mothers in most times and places, the first-born was an occasion for unmitigated joy. Her description of the birth reflects a full panoply of feelings: fear, pain, fortitude, relief, and happiness.

> *About nine I became sick enough. Began to feel discouraged, felt as if I almost wished I'd never been married. But there was no retreating. Meet it I must. About eleven I became quite discouraged. . . . But just as I supposed the worst was yet to come, my ears were saluted by the cry of my child. 'A son' was the salutation. Soon I forgot my misery in the joy of possessing a proper child. In that evening my husband returned with a thankful heart and plenty of kisses for me and my boy.*

Missionary wives, like Mary Richardson Walker, helped their husbands spread the Word among the various Indian tribes from the Sioux in the Dakotas, to the Nez Percés in the Northwest, and to other tribes such as the Winnebagos and the Kickappos in the far West. Of the 270 Presbyterian men sent to convert Native Americans between 1838 and 1869, only one of them was a bachelor. Because church politics insisted that a missionary should have a wife, not having one could be a distinct disadvantage for an aspiring cleric. As one Oregon missionary complained after he was refused a church position in Alaska: "That made the third time I have missed a good appointment because I did not have a wife."[21]

The story of Mary Richardson Walker has found its way into official history by virtue of her role as the wife of one of the first Christian missionaries in the Northwest. But there are many, many other stories of anonymous, or scarcely known women, who left behind no record at all or only a fragmentary one. Such was the case of Kitturah (Kit) Penton Belknap, a midwestern farm woman, whose journey to Oregon was vividly recorded in a few choice diary pages. Before leaving the state of Iowa with her husband George, she had borne four children and lost three of them. Her surviving son was one year old when she wrote in her journal in October 1847: "Now we have one little baby boy left. So now I will spend what little strength I have left getting ready to cross the Rockies."[22]

Preparation for the journey included making "four muslin shirts for George and two suits for the little boy (Jessie)," as well as "a piece of linen for a wagon cover and some sacks." Sewing the husband's shirts, the boy's suits, and food sacks is not surprising, but the thought of making the top of a covered wagon does give one pause! A few words picture the husband at her side during these preparations: "will spin mostly evenings while my husband reads to me." Husbands reading aloud to wives and children is one activity that regularly appears in the records of pioneer families. Kit's laconic entry suggests an affectionate relationship between the spouses; at least she did not refer to him as "Mr. Belknap," using the formula that proper middle-class wives employed when mentioning their husbands in letters, diaries, memoirs, and even in their speech.

When the Belknaps set out on their long journey, they traveled with five other families, each with one or two wagons and eight oxen to a wagon. Each wagon no larger than four by ten feet had to contain the entire provisions for a six months' journey. Kit filled her cloth sacks and wooden boxes (that would later serve as table tops and chests) with flour, cornmeal, "dried apples and peaches, beans, rice, sugar and coffee." Her spirit was decidedly hopeful as she anticipated the use of every possible inch of space. "There is a corner left for the wash-tub and the lunch basket will just fit in the tub. The dishes we want to use will all be in the basket. I am going to start with good earthen dishes and if they get broken have tin ones to take their place. Have made 4 nice little table cloths so am going to live just like I was at home."

The grueling trip ahead did indeed test Kit's optimism. Judging from her account and from those left by numerous men and women, no one survived the voyage unscathed. The experience of the death of fellow travelers, often babies and sometimes mothers in childbirth; of infectious diseases like typhoid, dysentery, smallpox, and the dreaded cholera; of windstorms and eye-burning dust; of skin infections and broken bones; of thirst and hunger under unforgiving skies; of heart-breaking separations with those who could not keep pace with the others or died en route—none of these memories could be forgotten.

At one point, when her son was "very sick with Mountain Fever," Kit Belknap was afraid she would lose her only remaining child. She kept a permanent record of her worst fear: "I thot in the night we would have to leave [the little boy] here and thot if we did I would be likely to stay with him." Fortunately, daylight brought "fresh courage."

Continuing on her journey and nursing her sick baby, Kit never mentioned that she was also—once again—pregnant. Being pregnant was a subject few women mentioned in writing; even letters to close family members referred to the subject so euphemistically that today's reader could easily miss the allusion. Though Kit Belknap's account of her journey ended on the Trail, we know from other sources that she and her small family made it to Oregon, where her new baby was born, and where she and her husband raised five children, before he died in 1897 and she in 1913.

The "Notes by the Wayside en Route to Oregon" left by Lydia A. Rudd document the constant presence of sickness and death along the Oregon trail. On May 9, 1852, she noted: "We passed a new made grave today dated May 4th, a man from Ohio. We also met a man that was going back; he had buried his wife. She died from the effects of measles."[23] Without his spouse, this unnamed man was apparently too despondent to continue the journey on his own. This was the case of numerous other "go-backs" after the death of a family member along the route.

On June 23, it was a member of Lydia's caravan who succumbed.

"Mr. Giftman died last night about 11 o'clock. He has left a wife without any relatives, but there are two fine men that was in company with her husband and brother that will take good care of her." The young widow would not want for suitors.

Over and over, Lydia Rudd recorded cases of illness, accident, and death. At one point she cried out poignantly, "Sickness and death in the States is hard but it is nothing to be compared with it on the plains."

The hardships pioneers endured on the trail did not necessarily end when they got to their destination. Elvina Apperson Fellows left a memoir documenting the horrors she suffered as a child bride in early Oregon.[24] After her father had died crossing the plains, her mother was left with "nine hungry mouths to fill in addition to her own." Arriving in Portland, the mother took in washing from the ships at dock and then started a boardinghouse. Difficult as her mother's lot was, it was nothing compared to her daughter's in her first marriage, as Mrs. Fellows told it in old age:

> In 1851 Mother was pretty hard run to earn enough money for us to live on, so when a man named Julius Thomas, a cook in a restaurant, offered to marry me, Mother thought I had better take him, so I did. He was 44 and I was 14.
>
> Back in 1851—that is 70 years ago—we had slavery of Negroes in the South, and we had slavery of wives all over the United States. . . . What could a girl of 14 do to protect herself from a man of 44, particularly if he drank most of the time, as my husband did? I still shudder when I think of the years of my girlhood, when I had to live with that husband. When he was drunk he often wanted to kill me, and he used to beat me until I thought I couldn't stand it.
>
> One time he came to my mother's house, where I had taken refuge. I locked the door. He tried to climb in at the window, but I held it down. This enraged him so, he took out his pistol and shot at me. The bullet passed just above my head. The glass fell on me and scared me so I dropped to the floor. He looked in, saw me lying on the floor, and, thinking he had killed me, put the end of the pistol barrel into his mouth and pulled the trigger and I was a widow.

Eventually, at the ripe age of twenty, Elvina met and married a "a fine man," Edward Fellows, a steamboat engineer, with whom she lived for the next half century.

A WESTERN ROMANCE

One of the most uplifting documents left by a pioneer woman are the journals kept by Mollie Dorsey Sanford between 1857 and 1866 in Nebraska and Colorado.[25] She began her journal at the age of eighteen in March 1857, as her family prepared to leave Indianapolis for Nebraska City. It is clear from the start that Mollie was a high-spirited, intelligent, young woman, who had received a decent education and a good Christian upbringing. She stated unequivocally: "We are a happy family," and, indeed, throughout the next three years with her mother, father, and seven younger siblings, Mollie's diary portrayed close and congenial family ties.

The family traveled by train from Indianapolis to St. Louis, then by boat to Nebraska. The trip took two weeks, during which Mollie made many acquaintances, including a "charming" young bride on her way to California and a young woman named Libbie whom Mollie was "fascinated with." When Libbie left the boat, Mollie confided to her diary: "She knows I love her. She is actually the most interesting girl I have ever met." It was not inappropriate for Victorian girls to express strong feelings for each other, to kiss one another, and exchange other tokens of affection.

By summer the family was homesteading in Nebraska on their own farm. This was to be an idyllic period in Mollie's life. Despite wind and thunder storms and the sparseness of their life, Mollie wrote mainly of glorious sunsets and spacious elm trees and the "bosom of the broad prairie." And her days were certainly enlivened by the man who was to become her husband.

Mollie had been advised by a friend to "set her cap" for Mr. By Sanford, a newcomer to Nebraska City from Indiana. When she first saw him, on May 5, she wrote in her diary, "I had a glimpse of him as I came out of the store today. A good-looking enough fellow." Then she added: "I do not know whether I will *ever* love any man well enough to marry him or not. If by the time I am twenty-one, I find a good sensible fellow that won't talk silly flattery, I may transfer my maiden heart to his keeping. . . . I so soon tire of the gentlemen, that is, if they get *too* sentimental."

Their three-year courtship proceeded with an ease that derived equally from their two affable characters and the freer circumstances of frontier society. As Mollie noted on June 29, 1857: "It is refreshing to meet a fellow like him after seeing so many flattering fops. It is wonderful how free and easy people become in this country." By October 15, when By had become a "hero" with her newly arrived grandparents by helping them after an accident, Mollie mused: "Grandma has taken it into her dear old head that he is my lover, and . . . I believe he is myself. I knew today when he came, and I had not seen him for so long, that I cared a great deal for him. We girls and he sat in the empty covered wagon until midnight last night talking and singing, and some way he found my hand and held it long and tenderly. No one knew it, unless my telltale face has betrayed me today."

Four months later, By moved to the level of a stolen kiss. In Mollie's words: "By has been to see me again. He looks splendidly, and his visit did me so much good. One night while here we went up to Grandpa's to spend a while. As we walked along the path admiring the starry heavens, he called my attention to a particular star, and as I turned to look, he kissed me on the cheek! It was *dreadfully* impertinent! and I tried to feel offended. He said he 'knew it was wrong and would take it back,' but someway, after all, I kept it, to think of, and it burns on my cheek ever since." However free from external constraints, Victorian courtship had inner ones that ruled out greater physical intimacy.

On March 1, 1858, Mollie received her first written declaration from By, which she confided to her journal. "I no longer stand in doubt. I have had a letter, a *sweet* letter. . . . By loves me tenderly, truly, and has asked my heart in return, and I know now that I can place my hand in his, and go with him thro life, be the path smooth or stormy. I feel like trusting him, more than any lover I ever had. No doubt or misgiving comes into my heart, and I have told him so. We did not fall madly in love as I had always expected to, but have gradually 'grown into love.' I hope that is an evidence that it will be lasting and eternal."

In June they became officially engaged, but without "definite plans for the future." By seems to have had a number of different ways of earning his livelihood, ranging from "teaming" to investing in lots. Mollie worked for several months as a seamstress under the direction of a married woman in Nebraska City. Always levelheaded, she wrote on June 1, 1859: "I will not marry until I am twenty-one, and by that time, we will be all ready with a home of our own. We will both work for that consummation."

There is a telling entry for February 15, 1859: "I had my 'valentine' from By and two or three from other sources. Sometimes I wish By was a little more demonstrative, a trifle more sentimental. He is very matter-of-fact, and yet I presume if he were, I would soon tire of him. *I know that he loves me, and that is enough for a sensible girl.*" Valentines were already in vogue in England and America, and could be sent not only by acknowledged sweethearts but also by scarcely known acquaintances as a way of indicating interest.

That spring Mollie opened a little school for twenty pupils aged six to nine, and every Sunday she met her fiancé, noting on May 15: "He is looking splendidly and *I love him more and more.*" Despite the attention of several other men, all with better financial prospects than By, Mollie remained true to her love.

Finally, in 1860, Mollie and By were married. On February 13, she wrote excitedly that By and his brother had gone "to Tecumseh, the county seat, to procure the license, since that legal document is necessary in this territory to fasten the nuptial tie. . . . I baked my own wedding cake and everything is prepared for the wedding at 2 o'clock P.M. tomorrow." But things did not proceed as she had planned. The account of her wedding day, penned a few days later, tells us a good deal about the uncertainties of life on the frontier.

> *Our wedding did not pass as quietly as I anticipated. Tuesday morning we were busy with preparations for dinner, receiving and entertaining our guests, and it is something to do that in as small quarters as we occupy. We were looking for By every moment, but after 10 o'clock I began to feel nervous. . . . Twelve! One! Two! Three! o'clock came, and no bridegroom. Many jokes were indulged in at my expense. I was fluctuating between hope and fear, but never doubting but that he was unavoidably delayed. . . . At three o'clock the folks were about starved and it was decided we 'eat, drink, and be merry.' . . . After the dinner was ended and evening approached, I could hardly stand the suspense.*

I would steal off and weep and pray, and come to the house and smile and be gay.

It wasn't until nighttime that Mollie heard the horse hoofs of her "truant lover" and hurried her "nearly frozen" sweetheart into the house. Somehow they managed to turn disaster into merriment by donning their wedding clothes in secret and suddenly appearing before their long-suffering guests. Mollie relates the finale with glee.

> *We came and stood outside the door, ready for the signal from Uncle Milton. Aunt stepped into where the company were, and said, 'We will not wait for Mr. Sanford any longer. Come out to prayers.' All marched solemnly into the kitchen. At a signal, the door opened, and stepping in, the ceremony was immediately begun, and Byron N. Sanford and Mary E. Dorsey were made man and wife together. Such a storm as followed, kisses and exclamations of surprise. Some of the best of the dinner had been preserved, and willing hands soon had a wedding supper with a genuine Bride and Groom at their posts of honor.*
>
> *And we were married in the kitchen! Start not! ye fairy brides. Beneath your veils and orange blossoms, in some home where wealth and fashion congregate, your vows are no truer, your heart no happier, than was this maiden's, in the kitchen of a log cabin in the wilderness of Nebraska. Time may change and I may have more attractive surroundings, and I may smile at this primitive wedding. I only trust my heart may ever be as brave and true as then and as happy as now.*

Her future would indeed try that hope severely.

Within two months of their marriage, Mollie and By left Nebraska and her beloved family for a new life in Colorado, where there were said to be more opportunities for an enterprising young man. It was a punishing trip, twenty miles per day under heat, rain, and wind, with sickness and accident looming at every stage of the way. Mollie noted on June 14, "I have been a bride four months tonight, but I'm too tired to expatiate much about it. The weather is so hot and we are so dusty and dirty. In fact we are about sick, all of us. Even the cattle and ponies seem drowsy. We have decided to rest for one day. Rest? Where *is* rest for us!"

Mollie and By's ten-week journey from Nebraska City to Denver was by no means as grueling as that of other pioneers who made the five- or six-month trek from Missouri to the Pacific Coast, but it was grueling enough. Arriving in Denver, where there were about five thousand people, Mollie and By camped with other "pilgrims" from the States. By worked again at teaming and devised "some sort of contrivance to be run by water power to grind the rocks to get the gold." Mollie took up sewing, for which she got "fabulous prices." Her hens kept her supplied with eggs, which she exchanged for meat, vegetables, and milk. It was an improvised life that called for ingenuity and a stout heart.

Soon they moved into a mountain cabin at Gold Hill, a small mining camp northwest of Boulder. For a time, Mollie became cook for the miners, a position she found "degrading"; she was "ashamed to be so homesick." December 17, on her twenty-second birthday, she was grateful mainly that she was still alive. February 14, on the first anniversary of her marriage, she was alone in their mountain cabin "so sorry to have By away." Finally, as on her wedding day, By appeared late at night. "He had walked 10 miles over that lonely road just to be with me on our first anniversary, and if anyone, or if I myself, ever thought him devoid of sentiment, that decides that he is not. He is lying on the bed resting, and I so happy I had to tell my Journal."

Mollie and By's vicissitudes continued for several years. One of the most traumatic events was the loss of their firstborn, "a beautiful boy" taken quickly by God "to his fold." Once again, Mollie felt lucky that her own life had been spared. For a time during the Civil War, By was a soldier with the Colorado Volunteers, and the couple settled into army barracks. On their second wedding anniversary, Molly wrote:

> *Two years married! We spent the afternoon in talking over the old times, bringing up each reminiscence of our lives since we first met. We have passed thro many vicissitudes and had some trials and hardships in our brief married life, but they have only cemented our hearts more closely together. We love and live for each other.*

Theirs was a true love story, a model romance for the ages, and one that ended well. In September 1862, Mollie gave birth to a second baby boy, "a marvel . . . of loveliness," who was later joined by a sister. By became an employee with the United States Mint in Denver, where he remained for forty years. Both Mollie and By lived into the twentieth century, he dying at eighty-eight and she at seventy-six. She was remembered by her family as a "tower of strength."

MARRIED LIFE IN THE SOUTHWEST

From the letters, diaries, and memoirs of many pioneers who went west along the California Trail, we are able to reconstruct the daily experiences of husbands and wives in early Southwestern mining communities. While the men panned for gold, their spouses took on all sorts of work. They ran boardinghouses, provided laundry service, became cooks, knitted woolen socks for the miners, and tended other people's children. It was possible for women to make money as they never had before.

Mary Ballou's letters to her son from a mining camp in California contained picturesque descriptions of her culinary feats in the makeshift kitchen of a primitive boardinghouse. She wrote in October 1852: "I will try to tell you what my work is here in this muddy Place. All the kitchen that I have is four posts stuck down into the ground and covered over the top with factory cloth no floor but the ground."[26] From this kitchen she provided an amazing variety of food:

> . . . somtimes I am making mince pie and Apple pie and squash pies. Somtimes frying mince turnovers and Donuts. I make Buiscuit and now and then Indian jonny cake and then again I am making minute puding filled with rasons and Indian Bake pudings and then again a nice Plum Puding and again I am Stuffing a Ham or pork that cost forty cents a pound. . . . Three times a day I set my Table which is about thirty feet in length and do all the little fixings about it such as filling pepper boxes and vinegar cruits and mustard pots and Butter cups. Somtimes I am feeding my chickens and then again I am scareing the Hogs out of my kitchen and Driving the mules out of my Dining room.

Her list of dishes continued: "I made a Bluberry puding to day for Dinner. Somtimes I am making soups and cramberry tarts and Baking chicken that cost four Dollars a head and cooking Eggs at three Dollars a Dozen. Somtimes boiling cabbage and Turnips and frying fritters and Broiling stake . . . and I cook squrrels."

In addition: "somtimes I am taking care of Babies and nursing at the rate of Fifty Dollars a week." Or she made items to be sold—soap, mattresses, sheets and flags (one Whig, one Democrat). Or she was busy washing the floor, scouring candle sticks, or separating quarreling men. Having left her beloved children behind so she could accompany their father west, Mrs. Ballou found herself "tired and almost sick" in a Californian Tower of Babel "among French and Duch and Scoth and Jews and Italions and Sweeds and Chineese and Indians and all manner of tongus and nations." Perhaps to reassure her son, she added, "but I am treated with due respect by them all." This energetic, humorous, unschooled woman appears to have transported the indomitable spirit of the Wife of Bath eight thousand miles from Canterbury all the way to the Pacific Coast. It staggers the imagination to think what she would have done with a Cuisinart!

A more literate version of life in a mining town fifteen years later shows how middle-class women could live in a style not so very distant from their sisters in the East.[27] Rachel Haskell, the wife of a toll-keeper in Aurora, Nevada, allowed herself the luxury of staying in bed on a Sunday morning because the ministers (both of them) were sick. She breakfasted at noon, washed her boys ("a good scouring all over"), and lay on the sofa reading a book. Her husband, always referred to as Mr. H., warmed the supper on the stove, and she washed the dishes. Afterward, "Came to sitting room, sat on a stool near piano while Ella [her daughter] accompanied songs by the family in chorus. Drew table in front of stove, resumed reading of 'Light' while children with bright happy faces filled up the gaps. Mr. H. after playing on floor with two younger ones lay on the lounge and read." It is an idyllic picture of domestic happiness, that could have come straight out of the pages of *Godey's Lady's Book*.

Monday, Mrs. H. gave Ella music lessons and practiced the multiplication table with her sons. Tuesday, she baked bread, "papered John's shelves nicely," and prepared a boiled dinner. Wednesday, she went calling on her friends in town. "Dressed in silk shirt and red waist, hat and red shawl. Had rather a hard tramp through snow. Called on Mrs. Levy, quite a pleasant chat and looked at her numerous sisters nine I think and fine portraits of her father and mother from Strasbourg on the Rhine. Went next to Mrs. Poors met Mrs. C. there. Would have me

Sentimental image of domestic life, from Godey's Lady's Book, May, 1859.

stay and spend afternoon. Sent for Mr. H. to eat supper and we had a lively pleasant time till dark." At Mrs. Cooper's there were several other guests, "and the jest ran high and the laughter loud." Returning home, Mr. and Mrs. H. found the little ones well taken care of by the older siblings, "John with Maney in his arms asleep." Sociability in mining camps had a high priority, since all the inhabitants were separated from their original families. In general, white newcomers, if they were not blatantly poor or eccentric, could count on a warm welcome, regardless of ethnicity and religion. Mrs. Levy, for example, was probably one of the Jewish settlers, who generally met with little prejudice in the Southwest.

Only one subject seemed to trouble Mrs. Haskell: her husband had the habit of spending many evenings in town with other men. One entry in her diary reads: "Mr. H. went up town with them, staid very late. I fell asleep on sofa waiting for him, but waked to find he had not yet come. Went to bed and fell asleep. Getting so blunted now on that subject it don't keep me awake, suffering in mind as formerly." Another entry starts with "Waked with rather a forlorn, angry feeling at heart" and ends with "Mr. H. seems much more affectionate."

Despite Rachel Haskell's concerns about her husband, they seem to have enjoyed a warm, companionate relationship bound by ties of affection to each other, to their children, and to their friends. Far from the cultural refinements of Boston or Charleston, this woman in the middle of a desert state seems to have found fulfillment in the roles of wife, mother, housekeeper, and friend.

When the pioneers pushed west, they came in contact with the Hispanic communities of California, New Mexico, and Texas. Protestants were often intrigued by the Spanish Catholic traditions so different from their own. California girls, carefully watched over by matrons with bright garments and tortoiseshell combs, were often married between the ages of thirteen and fifteen. Most marriages, especially in patrician families, were arranged, and most youth tended to abide by the conventions of their people. Girls amassed a hope chest according their means, grooms paid a dowry price—sometimes as much as a roll of gold coins—and priests sealed the marriage in a hallowed religious ceremony. The fiesta accompanying a wedding was renowned for its high-spirited mix of drink, music, dance, food, and general merriment.[28]

But not all women were happy with the practice of early marriage. The oral narratives recorded by Hubert Howe Bancroft in the 1870s contain examples of wives denouncing the earlier "hateful" custom of forcing very young girls to take on marital responsibilities before they were ready for them. Maria Inocent Pico de Avila, a member of the wealthy influential Pico family in Los Angeles, remembered bitterly:

> *Many girls never even finished these few studies, because their mothers nearly always took them from school to marry them off, because there was the bad custom of marrying girls very young, when they were called for. I only stayed in school until my fourteenth year; then my mother took me to the ranch to prepare me to work, and at 15 years and 8 months of age I was married.*[29]

With the arrival of more and more pioneers after the American conquest of the Southwest (1846–1848), there were more and more mixed unions. Many of these were "free union" marriages between male settlers and working-class Hispanic or Native American women. U.S. Army soldiers might sign conjugal contracts with the laundresses attached to their camps, but when they were discharged, there was nothing to prevent them from abandoning their common-law wives.

Among the Spanish elite, courting and marriage were elaborate rituals pitting Anglo and Hispanic gentlemen against one another for the hand of a prized wife. The letters of James Henry Gleason to his sister in the East bear witness to his efforts, ultimately successful, to wed a wealthy Spanish-speaking beauty.[30]

Monterey 30 May 1847
Night 11 o'clock
My affectionate Sister . . .
I have popped the question for the hand of that lovely girl Catarina Watson her parents wish me to wait for 18 months and then ask for her again as she is too young to marry only 14 years of age. She tells me that she will have me and none other. . . .
Her father is worth about 40,000$. I am now enjoying the happiest days of my life. . . .

Monterey Nov'r 15, '49
Dona Francesca Gleason, Plymouth
My dear sister
Well Fanny I'm married. My bonny Kate is now reclining over my shoulder. . . . I was married on the 7th of Oct at 3 Oc in the morning. A large dinner party was given by my father at his house in the afternoon and a dance followed in the evening. the expenses must have been nearly $1000. . . .

San Francisco Mar 31, 1850
My dear sister
My wife tells me to say that as she cannot write in English. You must excuse her and as a token of her deep affection . . . she will send a pina scarf . . . they are valued here at 125.$ each. She will also send her Deguerotype in her bridal dress and reclining on a harp as she was at a moment on the marriage eve. . . .

San Francisco, July 1, 1850
My dear sister Fanny
. . . I left my wife well in Monterey & should nothing occur to frustrate the workings of nature I shall be a Father in a few months, and then I am going home partly to see my old acquaintances and relations

& partly to get clear of a squalling baby. I like babys very much but not untill they arrive at a certain age. . . .

What I would give to have the musings of Catarina Watson Gleason during this same period! However enchanted she was with her suitor, did she live to regret marriage to a man who was obviously attracted as much by her fortune as by her good looks, and who was admittedly uncomfortable at the thought of a crying babe?

Marriages between Anglos and Hispanics at every level of society in the Southwest continued unabated from the moment of annexation onward. Within a generation, the practice of interethnic marriage was well on its way to producing the mixed-blood Latino-American population we know today.

The history of the men and women who braved the arduous journey to the North and Southwest has become part of the American heritage. But what of the people left beyond, the fiancées and wives who waited to be sent for? What do we know of their destinies?

A quilt, pieced together by Mary Carpenter Pickering in Ohio, speaks eloquently for the years she waited for John Bruce Bell, after he had gone to Oregon in 1850. Intricately embroidered and appliquéd with baskets and flowers, the quilt must have taken at least four years to make, according to quilt historian Marie Bywater Cross.[31] After eight years in the West, John returned, and the couple was married on September 3, 1861. By then, Mary had reached the ripe age of thirty. She and her husband started a family in Ohio, but moved as far West as Iowa in 1864.

A twenty-seven-page diary remains from the pen of Maria Abagail Henry Adams, who stayed with her small son in Dublin, New Hampshire, after her husband, Charles Wilson Adams, went to California. Between January 1860 and July 1861 she carefully noted the daily vicissitudes of the weather ("pleasant," "rained," "snowed," "blustering," "another cloudy dull day") along with the humdrum details of small-town life in New England (church attendance, weddings, funerals, blueberrying, drying apples, occasional sicknesses, visits to and from her relatives and friends).

Yet punctuating these sober entries are cries of longing for her distant husband. "Oh if I could only see him tonight. I feel so lonely. I feel

A Spanish colonial family, circa 1800. Anonymous painting from Mission San Diego de Alcala Museum. Copyright Kathleen Cohen.

as though I had not a friend in the world" (April 15, 1860). "Oh, I have felt so lonesome today, how I wish Charles was here" (May 16, 1860). "Oh! How I wish I could be with him but I cannot" (July 21, 1860). "It is two years today since I last saw Charles" (February 21, 1861).

What was the fate of this loving wife, separated from her husband by three thousand miles when she was still in her early twenties? Because her diary and a portrait of Charles and Maria Adams were bequeathed to the California Historical Association in San Francisco, one has reason to believe that she made the long journey from the Atlantic to the Pacific Coast and was eventually reunited with her husband.

MORMON PLURAL MARRIAGES

Any account of wives in the West must not overlook the special situation of Mormons practicing polygamy. Contrary to the popular view, not all Mormon families were polygamous—indeed, estimates suggest the figure was only 15 to 20 percent.[32] And of these, about two-thirds contained only two wives and 20 percent, three. Men with four or more wives were usually prominent church leaders, who indicated their adherence to Mormon theology by their conspicuous display of numerous wives and children.

Mormon doctrine professed that the more wives a man had and the more children a woman had, the more they would be rewarded in heaven. Marriages performed in Mormon temples were (and are) supposed to continue after death. Polygamy—or plural marriage, the preferred term—was a fundamental tenet of the sect between 1852, after the Mormons had settled in Utah, and 1890, when the president of the church bowed to U.S. anti-polygamy laws. For at least forty years, even

Mary Carpenter Pickering Bell Quilt, circa 1855. (Smithsonian Institution, Washington, D.C.)

wives who admitted to a personal preference for a monogamous union defended the system of plural marriage because it had been ordained by the church and was, in the words of one wife, "necessary to . . . salvation." "If polygamy is the Lord's order, we must carry it out," declared another plural wife.[33]

The typical polygamous family began with a man of about twenty-three marrying a woman three years his junior; this would be his only legal marriage. A dozen years later he would take as his second wife a woman eleven years younger than his first wife. If he took a third wife, she too would be in her early twenties at the time of marriage. Whether they were in polygamous or monogamous unions, Mormon wives had a high fertility rate, averaging seven to eight children.[34]

According to the husband's means and preferences, he would settle his wives in different rooms of the same house, or in different houses, sometimes quite far from each other. Mormon wives often found themselves in situations where they had to learn to live communally and cooperatively under the same roof with a co-wife or co-wives and chil-

Charles Wilson Adams and wife, Maria Abagail Henry Adams, mid–nineteenth century. (California Historical Society, San Francisco)

dren from various beds. This could create strong ties of sisterhood, especially in cases where a pair of sisters shared the same husband, as well as the potential for friction and jealousy.

If she was settled at a distance from her husband's headquarters, a Mormon wife was often remarkably independent. She had considerable autonomy in raising her children—indeed, the mother-child bond usually took precedence over the conjugal bond, since the husband was shared with other wives, often lived at a distance, and was frequently away on religious missions. It was not uncommon for a Mormon wife to work outside the house—the Mormon church encouraged women to be financially entrepreneurial and self-sufficient. Unlike Victorian middle-class wives of the larger society, Mormon wives were by no means restricted to domesticity; they worked as farmers, seamstresses, and businesswomen, and some even became nurses and doctors. Many were active in the Relief Society, an organization founded in 1842 as a support organization for religious, charitable, and cultural works. Later, between 1872 and 1914, some of the most progressive women produced a newspaper called the *Women's Exponent*, which expressed a wide range of concerns, including those associated with the fin de siècle "New Woman." Clearly nineteenth-century Mormon marriages were more complex than the popular view of them as "harems" catering to male lust.

The memoirs left by Mary Ann Hafen for her descendants give a vivid picture of her life as a plural wife in Utah and Nevada.[35] After the loss of her first husband (for whom she had been a second wife), she was urged by her parents to accept the offer of John Hafen. But he, too, had a first wife, Susette, who was not happy with the idea. Because of Susette's objections, it was only with the greatest reluctance and an abundance of tears that Mary Ann consented to the marriage. John Hafen was to take two more wives, and Mary Ann Hafen was to have seven children.

After the birth of her sixth child in 1891, Mary Ann moved to Nevada, while her husband and his other families remained in Utah. As she tells the story:

Because Santa Clara [Utah] had so little land for so many settlers, we decided it would be best for me to take my young family and move to Bunkerville [Nevada], where a settlement had been started and where there was more and cheaper land. . . .

I knew I was going to something of the same hardships I had known in childhood days; that my children were to grow up in a strange land with scarcely a relative near; and that they too would have to share in the hardships of subduing a new country. . . .

As soon as we could we planted corn, cane, cotton, squashes and melons in the field; and vegetables in the town lot. The brush fences were but poor protection from the stray animals that went foraging about. However we got a pretty good crop from everything planted that year. Albert [her son] dug up three young mulberry trees from Mesquite and planted them around our shadeless house.

Mary Ann initially missed the larger family in Santa Clara, and managed to make a trip back every year. At first, her husband visited regularly. "But being Bishop of Santa Clara," she tells us, "and with his other three families, he could not be with us much. So I had to care for my seven children mostly by myself." At the birth of her seventh child, "a fine husky boy, weighting 12½ pounds," she was assisted by the wife of the local Mormon Bishop, who came for the customary ten days. And where was her husband at this time? He came for a visit only after the baby had been born. The author volunteered with feisty pride: "I have never had a doctor at the birth of any of my children, nor at any other time for that matter, and I have never paid more than five dollars for the services of a mid-wife."

Mary Ann Hafen's story continues with an account of her work as a de facto head of family.

I did not want to be a burden on my husband, but tried with my family to be self-supporting. I picked cotton on shares to add to our income; would take my baby to the fields while the other children were at school, for I never took the children out of school if it could possibly be avoided. That cotton picking was very tiresome, back-breaking work but it helped to clothe my children.

I always kept a garden so we could have green things to eat. Keeping that free from weeds and watering it twice a week took lots of time. With a couple of pigs, a cow, and some chickens, we got along pretty well. . . .

This straightforward narrative attests to the self-sufficiency shown by many Mormon wives. There is scant self-pity, and only the slightest hint that polygamy could be stressful for both spouses. Other women expressed more jealousy and pain. For example, the plural wife Annie Clark Tanner wrote in her autobiography:

> *I am sure that women would never have accepted polygamy had it not been for their religion. No woman ever consented to its practice without great sacrifice on her part. There is something so sacred about the relationship of husband and wife that a third party in the family is sure to disturb the confidence and security that formerly existed.*[36]

Similarly, Jane Snyder Richards, first wife of the Mormon apostle Franklin D. Richards, recounted the trials she endured as a first wife obliged to welcome into her family ten other wives. Mrs. Hubert Howe Bancroft, who recorded Richards's story for her historian husband in 1880, concluded that Mormon women considered polygamy "a religious duty and schooled themselves to bear its discomforts as a sort of religious penance."[37]

Brigham Young, the religious leader who brought the Mormons to Utah, admitted that "women say they are unhappy" and that some men recognize the unhappiness brought into a first marriage by a second wife. Young insisted that Mormon men and women "embrace the Gospel—the whole of it," including plural marriages.[38] If not, there was the alternative of divorce. The Utah divorce law of February 4, 1852, was one of the most liberal in the nation, and was especially favorable to women. In addition to the usual reasons, divorces were granted to plaintiffs "when it shall be made to appear to the satisfaction of the court, that the parties cannot live in peace and union together, and that their welfare requires a separation."[39] Women finding themselves in intolerable marital situations often initiated divorce proceedings, whereas a husband had more difficulty obtaining a divorce, if his wife was opposed to it. But he did have the option of taking another wife.

Love does not seem to have been a major criterion in the choice of a Mormon husband or wife. If romance played a part, it is certainly not highlighted in women's reminiscences. Instead, Mormon women were taught to choose husbands with an eye toward family compatibility, financial responsibility, and the greater good of the community. In these ways, Mormon society departed from the ethos of romantic love and exclusive domesticity that was promoted for mainstream American women.

The case of Hannah Crosby exemplifies this marital philosophy. Her decision to marry into a plural family in Utah during the 1870s was greeted with disbelief by her nonpolygamous Mormon family. She admitted to them that she did not really love her intended husband "as lovers love, though I loved his wives and the spirit of their home." And indeed, it was the spirit of sisterhood among the co-wives that she prized most in her marriage. "We wives," she wrote, "had our work so systematized and so well ordered that we could, with ease, do a great deal. One would for a period superintend the cooking and kitchen work with the help of the girls, another make beds and sweep, another comb and wash all the children. At seven thirty all would be ready to sit down to breakfast."

During their pregnancies and confinement, all "stepped into the breach and helped each other." "For many years," she insisted, "we lived thus, working together cooking over the same large stove with the same great kettles, eating at the same long table without a word of unpleasantness. . . ." She spoke so little of her husband that he almost seems superfluous, though he was the patriarchal linchpin around which the marriage revolved. Still, when she contemplated the life promised her by Mormon theology, she thought only of her relationship with the two other wives. "To me it is a joy to know that we laid the foundation of a life to come while we lived in that plural marriage, that we three who loved each other more than sisters, will go hand in hand together down all eternity."

Hannah Crosby was an articulate spokesperson for the merits of plural marriage. "No one," she argued, "can tell the advantages of that system until he has lived it. We enjoyed many privileges that single wiferey never knew."[40]

A FEW GUARDED GENERALIZATIONS

Given the enormous diversity of Victorian women's lives, generalizations about marriage, such as I presented at the beginning of the last chapter, must always remain open to question. Did the ideology of separate spheres for husbands and wives prevail from London and Washington to Iowa and California? Did it regulate the lives of a New York proponent of women's rights, a Georgia plantation mistress, a cook in a California mining town, and a toll-keeper's wife in Nevada? It is obvious that the doctrine of separate spheres, with its associated corollary of domesticity for women, did not exist uniformly across class and geographical lines. The further one descended downward on the economic and social ladder, the less likely one was to discriminate between "men's" work and "women's" work. When it was a matter of survival, women, married or not, took whatever jobs they could to keep themselves and their families solvent. Similarly, the further one moved westward, the more likely one was to share work with one's husband, at least initially. Husbands and wives worked side by side as farmers in Kansas, as ranchers in Wyoming, and as boardinghouse operators in California. The frontier-breaking spirit that inspired many pioneer men and women in the first place often led to a subversion of gender boundaries as they moved westward.

Nonetheless, the ideology of separate spheres and the cult of domesticity did not give up ground so easily. Even on the overland trail, work was divided by gender: men drove the oxen and repaired the gear, women cooked, washed, sewed, and minded the babies.[41] Although women were often required to assume nontraditional activities—most notably, collecting buffalo dung for fuel—they were also expected to provide all the services that wives and mothers traditionally provided, without reciprocity from the men. Each day they had to "hurry scurry to get breakfast" and each evening they cooked "enough to last until the next night."[42]

If wives took on many male tasks during the journey, this did not mean that they shared equal authority with their husbands. The following incident told by Lavinia Porter illustrates the difficulty women had whenever they tried to challenge male leadership. Her husband had refused her request to veer toward a grove of trees half a mile away so she could gather firewood instead of buffalo dung. In a pique, she crawled into the wagon and told the men that "if they wanted fuel for the evening meal they could get it themselves and cook the meal also." Then she cried herself to sleep. Although her husband tried to make amends by waking her later with a dinner he had prepared himself, their relations were strained for weeks. As John Faragher and Christine Stansell point out in their version of this story, the traditional Victorian division of labor and authority between husbands and wives remained the backbone of marriage from the Atlantic to the Pacific, even if gender lines were more frequently crossed west of the Mississippi.[43]

A pioneer woman on the West Coast went into marriage with the same domestic expectations as her sister on the East Coast. Thus the relatively affluent fourteen-year-old bride, Bethenia Owens-Adair, married in Oregon on May 4, 1854, had a hope chest containing "four quilts . . . muslin for four sheets, two pairs of pillow-cases, two table-cloths, and four towels." Her father gave her "a fine riding mare," a cow, a calf, and a wagon and harness. Her mother gave her "a good feather bed, and pillows, a good straw bed, a pair of blankets and two extra quilts." Moreover, on the afternoon of her wedding day, the ceremony having taken place in the morning, she purchased on her father's account a full supply of groceries, cooking utensils, a churn, a washtub and board, a thirty-gallon iron pot for washing, and a water bucket and tin dipper. Her husband's possessions were a horse and saddle, a gun, and the small log cabin, twelve by fourteen, without floor or chimney, to which he brought his bride.[44]

In pioneer homes, a wife still had primary responsibility for the care of house and children, no matter what her other duties might have been. A husband would sometimes put a pot on the fire, but no one expected him to take charge of the household, even when his wife was sick or recuperating from childbirth. If he had to, for example when widowed, his very first thought was to procure another wife. Another question revolves around the spousal relationship as buttressed by two major patriarchal institutions—law and religion. This, too, varied greatly. If some women, notably Southern ones, expressed the view that they were happy with the status quo, indeed welcomed their domination by men, this was surely not the attitude of all women, even those in the South. Many wives found ways of subverting a husband's will, sometimes overtly, sometimes covertly.

One pioneer bride offered this analysis of her personal situation. "I already had ideas of my own about the husband being the head of the family. I had taken the precaution to sound him on 'obey' in the marriage pact and found he did not approve of the term. Approval or no approval, that word 'obey' would have to be left out. I had served my time of tutelage to my parents as all children are supposed to. I was a woman now and capable of being the other half of the head of the family. His word and my word would have equal strength."[45] Such, we imagine, was the position of many women, who chose their husbands for love and hoped for egalitarian unions.

Though many women in the North, South, Midwest, and West left enduring records of happy marriages, many others suffered through years of marital conflict that sometimes ended in desertion or divorce. Husbands left their wives and children for other women or because they drank or became depressed or were simply shiftless. Sometimes it was the wife who deserted, as evidenced by the newspaper ads for "runaway wives" that appeared in the "Missing" newspaper classifieds. Or she might petition for divorce, especially in the frontier territories, where the divorce code tended to be relatively liberal.

Often husbands and wives simply separated and did not bother with divorce proceedings unless one of the parties wanted to marry again. And even then, in a country as vast as the United States, it was easy enough to disappear into a new territory and create a new union without legally ending the old one. Bigamy seems to have been "a common social experience in early America."[46]

Few wives had the parental and internal resources to fall back on that helped Bethenia Owens-Adair leave her ne'er-do-well husband in Oregon. After four years of marriage, aged eighteen and the mother of a small child, Bethenia returned to her parents' home and filed for divorce. When an older woman asked why she had left her husband, Bethenia answered, "Because he whipped my baby unmercifully, and struck and choked me." At this dark moment, her difficulties seemed insurmountable—"a husband for whom I had lost all love and respect, a divorce, the stigma of which would cling to me all my future life, and a sickly babe of two years."[47]

Yet a truly remarkable life was ahead of her. First she went back to school to complete her primary education. Then she recruited sixteen pupils, whom she taught for a fee of two dollars each over a three-month period. When she and her son moved out of her parents' home, she pieced together a living out of teaching, doing laundry, and picking blueberries. For several years she ran a dressmaking and millinery business. By 1870, she was able, with her own money, to place her son in the University of California at Berkeley.

And it was at this point that her life took a dramatic turn. She got it in her head to study medicine. Borrowing a copy of *Gray's Anatomy* from a doctor, she taught herself the body's workings and arranged to enter the Eclectic School of Medicine in Philadelphia. Since women were not accepted in most reputable medical schools and since medicine was not considered a profession for women, her family felt "disgraced." Yet she managed to complete her medical training, not only at the Eclectic School, but also at the University of Michigan—one of the first universities to grant medical degrees to women. She received hers in 1880 at the age of forty, and went on to become a legendary "lady doctor" in her native Oregon for the next twenty-five years.

Bethenia Owens-Adair was fortunate to be an adult at a time when the patriarchal mold surrounding the lives of American and English wives was beginning to show its cracks. The legislation enacted in England from 1857 to 1882 and in America beginning in the 1840s granted married women greater measures of freedom, and new educational and work opportunities offered single and divorced women realistic alternatives to the career of wifehood.

SEVEN

The Woman Question and the New Woman

*I*n the third act of Ibsen's play *A Doll's House,* husband and wife Helmer and Nora have an extraordinary encounter. He says to her: "Before everything else, you're a wife and a mother." She responds: "I don't believe that any longer. I believe that before everything else I'm a human being—just as much as you are . . . or at any rate I shall try to become one."[1]

When the play had its first production at the Copenhagen Royal Theater in December 1879, it caused a scandal. The idea that a respectable woman should renounce her role as wife and mother, leave her husband and children, and strike out on her own was seen as an insult to society's most cherished values. In Ibsen's Norway, where the work was published a few weeks before its Danish premiere, his conservative enemies had found a perfect target. Although Ibsen usually reveled in adverse criticism, this time he was taken aback at the exceptionally vehement reactions throughout Scandinavia. For the German production, he even bowed to protest and changed the ending. In that version, Nora does not walk out of the house slamming the door behind her. Instead, she is forced by Helmer to take a look at her sleeping children, and, sinking to the floor before the curtain falls, she cries out: "Ah, though it is a sin against myself, I cannot leave them."

It was, of course, the original version that earned Ibsen the applause of progressive thinkers. Nora's struggle to break free from the "doll's house" where she had been only a "doll-wife" (and before that, her

Papa's "doll-child") reflected the struggle of many women to assume full citizenship in the human community. Almost immediately, Nora became synonymous with the conviction that a female person had the right to an autonomous existence, even if that meant denying the claims of wifehood and motherhood.

Like most literary masterpieces, *A Doll's House* speaks for its age and all ages. The protagonist, Nora, is simultaneously an upper-middle-class Norwegian wife bound by the social conventions of her time and place, and any woman of any age seeking personal fulfillment. Her particular story could have occurred only when it did, yet it is Everywoman's story.

Consider the times. During the second half of the nineteenth century, Scandinavia, like the rest of Europe, was embroiled in the Woman Question. The Norwegian novels of Camilla Collet (1813–1895) and the Swedish novels of Frederika Bremer (1801–1865) contributed significantly to an awareness of the one-sided privileges enjoyed by men. Did an unmarried woman have to leave all initiative to the male, waiting until he declared his intentions before she could express her love? Did marriage have to be a patriarchal institution that forced a single woman to exchange autonomy for protection? Did a wife have to be a minor in the eyes of the law, subject to her husband's guardianship? Did a woman have to give up all economic rights, except the right to the "lock and key," which meant responsibility for the care of the home? Did she have to marry at all?

In Sweden, to which Norway was united under a common sovereign, lively parliamentary debates on the Woman Question resulted in the law of 1874, which substantially changed the position of women. For the first time, married women were given some control over their private property. Wives who had been the recipients of sizable dowries or parental inheritances were almost always members of the upper ranks, wedded to men of their own class; yet whatever their social status, before 1874 they had no say whatsoever about the use of the property they might have brought into the marriage. The Scandinavian changes effected in the 1870s made it possible for Nora in *The Doll's House* to negotiate a bank loan without her husband's knowledge—a transaction that her confidante greeted with surprise. (She would have been even more surprised had she known that Nora had acquired the loan by forging her dying father's signature on a security note.)

The law of 1874 also permitted wives to possess their own earnings. This provision had special meaning for working-class women, many of whom were self-supporting in their premarital years. These women often delayed marriage until they had acquired a dowry on their own and were able to pay for a wedding—a costly ceremony that always devolved upon the bride or her family. During this "engagement" period, which could go on for years, Swedish working-class women often cohabited with their men, and even became mothers—practices that were unthinkable for middle- and upper-class women. Premarital cohabitation, practiced by an estimated 40 to 50 percent of all working-class couples, gave rise to the expression "Stockholm, marriage" for individuals living together without the blessings of church or state.[2]

Like priests' wives in the Middle Ages, lower-class women in "Stockholm marriages" were generally accepted by their communities, even if the clergy (predominantly Protestant) disapproved of such arrangements. Sometimes cohabiting men and women tried to camouflage their situation by pretending to be tenants in their partners' households, especially for official purposes like a census. Eventually most of these couples wed, and, if they had children, these were legitimized by their parents.

What we know of "Stockholm marriages" suggests that the women in these unions could be remarkably independent. Because they were not legally married, they were never under a husband's guardianship: they controlled their own earnings and were not dependent on the economic support of their partners. Throughout history, the independence of women seems to increase whenever they have access to money, either earned themselves or inherited. This economic independence has always made some men very nervous. Those who believe that society's ills in the late twentieth century derive from married women's work outside the home should take a good look at the late-nineteenth-century debate on the Woman Question. It is filled with many of the same concerns we still face today.

The European lineup in favor of progressive change for women included such literary luminaries as Henrik Ibsen and Bjørnstjerne Bjørnson in Norway; Frederika Bremer and Ellen Key in Sweden; the Russian-French diarist Marie Bashkirtseff; the French activists Marie Maugeret and Nelly Roussel; the South African novelist Olive

Schreiner; the Irish playwright Bernard Shaw; and the Austrian social critic Bertha von Suttner. In the opposing camp were equally formidable figures—the German philosopher Friedrich Nietzsche, the Swedish playwright August Strindberg, the Russian novelist Tolstoy, and a slew of Frenchmen. But no one probably had greater influence than Pope Leo XIII, who believed that married women should remain securely in the cage that patriarchy had always provided for them. His 1891 encyclical asserted that "a woman is by nature fitted for homework, and it is that which is best adapted at once to preserve her modesty, and to promote the good bringing up of children and the well-being of the family."[3]

Cartoonists had a field day with the New Woman as wife, and with her presumably downtrodden spouse. Following a long tradition of graphic satire aimed at the henpecked husband, they mercilessly ridiculed the idea of role reversal in marriage. An American version of the same theme, inspired by the idea of woman's suffrage, shows an elegantly dressed woman entering a carriage "manned" by two other

The Age of Iron, man as he expects to be. *Satirical lithograph exploring the possible consequences of the founding of the National Woman Suffrage Association in 1869. Currier and Ives. (Library of Congress, Washington, D.C.)*

MODERN MARRIAGE – MODERNE EHE
Anno 1900

She's **wearing the** *P***ants**
Sie **hat die** *H***osen an**

Modern Marriage—Moderne Ehe, *1900. European caricature of spousal relations with "the new woman."*

women, while the husbands stay at home to mind the baby and do the laundry. A German picture from 1900 titled "Modern Marriage" (*Moderne Ehe*) shows a scowling woman in pants brandishing a threatening shoe, while her husband, in a dress and bedroom slippers, holds the baby in one arm and a bottle in the other. The caption reads: "She's wearing the pants" (*Sie hat de Hosen an*).

THE NEW WOMAN IN ENGLAND

In England, during the 1880s and 1890s, the Woman Question reached its crescendo. Newspaper and magazine articles, novels and plays, public speeches and private conversations centered around the New Woman—an expression invented in 1894 to describe an already familiar phenomenon.[4] The New Woman was recognizable by her education, her independence, her tendency to flaunt traditional family values and blur the boundaries between conventional male and female behavior. She was, in the eyes of her admirers, the long-awaited feminine savior who would set things right between the sexes and bestow untold benefits upon family and society. But in the eyes of her detractors, she was no less than a reprehensible virago, a freak of nature bound to destroy the hallowed separation of gendered spheres and wreak havoc on such sacred institutions as marriage and motherhood.

Let there be no doubt about it—the New Woman scandal was rooted in anxieties over the future of the wife. While other issues, such as female sexuality, education, employment, and women's suffrage, became increasingly prominent, feminist protests were seen primarily as attacks on "true womanhood," that is, the self-sacrificing, all-caring spouse and mother. What would become of the family if married women had a truly egalitarian union with their husbands?

The first to bring this question to broad public attention in England was Mona Caird in her August 1888 article entitled "Marriage," published in the *Westminster Review.* Her piece provoked no less than 27,000 letters sent in less than two months to the *Daily Telegraph,* which had invited the public to comment on it.

What exactly had Caird written to initiate such an unprecedented epistolary outpouring, called by one of her contemporaries "the greatest newspaper controversy of modern times"?[5] In essence, she had drawn from feminist thinkers like Mary Wollstonecraft and John Stuart Mill the conviction that women had been kept in subjection for centuries because it suited men's purposes, and that marriage was the primary institution by which women continued to be held in bondage.

She attributed the idea of "possession in marriage" to the ancient practice of bride purchase, lingering on in the modern marriage market whereby a nubile Victorian woman effectively sold herself to the highest bidder.

In her brief and often arbitrary history, Caird reserved particular vitriol for Luther. It was he, she argued, who had denied the religious sanctity of marriage, turned it into a commercial contract, and "reduced it to something little above a licensed sin." She dismissed outright the view held by others "that Protestantism dignified marriage" and concluded that Reformation thinkers like Luther and Melanchthon were responsible for the belief, still current in Victorian society, that a woman's major duty in life was to bear children, even if she died from it.

Caird pronounced marriage "a failure." Because a wife was still subject to a "system of purchase," she was forced to develop her moral standards *"in accordance with her servitude to man."* A wife did not honor her own intelligence, education, or chastity, except to the extent that it was "relative" to her husband. Or, as Caird forcefully put it: *"The woman must protect the man's property in herself."* Conversely, because the wife's virtues "belong" to her husband, he sees himself "dishonoured" by any of her failings. The idea that a man's honor can be injured by his wife's infidelity is, in Caird's eyes, "a most naive proclamation of the theory of proprietorship." While it may hold up in a divorce court, given the law's tendency to equate wives with property, she asks a more fundamental existential question: "Is it possible to be really dishonoured by any action except one's own?" (That question could certainly be applied to *A Doll's House* and Helmer's worry that his wife's forgery would tarnish *his* reputation.)

Caird offered a number of radical proposals to alter this state of "degrading bondage." One solution was to reject marriage altogether. This was the option taken by "an increasing number of women . . . refusing a life of comparative ease in marriage, rather than enter upon it as a means of livelihood, for which their freedom has to be sacrificed."

But Caird did not really want to do away with marriage. What she wanted was not "destruction" but "rebirth," a process that would come about through the elimination of certain marital wrongs, including the legal obligation for spouses, even those unhappily married, to live together. Throughout the nineteenth century, proven adultery was the only grounds for divorce, and the legal costs involved made even that possibility prohibitive for most English men and women. Caird advocated more liberal divorce laws, as well as better education for girls so they could support themselves and not be obliged to marry for money. Marriage could then more easily become a matter of true choice based on love and friendship, rather than a sense of duty. These changes would be brought about by many people of both sexes who were, in her opinion, dissatisfied with present arrangements. Believing that a moral renaissance was in the making, Caird pointed to "the remarkable tumult of thought during the last few years, signs and wonders which seem to herald an awakening," and she invited her readers to join in the debate.

The selection of letters published in the *Daily Telegraph* in response to Caird's article came from wives, husbands, single women, bachelors, widows and widowers, curates, barmaids, physicians, sailors, a nurse, an artist, a physicist, an actress, a furrier, several lady clerks, and more. They were all members of the self-respecting middle class, except for a handful of working-class correspondents. Their letters either agreed wholeheartedly with Caird's views or disagreed just as wholeheartedly. They told their personal stories of happiness or misery, offered reasons why traditional marriage should not be tampered with, or made suggestions for its improvement. Many gave advice to a particular letter writer who had preceded them. This correspondence offers a remarkable panorama of British marriages at the end of the nineteenth century, including numerous miniature self-portraits. The following selection is divided into letters from 1) women who considered their marriages a failure, and 2) women who considered their marriages a success.

MARRIAGE FAILURES

I must say I concur in the suggestion that greater facilities should be afforded for divorce. Let me cite my own case. My husband is a helpless drunkard. It is true, he earns a good living and keeps me in comparative luxury; but is this an adequate consideration for the fact that I have to associate with a drunken, besotted husband five nights out of seven? LUCRETIA, Westbourne Park, Aug. 20.

I am one of those who have most unhappily found marriage a most dismal failure. Married when only a girl, after a few years I am practically a widow, having been obliged, from my husband's brutality, to seek a separation. This was not until, through his brutality, I lost an eye, principally owing to the very merciful law which compelled me to live with a man until I was maimed for life. . . . M.S., Bedford Street, Strand, Aug. 21.

I should indeed be grateful to Mrs. Mona Caird, or to anybody else, who would show us unhappily married folk a decent way out of our difficulties. Marriage, in my case, has been a miserable failure, simply because my husband and I do not suit each other. Ours is a clear case of incompatibility, proved beyond all doubt by the almost daily jarring and wrangling of some fourteen years. . . . We have both broken every vow we made to each other on our wedding day, save one; and being highly moral, if nothing else, we must still endure, wearing out our days in mutual misery, and darkening and embittering our children's lives by a loveless and joyless home. . . . A TIRED WIFE, Felpham, near Bognor, Aug. 21.

I myself am a deserted wife, and my husband has treated me with exceptional contempt and unkindness, but I am proud to say that so great is my reverence for the sanctity of the marriage vow, that if my husband sent for me to return to him to-morrow, I would go, and with a hearty will and friendly affection strive to do my duty to him. A City Merchant's Wife. Worthing, Sept. 10.

I married, unthinkingly, a man whom I did not love. I thought that perhaps I might grow to care for him, but I did not do so. . . . As I am his wife, I consider that I ought to stay with him, but my whole soul revolts against being tied to a man for whom I have no particle of love, and who, in tastes, character, and pursuits, is my direct opposite. I reflect how much better a woman I should have been had love and not duty, ruled me. . . . MATRIMONIAL ADVENTURER, Norwood Sept. 20.

My partner and I suffer from a total incompatibility of disposition. We do not quarrel but there is an absolute want of sympathy—an absolute antipathy of every thought and feeling. . . .

. . . I believe there would be fewer fretful, unhappy, and broken-down wives if husbands would see that their wives had amusements and occupations, apart from domestic matters. . . .

Another case of "Failure" in marriage is the objection English husbands have to their wives being independent in money matters. . . . Few men realise how humiliating it is to a woman of independent spirit to ask for every sixpence, nor the spirit of bitterness and rebellion that it engenders. . . . A LOST LIFE, Darenth, Kent, Sept. 26.

These letters and others from unhappy wives often attributed the cause of their misery to the husband, who was portrayed as brutal, contemptuous, unkind, and given to drink. The letter writer usually pictured herself as a person who had made every effort to be a "model wife," with "high notions of devotion and self-sacrifice," yet the circumstances of her union had defeated her, and all she desired was a way out that would be sanctioned by the laws of her land and the precepts of her religion. Still, none was willing to sin through adultery in order to get a divorce.

Some of the wives recognized incompatibility of character as the problem. They did not point the finger at their husbands any more than they pointed it at themselves. Indeed, one woman admitted that she was simply "unfit for marriage." Like the other correspondents, she protested against the laws that made it impossible for her and her husband to leave each other.

HAPPILY MARRIED

[W]ill you allow a married woman of twenty years' experience to say a few words? . . . Marriage was instituted, I humbly conceive, in the interest of the weaker portion of humanity, viz. women and children, and it works more to their advantage than otherwise. Men could probably content themselves very well—and ma.1y do—with a system of free, i.e., temporary marriage. . . . The woman, I suppose, was intended to be subject. "He shall rule over thee," was part of the curse pronounced on the first human sinner, Eve. . . . I write from a feminine standpoint only; and while admitting that marriage is often very disappointing, it cannot be considered a total failure so long as it carries on the race legitimately and surrounds the woman with the dignity—

*almost sanctity—of true wifehood and honourable motherhood. FAITH
AND HOPE, Brighton, Aug. 10.*

*If you are sensible, intelligent, and diplomatic women, and do not
expect too much of your husbands, you may be happy wives as a
rule. . . . Use your own judgment in the treatment of the particular
specimen of the genus homo on whom you bestow your affections.
Above all, recollect that there must always be something on both sides
to put up with, so bear and forbear; and if you get a decent fellow, he
will love, respect, and appreciate you for it. If you find that your husband is at all inclined to go astray, give him a latchkey; he will soon
tire of a liberty which is not disputed. Don't sit up for him. Go to your
rest contentedly, and meet him with a sweet, unsuspecting smile, and
no embarrassing questions on his return in the small hours of the
morning. . . . Under these circumstances your husbands will find no
sport at all, and I warrant, will return home nightly at regular and
respectable hours less than a month after. It rests with yourselves to a
great extent whether your marriage turn out failures or not. EMILY
COFFIN, London, Aug. 14.*

*On the eve of my marriage I made three mental vows. They were—
never to aggravate him, never to have a secret from him, nor by any
selfish or thoughtless act of mine to lead him one step towards bank-
ruptcy. Fifteen years afterwards I told him of those vows, and although
I have been a widow for ten years, I should blot this paper with my
tears if I attempted to put it in writing the love and tenderness of his
reply. . . . A BELIEVER IN THE SANCTITY OF MARRIAGE, Lincoln,
Aug. 20.*

*Will you give a workman's wife a chance to say a few words on the
marriage question? . . . Now, I am a married woman of forty years'
wedlock standing; therefore what I say is entitled to consideration. My
verdict is "Marriage is not a failure," and I will show you why I think so.
At fifteen, when I was an apprentice girl, I fell in love with my—
well, my old man. He was an apprentice boy, four years older. We were
very happy—happy as the finest swells that ever wooed, though neither
of us consulted our parents as to our choice, and we enjoyed courting on
the quiet, and we longed for the day when we could get married. As*

soon as he was out of his time we fixed the day; and one morning we both of us took a day off and marched away to church with a shopmate a-piece for witnesses and wedding train, and were united by a good-natured person, who seemed to relish the job of making so young and good-looking couple man and wife. My dowry was the love I had to give. His means were just what he could win week by week as a journeyman. With no bank account, and with but the slenderest sort of "establishment," we set up in matrimony, and we were as happy as was possible. Within a year my first boy was born. He has had eight brothers and sisters, and seven of them live in manhood and womanhood. . . . Why are we made men and women? Clearly to be partners one to the other, and to fulfill the divine mandate "Increase and multiply." We are not put on this earth by God merely to amuse ourselves, but to do a work. Woman's work is to be a mother, and form her children's minds and educate their hearts. But in acquitting herself of these duties she finds wondrous joys if she be a true woman. What greater prize can there be in life than to find, when the hair has grown white and the step is losing its spring, that the children one has borne return her love and care a hundredfold and that every day the interest on the outlay grows apace? I don't know of any; and I would not exchange the love of my sons and daughters, and the fireside quiet that is mine at near sixty, for the wealth of all the Rothschilds. . . . A WORKMAN'S WIFE, Plymouth, Sept. 6.

I had known my husband over three years before we were married, and saw a great deal of him; consequently we thought we understood each other's disposition sufficiently to live happily together. But we had not been man and wife many months before I found he was drifting away from me. . . . The advice from different friends was: "If he goes his way, you go yours." But I knew this was not the way to win him back; so, after bearing it pretty patiently for three years, I set about in my mind the best way to go to work. . . . I always met him at the door myself, as though nothing had happened, and paid the same little attentions I had always paid before we were married, took great care to study what friends he liked, and made a rule to ask one or two cheerful ones to dinner two or three times a week. . . . So by degrees, I was enabled to wean him from bad companions, and now, for the past year or more, we have been as happy as possible . . . MIDDLE-CLASS WOMAN, Croydon Sept. 12.

Before many years pass we hope to celebrate our golden wedding, please God, and we are not tired of one another yet. But I made many mistakes. . . .

I know how to manage my husband now, and have learned to double his pleasures, which are not many, by sharing in them. . . . WINNY JONES, Swaffham, Sept. 17.

On the whole, the happy wives were not so unequivocal as the unhappy ones. They assumed that marriage called for tolerance of a husband's weaknesses, and even wifely subjection. They believed it was their, rather than their husband's, duty to make the marriage work. One wife made three private vows of behavior on the eve of her wedding, which she kept for fifteen years before telling her spouse; another corrected her own youthful mistakes and learned in time to "manage" her husband; a third gradually weaned her husband away from "bad companions"; a fourth went so far as to give her husband a "latchkey" that allowed him to return at all hours of the night until he tired of his freedom. All subscribed to the view that the home should be a marital sanctuary, protecting a husband from the evils of the outside world, be it the aggressiveness of the workplace or the debauchery of drink and promiscuous sex. The "true woman" was devoted to her work as homemaker, wife, and mother.

Some of these wives were clearly influenced by traditional religious views of woman as the weaker vessel, destined by God to bow to her husband and bear numerous children. The most unusual correspondent of the group was the working man's wife so clearly conscious of her class difference from the majority of letter writers and so clearly content with her lot. It is noteworthy that this wife who had been married for forty years and the other older wives were the most happy. They had gotten through the difficult period of early marital adjustment, childbearing, pinched financial resources, and were, in their later years, cognizant of their blessings. Even this small sample seems to support the view, current in the work of some psychologists today, that old age can be "golden years" for couples who manage to stay together.[6]

FURTHER BRITISH AND CONTINENTAL
CONTROVERSY

The debate on the Woman Question continued long after the letters in the *Daily Telegraph*. British women reformists, such as Mona Caird, Sarah Grand, and Olive Schreiner, were attacked by anti-reformists, such as Eliza Lynn Linton, Mrs. Humphry Ward, and the popular novelist Ouida. Male writers, too, whether they were for or against changes in women's situation, also mirrored the turmoil surrounding the New Woman. Unlike the works of earlier fiction writers—for example, Austen, Brontë, Gaskell, and Dickens—the novels of the 1880s and 1890s no longer tended to end with marriage. Instead, a wedding might appear at the beginning or middle of a novel, followed by many pages devoted to its problems. Or a novel might end in no marriage at all.[7]

British novelists were somewhat behind their continental counterparts in abandoning the marital "happy end" for grimmer portraits of love, sex, and marriage. Already in 1832, the French novelist George Sand had shocked her contemporaries with *Indiana*—the story of a wife's flight from a brutal husband. The tomes comprising Balzac's *Human Comedy*, written in the thirties and forties, were replete with monomaniacal husbands and fathers responsible for the misery of their wives and daughters. In his *Mémoires de deux jeunes mariées,* Balzac offered prospective wives two marital models—the traditional marriage of convenience and the romantic marriage of passion. Two friends, released from their convent school, make totally different marriages, one based on family considerations, the other on the mandate of her heart. Despite Balzac's personal romantic orientation, he comes down on the side of the the woman who finds happiness in domesticity and motherhood, whereas the passionate heroine who loses her first husband through the excesses of voluptuous pleasure (!) and dies during a second marriage as a result of her own violent jealousy provides a sobering cautionary tale.

But it was Flaubert a generation later who established the prototype of the unhappy wife par excellence in *Madame Bovary.* Little did it matter that she was a pathetic provincial creature bred on the romantic illusions of her age; Flaubert turned her into a larger-than-life adulteress, more to be pitied than censured in her refusal to remain the faithful wife of a humdrum country doctor. The legal action brought by the conservative government of Napoleon III against Flaubert and his publishers in 1857 for their insult to morality foundered in the flood of words issuing from an eloquent defense attorney and a progressive judge, not to mention the tide of public opinion in favor of Madame Bovary.

It remained for Tolstoy to create a truly heroic adulteress in *Anna Karenina* (1875–1877). Beautiful, passionate, aristocratic, Anna Karenina leaves her cold husband and a beloved child for the handsome officer Count Vronsky. The consequences of this act are devastating for all concerned. Like Madame Bovary, Anna Karenina commits suicide, abandoning an illegitimate child as well as the son from her marriage. However much Flaubert and Tolstoy identified with their heroines, the wives were still made to pay in the end for their marital infidelities. Female adultery without ultimate punishment was still unthinkable.

By the 1880s, British novelists were catching up with continental writers in depicting the problematic nature of marital relations. Thomas Hardy led the pack of writers convinced that marriage, as practiced in his time, was a minefield for disaster. In *The Mayor of Casterbridge* (1866), the title character had in his youth committed the outrageous act of selling his wife and child to a seaman—an act that came back to haunt him when he was older and successful, and one that inevitably led to his downfall and death. *Tess of the d'Urbervilles* (1891) follows the history of a country girl seduced and made pregnant by her upper-class employer, then married to a man who deserts her when he learns of her past. In the end, Tess stabs her first lover and spends a few blissful days with the husband she has never stopped loving, before being arrested and hanged. *Jude the Obscure* (1894) combines a searing condemnation of British class-based society with a fatalistic vision of the unhappiness inherent in most heterosexual relations. Jude, a village stonemason, is tricked into an early, unfortunate marriage with a woman who soon abandons him. Then he falls in love with his cousin and lives with her illegally for several years. When their three children meet tragic ends, he and his cousin separate, and Jude dies a miserable death. It was the bleakest of Hardy's novels, and the least popular.

Numerous other British novelists critiqued the institution of marriage and addressed the Woman Question. Consider *The Odd Women* (1893) by George Gissing. "Odd women," also called "redundant women," were those half million females who had no chance of "making a pair" in late Victorian England, because women significantly outnumbered the men. Four of the central characters in Gissing's novel are unmarried women, and two of them—Rhoda Nunn and Mary Barfoot—remain unmarried by conviction in order to help other "odd women." They have set up a school to teach single women clerical skills so they may become economically self-sufficient. In the course of the book, one hears all the arguments for and against traditional womanhood and conventional marriage, though Gissing's heart is clearly on the side of the New Woman.

In the character of Rhoda Nunn (the family name is obviously symbolic), he created an imposing example of an independent, proud, intelligent person, who devoted herself to "the greatest movement of our time—that of emancipating her sex."[8] But lest we think of her as an "unwomanly" virago, Gissing made her sensitive to the love of a persistent suitor, Evrard Barfoot. Their verbal exchanges constitute a critique of marriage as it currently existed (a social "duty" held together by legal and commercial underpinnings) and a frank discussion of the merits of a "free union" (a nonlegal rapport based on passion and intellect.) Evrard speaks the language of sexual emancipation when he proposes to Rhoda:

> You can picture the kind of life I want you to share. You know me well enough to understand that my wife—if we use the old word—would be as free to live in her own way as I to live in mine. All the same, it is love that I am asking for. . . . the love of a man and a woman who can think intelligently may be the best thing life has to offer them.[9]

In the end, Rhoda Nunn chooses not to be a "wife" in any sense of the word because Evrard Barfoot turns out to have more conventional ideas on marriage than she does.

The two women in this novel who *do* marry represent the best and the worst of wifedom. Fanny Micklethwaite became a wife after a self-sacrificing engagement of seventeen years! After such fortitude, she and her husband both thrive in matrimony, despite their financial limitations. The other married woman, Monica Widdowson, accepted the proposal of an unprepossessing man twice her age, whom she scarcely knew, so as to escape the near poverty experienced by her two older, unmarried sisters. Within a year, the marriage proves to be an unmitigated disaster. Mr. Widdowson's old-fashioned middle-class views on the prerogatives of a husband, his pathological jealousy regarding his young wife, their total lack of understanding for one another—all combine to send her flying into the arms of a would-be lover. Though she does not act out her adulterous fantasies (only because the lover gets cold feet), she leaves her husband under a cloud of suspicion and dies giving birth to his child. So much for happy unions in Gissing's version of late-Victorian marriage.

On the other hand, the defenders of traditional marriage had hardly given up the ghost. Eliza Lynn Linton's 1891 articles on "The Wild Women" presented the conjugal home as a haven of "peace" and "love." She clung to the Victorian credo that "the man has the outside work to do, from governing the country to tilling the soil; the woman takes the inside, managing the family and regulating society. The more highly civilized a community is, the more completely differentiated are these two functions."[10] Linton dug her heels into the ground of separate spheres, despite the seismic shocks that were undermining that ground.

One of her major criticisms was reserved for the idea that women should be active in politics. "[W]here," she asked, "will be the peace of home when women, like men, plunge into the troubled sea of active political life?" Sounding the counter-alarm to cries for women's suffrage, Linton offered an argument that would be used for the next twenty-five years: the vote for women would be bad for marriage, since it would introduce another potentially divisive wedge between husband and wife. She asked her readers to "imagine the home to which a weary man of business, and an ardent politician to boot, will return when his wife has promised her vote to the other side. . . . [We] all know miserable cases where the wife has gone directly and publicly counter to the husband." Conservatives of Linton's generation, ranging from staunch Catholics, Protestants, and Jews to eugenicists and social Darwinists, applauded her efforts to maintain the conventional division of labor between the sexes. The New Woman, with her thirst for education and economic self-sufficiency, her refusal to be coerced into marriage, and her desire to limit the number of her children, threatened the very foundations of the old order.

THE WOMAN QUESTION IN AMERICA

In America, as in Europe, the late nineteenth century witnessed hundreds, if not thousands, of "New Women"—women inspired to seek greater autonomy for themselves with or without marriage. When in 1874 the reformist Abba Goold Woolson proclaimed, "I exist . . . not as a wife, not as a mother, not as a teacher, but first of all, as woman, with a right to existence for my own sake," she dared to articulate a thought that was barely conscious in the feminine mind, and one that most Victorians would have found appalling.[11] Yet within the next quarter century, American women would begin to respond in numerous ways to the call for greater female independence and equality with men. More and more women questioned the absolute need for marriage; as new opportunities for employment opened up, some even remained single by choice. Whereas domestic service was the major outlet for women workers (one half of all employed women according to the 1870 census), there were expanding opportunities for factory workers, seamstresses, and milliners, and, at a higher social level, for teachers, office workers, writers, and decorative artists. Women who were serious about their careers still had to decide whether to marry or work, for as Anna Lea Merritt put it in "A Letter to Artists: Especially Women Artists" (*Lippincott's Monthly Magazine*, 1900): "The chief obstacle to a woman's success is that she can never have a wife."

Some women, especially those with careers or independent means, did have "wives" in what was commonly known as "Boston marriages"—a term used for an enduring union between two single women.[12] Many of these women were professional pioneers, who supported each other's careers and social visions. The novelist Sarah Orne Jewett and her friend, the widowed Annie Fields, had such a relationship for almost thirty years. Mary Emma Wooley, the first female student at Brown University in 1891, shared her life with Jeannette Marks throughout Wooley's long tenure as President of Mount Holyoke College. Before the theories of Freud had gained currency in America, these relationships were not considered sexually "perverse"—indeed, they were presumed to be asexual. Society tolerated lesbian partnerships as long as they appeared to be devoid of physical intimacy.

Even in traditional heterosexual marriage, many American wives expected a greater degree of authority than that of previous generations. Often a late Victorian wife would find herself struggling for power not only against her husband and society, but also against herself. Although she wanted more say in the management of her person and family, she did not want to be associated with the "unsexed viragos" so frequently lampooned in cartoons and caricatures. A respectable middle-class woman believed in the institution of marriage, abhorred divorce, and would never embarrass her husband in public, but she also jockeyed with him in private for control over children, financial assets, and myriad other family decisions. Should they go to the seashore or her parents' home for the summer? Would her husband invest in yet another dubious business venture? Would they have to move once again to a locale of his choice? Did they have money for another servant? Shouldn't their daughter be educated as well as their son? Could she, the wife, join a women's club, go alone to a spa, or visit a friend in another city? Did he object to her earning money as a sometime writer or baker of cakes? Privately, if not publicly, middle-class American women were less likely to accept a husband's uncontested authority than their female forebears.

The life of Violet Blair Janin, retold on the basis of her letters and diaries by Virginia Laas, offers an example of an unusually strong-willed woman, who rejected submission in marriage and established with her husband Albert a peculiarly "modern" marriage.[13] Having reigned for several seasons as the acknowledged belle of Washington society, and having rejected twelve marriage proposals (an impressive number, even for one with her beauty, intelligence, and fortune), Violet Blair married Albert Janin in 1874—the same year that Woolson made her remarkable pronouncement on woman's right to exist as a noncontingent human being.

Six years earlier, at the age of twenty, Violet Blair had written in her diary: "I will never love & never marry—No man shall ever be my master—I will never promise to obey." A year later, reflecting on her tenth prospective proposal, she wondered: "What shall I do? I am so worried about all these men who are in love with me—I cannot marry them all & I don't want to marry any of them." Her diaries of 1870 registered the same anxieties: she admitted to herself, "I do not believe it is possible for me to love any man," and declared, "I will be no man's slave."

Yet at the same time she found herself attracted to Albert Janin, an intelligent lawyer from New Orleans with progressive ideas. He encouraged her interest in women's rights, even to the point of bringing her relevant books and pamphlets. He respected her unconventional views and considerable knowledge of several languages, and, most of all, he was willing to submit to her need for domination. She wrote approvingly in her diary on October 27, 1871: "He obeys me." Sometime that year she agreed to marry him.

The engagement remained secret at her request, and as she continued her endless flirtation with other suitors, he became distraught. In one letter he cried out: "I am rendered almost frantic by the possibility of losing you. My whole emotional being seems merged in yours; robbed of you I should be poor indeed. Though sad and lonely now, I esteem myself rich and blessed with the promise of future happiness. . . ." This was but one of many crises in their courtship. While it was common for Victorian women to test their suitors, few (if any) were as outrageously demanding as Violet, as she herself admitted on several occasions. "Oh! Bertie," she wrote, in 1872, "I may make your whole life miserable, a spoiled belle can't make a good wife." Finally, through dogged perseverance ("almost as faithfully as Jacob" in the words of one of Violet's friends), Albert succeeded in winning public acknowledgment of their engagement in the fall of 1872.

But this did not mean that Violet was prepared to accept a conventional marriage, and certainly not one that would force her into submission. Her terms were the following: "Nothing but absolute obedience can satisfy me. I reign now over my lovers & do you think I am willing to marry any man & bend my will to his. No! No! Never! . . . I was born to command not to obey." Albert accepted all her terms, including her right to control her own property and live in Washington while he was in New Orleans several months of the year. Her statement on the subject of separate residences sounds very modern indeed: "[You] would not be obliged to stay in the same city with me all the time. . . . You can always regulate your own movements & I mine." Some three years after promising to marry him, Violet became Mrs. Albert C. Janin.

The marriage was to last for fifty-four years. Like many long-term marriages, it saw various stages, ranging from extremely happy to mostly miserable. During the early years, Violet discovered a capacity for love that totally surprised her. When Albert was away, her letters were forthright with passion: "Oh, if you were only here to take me in your arms—I do long for you so—My heart aches to be with you again, my own beloved." Or again, "My own darling husband I don't know what makes me so spoony this evening, but I am so, & I don't mind telling you so." Still, she was not about to relinquish the terms of their original agreement. She made it clear that he was loved "as both husband and friend, but not as master."

They easily came to terms in financial matters. She was to invest her money as she saw fit, he to employ his as he deemed wisest. Unfortunately, Albert was almost never wise where money was concerned. He had a series of disastrous business and political ventures, all of which contributed to the erosion of their marital happiness. In addition, Violet's one attempt at motherhood resulted in the death of a premature baby girl.

By 1880, they were living apart most of the time, Albert in New Orleans, Violet in Washington. When he suggested she join him, she answered furiously: "You cannot support me. . . . How in the world could you keep me in New Orleans?" It was more than a year before they were to meet again.

Throughout the 1880s Albert worked to get himself out of debt, and Violet undertook to translate documents for her brother-in-law to supplement her income. She devoted herself increasingly to organizations, such as the National Woman's Suffrage Association, the Society for the Prevention of Cruelty to Animals, and the Daughters of the American Revolution. Violet and Albert led very cordial, largely separate, lives. In 1891, she noted in her diary, "I wonder if there is another respectable woman in this city—so slightly married as I— . . . At least we do not bore each other & we make no scandals."

There was a time, however, in the mid-eighties when Violet could have made a scandal. In 1883 she met the Austrian count William Lippe-Weissenfeld, and for several years enjoyed an extremely close friendship with him. She was clearly fascinated by the cultivated count, and did nothing to hide her fascination, even from her husband. But

Members of the Daughters of the American Revolution laying a cornerstone for the Memorial Continental Hall in Washington, D.C., on April 19, 1903. Photo by Frances Benjamin Johnston. (Library of Congress, Washington, D.C.)

she did hide his twice-weekly evening calls to her home, confiding to her diary in 1886, "If people knew *that* I would have to stop it." In the fall of 1887, Lippe was ordered to return to Austria. While the liaison does not seem to have been physically intimate (if we are to believe Violet's diaries), it was deeply satisfying to both parties on an emotional and intellectual level. Violet suffered from his departure, and Lippe never married.

Without Lippe to fall back on, Violet became increasingly disillusioned with her husband, who was invariably impecunious and, by the mid-nineties, dependent on her for support. Resigned to her husband's business failures and to the failure of their marriage, she wrote in her diary on December 31, 1897, a year-end summary statement: "My own marriage has not been happy, Heaven knows, but I have stuck to my bargain like an honest woman." And two weeks later she added a consoling note: "Bert at least does not meddle with me."

Just when Violet had given up all hope, Albert surprised everyone by taking over a piece of family property, the Mammoth Cave in Kentucky, and promoting it into a huge success. Although Violet continued to live on her own income and they were still separated most of the time, they found harmony and renewed affection in their later years. Albert wrote devotedly to Violet in 1905: "I have never known or seen any girl or woman who made upon me the slightest impression of the possibility of her being more desirable as a life companion for me than you with your superior charm of body and mind." Violet was to recognize their peculiar interdependence when she wrote in 1916: "As time goes on we need each other even more, I think. When are you coming?"

In his very last years, Albert became somewhat senile and often irascible. Nevertheless, Violet took over his care for months at a time in Kentucky and then loyally nursed him during his last year, in Washington. After his death in May 1928, she sold the Mammoth Cave for the substantial sum of $446,000, and turned over many of her assets to the Washington National Cathedral, before she died in January 1933. It had been, to say the least, an unconventional marriage. And yet, as her biographer has written, it was in many ways "a common story writ large." Her particular marriage magnified the tension between female autonomy and traditional wifehood that surfaced in the late nineteenth century, and that has by no means disappeared from our own era.

By the 1890s, it was impossible to ignore the many changes that were taking place for both single and married women in the urban middle class. The new women's colleges including Smith, Mount Holyoke, Bryn Mawr, Wellesley, and Vassar, the plethora of women's clubs and organizations, the acceptance of work for single women and, to a lesser extent, for wives, the belief that marriage did not have to put an end to a woman's interest in books, music, or sports (most notably tennis and bicycling)—all contributed to a heady atmosphere of female freedom and expectation.

The foremost symbol of women's liberation was the bicycle, its ubiquitous image appearing on posters and ads that lauded one brand over an other as "perfectly adapted for use by women." Victoria Bicycles promoted its "tilting saddle" for "those who experience difficulty in mounting," while Duplex Saddle Co., playing on women's anatomical fears, announced that "A WOMAN MUST NOT RIDE the ordinary bicycle saddle," according to the Boston Obstetrical Society of April 1895, and should purchase its own cushioned "safety saddle," whose indented pommel "does not even touch the body." The mother who may or may not have learned to ride a bicycle herself was instructed by such magazines as *Ladies' Home Journal* on the art of confectioning a riding outfit for her daughter.

Ladies' Home Journal and *Good Housekeeping,* both founded in the mid-1880s, kept women abreast of the latest fads and fashions. If in August 1884 the *Journal* could blandly assert that "the happiest women are those who lead the ordinary home life," a decade later it was responding more and more to the yearnings of married women for less ordinary lives. Articles titled "When Work Fits Woman," "Men as Lovers," and "Women and the Violin" (February 1896) extended the range of reading beyond traditional housekeeping hints and suggestions for married homemakers.

This is not to say that the basically conservative *Journal* had abandoned its glorification of the wife, mother, and housekeeper. It was simply obliged to recognize changing mores, often regretfully. Thus various articles bemoaned excessive talk "about the woman who never marries," the sensational publicity lavished upon divorces, and the frenzied activity of married women outside their homes. Ruth Ashmore, in her column "The Conservative Woman," offered the following picture of the perfect wife and mother—one that recapitulated the conventional Victorian ideal.

> She is the woman who with her husband and her sons is the best companion. She surrounds herself, unconsciously, with a spiritual atmosphere that is a rest to the weary, especially to the weary man. . . . Keeping always and ever in a man's heart a fresh spring of spirituality great enough to flood his whole system and worldliness and make him wholesome and clean is woman's noblest work. (February 1896)

Similarly, columnist Mrs. Lyman Abbott, responding to letters from her readers, clung to the view of marriage as a lifelong, sacred commitment, and considered divorce a "contagion" that had spread beyond the rich to people of moderate income (March 1896). When she was asked to comment on subjects that were clearly outside the domestic arena, Mrs. Abbot still managed to remind her readers of their feminine obligations. For example, she published a letter concerned with tax reform from a correspondent who was quick to state that she was "not a New

Woman," but nonetheless believed women should concern themselves with such issues, because "the vote of the country can be swayed more readily by the influence of earnest, intelligent women well beloved by men, whether as mother, wife, sister, sweetheart or acquaintance, than by the votes of the same women at the polls." It was a portrait of female contingency that corresponded exactly to Mrs. Abbott's own conservative ideas.

Editorials in the *Journal* made valiant efforts to stem the tide of progressive change for women. They decried the "mistaken rush of girls into the world of business and trade" and lauded efforts to "regard housekeeping as a science" and "lift the whole idea of domestic service to a higher plane" (February 1896). They praised the tendency for people to move to the suburbs, especially "young married couples who are moving into the country and building simple and pretty homes at the very start of their wedded life. . . . The more our girls breathe in the pure air which God intended for all, but which man in the cities pollutes, the better women we shall have: the fewer worried mothers we shall see" (December 1898). Suburban life, we know today, did not turn out to be the salvation of American wives and mothers.

Yet there is something so close to our present anxieties in these late nineteenth-century editorials that we cannot dismiss them outright as the monolithic musings of retrograde spirits. Take, for example, a January 1899 article titled "The Rush of American Women," which begins by asserting that a "sense of rush has taken hold of the American woman," which had proven detrimental to family life. "Outside interests have crowded out home affairs in the case of too many of our wives and mothers. . . . The whole business of women's clubs and women's organizations of every sort is being overdone." The writer reminds her married readers that governing a home allows for very little leisure time, and ends with a patronizing injunction:

> It is high time that our women should lead calmer lives, and get away from the notion that what we call "progress" in these days demands that they shall fill their thoughts and lives with matters at the cost of their health or peace of mind. Our homes must have more of a restful calm, and our wives must not be lured into nervous haste and

forgetfulness by wrong ambitions or foolish ideas of what the world expects of them.

Substitute the idea of paid employment and one hears the same critique of wives and mothers coming from conservative pundits a hundred years later. Yes, we agree, it is high time that our women should lead calmer lives. Unfortunately, most wives today cannot choose to make housekeeping an exclusive profession, even if they wanted to, and there are few alternatives to working forty hours per week outside the home and at least twenty more at home. Most husbands do not yet share housekeeping tasks equally with their wives, most families cannot afford substantial domestic help, and few community services are available to make the working couple's life less stressful. A hundred years ago, if we are to believe this editorial and similar documents, many middle-class women who were able to leave housekeeping tasks in the hands of their servants preferred the hustle and bustle of outside activity to the monotony of cleaning and cooking, regardless of the effect on their families and their own peace of mind.

While the conservative critics of the 1880s and 1890s directed their attacks against the restlessness of the New Woman and her abandonment of domesticity, radical and progressive thinkers defended her right to rebel against fixed sex roles and to strike out in the direction of greater independence. They emphasized the need for women to be able to support themselves through paid employment, which was seen less as a threat to marriage itself than an end to female degradation encountered in the "marriage market."[14] In his immensely popular *Theory of the Leisure Class* (1899), economist Thorstein Veblen offered a devastating portrait of the middle-class wife, whose lack of paid employment attested to her husband's social status. Veblen's term "conspicuous consumption" heralded an era of consumerism during which married women were increasingly targeted as buyers of household goods and personal items intended largely to display the family's wealth.

Among the intellectuals who conceptualized married women's situation within the context of capitalistic America, none was more insightful than Charlotte Perkins Gilman. Her reformist book, *Women and Economics* (1898), prefigured the work of Simone de Beauvoir a half

Advertisement for "Domestic Sewing Machine," circa 1882. (Library of Congress, Washington, D.C.)

century later in its insistence that female dependence upon male income was the primary reason for women's secondary status. Gilman was aware that the economic change she envisioned for women was already taking place. Her goal was to analyze that change and encourage it.

In Gilman's Darwinian view of things, the exodus of women from the home was an inevitable part of nineteenth-century industrialism: with machines replacing the labor of women on the farms, they no longer needed to be full-time housekeepers.[15] Outside work was seen as a liberating force for women, one that would enlarge their horizons and put them on an equal standing with men. Gilman was by no means an enemy of marriage, only of that form of marriage which restricted and weakened women's lives. In traditional marriage, she wrote, "The woman is narrowed by the home and the man is narrowed by the woman."[16]

Gilman recognized that the labor of women in their homes "has a genuine economic value," in that it "enables men to produce more wealth than they otherwise could." But this economic value was neither recognized by society nor equitably rewarded. "The women who do the most work get the least money, and the women who have the most money do the least work."[17] Her solution was not to pay women for their domestic and maternal labor, either in the form of an allowance from their husbands or a government stipend for each child, as in some European nations, but to encourage women to achieve economic independence on their own.

Although Gilman focused on economics as the key to liberation, her vision encompassed the broader aims of Abba Goold Woolson a generation earlier, who had proclaimed the right for women to live fully human, noncontingent lives in every respect. Work was honored as a fundamental means of self-fulfillment: "to do and to make not only gives deep pleasure, but is indispensable to healthy growth. Few girls to-day fail to manifest some signs of this desire for individual expression."[18] It was inevitable that modern women, with their celebration of individual differences, would reject an earlier, one-size-fits all, conjugal model.

Specialization was seen as a boon to family living. Not every wife need be cook, house cleaner, and nanny. Rather, with women entering the workforce in increasing numbers, many of their traditional housekeeping duties could be fulfilled by specialized workers. And here Gilman's vision of societal change has yet to be realized, for she imagined apartment houses for professional women with families, a common dining room, housecleaning done by efficient workers, "a roof garden, day nursery, and kindergarten, under well-trained professional nurses and teachers."[19] Ah, yes, working mothers then and now would flock to such a dwelling.

Gilman was both an acute social critic and an optimistic visionary. As she told an audience in 1903: "We shall have far happier marriages, happier homes, happier women and happier men when both sexes realize that they are human and that humanity has far wider duties and desires than those of the domestic relations."[20]

How these ideas played out in her personal life reveals the gap that always exists between the ideal and its practical reality. Gilman was married twice, first to the artist Charles Walter Stetson when she was twenty-four in 1884. A year later, she gave birth to a daughter, Katherine, who occasioned in her mother both profound joy and deep despair. Hers was more than a "normal" postpartum depression, for it reduced her to weeping, fatigue, and near psychosis. A regimen of total bed rest devoid of any intellectual stimulation, undertaken at the advice of neurologist Dr. S. Weir Mitchell, only worsened her despair. As presented in her autobiographical novella *The Yellow Wallpaper* (1892), she came to see her depression as a flight from marriage and motherhood, exacerbated by well-intentioned, but ultimately destructive, patriarchal figures.[21] Eventually she and her husband divorced, which did not prevent her from remarrying in 1900, this time to her lawyer cousin, George Houghton Gilman. This marriage seems to have been congenial, perhaps because it did not limit Gilman's active life as a writer and lecturer.

By the time of her second marriage, she had already established herself on the national scene. She was the renowned author of *Women and Economics,* to be followed in the decades to come by several other books, dozens of articles, and numerous public lectures. Between 1909 and 1916, she also published a monthly magazine, *The Forerunner,* for which she wrote most of the copy. Gilman's role as wife and mother took a backseat to her role as public figure. She even gave her daughter, Katherine, to Stetson and his second wife to raise, and did not take her back until she was grown. In later life, the New York household consisting of Charlotte and George Gilman, and her daughter, Katherine, seems to have been a happy one, perhaps because George—seven years Charlotte's junior—seems to have deferred to his wife's forceful personality.

One mark of Charlotte Perkins Gilman's strong will was the way she dealt with breast cancer at the end of her life. At a time when breast cancer was still a taboo subject, Gilman faced it with courage and equanimity. From 1932, when the disease was discovered, until 1934, when her husband died unexpectedly, she continued to write and lecture. Then she moved to California to live with her daughter, and, in 1935, aware that her cancer had not been arrested by the best medical efforts of her day, she ended her life with a dose of chloroform, leaving behind a suicide note that read: "I have preferred chloroform to cancer." The note appeared in her posthumously published autobiography *The Living of Charlotte Perkins Gilman* (1935).

Violet Blair Janin and Charlotte Perkins Gilman represent extreme forms of the married New Woman. Both were—in very different ways—products of an age that allowed middle- and upper-class women new possibilities for self-determination. Janin imposed her will on an adoring husband, lived a separate life from him in a different city, controlled her own money, and got involved in a number of women's clubs and organizations. Only toward the end of her life, when age and infirmity weakened her husband, did she assume the conventional responsibilities of a caring wife.

Charlotte Perkins Gilman was equally unsuited to traditional conjugality. She divorced one husband, gave up the care of her daughter, struck out for herself as a wage-earning writer, and established an egalitarian marriage with a younger man. In her life and work, she led the vanguard of change for married women. Like her British contemporary Cicely Hamilton, author of a widely read work titled *Marriage as a Trade* (1909), Gilman recognized that marriage would continue to be a compulsory career for most women, unless the doors of other occupations were open to them.

Before Gilman, no one had so clearly articulated the need for paid employment for married as well as single women. She noted that 3 million American women were already working by the turn of the century. In the agriculture sector, the Census of 1900 counted over 300,000 women as farmers, planters, or overseers, as well as 500,000 women (mostly black) who were farm laborers. By 1910, over a million wives worked as factory workers, clerks, saleswomen, teachers, bookkeepers and accountants, managers of business, and college professors, to name some of their major occupations.[22] Gilman was certainly correct in her prediction that women, including married women, would swell the ranks of the labor force as never before, though her prophecy was not to be fully realized until the last decades of the twentieth century.

But Gilman's prophecy that women's employment would result in "happier marriages, happier homes, happier women and happier men" is open to question. Like many visionaries, she did not foresee the problems that would be produced by the realization of her hopes.

EIGHT

Sex, Contraception, and Abortion in the United States, 1840–1940

We often speak of the dramatic changes that took place during the second half of the twentieth century as constituting a sexual revolution; yet like most revolutions, this one evolved gradually for decades before speeding up and overtaking traditional mores. The partisans of sexual freedom, the pill, and legal abortion in the 1960s and 1970s did not know it, but they were the distant inheritors of changing attitudes and practices that had begun more than a hundred years earlier. Let's go back to that earlier era to see how it experienced its own upheavals in the realms of sexuality, contraception, and abortion, and how it laid the subterranean foundations for today's sexual norms.

IDEOLOGY AND EXPERIENCE

Victorian women were commonly characterized as "angels in the house," ethereal spirits lacking sensual and sexual needs, less lusty and "purer" than men. This view was furthered not only by nineteenth-century novels featuring innocent brides and virtuous wives, but also by the medical treatises promoting an ideology of female sexlessness. The esteemed British doctor William Acton (cited earlier) was convinced that "many of the best mothers, wives, and managers of households know little of . . . sexual indulgence. Love of home, of children, and of domestic duties are the only passions that they feel." And Acton was by no means the only physician who characterized good women by their lack of sexual desire.[1]

In the 1870s and 1880s, as debate over the Woman Question became more vocal on both sides of the Atlantic, a new version of female sexuality began to refute the earlier one. Many thinkers of both genders allowed that women were not so different from men in the heat of desire. The American Elizabeth Evans, in *Abuse of Maternity* (1875), scoffed at the idea "that passion is much weaker in the female than in the male" and insisted that whatever difference there was resulted from "training" and "restraining circumstances." Challenging the received wisdom of Victorian society, she attributed women's chaste outward appearance to "the force of public opinion."[2] Similarly, reversing his previously expressed opinion that many women were basically frigid, even as wives, Dr. George H. Napheys later insisted: "It is a false notion, and contrary to nature, that this passion in a woman is a derogation to her sex." And accepting the mutual nature of desire between husband and wife, he concluded: "There should be no passion for one which is not shared by both."[3]

Other medical experts, presenting the case for anatomical knowledge as the key to satisfying sex, described the female genitalia with special attention to the clitoris; they recognized its primacy in female arousal, and, unlike Freud at the turn of the century, did not distinguish between "clitoral" and "vaginal" orgasm—an error in his thinking that had long-term negative consequences for many women who were made to feel they were not having the "right" kind. In the 1880s, doctors like Edward B. Foote (an outspoken proponent of birth control in America) wrote knowingly of "the clitoris and the erectile tissue of the vagina" as the parts that "induce sexual excitement" and bring about orgasm in women.[4]

What did married women themselves thinks of all these pronouncements? Did they try to be as sexless in the bedroom as some Victorian doctors told them they were? Or did they agree knowingly with the alternative picture of female passion? It is practically impossible to answer these questions, since neither wives nor single women left personal records of their sexual feelings and experiences. The conventions of their day precluded committing anything so intimate to paper. Yet there are a few sources that give us glimmers of insight into their private sexual worlds.

For one thing, there are the statements of married women within the Women's Christian Temperance Movement attesting to their husbands' amorous appetites, and to their own lofty indifference to the claims of sexuality. Perhaps they shunned sexual relations as a way of warding off another pregnancy, or perhaps they became truly fearful of a husband given to drink. Following the advice of purity manuals that counseled separate bedrooms for spouses and total continence during pregnancy and lactation, some wives were thus able to exert a measure of control over the marital bed. As one wife is reported to have said: "In my early married life, my husband and I learned how to live in holy relations, after God's ordinance. My husband lovingly consented to let me live apart from him during the time I carried his little daughter under my heart, and also while I was nursing her. . . . My husband and I were never so tenderly, so harmoniously, or so happily related to each other, and I never loved him more deeply than during these blessed months."[5] This wife sounds much like a Victorian reincarnation of Margery Kempe persuading her medieval husband to take a vow of chastity.

For more positive attitudes toward sex, our best source so far is the research conducted by Dr. Clelia Mosher between 1892 and 1920, which offers a unique picture of forty-five American wives reaching adulthood in the late nineteenth century.[6] As a gynecologist and university professor, Mosher asked a number of her patients to fill out lengthy questionnaires on their family history, general health, and sexual practices. Her respondents were mostly upper-middle-class wives with college education. She asked them specifically about the experience of intercourse—how often it occurred, how often they experienced "venereal orgasm," whether they enjoyed it, whether they used birth control, and what they considered the "true purpose" of intercourse.

Most reported they had intercourse about once a week, within a general range of two to eight times per month. An occasional woman spoke of greater frequency (three times per week or every night) especially during the first years of marriage. Some mentioned long periods of abstinence during pregnancy and lactation or when they were cautiously avoiding pregnancy, and several indicated that their marital relationships had waned over time. One woman, married for fifteen years, who had had intercourse twice a week early in her marriage, reported that intercourse had occurred "4 times for the last six years." Several women alluded to a diminishment of desire in later life, as in this statement by a fifty-three-year-old wife: "Although my passionate feeling has declined somewhat and the orgasm does not always occur, intercourse is still agreeable to me."

About three quarters of the women had experienced orgasm in marriage, with over a third saying they experienced it "always" or "usually." One woman responded "Never" and another "Never but once or twice." Another "had hardly experienced an orgasm until the fifth or sixth year of married life," then it occurred "half the time." Historian Carl Degler (who stumbled upon the Mosher papers in the Stanford University Archives) notes that this incidence of orgasm "compares favorably" with that reported by Kinsey in 1953.[7] The Mosher women were, of course, a small, highly select sample, and their sexual experience does not necessarily represent late Victorians at every level of society.

Forty-one of the forty-five wives used some form of birth control. The men practiced withdrawal or used condoms (referred to as a "thin rubber covering" or "rubber sheath"). The women relied on douches ("soap and water injection," "clean water with fountain syringe," "douches of bichloride," "cocoa butter & cold water douche") and various internal appliances ("Good-year rubber ring," "Rubber cap over uterus," "woman's shield—pessary cap given by Dr.") As discussed in the following pages, women of the middle and upper classes had no difficulty obtaining contraception from their doctors and pharmacists.

Most of the women considered reproduction to be the overriding purpose of intercourse, echoing the belief current among Christians and social Darwinians that "generation is a duty." Several felt that intercourse was *only* for procreation, as in the following statements: "Intercourse at desired intervals until pregnancy occurs, then abstinence until end of lactation." "Intercourse . . . until conception takes place. No intercourse during gestation and lactation." A thirty-one-year-old woman judged the ideal practice to be "total abstinence, with intercourse for reproduction only."

Yet even as they accepted their obligation to procreate, many of these women appreciated sex as an expression of love that created a special "spiritual" bond between husband and wife. Without much prompting, they wrote eloquently on this subject. "It seems to me to be a natural and physical sign of a spiritual union, a renewal of the marriage vows."

"The marriage relation should be nearer than any other. Sexual inter-course is the means which brings this about." "In my experience the habitual bodily expression of love has a deep psychological effect in making possible complete mental sympathy and perfecting the spiritual union that must be the lasting 'marriage' after the passion of love has passed away with the years." "The marital relation when *mutual* begets a certain bond of love and sympathy that is certainly peculiar only to those happily mated." "It is the one thing a woman gives which no one else can give—brings intimacy & closeness."

Some of the women attributed psychological benefits to regular sex-ual intercourse: it was credited with making the "marriage more stable" and the spouses more "normal." In language that sounds strangely like that of later-day health professionals, one wife declared: "A normal desire and a rational use of it tends to keep people healthier."

One woman in 1893 expressed a sexual credo that could have been written today: "The desire of both husband and wife for this expression of their union seems to me the first and highest reason for intercourse. The desire for offspring is a secondary, incidental, although entirely worthy motive but could never make intercourse right unless the mutual desire were also present. . . . My husband and I believe in inter-course for its own sake—we wish it for ourselves and spiritually miss it, rather than physically, when it does not occur, because it is the highest, most sacred expression of our oneness." Such a vision of sex having value in and of itself, apart from its procreative properties, would become increasingly common in the twentieth century.

CONTRACEPTION

But many Americans did not share the view of this woman and the forty-one wives in her cohort who practiced birth control. Those who believed that God or Nature had instituted copulation for the sole pur-pose of generation and who bemoaned the declining white birth rate (from seven babies per American-born white wife in 1800 to roughly half that number in 1900) were often staunch opponents of any form of contraception.

Knowledge about contraceptive devices had been seeping into American society since the 1820s from the fledgling birth control movement in England. The British concern about overpopulation articulated by Robert Malthus (1766–1834) and the attempts of Francis Place (1771–1854) to educate the masses influenced the first American efforts to disseminate contraceptive information.

In 1839, *Fruits of Philosophy; or, The Private Companion of Young Married People,* by Charles Knowlton, became the first American pamphlet on contraception published by a physician. Knowlton recommended postcoital douching as an effective means of evacuating the sperm. Women were advised to douche right after intercourse with a pint of water mixed with one of the following substances: alum, sulphate of zinc, sal eratus, vinegar, and liquid of soda. In Knowlton's opinion, these methods were sure, cheap, harmless, did not cause sterility, and did not interfere with coitus. Moreover, control was placed in the hands of the women, which was considered a good thing.

One of Knowlton's followers, the health writer Frederick Hollick, popularized douching and the rhythm method or "safe period," although medical knowledge was still confused about the fertile and infertile periods of the menstrual cycle. Since then, and especially after 1850, social reformers published books, pamphlets, tracts, and treatises advising women and men on the ways of avoiding an unwanted pregnancy.

James Ashton's influential *Book of Nature,* published in 1860 and reprinted several times thereafter, listed the five most popular methods of averting conception: "withdrawal, douching, the vaginal sponge, condoms, and the rhythm method."[8] He was unusually direct in his discussion of each method, and sensitive to the advantages or disadvantages for either the male or the female partner.

The increased visibility of contraceptive information and devices ran afoul of what came to be known as the "purity movement." During the second half of the nineteenth century, American and European purity activists, determined to control other people's sexuality, railed against male vice, prostitution, the spread of venereal disease, and the risks run by a chaste wife in the arms of a dissolute husband. They agitated against the availability of contraception under the assumption that such devices, because of their association with prostitution, would sully the home.

Societies for the "suppression of vice" were popular in a number of cities, including Boston, where blue bloods like the Cabots and the Lodges figured prominently in the campaign. In New York, with the

YMCA as headquarters, purity crusaders, including the fanatical Anthony Comstock, acted like medieval Christians engaged in a holy war. Comstock's dogged efforts resulted in the 1873 law passed by Congress that barred use of the postal system for the distribution of any "article or thing designed or intended for the prevention of contraception or procuring of abortion." Comstock was then appointed a special agent for the U.S. Post Office with the power to ferret out and destroy illegal mail—a position he pursued vigorously until he died in 1915.

One early victim of the Comstock laws was the physician Edward Bliss Foote, who had advocated the use of contraception in several books and pamphlets (*Medical Common Sense, Plain Home Talk, Home Encyclopedia, Words in Pearl*) and in his periodical the *Health Monthly* (1876–1883). In January 1876, he was indicted in the U.S. District Court of New York for the distribution through the mails of contraceptive information. Tried and found guilty, Foote was fined $3,000. When he appealed for financial help through his periodical, some three hundred donors responded, indicating substantial liberal support for his work. Nevertheless, after the prosecution, Foote became more cautious.[9]

Before the introduction of the Comstock laws, contraceptive devices were openly advertised in newspapers, tabloids, pamphlets, and health magazines. Condoms had become increasingly popular since the late 1830s, when vulcanized rubber (the invention of Charles Goodyear) began to replace the earlier sheepskin models, which had been used primarily to avoid venereal infections. In the 1840s, vaginal sponges also became increasingly available, not only from dubious sources like advertisements and traveling salesmen, but also from reputable druggists and physicians. The vaginal sponge, moistened with spermicide and containing a cord that facilitated withdrawal after intercourse, was one of the most effective known means of birth control.

While the diaphragm, invented in 1882 by the German physician, Wilhelm Peter Mensinga, did not make its way to the United States until the 1920s, similar American devices were being produced decades earlier. In 1846, a diaphragm-like article called "The Wife's Protector" was patented in the United States, and in the 1860s and 1870s, a wide assortment of pessaries (vaginal rubber caps) could be purchased at two to six dollars each.[10]

John D'Emilio and Estelle Freedman in their book *Intimate Matters* include several examples of married women sharing contraceptive knowledge. In 1876, Mary Hallock Foote wrote to her friend Helena Gilder that "a sure way of limiting one's family" was for her husband to "go to a physician and get shields of some kind. They are to be had also at some druggists. It sounds perfectly revolting, but one must face anything rather than the inevitable result of Nature's methods."[11]

In 1885, Rose Williams wrote from the Dakota Territory to her friend Allettie Mosher in Ohio: "I do not know whether you can get them out there. They are called Pessairre or female prevenative [sic]. They cost one dollar when Sis got hers it was before any of us went to Dak[ota]. She paid five dollars for it. The Directions are with it."[12] As these two letters indicate, women with and without advanced literacy managed to send information to their friends wanting to avoid pregnancy. By the last decades of the nineteenth century, as the Mosher study suggests, most middle-class couples were familiar with some form of contraception.[13]

The most common justification for limiting reproduction was that it was good for both the mother and the child. Dr. Napheys, for one, decried the disastrous effects of "*overproduction*—having *too many* children." In language worthy of an evangelical preacher, he spoke of "the evils of a too rapid succession of pregnancies," which resulted in "weakly infants." Similarly, Dr. W. R. D. Blackwood voiced a compassionate plea on behalf of needy wives: "Is it proper, is it human, is it desirable that the lot of a married female should be a continual round of impregnation, delivery, and lactation? . . . I do not hesitate for an instant to say NO! And I look with more than suspicion on the fulminations of those who, assuming superior virtue, condemn any and all attempts to control conception."[14]

In her highly popular *What Women Should Know* (1873), Eliza Duffey criticized "enforced child-bearing" and argued for "a limitation of the number of offspring" in the interest of the mother. Sounding a "pro-choice" note a hundred years before that term was invented, she insisted: "Surely, if there is any personal question which an individual has a right to decide, the woman should have a voice in the matter of childbearing. She has to endure the pains, penalties and responsibilities, both before and afterward, and she can best judge of her fitness and her powers of endurance."[15]

ABORTION

Duffey's support of a woman's right to choose did not, however, countenance abortion, which she unequivocally opposed. Like many of her generation, she had come to question the previously accepted view that human life begins at "quickening," that is, when a pregnant woman first feels fetal movement. During the eighteenth and early nineteenth centuries, this was the official position of the medical profession and the common law; consequently, abortions prior to quickening (around the fourth month of pregnancy) were not considered criminal offenses. If an early pregnancy ended, it was spoken of without reference to possible induction: it had simply "slipped away."[16]

Home remedies for abortion were passed on from one generation to the next, some brought from Europe, some learned from midwives, others from Native American healers. Brews mixed from the root of rue or leaves of the tansy plant were commonly ingested to produce abortion, as well as cathartics and potentially poisonous substances like calomel, aloes, ergot, prussic acid, iodine, and strychnine. Southern women wanting to miscarry were known to drink cottonseed tea. Home medical manuals characteristically contained information for unblocking "obstructed menses," such as bloodletting, bathing, iron and quinine concoctions, and other purgatives.[17] Physicians were often willing to help women "restore their periods," and Americans generally looked the other way when single women, anxious to avoid the disgrace of an illegitimate child, resorted to abortion. Only abortions after quickening were legally punishable, and even such cases were always difficult to prosecute.

But from the 1830s and 1840s onward, some states—for example, New York, Connecticut, Missouri, Illinois—began to enact more stringent antiabortion legislation and to question the distinction between the prequickening and the postquickening fetus. Did life begin at conception or at the moment of quickening? If life began at conception, then it was a crime for a woman to voluntarily abort at any time during her pregnancy. But if life began only at quickening, then it was not a crime to induce abortion before fetal movement was felt. As late as 1888, a Boston physician concluded that there was considerable confusion over whether "destruction of the infant" before quickening was a common law offense.[18]

Between 1860 and 1880, more than forty antiabortion laws were passed, some in states that had no prior ban on abortion. The antiabortion legislation relied on the support of medical doctors concerned with the increased incidence of abortion and the dangerous presence of quacks in the field. But there was another, equally pressing concern. After 1840, it became increasingly apparent that abortion was no longer confined to desperate single women. A high proportion of those obtaining abortions were "married, native-born, Protestant women, frequently of middle- or upper-class status."[19] As legal historian Lawrence M. Friedman has pointed out, it went against the ideology of sacred motherhood to countenance abortion for married women, especially if they were white and middle class.[20] Antiabortion activists condemned the "unnatural" woman who got rid of her offspring and blamed abortion for the decreasing birthrate of American-born, white children.

Doctors contributing to the midcentury repression of abortion fired off numerous salvos to their medical journals, expressing dismay that abortions were sought after by "married women, who have no apology for concealment, and who only desire to rid themselves of the prospective cares of maternity" (*Boston Medical and Surgical Journal*, 1854).[21] During the mid-1850s, the leading antiabortion crusader, Dr. Horatio Storer, went about gathering data on abortion, stillbirths, and maternal deaths from his medical colleagues. One of them wrote from the Minnesota Territory that "the practice of producing abortion is frequently resorted to in our vicinity and it is not infrequent for married women of high social position to apply for medicines which will produce abortion"—medicines they often obtained from "Regular physicians."[22] Armed with this information, Storer succeeded in persuading the American Medical Association to condemn abortion on the grounds that it was medically dangerous.

Despite the condemnation of abortion by the AMA, numerous physicians around the country continued to perform them, even after they were made illegal. In 1888, the *Chicago Times* exposé of abortion in the Windy City, home of the American Medical Association, documented the willingness of many doctors to help both married and unmarried women terminate a pregnancy.[23] The *Times* investigative report was a great embarrassment to the AMA, which had initiated the campaign to criminalize abortion, yet could not prevent its own members from making them available to women.

One of the findings of the *Times* report was that the abortion trade was not limited to the unwed. Wives from the middle and upper classes patronized abortionists more than lower-class single women, facts confirmed by the physicians themselves. One of them, Dr. Odelia Blinn, recalled that the vast majority of women who had asked her for an abortion were married. Unlike those who criticized such women for avoiding their wifely duties and for shamelessly committing a great evil, Dr. Blinn turned her criticism to the husband, the one who shared equal, if not greater, responsibility for the wife's pregnancy in the first place.

The use of abortion as a means of family limitation was, by the turn of the century, what one historian has called "an open secret."[24] That it was not confined to wealthy "society women" was apparent from the case of Frances Collins. As Leslie Reagan tells the story in *When Abortion Was a Crime,* Mrs. Collins was a working-class, married mother of two children. In April 1920, at the age of thirty-four, she went to a certain Dr. Warner's office in Chicago to have "her womb opened up." The doctor inserted an instrument into her womb, and she returned home, where she complained to her husband that she was "unwell." Later she became sick with vaginal bleeding, chills, and vomiting, and failed to improve, despite the ministrations of Dr. Warner, who treated her at home. By the end of April, Mrs. Collins was hospitalized by another doctor, the one who had delivered her two children and had advised her against procuring abortions. Shortly thereafter she died. Mr. and Mrs. Collins, like many other working-class families, had simply accepted abortion as a matter-of-fact method of preventing the birth of another child, the last time with tragic results.[25]

MARGARET SANGER AND THE BIRTH CONTROL MOVEMENT

In 1869, a twenty-one-year old woman named Anne Purcell married Michael Higgins in the state of New York. Both came from working-class, Irish-immigrant families, and though they were both nominally Catholic, only Anne was a believer. This may have accounted for her refusal to use any form of contraception, which was obtainable in her day, but specifically banned by Catholic doctrine. Anne Purcell was to have eleven children and to die, exhausted and consumptive, in 1899. One of these children was Margaret Sanger.[26]

The memory of her mother was undoubtedly a major factor in Margaret Sanger's work to make contraception legal and available to married women. Trained as a nurse and married in 1902 at the age of twenty-three to a young architect, Sanger limited her own progeny to three children during a period of eight years. When her family moved from Hastings, New York, to the city in 1910, she took up work as a part-time nurse in the immigrant districts of New York's Lower East Side. The plight of women who, like her mother, wore themselves out with continuous childbirth awakened her social conscience.

She was particularly moved at the sight of women with shawls over their heads lining up outside the office of a five-dollar abortionist, and even more so at the sight of the patients she nursed after the complications of an illegal abortion. One in particular, Sadie Sachs, remained in her memory for half a century as the archetypal immigrant wife who died from septicemia following a self-induced abortion. This woman had been told by her physician that the only reliable contraceptive was to have her husband "sleep on the roof."

By 1911 Sanger was offering public lectures on sexuality and reproduction under the auspices of the Socialist Party, and in 1912 she began a weekly column called "What Every Girl Should Know" for the Socialist newspaper *The Call*. In it she discussed such daring subjects as menstruation, masturbation, pregnancy, contraception, and abortion— columns that provoked an outpouring of heated responses (both negative and positive) from *The Call*'s readership. Her article on venereal disease brought her into direct confrontation with her antagonist and nemesis, Anthony Comstock, who outlawed her column in 1913. Comstock's efforts to turn back the tide of freer sexual information and practices were destined to failure, but he and his like undeniably slowed its progress.

From this point on, Sanger was often in conflict with the law. Her arrests, flights from justice, trials, fines, and imprisonments were the subject of both public outrage and mounting support. When she was tried in 1917 for distributing birth control information and devices to immigrant women from a clinic she had established in a Brooklyn storefront, thirty of her clients were subpoenaed and came to the courtroom with numerous babies in tow, presumably to indicate their need for family limitation. Found guilty and given the choice of a $5,000 fine or thirty days in prison, Sanger chose the latter.

The saga of her trial continued into January 1918, when, in response to an appeal, her original conviction was upheld under the state's obscenity law. However, the judge allowed that contraception could be used to prevent venereal disease, and for other broadly defined medical purposes. This interpretation would allow Sanger and other birth control advocates some leeway in the decades to come.

Sanger's marriage did not survive the turmoil of those early, strife-filled years. Unlike Elizabeth Cady Stanton in the nineteenth century, Sanger was not about to raise a brood of children, support a financially failing husband from the revenues of her lectures and publications, and remain sexually "pure." The times were different, and they were heady indeed for a perky woman of Irish extraction, drawn to left-wing politics and the free-love circles of American and European bohemia. Suffice it to say that her lovers included such distinguished figures as the sexologist Havelock Ellis and the writer H. G. Wells, both of whom added to her intellectual capital. Ellis wrote an introduction to her first book, *Woman and the New Race,* and Wells, an introduction to the one that followed, *The Pivot of Civilization.* Together the two books sold more than a half million copies during the 1920s. In these and other works, Sanger argued not only for birth control as an indispensable right for married women, but also for the new sexual ethics that were gaining ground in the twenties. Free to control the number of her children, a wife would presumably be more able to enter into public life and help solve the pressing problems of war, poverty, and class conflict. While Sanger's broad hopes for humankind are still to be realized, she left her personal mark on history as the founder of the birth control movement in America.

Despite ongoing opposition, the movement found many allies in unlikely places, including some of the more progressive religions. In 1930, the bishops of the Anglican church issued from London a carefully worded statement condoning the use of artificial contraception within marriage when spouses felt a moral obligation to limit parenthood. A year later, the Federal Council of the Churches of Christ in America, chaired by theologian Reinhold Niebuhr and representing some 22 million Protestants, formally endorsed birth control on medical and economic grounds. Echoing words that had been penned fifty years earlier, birth control was seen as protection for the health of women and children and as a deterrent to poverty and overpopulation. But this view was not accepted unanimously among all American Protestant sects; conservative members, including some Methodists, Presbyterians, and Lutherans, turned their backs on it and did not reverse their position until the 1950s.

The Catholic church continued to oppose all forms of contraception. In his 1930 encyclical *Casti Conubii* (Of Chaste Marriage), Pope Pius XI declared that any human effort that deprived marriage "of its natural power of procreating life, violates the law of God and nature, and those who do such a thing are stained by a grave and mortal flaw." Yet in one way, the encyclical clarified centuries of confusion over intercourse between spouses; it stated explicitly that marital sex bears "no taint of evil." While emphatically upholding procreation as the primary purpose of sex and emphatically condemning the use of contraception, the pope allowed for the "secondary ends" of marriage in "mutual aid, the cultivating of mutual love, and the quieting of concupiscence." In this vein, the pope also recognized the right of married couples to continue sexual relations after menopause.

Although the church officially opposed birth control, some Catholics went so far as to propose the rhythm method as an acceptable contraceptive practice for the faithful. This practice had been recommended outside the church by a few secular thinkers since the mid-nineteenth century, but it was not until 1929 that scientists fully understood how it works: ovulation occurs sixteen to twelve days before the onset of menstruation, and a woman must abstain from intercourse for at least eight days before ovulation and three days after. (Even so, this method is by no means infallible.) In 1932, a book titled *The Rhythm of Sterility and Fertility in Women*, published by a Catholic physician with the support of prominent Catholics in Chicago, advised women to keep a calendar and limit sexual activity to the sterile period. It took another twenty years before the church officially accepted the use of the rhythm method when absolutely necessary for medical, eugenic, or economic reasons (Pope Pius XII's *Moral Questions Affecting Married Life.*)

THE NEW SEXUALITY

The birth control movement and the more liberal stance adopted by most Judeo-Christian denominations by the mid-twentieth century corresponded to a new marital vision that had been developing for decades. Americans were moving away from procreation-centered marriage to the ideal of a union based on love, companionship, and the enjoyment of sex, within the context of a society increasingly dominated by "consumption, gratification, and pleasure."[27] The idea that sex should be frankly pleasurable, instead of inherently shameful, and that it should be enjoyed by both parties was a driving force in the trend toward egalitarian marriages.

More positive attitudes toward sex, expressed in films, fiction, and nonfiction, were filtering into the American consciousness. Some of the impetus came from abroad, from the pioneering work of Sigmund Freud and Havelock Ellis, who located the major source of personal unhappiness in sexual repression. While Freud concurred with many of his contemporaries that women should be spared competitive labor outside the home and should maintain their preeminent place in the family, Ellis championed women's sexuality and their right to be both domestic and public creatures.

How did these burgeoning theories and movements affect the sexual sensibilities and practices of American wives? Unfortunately, we do not find in female-authored writing from this period much greater willingness to express personal sexual feelings and experiences than we did in the Victorian era—at least not in anything intended for another person's eyes, like an autobiography, a poem, or a piece of fiction. Women in the modern Anglo-American world simply did not write about such things until the late twentieth century. Oh, yes, there were a few pioneers like the Southern writer Kate Chopin in her novel *The Awakening* (1899) and the British author Radclyffe Hall in *The Well of Loneliness* (1928). Chopin portrayed a passionate mother in a stifling marriage, determined to have a fate different from the other wives "who idolized their children, worshipped their husbands, and esteemed it a holy privilege to efface themselves."[28] Hall took on the even more shocking subject of lesbianism, a subject so taboo that her book was banned in England, though it was sold in France and America. While Chopin expressed the marital claustrophobia and inner turmoil that some wives undoubtedly felt at the turn of the century, and Hall gave expression to the new sexual freedom of the flapper era, both writers were clearly far from the mainstream.

Mainstream America was still committed to the ideals of premarital chastity for women and postmarital satisfaction in their roles as wives and mothers. Only notorious vamps and other "evil sisters"—staples of the early film industry—defied the image of the wholesome help-meet.[29] If a respectable woman took pleasure in marital lovemaking, as she was now entitled to, it was still considered inappropriate for her to talk or write about the secrets of the bedroom.

The most revealing documents on female sexuality during this period are found in the newly created sex surveys: for instance, Katherine Bement Davis's *Factors in the Sex Lives of Twenty-two Hundred Women* and Gilbert Hamilton's *A Research in Marriage,* both published in 1929. These studies bear witness to the ongoing sexual evolution that preceded the sexual revolution of the 1960s and 1970s.

Whereas Victorians believed that sex should be strictly limited to marriage and that its preponderant goal was reproduction, Americans emerged from World War I with more tolerant views on a variety of nonprocreative forms of sexuality. Whereas Victorians believed that passion was considerably less significant for women than for men, by the 1920s it was widely recognized that women, too, had strong cravings, if not identical ones to men. Whereas the Mosher survey representing turn-of-the-century wives documented the transition between the Victorian ideal of sex in the service of reproduction and the new ideal of marital sex for its own sake, Davis's and Hamilton's work in 1929 suggested that the transition was basically complete: sex was widely accepted as a conjugal good, irrespective of its procreative possibility.

A closer look at the Davis survey reveals the following. Most wives reported intercourse on a weekly basis, and 74 percent of them practiced some form of contraception. Although a quarter of the women reported that their initial experience of marital sex repelled them, more than half came to enjoy sex as the marriage progressed. Thirty percent of the wives judged their sexual appetites to be as strong as their husbands'.[30]

Davis's survey also tells us something about nonmarital sexual activities: 7 percent of the wives admitted to having had premarital sex, 40 percent of the married women and 65 percent of the single women reported having practiced masturbation, and a large number of unmarried college graduates reported having had a homosexual experience. Davis's presentation of this information shows the extent to which sex—even aspects that would be considered "immoral" or "abnormal" by most Americans—could now be investigated, at least in scientific surveys.

In the other 1929 survey, Dr. Hamilton attempted to measure the correlation between sexual satisfaction and marital happiness. Like many of his generation, he assumed that sex was beneficial to marriage, and that sexual dissatisfaction led to severe marital problems. Following Freud, he concerned himself largely with "orgasm inadequacy" on the part of the wife. Since Hamilton's questionnaire looked for marital problems, it is not surprising that he found them. Thirty-five percent of the wives in his sample felt reluctance or aversion to sex the first time it occurred in marriage. Many of them never experienced orgasm, and one-fifth of them were "serious psychoneurotic cases." All of them, except those who were sterile or wanted to become pregnant, used contraception.[31]

The Davis and Hamilton surveys are in some ways contradictory. Davis suggests that wives were generally satisfied with their sexual experiences. Hamilton focused on the problems, and, like other medical experts of his day, he contributed to a new kind of anxiety surrounding female sexuality. In the mid-nineteenth century, wives may have been anxious when they experienced intense desire because society told them they were not supposed to have any. A century later, wives were made to feel anxious if they did *not* experience sexual desire and satisfaction—which for Hamilton and other Freudians meant if they did not achieve "vaginal orgasm" through male penetration. The major similarities between the Davis and Hamilton surveys are the central place accorded to sex in marriage, and the use of contraception by husbands and wives.

The changing sexual attitudes of the early twentieth century must be understood within the context of other fundamental societal changes affecting women. With female suffrage finally a reality in 1920, with more women entering higher education and finding employment, with religion giving way to secular expertise, the New Woman had come of age. Researcher Alfred Kinsey, in his later studies of male and female sexual behavior (to be discussed in chapter 10), would look back to the roaring twenties as the decisive period of change in American sexual attitudes and practices.

Popularizations of the new sexual morality could be found in numerous American magazine articles, advertisements, books, and films. One such book that had wide distribution was *The Hygiene of Marriage* (1932), by Millard Everett from the Central YMCA College in Chicago.[32] His openness in discussing such subjects as the male and female genitalia, venereal diseases, childbirth, and birth control reflected the tenor of the times among liberal-thinking Americans. Procreation took a backseat to sex, now considered "an end in itself" and "one of the chief constituents of happiness." On this point Everett wrote unequivocally: "Reproduction is neither the sole nor the chief purpose of marriage. If one wishes to assign any one supreme purpose to marriage, . . . he will find that it is the desire for sexual communion and companionship."

Ideal marriage, as Everett presented it, bears a close relationship to what some of the Mosher women believed at the turn of the century and to what most Americans believe today. He recognized the need for romantic love in the initial stages of a relationship, and sexual freedom within the marital bed for both parties, but even more so, he focused heavily on the "fundamental equality" of husbands and wives. He counseled men and women "to enter marriage with the same background of experience in every respect." He advised women to attain "economic independence, not only because it will make men and women better companions . . . but also because they will possess greater freedom and therefore be less constrained to endure the injustice or overbearing ways of men." He recommended that husbands and wives, "unless they are hopelessly enslaved to a medieval tradition" (by which he meant Catholicism), should be knowledgeable about contraception. And he looked forward to the day "when men and women share the work of the world alike; when women, merely because of the few times when their function of childbearing is exercised will not be excluded from a life of stimulating, purposeful activity . . . and when neither man nor woman will be 'head of the house' but marriage will be a genuine partnership."

While this hopeful picture of egalitarian marriage undoubtedly did not represent the views of all, or even most, Americans in Everett's day, it is significant that it had the imprimatur of the YMCA—a bastion of white, middle-class, Protestant values. Wives from that sector of American society were being led to believe that sexual pleasure was their right; that employment, marriage, and children could be combined; and that complete equality with their spouses was just around the corner.

But the following years probably set back this vision in several important ways. Nonrepressive sexuality, egalitarian marriages, working wives were simply not a top priority during the economically depressed thirties. Most people were downright grateful if one person, usually the husband, had a job. As public sentiment blamed working wives for taking jobs away from men, state legislatures even enacted laws restricting the employment of married women.[33] Both wives who worked outside the home and wives who did not struggled to limit their household expenses *and* the number of their children.

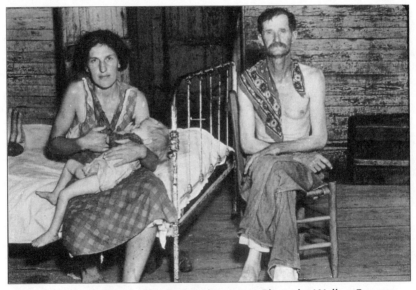

Poor rural couple during the Depression years. Photo by Walker Evans, 1935. (Library of Congress, Washington, D.C.)

CONTRACEPTION AND ABORTION:
THE DEPRESSION YEARS

Although the federal Comstock laws prohibited the use of the postal service for distributing contraceptive information and devices, and about half the states had passed their own anti-contraceptive laws, a growing number of individuals, led by Margaret Sanger, were actively campaigning to make contraception legal and freely available to married women. Throughout the depressed 1930s, birth control activists underscored the need for fertility limitation, especially in families who could not provide for the children they already had. The fear that one could not support one's children or that poor families with numerous children would become dependent on the state persuaded many Americans to accept the need for contraception.

Several legislative victories loosened the Comstock stranglehold on the dissemination of contraceptives. By the mid-1930s, millions of condoms were being produced and sold in any number of venues (drugstores, gas stations, barbershops) to men of all classes, and other forms of birth control, such as the diaphragm, were becoming more readily available to poor as well as middle-class wives.

Much of the change in contraceptive practices must be attributed to the birth control clinics modeled throughout the nation on the one Sanger had established in New York City. In 1930 there were fifty-five of them sponsored in fifteen states by the American Birth Control League. By 1938 there were over five hundred. D'Emilio and Freedman, analyzing Kinsey's research on female sexual behavior during these years, point to the difference between the contraceptive practices of older and younger women.[34] The older group relied primarily on the condom (40 percent), then on the diaphragm (31 percent), and then on douching and withdrawal. By contrast, the younger women relied primarily on the diaphragm (61 percent), and, to a lesser extent, the condom, but douching and withdrawal had become almost negligible. Birth control advocates, who promoted the diaphragm as the most dependable form of contraception, had reason to take heart.

By the end of the 1930s, probably because of the Depression, effective contraception had become more common at all levels of society. Public attitudes toward contraception had shifted from outright condemnation or moral uncertainty to general acceptance. In 1937, the

Cervical caps, 1925. (Wellcome Medical Library, London)

American Medical Association officially abandoned its opposition to birth control. In 1938, a poll conducted by the *Ladies' Home Journal* revealed that 79 percent of American women approved the use of contraception.

In contrast to the openness surrounding contraception, abortion remained a backstairs issue, and it remained so despite a dramatic rise in the number of abortions performed during the Depression. In 1931, Dr. Fred J. Taussig stated in *The American Journal of Obstetrics and Gynecology* that abortions had been steadily increasing, especially among mothers who had borne three or four children. He estimated the number of abortions at 700,000 per year, and the annual mortality of women from this cause at 15,000.[35]

Numerous medical studies attributed the steep rise in abortion to the economic hardships experienced during the Depression by both single and married women. Married women were not only aborting their fourth or fifth child, but first pregnancies as well. One female doctor who interviewed almost a thousand women at a New York City birth control clinic in 1931 and 1932 concluded that wives resorted to abortion when they were the family breadwinners and could not afford to lose their jobs, or when they were simply unable to feed another mouth. Even white, middle-, and upper-class wives had a higher incidence of abortion than ever before.[36]

Like their white counterparts, married black women also used abortion more during the Depression. An African-American surgeon in Cleveland commented in 1932 that "there has been a very definite increase in the numbers of abortions, criminally performed, among the married." Black and white married women of the same class seem to have had abortions at the same rate, but unmarried white women were more likely to abort than unmarried black women, probably because the latter were less ostracized by their communities in the event of an out-of-wedlock birth.

During the early thirties, physicians and hospitals began to see more women coming in for emergency care after a botched abortion. In 1935, the Harlem Hospital in New York opened a separate ward specifically for such women. In 1939, the Cook County Hospital in Chicago treated over a thousand women for abortion-related complications. Though a few physicians were so alarmed by the consequences of this trend that they spoke out in favor of legalizing abortion, the publishing world responded mainly with censure and silence.[37] Members of Sanger's birth control movement were also unwilling to support legalized abortion, for fear they would be tainted through association with a criminal practice.

Despite the public taboo on abortion, quite a few members of the medical profession were willing to perform them, for monetary and/or humanitarian reasons. Historian Leslie J. Reagan, tracing the practice of Dr. Josephine Gabber, a well-trained, highly successful abortion specialist in Chicago, figures that Gabber's State Street clinic performed over 18,000 abortions between 1932 and 1941. The majority of the patients—a full 80 percent—were married. This matches the findings of other studies that suggest that the majority of women who had abortions before World War II were wives.[38] From a small subset of seventy patients records, Reagan was able to determine that most of the married women were homemakers, though about a fourth of them worked outside the home.

The women were either referred by another doctor, or they found the abortionist's name from personal contacts—a friend, a hairdresser, a pharmacist, or a nurse. Most of the wives came early in their pregnancies, which made the procedure easier and safer than if they had come after the first two or three months. The abortions, performed in Gabber's clinic operating room, resembled any other surgical procedure undertaken by a skilled practitioner. Patients left with a list of instructions, including an admonishment to call the office at any time in the event of a problem and to return for a checkup, either the next day or sometime in the next few weeks.

In other cities—New York and Baltimore, for example—reputable physicians were also willing to perform abortions. Reagan concludes that "thousands of women obtained abortions from physicians in con-

ventional medical settings and suffered no complications afterwards."[39]

But many other women, those without sufficient money or a referral
source, were not so lucky as to obtain competent medical treatment in
their time of need. The horror stories of back-alley treatments performed by quacks, and self-induced abortions with dangerous objects
like coat hangers or bleach douches, came out into the open during the
1970s crusade to make abortion legal. Between the late 1920s, when
abortion rates began to rise, and 1973, when abortion was decriminal-
ized, tens of thousands of women every year needed emergency care
following an illegal abortion.

In the decades preceding World War II, married women underwent
considerable change in their sexual and contraceptive practices. By
the 1930s it was a given, among liberal-thinking women, that they
had a right to sexual pleasure in marriage and to birth control. The
two were intricately related. It was a commonplace of reformist rhetoric to argue that only a woman freed by reliable contraception from
the consequence of childbearing could enjoy making love. Similarly,
only a wife free to limit the number of her offspring and to space
them according to her physical and economic needs could raise
sound children. When Planned Parenthood was formed in 1942,
mid-America had come to believe that birth control was an aid to the
realization of marital happiness. Though abortion was not yet part of
the legal repertoire, women could already enter marriage with a better
chance at separating sex from reproduction than at any previous time
in American history.

N I N E
Wives, War, and Work, 1940–1950

"Mrs. John Doe We Need You!"
Women's Home Companion, July 1942

"I'm Proud of My Wife's War Job"
McCall's, September 1943

"I'm Proud . . . my husband wants me to do my part."
World War II poster

*E*velyn Guthrie, the wife of a navy officer, accompanied her husband "Hal" to Hawaii when he was stationed there in 1941. While Hal spent his work hours aboard ship, Evelyn devoted her days to the Honolulu Red Cross Motor Corps, taking military hospital patients out for drives and squiring about air corps trainees from Australia and New Zealand.

The Guthries saw the war coming and prepared for it. As she tells it in her unpublished memoirs: "On December 5, Hal and I went to a lawyer's office and each signed our last will and testament. . . . I drove him to Pearl Harbor and his ship left port at 12:01 on December 6 to take planes to the marines at Midway, although at the time I did not know where the ship was headed."[1]

On the morning of December 7, as she was leaving her apartment, her landlady called out to her that Pearl Harbor was under attack. She quickly changed into her Red Cross uniform, grabbed her first-aid kit, and headed toward her car. On the way, she picked up several naval officers who were also in a hurry to get to Pearl Harbor. What they found when they were finally able to reach the landing was a "sight of unbelievable horror. . . . Some of the ships were afire. There were men trying to swim through fiery oil in the water."

Stunned by the spectacle of the surprise attack, Mrs. Guthrie barely escaped with her own life. Before her eyes, a Japanese plane zoomed down on the battleship Pennsylvania and managed to drop a bomb on a destroyer tied up in front of the ship. "The bomb blew off the bow of the destroyer and due to the repercussion, my car . . . careened back and forth across the dock." When she was able to get it under control, she drove to Motor Corps Headquarters, where she picked up a few other Red Cross members, and then headed to Civilian Defense Headquarters.

> Here we found great activity. Trucks of all types and sizes were being stripped for use as ambulances as a desperate call had come from Hickham Field. We were told help was needed at Tripler Army Hospital. Four of us using my car drove to Tripler and reported for duty in the hospital. As the wounded from Hickam Field were brought in on stretchers, we cut clothing from the area of their wounds and they were taken directly to an operating room. We then split up and each one was sent to a hospital ward in order to help in any way possible with the wounded.
>
> . . . At infrequent periods, a nurse or a doctor of the regular hospital staff would arrive to give them some attention but there was little that could be done for them. All of those who had lost an arm or leg died that day. From the hours of about ten in the morning when I arrived in the ward until late afternoon when some relief nurses arrived as volunteers, I felt completely helpless. I could only hold the hand of a dying man, give another a drink of water or keep the excited hospital corpsman busy wiping up the blood from the floor so no one would slip.

During the next few days, Mrs. Guthrie transported medical items to and from the naval and army hospitals. Another duty that became routine was to help the civilian hospitals with the stream of blood donors who had responded to a radio appeal. She also had "the very sad duty of driving a navy chaplain who was detailed to make arrangements for the burial of the dead service personnel."

Since the "service wives" had husbands aboard ships, they volunteered to take night duty at headquarters so the "civilian wives" could be home with their families. For three weeks, Mrs. Guthrie heard nothing from her husband. Then an enlisted man came to her apartment and informed her that Hal was all right but had been too busy to come ashore even to phone.

". . . Just before Christmas, one of the Matson liners arrived in port to evacuate service women and children. It was quite different from former times when the band played Aloha and people left burdened with leis."

After several months, when most of the service wives with children and many others had been evacuated, it was decided that no wives could stay behind unless they were employed by the government in some type of war work. In order to remain, Mrs. Guthrie took a job working six days a week censoring mail in the Honolulu Post office. She censored about 130 letters a day, removing any sensitive material that might give aid to the enemy.

Occasionally the work had its lighter moments, as in this memory. "One time I had two letters to censor both from the same man, one was to his wife and the other apparently to a girl friend. He enclosed a [war] bond for the girl friend and it was a real temptation not to switch it to the wife's letter."

During this time, for over a hundred days, she had no idea where her husband was. In May, his ship returned to Hawaii after the Battle of the Coral Sea, and a much thinner man came ashore. After a few days in port, he was off to sea again. Evelyn Guthrie celebrated their twentieth wedding anniversary without him.

A month later an even thinner husband returned from the Battle of Midway. Friends came "to congratulate Hal on being alive rather than the usual type of celebration." While he was recuperating, she kept working in the censor's office. In early December, a year after Pearl Harbor, she received a phone call from California informing her that her mother had suffered a heart attack and might not survive. "Being an only child and her sole relative, there was no other decision to make but return to the mainland. If I left Hawaii, I would not be allowed to return. . . . I said goodbye to Hal not knowing when or if I would see him again."

Fortunately, her husband, too, was soon sent to the mainland, with a promotion and a new assignment. The Guthries both survived the war and lived many years thereafter. Her experiences as a "service wife" were indeed marked by service in more than the limited sense of the term.

To have probably been the only woman at Pearl Harbor during the fateful 1941 attack was a significant milestone in Mrs. Guthrie's life story. Characteristic of military wives, she worked as a volunteer in the Red Cross and served, it appears, with distinction. Uncharacteristic of wives of her class, she also took on a paid job in response to the demands of war. She was one of the millions of wives from every walk of life who contributed to the wartime rise in married women's employment—from 15 percent in 1940 to more than 24 percent in 1945.[2]

World War II, one can argue, merely accelerated a trend that was already in progress, since the overall female workforce had been steadily increasing since the turn of the century. One can also argue that World War II acted as a catalyst for unprecedented change in female employment, especially for married women. Of the 6,500,000 *new* women workers hired during the war, 3,700,000 were wives. For the first time in U.S. history, there were more married than single women in the labor force.

The preponderance of married women resulted, in part, from the sense of urgency that propelled brides and grooms to the altar throughout the war years. As streams of soldiers said good-bye to their loved ones or came home on leave, approximately one million more marriages took place than would have been expected at prewar rates. As one of the multitude of brides marrying in 1942 remembered fifty years later: "We would probably *not* have married so quickly if it had not been wartime."[3] By 1944 there were 2,500,000 more married women than there had been in 1940.

Initially, the War Manpower Commission was reluctant to encourage homemakers to seek employment, and stressed, instead, their responsibilities to their families. But many patriotic citizens, organizations, and magazines urged wives, as well as single women, to take up the jobs left vacant by servicemen and to fill the new jobs required by the war industry. One of many posters published by the U.S. government printing office asked, "Should your wife take a war job?" The poster, ostensibly addressed to the husband, showed him reading a

Should Your Wife Take a War Job? *World War II poster. (Hoover Institution, Stanford University)*

newspaper to his wife, juxtaposed beside photos of a woman at a sewing machine and a woman in a factory. In answer to its bold-faced question, the poster answered, "Every woman over 18, who is physically fit and has no children under 14, should be prepared to take a war job."

A one-minute radio spot enlisted the voices of local women to broad-cast the following message: "This is (name) . . . speaking earnestly to the housewives of (city). I'm a housewife, too . . . never worked outside my home until this year. Feeding my family and buying war bonds just didn't seem enough. So I got an 8-hour-a-day job, and managed to run my home besides. . . . My husband's proud of me . . . and I've never been happier. I feel I'm *really* helping to make the war end sooner."[4]

If, during the Depression, the working wife had been the object of widespread disapproval for "taking away a man's job," now, with the labor shortage, she was courted and praised. Rosie the Riveter, house-wife–turned–factory worker, became a national icon. Like the Revolu-tionary War wife "Mollie Pitcher," who had joined her husband on the battlefield, Rosie was honored for filling in for a man. But as Leila J. Rupp reminds us in her study of wartime propaganda, transformation was intended to be temporary. Everyone understood that as soon as the war was over, she would return to her primary occupation as wife, mother, and homemaker.[5]

The employment of married women in large numbers represented what historian William Chafe has called a "drastic change in policy by business and government."[6] Previous bans against the employment of wives were now discarded, as were policies that discriminated against older women—that is, women over thirty-five. These older women, most of whom were married, brought a new dimension to the work-force. With their children in school or already grown, they relished the opportunity to exchange their pots and pans for filing cabinets and riv-eting machines. Women like these, with comparatively light homemak-ing and childcare responsibilities, swelled the ranks of the female labor force.[7] For every two working women over thirty-five in 1940, by the end of the war there were three.

Another change was the increased employment of women with small children. At first, the War Manpower Commission expressed the preva-lent belief that a mother's overriding duty was to stay at home with her offspring, but before long it changed its attitude: everyone, with or without children, was needed for the war effort. Responding, however, to concerns about the children's well-being, the WMC directed govern-ment agencies "to develop, integrate, and co-ordinate federal programs for the day care of children of working mothers."[8]

Some nursery schools had already been provided through the Work Projects Administration for children from low-income families— 180,000 preschool and school-age children were enrolled in these in 1942–1943. After June 1943, the WPA nursery school project was discontinued, and a new program was established under the provisions of the Lanham Act for the children of mothers in the defense industry. At its peak, this federally subsidized program cared for 130,000 children in 3,000 centers. At the same time, other programs were initiated by state, local, and private agencies throughout the country, but never enough to care for the estimated 2 million youngsters needing some form of assistance, according to the WMC in 1943.

The fault was not entirely with government policy. American mothers were initially wary of collective solutions to their childcare problems, and, whenever possible, preferred to make their own arrangements, either with family members, neighbors, or friends. William Tuttle's *"Daddy's Gone to War"* documents the diverse childcare solutions mothers improvised.[9] Some worked the night shift and left their children with a father who worked a day shift, or with grandparents, or with older siblings, or alone. One homefront child remembered that her mother worked a night shift so that her daughter-in-law could work days, and they could both share the baby-sitting. Other mothers worked the day shift and left their children to fend for themselves after school.

These "latchkey" children provoked anxiety in the hearts of worried Americans. "Who's going to take care of me, Mother, if you take a war-plant job," asked a fair-haired boy in the May 1943 issue of *Better Homes and Gardens*. Similarly, a patriotic and self-serving ad for Adel Precision Products pictured a fair-haired girl asking her mother dressed in overalls: "Mother, when will you stay home again?" To which the mother optimistically replied: "Some jubilant day mother will stay home again, doing the job she likes best—making a home for you and daddy when he gets back. She knows that all the hydraulic valves, line support clips and blocks and anti-icing equipment that ADEL turns out for airplanes are helping bring that day closer."

This fictitious mother's reply notwithstanding, there was reason to worry. Some children were clearly being neglected, at least according to popular magazine articles. Mothers coming home from work exhausted were often unable to give their children anything but minimal care. And their job performance also suffered; absenteeism was high among working mothers, who were often obliged to take time off for a sick child or to quit working altogether.

Individual defense plants resorted to innovative measures to keep their female employees. For example, Los Angeles aircraft manufacturers petitioned the city to keep the schools open in summer, since many working mothers needed to be home with their children during the vacation months. A more foresighted plan was undertaken in Portland, Oregon, by the Kaiser Company, which established on-site, round-the-clock centers at its two plants for children aged eighteen months to six years. With 25,000 women workers in its shipyards and progressive thinking on the part of its leaders, the Kaiser Child Service Centers "still stand as an example of what private industry might accomplish to alleviate the pressures on working mothers while providing real care for the children."[10]

Despite this and other corporate and community initiatives, adequate child care never kept up with the need. The United States did not follow the lead of its British ally, which provided a large range of services for its working wives and mothers: day care centers, home-helps, canteens, prepared meals, and one free afternoon a week for shopping.[11] Moreover, Great Britain worked out a system of part-time work for married women, allowing two part-timers to perform the work of one-full-time employee. This system was a boon to the British war effort—and to working wives.

The household responsibilities of America's wartime wives did not disappear when they went off to the factory with their overalls and lunch boxes or to the office with their stockings and gloves. Then as now, women simply added one job to another, and tried not to collapse under the strain. Why did these women take on five- and six-day-a-week schedules, often on swing and night shifts, in addition to their workload at home?

Many were undoubtedly inspired by patriotic feelings. Those with husbands and sweethearts in the armed forces hoped their work would help shorten the war and have a direct impact on the lives of their men abroad. They believed the posters that read: "Longing won't bring him home sooner. . . . Get a War Job!" and "Do the job he left behind."

Another reason was economic. Servicemen's wives existing on a meager government allotment often had difficulty making ends meet. In Athol, Massachusetts, one navy wife and mother, with a second baby on the way, figured that after she had paid for rent ($20), electricity ($3.75), telephone ($2.00), milk ($6.50), laundry ($4), groceries ($30), insurance ($2.95), and oil ($2.80), she had only $8 left from her $80 monthly allowance for "clothing, medicine, heat in winter months, newspapers, periodicals, amusement, etc."[12] By 1944, a total of 1,360,000 women with husbands in the armed forces were working for pay, out of approximately 4 million servicemen's wives.[13]

Whether one had a husband in the service or not, women and whole families flocked to the new wartime centers in search of jobs. They migrated from Appalachia, the South, and the plains states to the West, the East Coast, and the Great Lakes region. They left rural farms for booming cities, like Detroit, which built the largest plant in the world at Willow Run, producing bombers in unprecedented numbers and with record speed. They crowded into substandard housing and trailer parks, and sent money back home for their relatives and friends to join them.[14]

Wartime pay was good, better than ever before in American history, and that pay was now being offered to women for jobs that would previously have been reserved for men. Wives who had depended on their husbands for support could now contribute to the family economy—to the purchase of new furniture or clothes or even a house. Some were proud to be earning money for the first time in their lives, and to have some say in how that money was spent. Those who could afford it bought china and silver on the installment plan, sent gifts to their parents back home, bought war bonds, and saved for their children's college education. Many of them were simply glad to be out of the house. As one worker at the Puget Sound Navy Yard put it, "Somehow the kitchen lacks the glamour of a bustling shipyard."[15]

The war permanently affected the composition of the female workforce. Before the war it had been dominated by single, young women; afterward a majority of the women were married and middle-aged. In 1940, 6,380,000 single women and 4,680,000 married women were gainfully employed. Ten years later, the ratio had changed to 5,270,000 single and 8,640,000 married women.[16] The wartime wives had, on the whole, more work experience than women who had married in the

1920s and 1930s, and were more likely to work after marriage, despite a drop in overall female employment during the immediate postwar years.[17]

During the next half century, the percentage of women combining work and homemaking soared to unimaginable heights. A girl born in 1950, when only one out of four married women worked for pay, would have had a very different picture of womanhood from one born today, when more than three out of five married women are employed in virtually every occupation. And if one considers women with children—married and unmarried—the proportion rises to approximately four out of five. In the following pages, I will look more closely at wartime wives working in different sectors of the economy and different regions of the country.

SHIPBUILDING WIVES

During World War II, shipbuilding, one of the highest paid industries in the country, opened its doors to women—single and married, younger and older, with and without children. Consider the case at the Commercial Iron Works in Portland, Oregon. Throughout 1942 it explicitly refused to hire women, but by March 1943, it had taken on 500 women as industrial workers. One of them, Berenice Thompson, a wife with grown children, had opposed her husband's express wishes when she went to work at the shipyards. "I had been very poor," she recalled, ". . . and it meant a lot just to prove myself. My husband was from Kentucky. He didn't think women knew anything. So I showed him." Eventually he had to accept her upgraded status when her wages paid for their new home.[18]

Rosa Dickson's husband, who worked at the shipyards, thought it was a bad place for women. According to his wife, he said, "Oh you cannot work down there in the shipyards. They're too rough and the language is bad." After looking for employment in a store that paid modest wages, she said, "Well, I'm not gonna take a job like that because the shipyards are paying the big money." With three of her five children still at home, she took a job as a welder at a small shipyard in the Portland area, then became a pipe fitter's helper, and held various jobs until 1946. The Dicksons' combined earnings made it possible for them to buy the house they lived in till the end of their lives.[19]

Even when a husband didn't object, women had to overcome blatant sexism among the male workers, many of whom continued to believe that females didn't belong in shipbuilding. It was no easy task to prove themselves as welders, riveters, shipfitters, electricians, painters, machinists, and boilermakers in a male bastion that was hostile to the very idea of women as coworkers.

An article written by Virginia Snow Wilkinson, titled "From Housewife to Shipfitter" and published in the September 1943 issue of *Harper's Magazine,* offers a lively account of one woman's experience in the shipyards. Virginia Wilkinson's husband had apparently not objected to her new employment; indeed, sharing her excitement, he and their children asked to be awakened with her at five-thirty the first day she went off to the Kaiser Shipyards in Richmond, California.[20]

With six other women, she was greeted incredulously by the man in charge of new workers: "Oh, my God! Women shipfitters! Why do they treat me like this?" Because Mrs. Wilkerson had already attended a defense class, she was immediately given a variety of small assignments as a shipfitter's helper, but most of the time, like the rest of the workers, she just stood around waiting. Shipbuilding, it appears, did not proceed with the efficiency of the assembly line.

Why so much idle time? Mrs. Wilkinson's foreman explained that the management employed more men and women than it could put to work at the same time. "You've got to have a lot of people to draw from in order to get even some good workmen." He also explained to her the place of women in shipbuilding.

"And the women too have got to be used. The men don't like the idea; they voted against it in their unions; but they'll get used to women in time and think nothing of it. They used to feel the same way about women in the plate shop, but it's full of women now—they run the show—and there's no real hostility there toward them any more. Women haven't been seen much on ships yet but they'll be seen as the war goes on."

While she accustomed herself to the men who called her "duchess" and "darling," Virginia Wilkinson was unprepared for an incident of outright sexism. When three shipfitting women, including the author, were given their own unit to work on, their enthusiasm and efficiency went hand in hand. "We became integrated persons working together on a project which focused all our interests. I noticed how quickly we ran our own errands, how conscientious we were in checking, how we abhorred sloppy measurements. For once we had been given responsibility, for once we had been put on our own, for once we had enough to do."

But the female team was not to last. By late afternoon, the three women "became gradually aware of the hostility of the men. . . . They were 'seething with resentment' that women should be given a unit to construct . . . this was the first time that we had been seen in the light of competitors. . . . The next day, with no explanation, our XAK, 'our baby,' was taken from us and given to the men. We had to stand aside and see the men working on what we felt was our project."

One of the female workers said the men were afraid that the ship units would become "overrun by women," like the plate shop. Mrs. Wilkinson generously conceded that it must have been hard for the men "who were heads of families, straining to take care of several dependents," to see their jobs taken up by women lacking in experience and earning the same money as the men. She had started out at ninety-five cents an hour.

After six weeks she was given her own unit to direct. This entailed measuring and locating the steel material for her unit, labeling it with chalk and engaging the riggers to lift it, finding a flanger and a welder to put the steel in place. Watching the crane lifting the material, and later looking out to sea where a troopship on which she had worked was being towed by, Virginia Wilkinson felt a keen sense of exhilaration. "It was good," she wrote, "this working together on a ship."

Although this story ended on the requisite upbeat note, it did not hide the misogyny endemic to the shipbuilding industry. Before the war, in 1939, only 2 percent of the entire shipyard industry was female. Any woman who ventured on the grounds was traditionally greeted with whistles and catcalls.[21] The influx of women into the shipyards changed the statistics and the atmosphere: by 1944, 10 to 20 percent of the shipbuilding workforce was female, and most of the men had learned to treat the women with respect, however grudgingly.

A few women in the shipbuilding industry even advanced to supervisory levels. For example, at the Dry Docks and Shipbuilding Company in Mobile, Alabama, thirteen women were promoted to much publicized leadership positions. One of them, a wife, supervised a crew of fourteen workers, including several men.[22]

Not all women working in the shipyards were shipbuilders; many were secretaries, accountants, cleaners, cooks, canteen operators, and groundsmen. Polly Crow, a thirty-year-old wife and mother whose army husband was shipped to Europe in 1944, took an office job at the Jefferson Boat and Machine Company near Anderson, Indiana, while she was living with his parents in Louisville, Kentucky. Her letters to her husband provide a window into the experiences of one working mother whose small son was well cared for by his paternal grandmother.

> *Louisville, June 12, 1944*
>
> *Darlin':*
>
> *You are now the husband of a career woman—just call me your little Ship Yard Babe! Yeh! I made up my mind that I wanted to work from 4:00 p.m. 'till midnight so's I could have my cake and eat it too. I wanted to work but didn't want to leave Bill all day—in the first place it would be too much for Mother altho' she was perfectly willing and then Bill needs me. This way Mother will just have to feed him once and tuck him in. . . . I finally ended up with just what I wanted. Comptometer [calculator] job—4:00 'till midnite—70 cents an hour to start which amounts to $36.40 a week, $145.60 per month, increase in two months if I'm any good and I know I will be. . . .*
>
> *Opening my little checking account too and it's a grand and a glorious feeling to write a check all your own and not have to ask for one. . . .*
>
> *Good nite, Darlin'*
> *I love you, Polly*[23]

Polly was lucky to have a mother-in-law willing to take care of her son, Bill. Her major worry was getting to and from work, which took forty-five minutes, but once that problem was solved, she was enthusiastic about her new life as a defense worker. "I like it here," she wrote to her husband on November 9, 1944 ". . . and am out for every penny I can get while the getting [sic] good." By then she had put away $780 in the bank—enough for a small family to live modestly on for six months.

The experiences of Polly Crow and Virginia Wilkinson, one the mother of a small child, the other the mother of five children, suggest that employment in the shipyards was a rich and satisfying experience for white women with backup support, despite the difficulties of childcare, transportation, and lingering sexism on the work site. But if one were African-American, work in the shipyards was almost always compounded by deep-rooted racism. Before the war, black women throughout the land had been largely limited to employment as maids, waitresses, agricultural workers, and other low-status positions. When well-paying jobs in war production became nominally open to them, thousands of black women were quick to leave their former employment, even if that meant traveling long distances to the new work sites. Many flocked to the burgeoning West Coast shipbuilding centers.

The oral histories of Portland/Vancouver shipbuilding women recorded by Amy Kesselman include the stories of several African-American women who experienced severe racial discrimination in the workplace. Six black women welders, having complained to their supervisor that their lead man called them "niggers" and treated them unfairly, were all inexplicably transferred from the graveyard to the swing shift. Then they were given discharge notices and told they could work only on the day shift. Since they all had children and had made childcare arrangements for the graveyard shift, the revised schedule created real hardships for them. One of the women remembered: "I told them it would be impossible to work days with two small children, one school age and the other too young to attend a nursery, my husband gone to service . . . but my request went unheeded." In the end, the protests they placed before the Kaiser Vancouver management and the War Manpower Commission were of no avail.[24]

Similar incidents occurred to other African-Americans throughout the country. Some defense training programs simply would not accept black women, and many war plants either refused to hire them, or segregated them into low-status occupations once they were hired. Management justified these practices by arguing that white workers would not accept working alongside "colored" women. At the Edgewood Arsenal near Baltimore, there were walkouts and widespread protest when black women were first employed.[25]

SOUTHERN WOMEN AS DEFENSE WORKERS

The differential treatment of African-American and white women was endemic to the South. Consider the case of the female defense workers of Alabama, as recorded by Mary Thomas in *Riveting and Rationing in Dixie*.[26] Before the war, few white wives were employed outside the home. Characteristically, they worked a few years before marriage, and then devoted themselves exclusively to their families. White women who worked because their husbands did not earn enough to support them were looked down upon by more affluent Southern women. It was simply not socially acceptable for a middle-class wife to be employed.

African-American women, single or married, were in a totally different situation. They had to work for economic reasons, and about half of them did, mainly as domestic and agricultural laborers. When the defense factories opened their doors in various parts of Alabama, many of these women would have been glad to exchange their menial, low-paying jobs for work that paid at least two to three times what they had been earning before.

The Air Service Command at Brookley Field in Mobile, Alabama, which was to become the largest employer of women in the state, actively recruited only white employees. Within that color code, it recruited single women, married women, older people, and handicapped persons. By 1943 it employed 17,000 people, half of whom were women and 800 of whom were physically handicapped. But it took complaints lodged with the Fair Employment Practices Commission for them to hire some black women, and then primarily in low-paying and low-skilled jobs.

Mobile was one of the new boomtowns that drew an unprecedented number of women from the Alabama countryside and neighboring states. Many women followed their civilian husbands to the defense centers, where they too found employment. One wife who had joined her husband in Mobile was hired by the Civilian Welfare Association and eventually became its chief clerk. Another, who had thought of herself exclusively as a wife devoted to housework, cooking, and playing bridge, went to work as a supervisor in maintenance, and discovered that she loved being a paid employee. An older woman, who had worked prior to marriage and then again after she had raised two daughters, was hired as chief of the Central File Section. She left this advice for younger women: "If you get married young, you can raise your family and all that sort of thing and still have plenty of time left to have a good time. Just because you happen to be a grandmother doesn't mean it's a sign to curl up around the edges."[27]

Elsewhere in the South, as in other parts of the nation, women motivated both by patriotism and economic necessity went from home to factory with a sense of excitement and purpose. For many, it was a welcome change from the drudgery of full-time housework. Karen Anderson, in her study of wartime women, recorded the feelings ranging from relief to elation experienced by several women working in Baltimore. One, a machine operator, was grateful to exchange her precarious situation as a coal miner's wife in West Virginia for a well-paying city job. A hand driller at Eastern Aircraft said she needed a change when her husband went into the service because "staying at home— emotionally and temperamentally does not suit me." Another admitted that leaving her factory job at her husband's insistence had made her so nervous that she went back to work on the advice of her doctor.[28]

Women's entry into the defense industry allowed Baltimore women to work in a variety of formerly sex-segregated occupations. Even though the traditionally female arena of clerical work paid somewhat less than factory work, it held on to its women workers because "it had shorter hours than factory jobs, was less strenuous physically than the assembly lines, offered the status of a white-collar job, provided more job security than the war-inflated manufacturing sector," and was less threatening to conventional ideas about gender roles.[29] Even African-American women, denied the training and employment that was open to their white counterparts, profited from the wartime economy; the number of black women in Baltimore previously employed as maids was reduced by almost half during the war years because they were able to find jobs in other fields.[30] They fared better than the black women of Alabama, not only because of engrained prejudice in the deep South, but also because they were closer to Washington, D.C., where the shortage of workers was acute.

War is nothing that any sane person ever welcomes. This is particularly true of women, whose lives have traditionally been devoted to nurturing life rather than destroying it. Yet it is also true that war has sometimes provided new opportunities for women, thrusting them into positions of responsibility and independence that were previously unthinkable. The absence of men and the shortage of manpower, forced and voluntary dislocations, the spirit of patriotism and adventure, the blurring of gender boundaries in previously sex-segregated occupations, and the creation of new organizations for women—all of these factors catapulted women into unfamiliar landscapes where they had to find their way with few guiding lights.

WACS AND WAVES

Take, for example, two new organizations "manned" exclusively by women: the Women's Auxiliary Army Corps (WAAC), authorized by President Roosevelt in May 1942 and renamed the Women's Army Corps (WAC) the following year, and the Women Accepted for Voluntary Emergency Service of the U.S. Navy (WAVES), founded in July 1942. These two military organizations, followed by the SPARS (U.S. Coast Guard) and WAFS (Women's Auxiliary Ferry Squadron), were not greeted unambiguously by all Americans. The same people who bemoaned the sight of women in factory overalls were equally unnerved by the vision of women in uniforms replacing men not only as typists, cooks, postal workers, telephone operators, and drivers, but also as intelligence officers, translators, radar specialists, medical technicians, control tower operators, aerial gunnery instructors, and photographers. Though all of these women were barred from active combat, they did eventually serve in dangerous areas, where some were wounded or killed.

Married women served alongside single women in all of these organizations, though in fewer numbers. Typically, a young married woman would enlist in the WACS or WAVES when her husband was shipped overseas. The following vignettes follow three such wives in their tours of duty.

In 1942, soon after the WAACS had been formed, Gertrude Morris was a recent bride living with her lieutenant husband near Fort Bragg, North Carolina. When Lieutenant Morris was sent to North Africa two months after their wedding, Gertrude Morris enlisted in the WAACS. Her memories evoke the makeshift nature of basic training for women at Fort Des Moines, Iowa, during the early stages of the war: ". . . falling out for reveille at 6:00 A.M. in dark, below-zero weather in deep snow . . . the oversized man's GI overcoat, which I wore over a thin fatigue dress."[31]

After basic training she was sent to Georgia, then to Missouri, then to Texas. She did clerical work, learned Morse code, and had her "most exciting job" directing the traffic in an air control tower. In the fall of 1944, after her husband had fought his way from North Africa to Sicily, France, and Germany, she too was scheduled to go overseas. She recalled: "My excitement was intense—not only was I to go overseas, but perhaps I would by some fantastic stroke of luck cross paths with my husband. . . . Of course, irony and the army's logic prevailed, and my orders came through for the Pacific theatre." She was sent to New Guinea and ended up in the Philippines, "never too far behind the advancing troops but . . . not exposed to any real danger."

Even after the war had ended and Gertrude's husband had returned from Europe, she was still in the Pacific awaiting transport home. Despite her husband's efforts to influence the WAC commandant, Oveta Culp Hobby, in Washington, Gertrude Morris did not come home till October 1945. Reunited with her husband, she went back to teaching, had two daughters, and would always remember her wartime experience as a "a time of adventure, opportunity for development, and above all service."

Alvira "Pat" Vahlenkamp married Charles "Chuck" Melvin, an air force pilot, in September 1943. When he was sent to France in the spring of 1944, Pat enlisted in the WACS under the assumption that another serviceman would then be freed to go overseas. Though her husband was not initially happy with her decision, he later became very proud of her. Her letters to him evoked the daily exertions demanded of women in basic training and her dream-time worries about her husband.

Fort Des Moines, Aug. 13, 1944

Darling Hubby,

. . .

Sunday was just another day here for we G.I. gals. Only, we were able to sleep until 6:30. Ate at 8:00. Drilled until noon mess. Lecture at 3:00 until mess. Then we were off. We all have our uniforms now. So five of we girls went to the P.X. and Service Club. Didn't stay longer than an hour. . . .

Darling, please, keep on loving me. Will you? That's all I want. That's all I need. I miss you dreadfully and I think of you constantly. I dreamed last nite that you didn't love me any more. It was awful. . . . If only right now you were with me and we could live our lives together alone, I would be so happy.

Love, Pat[32]

From her barracks on the base, Pat wrote that she had an upper bunk where it was "nice and cool" in the summer, that she had survived KP (kitchen duty), and that the army "is getting better every day." Pat didn't hide from her husband the satisfaction she derived from her work as a WAC, even as she tried to reassure him that she was still, first and foremost, a devoted and faithful wife. "Of course, I know what my husband thinks of the WACs. But, Darling, always remember your wife is still your wife. WAC or no WAC and she loves you and you alone."

Dorothy Barnes and James R. Stephens graduated from college in California in June 1942 and, with the cloud of war over their heads, they eloped to Arizona three months later. When J.R. was called up for active duty as a Signal Corps photographer, Dorothy decided to enlist in the WAVES.[33]

She spent boot camp at Hunter College in New York City, an experience that left her with few fond memories. "We hit the deck before dawn and fell exhausted into bed at 2200 (10:00 P.M.) Spud locker detail (as the navy called it) working in ankle-deep water peeling beets and potatoes, guard duty where I actually was given a baton and told to guard a gate, classes in military organization, and learning navy songs used up the day. After lights out I'd cry into my pillow."

Somehow she survived basic training and then radio school in Ohio, before being posted to Treasure Island Naval Station in San Francisco. During this time J. R. was sent to the Pacific, and there were long periods of silence when Dorothy did not know whether he was dead or alive. When the news came that he had made it back to Hawaii, she excitedly applied for a transfer to the islands.

"The big hurdle," as she recounted years later, "was the interview with the captain, commanding officer at Treasure Island Naval Station.

I'd heard he was very strict about whom he'd approve, that one had to convince him of selfless intentions to get an assignment there, so for my interview I had imagined a little patriotic speech."

But, instead, she blurted out the truth—that she wanted to be with her husband. The captain, surprisingly, approved her request, with the caveat that the reason for her transfer remain between the two of them. Once they were both stationed in Hawaii, Dorothy and her husband had to overcome numerous obstacles for their off-base meetings in makeshift accommodations. Before long she was pregnant. In that pregnancy was considered a major infraction for women in service, Dorothy was relieved to be discharged from the navy a few months later.

"FOR THE DURATION"

The patriotic stories of women shipbuilders, airplane repairers, WACS, and WAVES received much public attention during the war years, so much so that they overshadowed the efforts of women with more mundane occupations. Most married women were full-time housekeepers. For every one wife working for pay at the height of the war, three others remained unsalaried at home. Mrs. Keith Frazier Somerville, in her bimonthly newspaper column from Cleveland, Mississippi, acknowledged a definite wistfulness on the part of those who were out of the limelight: "I and all the other non-military housewives here about who neither rivet nor weld but remain behind to keep the home fires burning! We are to be called W.I.N.K.S.—"Winks" . . . Women in Numerous Kitchens!"[34]

Mrs. Somerville's "Dear Boys" column for the *Bolivar Commercial* weekly was addressed to servicemen from Bolivar County in all parts of the world. A former schoolteacher and active community member, the writer was well situated to keep them informed of their loved ones at home and their friends abroad. The "Dear Boys" columns sketched the scene in small-town America at a time when everyone—except for some stay-at-home wives and mothers—seemed to be on the move.

Local soldiers were constantly being transported from training camps and specialized programs throughout the land to posts abroad in Europe and the Pacific. Their sweethearts and wives met them wherever they could, in boomtowns that had no rooms to rent, in temporary housing with shared kitchens and bathrooms, in their own homes when the servicemen had precious leave.

In column after column, Mrs. Somerville reported the flood of weddings that was sweeping through the nation. On June 18, 1943, she wrote:

> *Dear Boys:*
>
> *"America is on a matrimonial spree," says Kate Burr [a journalist and radio commentator]. "Every month, 150,000 couples are married! Despite other shortages, there seems to be no priority on love!" Well, our Bolivar County youngsters are no exception to the general rule. They're at this marrying business, too, as I've told you before. Last Monday, out at San Diego, California, Bill Lowery and Myrtle Lindsey were quietly married. . . . Billy is feeling super fine these days, but the Navy still has him doing "limited service." You know he . . . was one of the first of our boys to be wounded in action. Well, a pretty Delta bride should be all the tonic he needs! . . .*
>
> *On Friday, pretty Joyce Shular (fortunately entirely well now from a recent appendectomy which postponed her wedding) is to be married to Robert Hays, formerly of Port Gibson, but now working for the A.A.A. [Agricultural Adjustment Administration] in Washington. . . .*
>
> *And as soon as he gets his wings (sometime this week) out at the Corpus Christi Naval Air Base, Nevin Sledge is coming home to wed that talented Brenda Wilson. . . .*
>
> *That marrying bug has struck Pace [neighboring town] too. Had you heard that Robert Grantham, home on a twenty-day leave after a year in Hawaii, married attractive Edith Lott last week? He couldn't be letting brother Gray (a cook at the Port of Embarkation, New York) get ahead of him. . . . You know Gray married Ethel Quinton when he was home last December! And Rufus Aycock married recently too, a pretty Georgia girl. He's paratrooper, up in North Carolina now. . . .*
>
> *But I'm not through with Pace's wedding yet! Frank Thompson graduated from the Glider School at Lubbock, Texas this spring and married Betsy Worrel the very same day!*

Brides were invariably portrayed as "pretty," "talented," or "attractive." Almost every column announced another war-hastened wedding, always with approval. As Mrs. Somerville opined on July 2, 1943: "With all its ups and downs, marriage is still a pretty good institution, preferable with all its imperfections to unmarried bliss!" On December 3, she noted that the latest statistics suggest "at least two million new brides in 1943, or about fourteen marriages per 1000 population. During World War I, we had eleven marriages per thousand, so you boys are doing better than your dads did!"

Babies, too, were being produced in record numbers, with the birth rate climbing from 2,466,000 births in 1939, to 2,703,000 in 1941, to 3,104,000 in 1943. Although some Americans voiced concern over the future of these children, many of whom would be fatherless after the war, the overwhelming consensus was that babies, like marriage, were good for the nation.[35]

Taking note of the increased birth rate, Mrs. Somerville wrote on March 12, 1943: "Have you heard about the Boom in Babies? . . . a bunch of our servicemen are new fathers! 'Jimmie' Newman (Lt. James V.) from out Pace way was home from Keesler Field not long ago for the arrival of his wee daughter, and 'Pete' Gammil (Lt. Tom L.) flew home to Skene from Phoenix, Arizona, with his month old twins, a four pound girl and a five pound boy! Naturally his wife (Frances Foster of Greenwood, a Delta State girl) came along to show the home folks their treasures! . . . And a sure 'proud papa' is Ralph Collins Reed, home from Camp Pendleton (the biggest Marine camp of all, at Oceanside, California) to visit with his son and wife (Lorraine Ruscoe)."

After another list of weddings and babies reported on January 7, 1944, Mrs. Somerville added this interesting piece of information: "You knew, didn't you, that if a baby is born after the father goes overseas, Uncle Sam will send its picture by V-mail [a special wartime letter] to the dad!"

On December 3, 1943, she noted that Elaine Tyler had come home from Camp McCain, Mississippi, with her daughter and baby son "for the duration," while her lieutenant husband continued to serve his country. "For the duration" was a common wartime expression implying that the present situation, while uncertain in length, was only temporary. Wives and families hunkered down with the expectation of resuming a "normal" life at war's end. In the meantime, they would do their best to take care of themselves and—like Mrs. Somerville—send smiling pictures to their far-flung "boys."

HOUSEKEEPING ON THE HOME FRONT

Nonworking wives and mothers (that is, three out of four married women) stayed at home caring for the new wartime babies and children of all ages. Sometimes they had the care of their parents as well. It was no easy task to be a homemaker in a wartime economy, when household help was hard to come by, even for those who had the money, and store-bought items were pricey and scarce. Rationing of gas, meat, sugar, coffee, butter, and other fats made transportation chancy and meal preparation challenging.

The 1942 edition of *The Good Housekeeping Cookbook* acknowledged that "the war is bringing new problems into the home kitchen." These included "food rationing, changing prices, scarcity of some food, and gaps on grocers' shelves because our government had needed almost the entire supply of certain food for our armed forces and our allies."[36] The cookbook contained a Wartime Supplement that told homemakers how to cope with some of these problems. They were advised to buy in quantities that leave a minimum of leftovers, to plan meals for two or three days so as to cut down on trips to the market, to be sure that daily meals are adequately nutritious, and to "cheat the garbage can in every conceivable way."

In italics, cooks were admonished: *"Save every scrap of fat that you would ordinarily throw out."* These could be strained into a container, put in the refrigerator, sold to the butcher, and ultimately used in the making of explosives. A poster issued by the U.S. government printing office graphically showed fat dripping from a frying pan that was funneled into explosives. The caption read "Housewives! Save waste fats for explosives! Take them to your meat dealer."

Tin cans had become precious because they were made of materials that were needed for war production. *The Good Housekeeping Cookbook* reminded housewives to "save every can. Remove labels, and wash thoroughly, as cans cannot be used unless they are very clean. Remove both top and bottom of can, flatten each can with the foot until the sides nearly meet." Then they were to be taken to the collecting center.

A special section of the cookbook contained a list of fourteen suggestions for the "The Business Housekeeper," a euphemism for the working wife. She was advised to keep her menus simple and to take advantage of packaged quick-frozen vegetables, fish, meats, and fruits, as well as prepared biscuit, muffin, and griddle cake mixes, and canned breads. At the end of the list of timesaving hints, the fourteenth suggestion reminded the housekeeper to keep up her appearance. "Never fail to smooth your hair and to powder your nose before you announce dinner.

Advertising exploited the worry that wartime activities would tarnish the looks of servicemen's wives and sweethearts, as in this Palmolive soap ad that promoted beauty care as a form of patriotism.

World War II poster encouraging housewives to grow and can their own fruits and vegetables. (Hoover Institution, Stanford University)

Then you can greet your family and guests with a smile that isn't put on." Throughout the war years, whether in factories or in homes, women were told that looks counted and that their looking good (i.e., feminine and even glamorous) contributed to the national morale.

While few food items were officially rationed—Americans never faced the privations known to our allies in Britain and France, or our enemies for that matter—many items were in short supply. The shortage of fresh and canned vegetables and fruits impelled many homemakers to grow "victory gardens" and can their own produce. The shortage of butter led to the introduction of margarine on the American table. Initially, the dairy industry prevented manufacturers from giving margarine the same color as butter, and one had to add a pellet of dye to transform its unappetizing white substance into a glowing yellow.

The shortage of clothing obliged many women to mend and sew and resize clothes passed down from older siblings and friends. Finding shoes for growing children was an ongoing challenge. Household appliances like toasters, egg beaters, refrigerators, and washing machines were all in short supply.

A *Harper's Magazine* article of April 1944 titled "Housekeeping after the War" took note of the many difficulties homemakers were facing, especially in the service sector. "Commercial laundries collect and deliver less frequently than they did. . . . It takes forever to get a vacuum cleaner, or iron, or leaky faucet fixed. . . . The grocer and butcher have in many cases stopped delivering. Shopping—with fewer clerks in the stores and with many transactions complicated by ration coupons and tokens—takes longer than ever. Getting to market, taking small children to school, and many other errands that used to be done easily and quickly by car now have to be done on foot, or by bus and trolley. And the supply of domestic workers is drying up so rapidly that fewer housewives than ever have anyone to help get the work done."[37] The privileged 10 percent of American families with full-time servants before the war were probably reduced to half that number by 1944.

In middle- and lower-class homes, where maids were extremely rare (except in Southern cities serviced by black domestics), there was often a new presence—that of the wartime boarder. With acute housing shortages in certain locales, the National Housing Agency launched a "Share Your Home" campaign destined to produce some 1.5 million shared homes. Families took in boarders to help ease the housing shortage and to bring in extra income.

Sometimes the boarders became good family friends, people to count on for baby-sitting and emergencies. This was the case for a migrant family in Fort Worth, Texas, who had moved in with another family of war workers. Both fathers worked nights, and "it was great to have two mothers" during the day, as one of the children remembered years later.[38] This was also the case for an African-American family in Berkeley, California, who took in five roomers—a young black man, his wife, and their baby residing in the kitchen, and two young men in a room upstairs. Because the landlady and her husband both worked in the post office and she had a job six days a week from 7 A.M. to 3:30 P.M., she was glad to have another woman in the house while she was away at work.[39]

The "landlady" has a very long history. For centuries, wives, widows, and single women have rented rooms in their homes or run boardinghouses to support themselves and their families. For the most part, brothels notwithstanding, the work of the landlady was considered a respectable female occupation, and in wartime, an honorable one as well.

VOLUNTEERISM

Wartime wives and mothers were also asked to participate in a variety of community activities. Mrs. Somerville's columns highlighted those women whose volunteer work aided the war effort. Kudos for "Mrs. Albert Smith, County Chairman of Women at War. With her happy smile and enthusiasm, it is no wonder that her bond drive is being crowned with the success that always accompanies her efforts along any line" (April 9, 1943). Kudos for Mrs. Ed Kossman, who taught a Red Cross knitting class to fifteen ladies "at the lovely home of Mrs. Tom Boschert" (May 7, 1943). And kudos for Mrs. Lois Hardee, who worked in the local Ration Board (May 21, 1943).

Women's clubs, with their 12 million members, gave themselves wholeheartedly to defense activities.[40] For once, a common goal united such diverse organizations as the National Federation of Business and Professional Women, the Daughters of the American Revolution, the Young Women's Christian Association, the National Council of Catholic, or Jewish, or Negro Women, the American Association of College Women, the 4-H, the Homemakers' Clubs, and the Junior League, to name only a few of the most prominent. Every local garden club and reading group found some way to contribute: by leading a war bond drive, by organizing the salvage of newspapers and tin cans, by knitting socks for the servicemen, by preparing for emergencies. New organizations and drives sprung up to meet war-related problems. In Texas, the Federation of Women's Clubs organized a statewide nutrition campaign in keeping with governmental efforts to promote healthful diets. In Cincinnati, San Francisco, and several other cities, groups were formed to assess housing needs for defense workers.

In the coastal cities, where there was widespread fear of enemy attacks, women and men prepared for civil defense. They went to their posts as air raid wardens and plane spotters. Behind them stood thousands of women trained as nurses, nurse's aides, ambulance drivers, and communications operators, many under the auspices of the Red Cross. In some areas they prepared for evacuation, with special attention to children, the aged, and the handicapped. And all the while they were told that they were responsible, first and foremost, for the well-being of their families. "The first task of every American mother is the adequate training and discipline of her own household."[41]

The American Red Cross contained the largest number of volunteers in the nation. Founded in 1881 by Clara Barton, it had a history of emergency aid that depended primarily on women serving as nurses, chauffeurs, ambulance drivers, canteen operators, telephone and telegraph personnel, liaison with military families, and relief workers for needy civilians.

For thousands of women, the Red Cross became a way of life during the war years. Typically these women were, like Evelyn Guthrie, married, middle or upper class and middle-aged. But younger women, too, of lesser social standing, found in the Red Cross an outlet for their patriotic urges, especially when their husbands were stationed away from home.

Marjorie Reid Killpack, a former elementary school teacher from Utah, followed her husband to various postings from coast to coast during his first two years in the Marines. When he was shipped to the Pacific she returned to Utah, where she decided to volunteer time to the Red Cross. Though her letter of March 8, 1944, shows the deference she always paid to her husband, there is also an incipient new spirit of independence related to the Red Cross work.

> *Dearest Husband:*
>
> *. . . Elliot, I've had something happen today. I hope will meet your approval. Margaret Keller told me to call this Mrs. Greenwell of the American Red Cross. They were in need of case workers. I did and am beginning in the morning for a trial period for the balance of this month. It is something that will be completely absorbingly new and that which I've wanted to try for a long time. . . .*
>
> *I have to stand by for night telegrams every other week and have duty every other week end, but both girls who are working there say there's constantly something interesting happening—and it's absorbing.*
>
> *Elliott, I have tried my best to make good decisions. This is not certain I'll stay with the Red Cross but at any time it would be a good recommendation for other work. Hope you'll think it's okay—if you don't want me to, let me know as soon as possible. Your approval is necessary to my happiness and peace of mind. . . .*
>
> *Goodnite dear one, heaven's blessings on you.*
> *Yours devotedly, Marjorie*[42]

A month later, Marjorie had settled into a schedule of Red Cross work on Monday, Saturday, and Sunday, a schedule that would probably have been impossible for a wife with a resident husband and/or children. Work kept her mind off her husband's dangerous combat duties and her loneliness without him. "Well, dear," she wrote on November 1, 1944, "my life goes on, busily but certainly my days are not complete, for you are gone. It's good I can't think too much as I'd spend my time in trying to heal a very lonely and empty heart."

As the war progressed and many servicemen returned home wounded, the Red Cross played an important role in rehabilitation programs. Under Red Corps auspices, membership in the "Gray Ladies" became the pride of older women trained to help the men on their road to recovery. At Dibble General Hospital in Menlo Park, California, they and the other Red Cross volunteers spent countless hours at the bedside of the severely wounded, helping them keep up their morale in the face of lost limbs, devastating burns, and blindness. They organized recreational programs featuring local and nationally known entertainers. They helped out in occupational therapy, where the men learned skills in weaving, leather work, jewelry making, ceramics, woodworking, and radio repair. They were there to provide those extras that paid staff are often too busy to provide.

From the unpublished diary of Mrs. Maybelle Hargrove, who pioneered Red Cross Activities at Dibble, one reads of her initial work sewing on insignias for the men who were going out of the hospital on passes (Sept. 16, 1944):

> First the boy with an Asiatic ribbon, who had won a good conduct. . . . Then the good looking boy who wondered why men couldn't have wedding rings too? I told him he should feel complimented because his wife trusted him. That when I was married during World War I "You bet I labeled my soldier with a wedding ring!" . . . A colored boy came up and wanted an airforce insignia sewed on his shoulder. Told him that looked familiar 'cause my boy was in the A.A.F. . . . A Jewish boy sat watching me. Asked if he had something to be sewed—"No, I was a tailor before I landed in the quartermaster dept." . . . Then there was the boy I would like to have brought home with me—Gonzales was his name. Showed me the pictures of his family. His father lived in Colorado—his mother and married sister in Long Beach. He had never been in Northern Calif. . . . I fastened a gold star to his ribbons—one a purple heart ribbon, good conduct too. He was coming back to the hospital to sleep because he had no place to go in P.A. [Palo Alto].[43]

Mrs. Hargrove's diary gives us a good cross section of the "boys" aided by Red Cross women: Asian-Americans, African-Americans, Jews, and Latinos, as well as whites of varying European ancestry. Though she took note of their ethnic and religious inheritance, Mrs. Hargrove seems to have been above prejudice when it came to the treatment of wounded servicemen.

An article in a local Bay Area newspaper reported in December 1944,

Around a million American soldiers in Europe and Asia married "war brides." This bride and groom at the U.S. Consulate in Tokyo on February 10, 1951 were the last couple to be married under public law 717, which made possible more than 1,300 G.I.-Japanese marriages. (Library of Congress, Washington, D.C.)

A well-earned Christmas rest is being enjoyed today by the Red Cross women of the three peninsula chapters. . . . The Red Cross provided and trimmed 47 trees for Dibble, 43 small ones for the wards and four large trees that tower in the recreation and mess hall. The arts and crafts corps spent uncounted hours teaching the patients to make tree ornaments of scrap tin, highlighted with paint, that turned out to be glistening, modernistic decorations.

A total of 1,600 gifts for the men, bought with funds donated by local organizations, were selected and delivered by the Red Cross. Heading

the list of wanted presents were shaving lotion, pocket picture frames,
writing cases and GI socks and ties. Sixteen hundred red, green and
white tarleton bags stitched in red wool were also delivered to Dibble.
They were filled with candy (much of which was contributed by the
public) and two packages of cigarets, the gift of the Red Cross.

POSTWAR WIVES

Nearly one million foreign brides wed American servicemen during
and after World War II.[44] Though the U.S. government discouraged
such marriages and put up endless bureaucratic barriers, love-struck
G.I.s were not to be dissuaded. In Europe they married women mainly
from Great Britain (a record number in the spring of 1944 before the
invasion), France, and Italy. During the occupation, despite an official
non-fraternization policy, they married Germans and Austrians. In the
Pacific arena, they married women from Australia and New Zealand,
and after the War Brides Act of 1945 overturned previous legislation
designed to exclude Asian immigrants, they married women from
China, Japan, and the Philippines. Seventy-five percent of these brides
eventually came to America.

With the liberation of Europe, Americans began planning for the
postwar period. Questions about the end of hostilities and the returning soldiers were linked to questions about their wives and families.
The 1944 *Harper's* article "Housekeeping after the War" (referred to earlier) took a progressive view of women's future possibilities. It asked
whether women would continue to be "mere servants of their husbands
and children," or whether some system could be devised that would
enable wives "to do a good job of housekeeping and still have time to
hold down an outside job." The authors came up with a number of suggestions for "living pleasantly without servants" under the (correct)
assumption that fewer and fewer people would have them. Some of
their predictions have come to pass, but some of the most important—
those dealing with communal housing and childcare—have not.

For one thing, postwar manufacturers did produce better and
cheaper vacuum cleaners, toasters, electric mixers, washing machines,
even sturdy dishwashing machines to replace the inefficient prewar
models, and other timesaving appliances, although, as the article pre-
dicted, these items would still need to be constantly cleaned and occa-

sionally repaired. Another anticipated boon was the rise of the commercial cleaning service, with a team of bonded, well-equipped workers arriving on a regular schedule. Also, the steady increase of ready-to-serve food, accelerated during the war years, continued in the postwar years ad nauseam.

But the field where the authors saw "the greatest opportunity for organized service," in the creation and improvement of nursery schools and childcare centers, did not keep up with the need. Wives in postwar America were as much on their own in finding adequate childcare as their mothers had been a generation earlier. The lessons of federally subsidized childcare and on-location centers were lost with the war's end.

The popular sentiment (*Harper's* notwithstanding) was that women should go home and resume their roles as wives, mothers, and homemakers. Now that the men were back, there was ostensibly no need for married women to work. And with unemployment greeting thousands of returning servicemen, women were asked, once again, not to take a job away from a man.

After all, these men were returning from untold horrors and had every right to expect the rewards of guaranteed work and loving homes. Not all men were so lucky. Some found that employment in their home locale or in their chosen field was not available, and had to make major adjustments in their career expectations. In addition, the housing shortage forced many couples to live with their parents, adding intergenerational stress to the marriage. One wartime wife recalled:

> *Money was scarce and apartments were nil, and we were going to stick it out and live with Mom. . . . My sister, who is two years older than me, she is there with her new husband out of the Army and her first baby. . . . Here you have two married couples. I have a baby on the way, my sister has a baby, so it was insanity, insanity. I couldn't wait to get out of there.*[45]

It was often hard for mothers who had headed households during the war to relinquish their authority to husbands unfamiliar with their own children and the family codes. Remembering her husband's return after two years in the war to a son he didn't know, one wife spoke of her family's "difficult adjustment period. . . . All of a sudden from having one parent, one boss saying 'no,' now there are two people there to say 'no.' "[46]

Many military husbands and their wives, who had rushed into hasty marriages and then been separated for months and years, had real problems getting used to living together once they were finally reunited in peacetime. By 1946, the divorce rate rose to a new high of one in four marriages.[47]

One issue that caused problems for some married women was their desire to continue working. They had experienced the independence that comes with a paycheck and were reluctant to exchange it for a husband's largesse. Their husbands, however, feared they would be seen as inadequate providers if their wives continued to work. Many men were still marked by anxieties from the Depression years, when a successful breadwinning husband took pride in his ability to support a stay-at-home wife. And even with a husband's consent, wives were not always able to hold on to their wartime jobs. They were laid off from obsolete, war-industry jobs and eliminated from other sectors of the economy in preference to returning veterans.

On the other hand, many previously employed women *chose* to join the ranks of the housewives, and devote themselves exclusively to home and hearth after the trials of the war years. Women born two or three decades before the war had been socialized to believe in well-defined roles for husbands and wives, and especially for mothers, as one of them recalled many years later: "I was totally into motherhood, completely into motherhood. I was never career minded, and women of my generation were always raised to be mothers. That was your goal in life."[48]

Another looked back with pride on how well she had performed her role as wife and mother. "I never had to work . . . I raised the kids . . . I liked to be a homemaker. . . . A woman wants a lot of affection, she wants to know she's important in the man's life. . . . When he came home from work, I dolled up like I was going on a date. I always did that."[49]

Housewifely and maternal images propagated by government, business, and the ladies' magazines continued to reinforce a domestic ideology. As early as June 1944 a *A Ladies' Home Journal* article argued that most women workers wanted to be full-time homemakers after the war. The author, Nell Giles, summing up the results of a national study, wrote: "If the American woman can find a man she wants to marry, who can support her, a job fades into insignificance beside the vital business of staying at home and raising a family—three children is the ideal number. . . ."[50]

The *Journal* repeated this message often, as in April 1945, when the "How America Lives" section featured the story of Mrs. Eck, who had given up her concert career for the sake of her husband and children. Whatever qualms she might have had about that choice were hidden under a rhetoric of consumeristic satisfaction: "The sooner a woman makes a real home for a man, the sooner he will became successful and can give her a better house, servants, lovely clothes and so on. . . . Few men ever amount to much when their wives work."[51] Implicit in this and similar assessments intended for a female readership was the belief that a wife was responsible not only for her children's well-being and her husband's comfort, but for his career as well. If he didn't succeed, it was undoubtedly her fault.

Five years later, in a September 1950 *Journal* article titled "Making Marriage Work," wives were advised "Cater to his tastes—in food, in household arrangements, even in your appearance. Indulging his wishes, even if they are whims, is a sure way of convincing him that you really want to please him."[52] One wonders if any of the *Journal's* readers were aware that this was the exact same message American and English wives had been fed a hundred years earlier.

There were, however, a few signs that American housewives were not all experiencing domestic bliss. For example, a 1947 *Life Magazine* spread, "The American Woman's Dilemma," recognized that many wives and mothers who enjoyed their families still wanted to participate in the outside world. How could they fulfill their domestic obligations and simultaneously work or volunteer beyond the home? Certainly society was not prepared to help them resolve this dilemma in any appreciable way. Although, as William Chafe points out, the conflict may have been exaggerated and limited primarily to white, middle-class women, the *Life* editors had put their fingers on a problem that was not going to go away.[53]

TEN

Toward the New Wife, 1950–2000

"I'll have a husband, which, as everybody knows, a woman should have at least one before the end of the story."
Grace Paley, "Goodbye and Good Luck," 1956

"Every working woman needs a Wife."
Late–twentieth-century popular saying

*I*t's no secret that the American wife has been radically transformed during the past half century. Fifty years ago, a white middle-class woman was likely to enter marriage with a man from her own region, ethnicity, race, and religion, hoping for three to four children, two cars, and wall-to-wall carpeting. Prior to marriage, she had probably engaged in some pretty heavy petting, but for fear of "losing her reputation" or, worse yet, of becoming pregnant, she would not have "gone all the way," at least not until an engagement ring was on her finger. Marriage usually put a halt to her education, and a baby meant the end of paid employment. She knew few people who had been divorced, and had every good reason to expect her own marriage to endure until death. For the rest of her life, even if divorced or widowed, people would address her as "Mrs.," which was considered an improvement over "Miss."

Today, few women of any class or color enter marriage without having had sexual intercourse beforehand. It is so commonplace for single women to live with a lover—both before and in lieu of marriage—that

A fifties June bride and her mother.

cohabitation has practically become the norm. If women become pregnant while single, they do not necessarily hurry to the altar—a full 40 percent of first babies are born out of wedlock. When women marry, they do so on the average of five years later than the women of the fifties, at age twenty-five instead of twenty. Many marry men from different religions, races, regions, or ethnic backgrounds. Most continue to work after marriage and the birth of their children. North American mothers now bear roughly two children which is also the average in

Europe, Russia, China, Japan, Australia, and New Zealand, but considerably less than the fertility rates in Latin America and Africa. One out of two American wives will see her first marriage end in divorce. This will not prevent many of them from becoming wives again in second, and even third, marriages. And in all of these cases, a married woman, like a single woman, may be addressed with the neutral term "Ms."[1]

Of course, these scenarios vary greatly according to one's ethnicity, race, religion, and personal idiosyncrasies. For example, sexually active white women who become pregnant are more like to marry before giving birth than either African-American or Hispanic-American women. Japanese-Americans intermarry more often than Chinese-Americans. Jews frequently marry non-Jews. Muslim men outmarry more often than Muslim women. Divorce is more common in big cities, such as New York and Los Angeles, than in rural locales. Children of divorce are less likely to marry than children of nondivorced parents, and divorced adults are more likely to live together in subsequent relationships than remarry. Yet despite significant differences between specific groups, overall trends point in the same direction for all American wives: more premarital and extramarital sex, more economic independence, more divorce, more serial marriage.

These trends did not start yesterday, nor in the turbulent sixties or feminist seventies. They are rooted in historical changes that began more than a hundred years ago, most notably in the sexual attitudes and experiences of American couples, and in work opportunities for women outside the home. A long-term shift in the meaning of sex, from an emphasis on procreation to an emphasis on pleasure, and the increasing presence of women in the workforce have been key components in the making of the "New Wife."

As we consider these changes, it is useful to remember that a wife is not a single photo, but a series of photos as one would find in a family album. The women of the fifties were not frozen into perpetual domesticity, nor were their daughters—adults in the seventies and eighties—congealed forever in the molds of feminism and sexual freedom that were characteristic of those decades. People change with the times, both *with* and *against* the currents they encounter. They change because they interact with members of the next generation, who force them to confront new values and behaviors. And most of all, they change because they themselves age and reach different developmental stages.

Studying wives of the past half century, I was, for the first time in this book, able to look at living examples. Many of the wives who confided their marital stories to me are today in their thirties, forties, fifties, sixties, even a few in their seventies and eighties. I have been struck over and over again by the adaptability of the American wife. Older mothers have accepted behaviors for their daughters that were unthinkable for themselves, and they have sometimes even followed their daughters' lead in changing their own lives. How many wives have gone back to school in middle age, taken jobs, had sexual encounters, divorced, remarried, or moved toward more egalitarian relations with their husbands because their daughters and other young people made them see the world differently?

What follows is an all-too-quick run through the past half century, when married women have evolved so dramatically that the word "wife" has lost many of its past associations and taken on others that have not yet endured the test of time.

THE SEXUAL REVOLUTION: FROM THE *KINSEY* TO THE *COSMO REPORT*

From midcentury onward, American sexuality has been well documented by numerous investigators. Alfred Kinsey's books on male and female sexual behavior became best-sellers in 1948 and 1953 and established a baseline for all future sexologists.[2] His findings flew in the face of traditional religious and moral teachings. He found that almost all adult males had a history of masturbation, that 90 percent of them had engaged in premarital sex and half in extramarital sex, and that a third had experienced some form of homosexual encounter. Women, too, were no longer constrained by Victorian ideals. About three-fifths of Kinsey's sample of 5,940 white women had masturbated, nearly 50 percent had sexual experience before marriage, and a quarter had engaged in extramarital relations. Between 3 and 12 percent of the single women were lesbians (depending on how you defined "lesbian"), and 20 to 25 percent of the married women had had criminal abortions.

Kinsey's women spanned four decades, from women born before 1899 to women born before 1929. While the frequency of marital intercourse remained fairly similar from one decade to the next, wives reported an increase in the incidence of orgasm starting with the generation born between 1900 and 1909 and married in the 1920s. These women had responded to the growing consensus that the marital bed was made primarily for sexual satisfaction. Kinsey linked the greater frequency of orgasm to the sexual revolution that had taken place in the roaring twenties, and attributed its ongoing effects to the "franker attitudes and the freer discussion of sex which we have had in the United States during the past twenty years."[3]

Although Kinsey's hallmark was statistical data, he made it clear that numbers did not tell the entire story. For example, the "nearly 50 percent" of married women who had had premarital sex did not mean that American women were promiscuous. A "considerable portion of the pre-marital coitus had been had in the year or two immediately preceding marriage" and was confined to the fiancé.[4] Americans, traditionally rigid on the subject of sex outside marriage, had a history of looking the other way when couples were engaged.

Once married, there was considerable variety in what couples did or did not do in bed. The range of foreplay included kissing, practiced by 99.4 percent of spouses; manual and oral stimulation of the female breast by the male (95 and 93 percent); manual stimulation of the male genitalia by the female (91 percent); oral stimulation of the female genitalia by the male (54 percent) and of the male genitalia by the female (49 percent). Some couples spent only three minutes in foreplay, others as long as half an hour, an hour, or more; most were in the four to twenty-minute range. Extensive foreplay seemed to be more prevalent "among the better educated groups."[5] While the old-fashioned missionary position in intercourse with the man on top was still the most prevalent, the reverse position with the woman on top was becoming more common among younger women. Younger wives were also more prone to engage in sex in the nude, as opposed to women born before 1900, who were more likely to be clothed during intercourse.

Kinsey believed his study would be especially beneficial to those married persons, who need "additional information to meet some of the sexual problems which arise in their marriages." He estimated that in "perhaps three-quarters of the divorces recorded in our case histories, sexual factors were among those which had led to the divorce," and he invoked the authority of pastors, teachers, physicians, and other clinicians to support the view that "improved sexual relationships might contribute to the improvement of our modern marriages."[6] Kinsey added academic credibility to the increasingly popular belief that satisfying sex was the cornerstone of an enduring marriage.

Though Kinsey was publicly hailed as a brilliant researcher who had brought together more data on human sexuality than had ever been amassed before, many critics were uncomfortable with his findings. Millicent McIntosh, president of Barnard College, feared that the wide distribution of his book "has added greatly to the confusion in the moral climate of our time." She worried that young people would feel "trapped by these statistics" and try to emulate them in order to appear "normal."[7] Other critics lamented Kinsey's amoral stance or his failure to interpret the meaning of his large body of data. But "the important thing," as University of Pennsylvania Medical School marriage counselor Emily Mudd wrote in 1954, is that "women emerge from all those pages of careful analysis with far more sexual drive than they have ever been given credit for."[8] Significantly, sexual drive was now seen as something acceptable and even desirable in a woman.

When the Kinsey report on female sexuality first appeared in 1953, there was already a new generation of wives born after 1930, who would marry at an early age, bear their children when they were young, and generally finish childbearing by the end of their twenties.[9] Their adult identities would be largely determined by their marital and maternal situations. As the distinguished sociologist Talcott Parsons stated boldly: "The woman's fundamental status is that of her husband's wife, the mother of his children."[10] Indeed, according to polls of the time, young women aspired first and foremost to become the wives of prominent men and the mothers of successful children. Their own sense of self was dependent on their husbands' careers and their children's accomplishments.

In becoming wives and mothers, these women of the fifties also depended heavily on their gynecologists and obstetricians, who were almost always male. In the doctor's office, they went through routine fittings for a diaphragm to prevent conception and urine tests that would determine if they were pregnant. Once a women knew she was pregnant, she counted on her doctor to sustain her through the months ahead and to be available when she went into labor. Trained with the

latest obstetrical methods, American doctors were generally not interested in the new ideas of "natural childbirth" that were gaining ground
in Europe, especially in England under the influence of London obste-
trician Grantly Dick-Read. Instead of encouraging women to be active
participants in the childbirth process, they told their patients to leave
things in professional hands. Many women went into childbirth knowing nothing about proper breathing techniques, or the eventualities of
anesthesia, epesiotomies, and Cesarean section. There were no classes
for pregnant women, no Lamaze groups, no midwives, only Dr. Benjamin Spock's *Common Sense Book of Baby Care* (1946), republished in
paperback as *Baby and Child Care* (1954), to give practical advice to the
novice mother.

When it came to breast-feeding, most American doctors were indifferent, if not hostile, to the idea. With the introduction of baby formula
in the 1930s, most American women stopped nursing their babies;
only 25 percent did so between 1940 and 1970. The medical establishment saw little need for women to nurse their infants, since formula
was considered a perfectly adequate substitute. It would take another
generation before American women rediscovered the benefits of giving
their babies mother's milk.[11]

America took pride in the health record of its postwar mothers and
children. From 1940 to 1949, maternal mortality and infant deaths
dropped dramatically. Women who gave birth in the hospital—that is,
close to 90 percent of mothers in the fifties—had every reason to expect
a safe delivery and a healthy baby.[12]

The popular media of this period projected images of women determined to catch and preserve a husband. Gone were the career-women
films of the thirties and forties, where stars such as Katharine Hepburn
and Rosalind Russell triumphed as confident airplane pilots, lawyers,
and journalists. Instead, cute coeds and spunky wives, played by Doris
Day and Debbie Reynolds, incarnated the American ideal—upbeat,
earnest, and coyly sexual. Even such superstars as Elizabeth Taylor and
Marilyn Monroe, who exuded polymorphous sexuality, were generally
crowned with wedding veils by the end of the film. (Significantly, Marilyn Monroe was to have three husbands in her short life, and Elizabeth
Taylor had seven, one of whom—Richard Burton—she married twice.)

The 1950s television sitcoms featured families of the *Father Knows*

Best, I Love Lucy, and *Ozzie and Harriet* variety. Lovable stay-at-home wives sparred with breadwinning husbands, usually besting the men with a lighthearted touch. Lucy, however, was unsuccessful in overriding her TV husband's refusal to let her work in show business. But in real life, the star was a top moneymaker—she even managed to continue working throughout her pregnancy at a time when CBS would not even allow the word "pregnant" to be used on TV—and she gave birth to Little Ricky as a part of the television drama.[13]

Spotless TV moms reigned over superclean homes and superclean children. That artifical image projected into the living rooms of rich and poor was bound to make some people question their own less than perfect homes. As a child, the black writer Assata Shakur asked herself:

> *Why didn't my mother have freshly baked cookies ready when I came home from school. Why didn't we live in a house with a backyard and a front yard instead of an ole apartment? I remember looking at my mother as she cleaned the house in her raggedy housecoat with her hair in curlers. "How disgusting," I would think. Why didn't she clean the house in high heels and shirtwaist dresses like they did on television?*[14]

Television, Hollywood, and advertisements catered to the fantasy of the beautifully dressed, perfectly coiffed, nonharried housewife. After all, with the many labor-saving appliances and packaged foods available in the postwar years, housekeeping was supposed to be practically effortless. But in fact, the new products did not reduce the amount of time women devoted to housework: full-time housewives averaged between fifty-one and fifty-six hours per week on household tasks from the 1920s to the 1960s, while women with jobs outside the home still spent thirty-four hours a week on housekeeping.[15] Higher standards of household cleanliness and personal attractiveness, promoted by TV, the women's magazines, domestic advice literature, and consumer ads gave homemakers more to do and more to worry about. One wife complained in *Redbook* magazine (September 1960) that after ten years of marriage, her husband still expected her to be "a combination of Fanny Farmer and Marilyn Monroe." Another, with her finicky spouse in mind, confessed: "I get terribly defensive if I serve dinner late or he comes home early and my hair's still in curlers." Domesticity was back

An ecstatic housewife producing wonders with her Gibson Ultra 600 Electric Range, late 1950s.

in fashion, and was expected to fulfill a wife's fundamental needs. If it did not, the assumption was that something was wrong with her.

Psychologists and psychiatrists following Freud (for this was the golden age of Freudians in America) believed that women should be able to find fulfillment in their roles as wives and mothers, without the extra burdens of paid employment. In this respect, little had changed in psychoanalytic thinking since Freud had written to his own fiancée in the 1880s denouncing the feminist views of John Stuart Mill. Freud found it "unrealistic to send women into the struggle for existence in the same way as men" and was determined to transfer his bride from "the competitive role into the quiet, undisturbed activity of my home," where she could enjoy being "a beloved wife."[16]

Seventy years later, in the early 1950s, British analyst John Bowlby followed Freud's line of thinking in developing his influential attachment theory. Bowlby argued that the mothers of small children should devote themselves exclusively to nurturing their offspring and that employment at this time of life was inadvisable. In his words: "The mother of young children is not free, or at least should not be free, to earn."[17]

Women with an acute case of "penis envy" (an obsolete Freudian idea that hung on well into the seventies) obviously wanted to compete with, rather than nurture, the men in their lives, be it coworkers, husbands, or sons. Although a few iconoclastic psychoanalysts, namely Karen Horney and Clara Thompson, understood penis envy symbolically as women's desire to acquire the privileges that traditionally accrue to men, most psychiatrists accepted Freud's formulations literally.

Sylvia Plath's portrait of an obtuse male psychiatrist in her 1963 novel *The Bell Jar*, based on her experience of mental breakdown ten years earlier, was only an exaggerated version of contemporary psychiatric language and practice. With the photo of his beautiful wife and two children on his desk, Dr. Gordon was totally incapable of understanding the anxieties that had driven *The Bell Jar*'s protagonist, Esther Greenwood, to the verge of madness. Esther's collapse (like Sylvia's) was related to her father's early death, leaving her vulnerable for the rest of her life, and to conflicts she experienced at a very deep level between her desire to be a writer and social imperatives for her to become a wife and mother.[18] Dr. Gordon's prescription of shock treatment, instead of improving her condition, pushed her over the edge into a suicide attempt.

Esther had better fortune in the choice of her second psychiatrist, Dr. Nolan, a woman. Yet she, too, could not get away from the psychoanalytic clichés of her day. She rewarded Esther for being able to say that she hated her mother. It was the heyday of mother vilification, which had found popular expression in Philip Wylie's best-selling *Generation of Vipers* (1942) and in psychiatrist Edward Strecker's theory that overprotective mothering was responsible for the 2 million men who had been turned down by the draft in World War II. With little understanding of the genetic nature of schizophrenia, psychiatrists embraced the term "schizophrenogenic mother" to account for schizophrenic children, and for any number of family and social ills as well.

Wives were seen as key to the success or failure not only of their children, but also of their marriages. If a marriage went bad, it was primarily *her* fault, not his. A senior Harvard psychiatrist could write with impunity in the early sixties: "Just as the fate of personality development hangs largely on the effect of mother on child, so, I believe, the fate of a marriage hangs largely on the effect of wife on husband. . . . overwhelmingly the flow of crucial influence is from the woman to the man, requiring adaptation or defense on his part. . . . It is the woman who 'makes or breaks' a marriage."[19] Consciously and unconsciously, most married women knew they would be blamed more than their husbands if the marriage broke down, and most did not want to resemble the bitchy wives, dissatisfied with their lives and intent upon destroying their husbands, pictured in such popular fiction as Hemingway's "The Short Happy Life of Francis Macomber" (1938) and Sloan Wilson's *The Man in the Gray Flannel Suit* (1955).

A totally different picture of women appeared in Simone de Beauvoir's *The Second Sex,* published in France in 1949 and translated into English in 1953. This work, the longest and most incisive French study of women's situation, can be credited with the beginning of what was subsequently called the second wave of feminism. De Beauvoir took a dim view of marriage—she and Jean-Paul Sartre, her companion from 1929 until 1980, rejected it outright as a bourgeois institution incompatible with existential freedom. She was even harder on motherhood, which she believed made women passive vessels of procreation rather than active creators of their own destinies. In some ways her analysis seems dated, but she was right on the mark in at least two respects: her understanding that gender is almost entirely socially constructed, as she phrased it in the now famous statement, "One is not born, but rather becomes a woman," and her conviction that women would always be the second sex as long as they depended on men for economic support. Both of these positions became credos of the feminist movement in the decades to come.

But neither de Beauvoir in France nor Sylvia Plath in America could be considered "representative" women of their time and place. A more likely candidate in America might be the First Lady, Mamie Eisenhower, depicted in the July 1953 issue of *Woman's Home Companion* as "no bluestocking feminist" and praised by *Better Homes and Gardens* for not attempting "to become an intellectual."[20] Implicity, she was being compared with former First Lady Eleanor Roosevelt, who had allied herself with several liberal causes, including the Equal Rights Amendments (ERA).

Throughout the fifties, liberals and conservatives opposed each other on numerous women's issues, some of which are still with us today. The legality of contraception was still being debated in Connecticut in the early fifties, and an unwritten ban on contraceptive counseling in New York public hospitals was not removed until the end of the decade. In 1960, the Food and Drug Administration approved an oral contraceptive (Enovid and Norlutin) for the subsequent year. Henceforth the pill would be the preferred mode of contraception for American females. It was easier to use than the clunky diaphram and provided almost 100 percent protection. Whatever health risks it entailed for long-term users were not yet known. In many ways, the introduction of the pill marked the end of the fifties, both literally and figuratively.

In her aptly titled book, *The Way We Never Were,* Stephanie Coontz revealed the underside of the mythical fifties.[21] Alcoholism, suicide, madness, family violence, and wife and child abuse were all known to social workers, psychiatrists, ministers, priests, and rabbis, but they were, for the most part, hidden from the general public. Even the professionals did not take some of these subjects seriously. In fact, there was virtually no scholarly research into domestic violence until the late seventies; previously it had not only been ignored by social scientists, the medical profession, and police officers, but "explained away" as the

inevitable consequence of wives who relentlessly goaded their husbands. Psychiatrist Helene Deutsch gave credence to this blame-the-
victim view with her elaborate theories of female passivity and
masochism. Similarly, psychoanalysts were wont to understand incest
as provoked by a "seductive" girl child. Marital unhappiness caused by
these and other sources would result in the eventual divorce of between
one-quarter and one-third of all couples married in the 1950s.

Some inkling that a significant number of American wives were dissatisfied with domesticity was beginning to seep into the popular press.
In 1956, McCall's ran a piece titled "The Mother Who Ran Away," and
Ladies' Home Journal devoted an issue to "The Plight of the Young
Mother."[22] In September 1960, a Redbook article entitled "Why Mothers
Feel Trapped" painted a picture of "desperately anxious" homemakers
who felt "pushed and pulled" by the multiple demands of their roles as
wives, mothers, and community members. One Redbook housewife
described her typical morning as resembling an old Marx Brothers
comedy.

> I wash the dishes, rush the older children off to school, dash out in
> the yard to cultivate the chrysanthemums, run back in to make a phone
> call about a committee meeting, help my youngest child build a block-
> house, spend fifteen minutes skimming the newspapers so I can be well
> informed, then scamper down to the washing machine where my thrice-
> weekly laundry includes enough clothes to keep a primitive village
> going for an entire year. By noon I'm ready for a padded cell.

In contrast to the middle-class readers of Ladies' Home Journal and
Redbook, working-class women accepted their roles as housewives more
easily, according to Mirra Komarovsky in her groundbreaking 1962
book. Kamorovsky found "little evidence of status frustrations" and
"hardly a trace . . . of the low prestige that educated housewives sometimes attach to their role."[23] Gender roles were clear-cut: men were
expected to be "good providers" and women to be full-time wives and
mothers. For the most part, the men did not want their wives to work
outside the home, since it reflected badly on the husband's earning
power. He, in turn, considered it inappropriate to pitch into housekeeping once he came home from work. In about four-fifths of the
families, cooking, laundry and cleaning were exclusively feminine

occupations. About a third of the husbands sometimes helped with the dishes. One wife remarked that she didn't ask her husband to participate in that daily chore because of the cartoons showing henpecked husbands doing the dishes. About 20 percent of the couples had arguments over the failure of the husband to help with what he perceived to be a feminine task. When it came to the father's involvement in child-care, the husbands were divided into three nearly equal groups: one third hardly ever helped, another third helped occasionally, and the others helped frequently or regularly.

Typically, a working-class wife's day started very early, when she rose to make breakfast for her family and send the children off to school. Then she cleaned house and took care of the laundry and ironing. If there were small children and the weather permitted, she might take them to the park or to a shopping area. Sometimes she would stop in on a friend for a cup of coffee. She would need to be home in time to prepare and serve supper soon after her husband returned from work, around 5:00 or 5:30.

While the majority of spouses believed that a woman's place was in the home, a small group of wives were employed. Some of these were clearly overburdened by their double jobs, and would have gladly stayed at home, if the family didn't need their salary. This situation could be compounded by the negative attitude of the husband, who resented the fact that his wife *had* to work because of his insufficient income. On the other hand, about a third of the full-time homemakers would have liked to work for pay, preferably part-time, just to get out of the house.

Middle- and upper-class wives had various time-honored ways of getting out. There was volunteer work to be done in local churches, synagogues, hospitals, museums, and such organizations as the League of Women Voters, Planned Parenthood, and the upper-crust Junior League. Many wives belonged to auxiliaries supporting male organizations, like the Masons, the American Legion, and various professional groups. Such volunteer work provided a sense of purpose and a social community outside the home. At the same time, membership in a bridge, garden, or book club offered an outlet for one's cultural and intellectual interests.

Some wives entered paid employment, even when they did not

have to. The proportion of working wives continued to rise after the war: by 1960, 30 percent of married women were in the labor force, double the percentage of 1940. Interestingly, the greatest growth took place among well-educated wives from families where the husband earned from $7,000 to $10,000 a year, a comfortable income for the times.[24]

One woman, married in 1940, recalled with pleasure her work as a teacher. "I was gonna work for a year, and I lasted twenty-five years. I loved it. I loved every bit of it. It was not easy. . . . He didn't like it in the beginning, but he saw that I enjoyed it."[25]

Some worked because they were simply too unhappy staying at home. This is how one wife described her decision to reenter the workforce.

"My youngest . . . was about ten years old. . . . I found myself screaming my head off at her, because she left a finger mark on the wall. And it kind of brought me up short. . . . I wasn't running a house, the house was running me."

She told her husband she wanted to go back to work. "I'm gonna go get a job, because my life has closed in on me to the point where I've lost my sense of values. I have to get out of this house! I have to be with other adults."

> His reaction was to put his hand in his pocket, and he said "Here's money. What is it you want to buy? Go buy it." And I tried to explain to him that it had nothing to do with money. . . . All I can talk about is when I washed the floor last or the best buy in the supermarket. I felt stupid. I was beginning to feel as though my brains were drying up. . . . And when I made him understand that, he was not thrilled, but he agreed that if that's what I wanted to do, then he would support me in whatever way he could.[26]

Husbands, like this one, who loved their wives and wanted to see them happy, had to accept a very different lifestyle from the one they had expected in marriage.

A study of some 900 wives in Detroit and the nearby farm country conducted at the University of Michigan and published in 1960 under the title *Husbands and Wives* examined prevailing marital mores at different levels of society.[27] The findings pointed in the direction of more egalitarian decision making between husbands and wives, with the balance still slightly in the husband's favor. Debunking the myth of "momism," the survey showed that the domination of husbands and children by wives and mothers had been greatly exaggerated. Not surprisingly, white-collar men possessed more authority at home than working-class men: the more money a man made and the higher his prestige in the community, the more decisions he controlled in the home. Yet these same prestigious husbands did more chores around the home than husbands with lesser status. It's as if the successful white-collar men had enough confidence to dismiss the fear that "women's work" would taint them.

As wage earners, few husbands were rivaled by their wives. Although one out of three wives in low-income families worked for pay, only one out of twenty did so at the other end of the scale. The wives in high-income families believed that their support, advice, and domestic skills contributed substantially to their husbands' success.

When asked to list the benefits of marriage in order of importance, the wives answered: 1) companionship; 2) the chance to have children; 3) understanding and emotional support; 4) love and affection; 5) financial benefit. While the wives may have been reluctant to give financial benefit a higher priority for fear of appearing crass and materialistic, it is surprising that love and affection ranked only fourth. These Michigan women seemed to have been a practical and realistic lot: companionship and children were what they appreciated most in being wives.

Yet children were by no means seen as an unadulterated blessing. However much children added to marriage, they also put strains on it. A common pattern emerged of children diverting attention away from the couple per se, causing spousal conflict, as well as worries about child-rearing, illness, and finances. Nearly all wives were less satisfied with the companionship of their husbands after a few years of marriage than they formerly were. With the advent of children, many husbands felt the necessity to work harder and longer, and many wives complained of a loss of spousal intimacy. This dissatisfaction reached a low point when the children were adolescents. In statistical terms, in the first two years of marriage, 52 percent of the wives were very satisfied with their marriages and none notably dissatisfied, as compared to twenty years later, when only 6 percent were still very satisfied and 21 percent were conspicuously dissatisfied.

Even though the course of marital satisfaction ran downhill for the first two decades, the survey indicated that eventually it turned upward again. Once the children had been launched, marital problems diminished. Having weathered the *Sturm und Drang* of the child-rearing years, the couples who survived experienced what the researchers called a second honeymoon. This is exactly the same marital trajectory that some researchers would find forty years later.

During the second half of the twentieth century, the baneful expression "just a housewife" reflected the diminished status of the stay-at-home wife.[28] One sixties' housewife from a Chicago suburb candidly described her situation in an interview with radio personality Studs Terkel: "A housewife is a housewife, that's all. Low on the totem pole. . . . Someone who goes out and works for a living is more important than somebody who doesn't. . . . I don't like putting a housewife down, but everybody has done it for so long." Nonetheless, she added: "Deep down, I feel what I'm doing is important. . . . I love being a housewife." This woman expressed the ambivalence many housewives felt about their lot: because they incorporated into their self-assessments society's low regard for homemakers, they felt "guilty" for not working for pay, even if they enjoyed cooking and cleaning and caring for their families, as this woman obviously did.[29]

A General Mills ad picturing a wife making Christmas cookies was titled "Just a housewife?" Underneath that rhetorical question, a lengthy text tried to make the much maligned housewife feel better about herself, and, not incidentally, keep her baking cookies.

> . . . *her career is the most important one a woman can choose. . . . Her job is to keep her family well fed and patched and clean behind the ears. Her ambition is to build good citizens . . . to make them happy and comfortable and proud of the way they live. . . . Her working day often begins before dawn and may last right up until bedtime—seven days a week. Her pay? The pay she values the most is the loving appreciation of her family.*

Despite such efforts to bolster up the housewife's self-esteem, in real life, many housewives resented the monotony, drudgery, and isolation of their daily lives. All the consumer products intended to make their work easier and their lives more pleasant (according to the marketing mavens of their day), all the newly fabricated mood pills like Dexedrine prescribed by indulgent doctors, all the talk of woman's biological destiny and sacred place in the family could not hide the sense of frustration and alienation that some wives were feeling in their suburban cages. Little wonder that Betty Friedan's *Feminine Mystique* (1963), with its passionate exposé of the housewife's plight, hit a nerve among thinking Americans and sold more than a million copies.

Friedan's naming of "the problem that has no name" has been credited with relaunching the American feminist movement. And, indeed, unlike de Beauvoir's *Second Sex,* which had appeared fourteen years earlier in France, *The Feminine Mystique* led to political action. Whereas de Beauvoir's France in 1949 was still licking its war wounds, Friedan's America in 1963 was ripe for social change.

Nineteen sixty-three was the year of the civil rights march in Birmingham, Alabama, and Martin Luther King Jr.'s "I have a dream" speech in Washington, D.C. In 1964, President Lyndon Johnson signed the landmark Civil Rights Act, which included a prohibition against discrimination in employment on the basis of sex. In 1965, 15,000 students marched in Washington to protest the war in Vietnam.

It was within this context of heightened political awareness that the women's movement was born. In 1966, the National Organization for Women (NOW) was founded, with Betty Friedan as its first president. The event was by no means headline news, although the conservative *National Observer* published a front-page article that began:

> *Warning to all American husbands: the days of male supremacy are numbered. Your wives, victimized and degraded by a double standard in law and custom, have found a new champion. It is NOW— the National Organization for Women—a militant new women's rights movement envisioned as becoming a mass-based pressure group capable of fulfilling the dream of emancipation of womanhood held out by the Nineteenth Century suffragettes.*[30]

NOW had learned from the civil rights movement how to lobby and litigate on behalf of women, so as to bring them into employment and public life on a more equal footing with men. Among other initiatives, it inaugurated a campaign to end the practice of advertising jobs on the basis of sex. It supported passage of the Equal Rights Amendment (ERA). And it endorsed the legalization of abortion.

NOW's agenda was too radical for most Americans. Journalist and publisher's wife Clare Booth Luce in a 1967 *McCall's* article titled "Is It NOW or Never for Women?" expressed the public's general reluctance to share NOW's concerns "about the so-called overall 'inferior' status of women in economic and social life." Luce maintained that most women would be satisfied with their lot, if their spouses just showed a little more appreciation: "Husbands, praise your wives! and marvel at how quickly they stop complaining about discrimination."[31]

Nineteen sixty-eight was a tumultuous year for the women's movement, as it was for the entire nation. Martin Luther King was assassinated in Memphis. Robert Kennedy was assassinated in Los Angeles. Women's liberation groups demonstrated against the Miss America Beauty Contest in Atlantic City.

Conservatives, appalled by these threats to traditional values, fought back on all fronts. In 1968 the Pope's encyclical *Humanae Vitae* ruled against the use of artificial methods of birth control, including the pill. In 1969, the John Birch Society called for active opposition to programs for sex education in the schools. In 1970 the National Right to Life Committee was established to try to block the liberalization of abortion.

Yet nothing could turn back the tide of protest that was sweeping across the country—protest against racial and sexual discrimination, against antiabortion laws, and, increasingly, against the Vietnam War. Married women marched in countless antiwar demonstrations. Black and white, they marched in civil rights protests in the South. They clamored at the White House on Mother's Day for "Rights, Not Roses." Not since the suffragist movement had so many women, single and married, taken to the streets.

A later cartoon captured the paradox of married women as political demonstrators. Wearing an "ERA NOW" T-shirt and holding an "ERA YES" sign, a middle-aged wife sits dejectedly on the front porch of her house. Her husband in bedroom slippers, with a newspaper in his hand

and a dog at his side, speaks to her in two separate captions. "You have fought a good fight, Madeline. . . . You have finished the course. . . . You have kept the faith. . . . But now it's time for you to get your carcass into the house and cook supper!"[32] Whatever the extent of their wives' political involvement and public activity, many men wanted them back in the kitchen.

Yet by 1970, 40 percent of wives and two-thirds of mothers with children under the age of six were in the labor force.[33] The expanding female presence in the workplace was steadily contributing to a new picture of American womanhood, one that showed up in an early 1970s poll: nearly 70 percent of college women agreed with the statement that "the idea that a woman's place is in the home is nonsense."[34]

The seventies began with a spate of books that laid out controversial theories on women's liberation. Shulamith Firestone's radical *Dialects of Sex* (1970) argued that the only way to free women from male oppression was to diffuse the burden of childbearing and child-rearing to society as a whole. She went so far as to propose test-tube babies maturing outside the female body—a *Brave New World* solution that even other

ERA YES. *Political cartoon by Kate Palmer, 1982.*

feminists were not quick to embrace. Kate Millett's *Sexual Politics* (1970) revolutionized the reading of certain male authors, such as D. H. Lawrence and Henry Miller, by showing to what extent their depictions of sex were sadistically violent to women. Germaine Greer's *Female Eunuch* (1971) turned men, rather than women, into sex objects. Women, she argued, would not be fully liberated until they adopted the same sexual freedom that men enjoyed, unencumbered by family and marriage.[35]

Gloria Steinem launched the magazine *Ms.* that was to play such a crucial role in consciousness-raising throughout the nation. Its preview issue of December 1971 included such stories as "The Housewife's Moment of Truth," "Raising Kids without Sex Roles," "Women Tell the Truth about their Abortions," "Welfare is a Woman's Issue," and the classic essay "Why I Want a Wife." The cover showed a pregnant woman with eight arms, each one holding either a frying pan, a clock, a duster, a typewriter, a steering wheel, an iron, a telephone, and a mirror. Like Friedan's book eight years earlier, Steinem's magazine pressed an alarm button in tens of thousands of American homes.

The most popular representation of liberated womanhood, and one that marked a turning point in women's fiction, was Erica Jong's *Fear of Flying* (1972). The novel's married heroine wrestles with the two conflicting imperatives of her age—to be a free sexual being and to be a wife. While she fantasizes (like a man) of sex on the run, she cannot free herself from notions of dependency and commitment. In the end, she returns to her husband . . . but not without titillating a whole generation of female readers who were asking similar questions about themselves.

Alex Comfort's *Joy of Sex* (1972), while neither feminist nor female-authored, offered a how-to manual that inspired men and women to experiment in lovemaking as if they were concocting a delectable meal. The Boston Women's Health Collective's *Our Bodies, Ourselves* (1973) not only taught women to look at themselves through their own eyes, instead of through the eyes of male doctors, but also launched a grassroots movement that would bring to public attention women's health issues, such as breast-feeding, breast cancer, and the underrepresentation of women in medical research.

The early seventies produced many significant changes affecting women, and none more significant than the 1973 U.S. Supreme Court decision in

Roe v. Wade that invalidated all state laws restricting abortion in the first three months of pregnancy. The decision to abort in the first trimester of pregnancy was to be left to the woman and her doctor. During the second trimester, the states could regulate the abortion procedure in the interest of protecting the health of the woman, and in the third trimester, they could even prohibit it. For the first time in American history, the highest court laid out legal guidelines permitting abortion. Although numerous conservative and right-wing individuals and organizations have since agitated against this decision and made abortion difficult to obtain, *Roe v. Wade* remains a landmark moment in the ongoing struggle for women to acquire reproductive control over their bodies.

The *Roe v. Wade* decision was related to the freer sexuality that had been gaining ground in America since the revelations of the Kinsey reports. By the time that Masters and Johnson (Dr. William H. and Dr. Virginia E.) were amassing data for their books on sexuality in the sixties, it was no longer a matter of interviewing subjects about their sexual proclivities, but of recording their arousal and climax in live performances.[36] From their laboratory, where they monitored individuals with sophisticated recording systems, Masters and Johnson studied the techniques that did or did not lead to male and female orgasm. For one thing, they thoroughly debunked the idea of two types of female orgasm: there was only one type, and that occurred most easily through direct stimulation of the clitoris. By deemphasizing penetration and the goal of simultaneous orgasm, Masters and Johnson gave many women permission to achieve orgasm in ways other than the missionary position. Moreover, if female orgasm was largely a matter of technique, then failure to orgasm was treatable. Like Kinsey and others before them, Masters and Johnson believed that sexual problems caused the majority of divorces, and that sex therapy—a field they helped to create—could help couples stay together.

Throughout the seventies, many surveys tracked women's sexuality. The 1976 *Hite Report*, instead of emphasizing heterosexual intercourse, counseled women to use whatever means best suited them—masturbation, a vibrator, oral sex, anything that brought about the elusive orgasm, with or without a male partner.

In response to the *Hite Report*, *Redbook* magazine conducted its own survey. It drew an amazing 100,000 responses from married women and painted a picture of overall sexual satisfaction: 63 percent of the

Redbook respondents reported they experienced orgasm always or almost always with their male partners. Thirty-percent would have liked even more sex.

My own contribution to this type of investigation began in the late seventies at the Center for Research on Women (now the Institute for Research on Women and Gender) at Stanford University. With two graduate student researchers, I queried married women alumnae from the class of 1954 at Stanford University and Wellesley College, each of whom had at least one college-aged daughter.[37] A total of 141 mothers—93 from Stanford and 48 from Wellesley—completed a questionnaire that provided information about their sexual attitudes and behavior from their high school years until the time of the survey.

The mothers were typically forty-five- or forty-six-year-old homemakers who, in two out of three cases, worked part- or full-time outside the house. They were, for the most part, still married to their first husbands, who pursued careers in business and the professions. They had on average three or four children, although some had as many as eight and some as few as one. This largely upper-middle-class white sample differed in one major respect from the Kinsey women: only 6 percent said they had experienced sexual intercourse before marriage, though they had engaged in kissing and petting to a considerable extent. Did this low incidence of premarital sex mean that the Wellesley and Stanford women were not telling the truth, or that they were more protected, or that they exercized more self-control than other women of their time? Their most positive experience was not of sex, but of the birth of their first child (91 percent), followed by their first love experience (86 percent).

When they considered their present lives in early middle age, there were both losses and gains. On the negative side of the ledger, some women felt themselves "waning" as sexual beings. They expressed concerns around a sense of physical decline in appearance, in health, and in other premenopausal problems that contributed to a feeling of sexual inadequacy. They also felt vulnerable to the possibility of divorce, which had notably increased throughout America in the twenty-five years since they had left college. On the positive side, the majority of women indicated they were more comfortable with themselves. Their experience as wives and mothers had, for the most part, contributed to an overall sense of self-confidence and self-acceptance, including their sexual selves.

Seventy-four percent of the respondents believed their sexual attitudes had become more liberal since they were in college. They attributed much of this change to their daughters. While expressing concerns that their daughters were too sexually free, they were inclined to accept the changing mores. For example, the large majority of mothers said they would assist their unmarried daughters in obtaining contraception if they knew their daughters were sexually active. Half of the mothers said they would counsel their daughters to have abortions if they knew their daughters were pregnant and unmarried. Less than half of the mothers expected their daughters to remain virgins until married. Homosexuality, however, was the one area where increased sexual liberality was not in evidence. While the mothers tolerated their daughters' premarital sexual experiences with males, they were not ready to accept lesbian relationships. Ninety percent responded "very negative" or "negative" to the question "How would you feel if your daughter had a homosexual experience?"

This picture of intellectually privileged, economically secure, married mothers who were in their late forties twenty years ago points to the adaptability of the American wife during the sexual revolution of the 1960s and 1970s. While they themselves had come of age in a period of relative sexual restraint, they had to adapt to the new sexual mores of their daughters. Most moved with the times and accepted for their daughters a mode of premarital freedom that they themselves had not known.

The world their daughters were facing was widely documented in the 1980 survey conducted by *Cosmopolitan* magazine. Outdoing even *Redbook* in numbers and shock value, the *Cosmo Report* was based on some 106,000 responses from sexually active single and married women. Their major findings confirmed the worst fears of those who believed the sexual revolution had gone too far. The great majority of women (95 percent in this survey) had sex before marriage. In comparison, Kinsey's 50 percent now looked modest. Moreover, as Linda Wolfe noted in chapter one of the *Cosmo Report:* "there is little social stigma attached to premarital sex."[38]

The overall findings reported in the *Cosmo Report* were not broken down into married and nonmarried, but a number of the letter writers identified themselves as wives. Anonymously, they spoke freely about their sexual experiences with their husbands and lovers. Oral sex? "Nothing could be better." Anal sex? "Have enormous orgasms that way." Solo sex? "Go to bed at night with Victor—my vibrator." Faking orgasm? "Don't see any harm in this, really." Mate swapping? "We are doing it even in Virginia."

Although most of the respondents were under forty, there were several older wives eager to share their most intimate activities. For example:

> *Seventy-two years. Best of health. Husband, 74. Also best of health. Married fifty years. Several children. All married. Very good sex life. At least five times a week until past 60. Now twice a week. Always enjoyed sex but had first real orgasm at 69. A big thrill. As husband has slowed down some, he spends more time stimulating me. —A woman from Minnesota*

Quite a few women wrote of extramarital affairs. One, a twenty-six-year-old market researcher from Connecticut, began an affair with a coworker that had lasted for three years. She mused: "I never thought when I kept working after I got married . . . that work was going to bring me such fringe benefits."

A forty-one-year-old from Pennsylvania, married for twenty years, told a much grimmer story.

> *I grew up in a small steel town where almost everyone was Polish and everyone knew everyone else's business . . . right after high school I made love in a car and got pregnant and got married. . . .*
>
> *One day I met a telephone service repair man by accident and he started coming over for quickies in the afternoon. He wasn't much warmer than my husband but still, it was quite a change from my drab life. Then some years later I met another man, different from the others. He brought me things, complimented me, wanted to take me places, and in bed he could hold out until I was completely satisfied. But he told his wife about us, and she in turn told my husband, and [he] threatened to kill us and that was the end of that. . . .*
>
> *. . . We have three kids and two big dogs. I never get to go out with*

friends for an evening, never have sex, have no allowance or even much money to spend on groceries, am beginning to drink, am fifteen pounds overweight and have just about given up on life.

A fifty-eight-year-old grandmother, married at age twenty-six, remembered: "The double standard was very strong in those days, so although he had had a lot of sexual experience he expected to marry a virgin. And he did. He was my first and only lover until six months ago. . . ." At that point she met a man who shared more interests with her than her husband, and they began an adulterous affair. Although she said she did not feel guilty, she added: "I could never leave my husband. After all these years of our being together, I think it would kill him."

Sometimes the affair led to the breakup of the first marriage and to a second relationship, that was more satisfying. Consider the following four examples.

It took me five years and three affairs to get up the gumption to let go of my first marriage. Now I've been married for the second time for five years, with no affairs. Why? Because I love my second husband. —A thirty-two-year-old woman from Georgia

I had been programmed, in my typical middle-class Catholic upbringing, to believe that the ultimate life goals were being a faithful wife and a devoted mother, and having a beautiful suburban home. No divorce. No working mothers. . . . I was miserable. What could I do about it? Since I had six years of solid secretarial experience behind me, work seemed the most logical place to start. . . . I went to call on a prospective client, one thing led to another, and suddenly this nice 27-year-old wife and mother found herself in bed with someone's else's nice husband. . . . Six months later I left my husband and moved in with my lover. I am still with him now. —A secretary from Texas

My spouse asked how I could have kept such a vile secret from him. . . . When we'd watch TV, or even when we'd make love, he'd ask how sex had felt with my father. . . . Later, all hell broke loose. He began to stay out late and come in staggering drunk and accuse me of infidelity and beat me, even in front of our three tiny babies, who screamed and screamed in fear. Finally I came to the realization that I did not deserve this punishment, that what I had done with my father wasn't my fault. And finally, slowly, I determined to live alone and raise the babies myself. I moved out. And I started a new job. Within months, I began to gain confidence, and the day even came when I allowed another man into my life. I emptied out my problem to him right from the beginning, and his only reply was, "I love you and all of that doesn't change my love one iota." This man and I have presently been married for three years. Our love grows greater daily. —A woman from Colorado

After three years of being single since a divorce at age 27, after three years of being sexually liberated and having a large number and variety of lovers, several threesomes, and always no commitments, no tomorrows, I'm in love. And my lover is in love with me! I'm 30 years old, a good mother, a successful business woman and now, much to the shock of my friends, a one-man woman.

I am gladly leaving the battleground of the sexual revolution— A thirty-year-old raised in Iowa

When we think about these letters in comparison to those sent to the *Daily Telegraph* in 1888, it's as if the two sets of women came from different planets. In less than a hundred years, wives had gone from thinking of marriage as a religious duty to an arena for sexual satisfaction. And if the husband wasn't satisfying enough, he could sometimes be exchanged for a lover or second husband. Without denying that the two sets of letters were instigated under very different circumstances— the first in response to a staid British newspaper article on the failure of marriage, the second in response to an American women's magazine questionnaire designed for sexually liberated women—still, the contrast is staggering.

How much of the exuberance exhibited by the 1980 letter writers was grounded in the availability of birth control pills? How much was traceable to the legalization of abortion that resulted from the 1973 *Roe v. Wade* Supreme Court decision? Surely access to effective contraception and legal abortion made it possible for many women to enjoy sex without worrying about the risks of pregnancy. But that is by no means the whole story.

The letters indicate that even at the height of the sexual revolution, most wives were asking for something more than good sex. They wanted love, warmth, respect, friendship, common interests, commitment. Or, put another way, good marital sex presupposed a good relationship. As for the younger wives, most of whom had slept with their mates prior to marriage, they at least knew whether they and their partners were minimally compatible in bed, and hoped that marriage would not only afford continued sexual gratification but also other forms of fulfillment, such as companionship, economic stability, and children. Or else, why marry?

One of the revelations of the *Cosmo Report* was that the sexual revolution was not confined to younger single women. The new sexual permissiveness had spilled over to older married women, some of whom started new relationships in their forties, fifties, and sixties, and one of whom was explicit about the joy she and her husband derived from sex in their seventies. There was little expression of guilt associated with extramarital affairs for either the younger or older wives.

Some of the darker secrets, gingerly alluded to by Victorian wives, came out in the open a hundred years later. Drink was still associated with what Victorians euphemistically alluded to as "brutality" and what the generation of 1980 frankly called wife beating and rape. Father-daughter incest was also confronted by adult women whose marriages were often marred by the lasting effects of their traumatic childhood experiences.

The openness to sexual experimentation and the willingness for women to discuss such matters in a public forum put an end to Victorian repression. In its place, however, new societal problems were in the making: the rising incidence of teenaged mothers, the spread of venereal diseases, including AIDS, and the increase in divorce and single parenting.

THE WORK REVOLUTION: THE RISE OF THE DUAL-EARNER COUPLE

The greater sexual freedom women experienced from the sixties onward was paralleled by, if not intertwined with, their greater participation in the workforce. As we have seen, both of these trends were already in motion earlier in the century, but they accelerated during World War II, and developed exponentially in the context of the postwar political movements, especially the women's movement. In 1960, 30 percent of wives were in the labor force. Twenty five years later, it was 54 percent. By the mid-1990s, 60 percent of American families had dual earners, 30 percent followed the traditional breadwinner/homemaker model, and 10 percent had either no earners or one part-time earner. European women were also following this trend, especially in the Scandinavian countries, France, and Great Britain, where employment for wives has by now become the norm.[39]

Between the 1960s and the 1980s, the growing number of wives working outside the home began to alter the fabric of American marriage. It was not only that more wives had become breadwinners, since some working-class women had always contributed to the family income. What began to change in the 1960s was the belief that a wife's employment had to be secondary to her husband's, that she had to subordinate her professional needs to his. Indeed, by 1969 the term "dual-career family" had been invented to designate a type of family structure in which the husband and the wife both took their work seriously and did not necessarily advance his at the expense of hers.[40] As opposed to the "two-person career couple," where the wife traditionally devotes herself to promoting her husband's career, the dual-career couple ostensibly invests equally in both the wife's and the husband's professional development. Even with time off for childbirth and the nurturing of small children, many wives from the sixties onward began to think of their work outside the home as a "career" demanding long-term commitment, rather than as a piecemeal series of jobs. Sometimes, promoting both partners' careers means that couples have had to live apart, and even well-intentioned individuals have discovered that not all marriages can survive under those circumstances.

Despite the egalitarian philosophy underpinning dual-career families, wives have continued to bear the greater burden of responsibility for homecare and childcare, and this disparity has been an ongoing source of contention for working couples. Back in the 1970s, the feminist slogan "the personal is political" led many women to believe that societal change would begin in the household. While wives became lawyers, doctors, computer programmers, cab and bus drivers, managers, and mayors, husbands were asked to become housecleaners and baby-sitters. Understandably, many men balked at performing these low-status occupations traditionally relegated to the feminine sphere. Yet gradually, some began to help around the house: taking out the trash, shopping for groceries, and doing the dishes were the first stages in the domestification of the American husband.

Another revolution was taking place, one that was not heralded as much as the sexual revolution, but one that had (and has) the promise of fundamentally transforming family life. The sons of fathers who had rarely lifted a housekeeping finger in the fifties were learning to put food on the table and clean up after themselves during the seventies and eighties. It's been a slow revolution, counted in hours and percentage points by social scientists, who keep reminding us that the men are not yet pulling their full weight.[41] Yet inch by inch, many husbands are getting used to the idea that they, too, are responsible for housekeeping, even if they spend less time on it than their wives.

Friction can and does arise between spouses over housework. A 1989 study of husbands' and wives' perceptions of the division of labor disclosed "a major discrepancy between expectations and behavior."[42] Both husbands and wives saw themselves participating more than their spouses thought they did. They agreed, however, that husbands were primarily responsible for money management, household repairs, and yard work in the majority of cases, and that about a third of the husbands performed some regular household tasks.

Highly educated husbands were more likely to take on the responsibility for housework than husbands with little education.[43] A 1991–1992 Stanford University questionnaire sent to members of the class of 1981 deemed they were were "at the forefront of change with regard to sharing household tasks," with almost half the husbands and wives performing household tasks about equally with their partners.[44] Since highly educated husbands often have working wives with similar educational backgrounds and earning power, these men have little grounds for maintaining a traditional male wage-earner/female housekeeper model.

Equally radical changes have taken place in the ideals and practices of fatherhood. Beginning with the pregnancy of their wives, men have been encouraged to participate more actively in the childbirth process. Once they were shunted out of the delivery room, indeed considered taboo. Today they help their pregnant wives learn breathing techniques and are often present at the birth of their babies. Many are involved in feeding and changing their offspring on a regular basis. One sign of the times are the babies' changing tables in men's restrooms at airports throughout the nation.

Fathers carry their infants in frontal pouches that seemed odd just a decade ago, but now cause no second looks. They take hikes with their babies in front- and backpacks, push their toddlers in a variety of wheeled contraptions, strap their youngsters into car seats, and bicycle with children in tow.

Once upon a time a father charged with tending a baby was mercilessly ridiculed. The French caricaturist Honoré Daumier (1808–1879) made fun of the bluestocking's husband shown cradling his baby and explaining to a top-hatted visitor: "Monsieur, my wife is inspired this

Married couple with twin daughters in frontal packs. Northern California, 2000. (Photo by Reid Yalom.)

morning . . . impossible to see her. I am, as you see, obliged to give my attention to the last work we collaborated on" (*Moeurs Conjugales,* no. 46). By the late nineteenth century, hundreds of cartoons and satirical images, such as the German and American illustrations reproduced in chapter 7, ridiculed the reversal of spousal roles.

Even with such films as *Mr. Mom* (1983) *Three Men and a Baby* (1987), and *Mrs. Doubtfire* (1993) that poked fun at men performing traditionally feminine tasks, Americans in the last decades of the twentieth century have gotten used to the caretaking father and the bread-earning mother. Two new terms have crept into the vocabulary: the "househusband" and the "stay-at-home dad." He may be an artist or writer or just an unemployed bloke, whose wife is a successful lawyer, doctor, dentist, businesswoman, engineer, manager, or academic. Neither of them may be fully satisfied with the situation, but it does not necessarily lead to the breakup of a family.

The are currently around 2 million fathers looking after children full time while their wives work, and another 3 million who do part-time day care. Conventions, support groups, newsletters, and web sites now cater to the needs of "At Home Fathers" (*New York Times,* January 2, 2000). While many of these men speak of the satisfactions they find in their new role as primary caretakers, they also complain of isolation, depression, and lack of status—complaints that have been voiced for a long time by innumerable American housewives.

In response to the *Times* article, a letter on the op-ed page (January 5, 2000) from a stay-at-home dad expressed the belief "that the rearing of children is the most difficult and thankless job there is." He added: "After three and a half years at the helm of a household, I can attest to the truth of the adage 'A woman's work is never done.' " This father had come to appreciate "the vital role that mothers play in the shaping of a civilized world" through assuming that role himself.

It is still rare for an employed woman to have a househusband. Most wives negotiate, with difficulty, their two "shifts" in two different locales. Especially when there are children, work/family conflicts produce continual problems that are never definitively resolved. Psychologist Ruthellen Josselson, studying a group of thirty women including thirteen working mothers over a twenty-year period beginning in 1972, reports that all women with careers and children feel squeezed between professional and parental obligations, especially when their children are young. Yet those working mothers are, according to Josellson, "happier with their work than the non-mothers." They enjoy the variety of their life experiences, however hectic, and do not feel they would have been more successful in their careers, had they not had children. If anything, their family life motivates them in the workplace.[45]

Josellson's sample was a small one and her interpretation may reflect the bias of its investigator, who, like many social critics of the moment, including myself, tend to see paid work for married women and mothers not only as inevitable, but also as beneficial. Yet there is undoubtedly another point of view, one held by wives who choose to be full-time homemakers. A member of the Stanford class of 1981, electing to stay home full-time with her children, wrote on her 1991–1992 questionnaire: "[Homemaking] is not prestigious, but it is important. Putting the welfare of one's children before one's own self-aggrandizement is worthwhile and should be recognized." Another full-time homemaker from this cohort was less grandiloquent: "I decided that it is too difficult to work and raise children at the same time, so I quit my job."[46] For the most part, the full-time homemakers were satisfied with the decisions they had made, though they sometimes missed the intellectual challenge and the adult interaction of the workplace.

The authors of the Stanford study, Myra Strober and Agnes Chan, noted little difference in the income of the husbands of stay-at-home mothers and the husbands of employed mothers. There was, however, considerable difference in the class origins of the wives. Coming from an upper-class family "made them more likely than their classmates to become full-time homemakers," perhaps because they had internalized the model of an affluent family with a successful father and because they could fall back on their parents in the event of divorce.[47]

Only a third of the Stanford mothers from the class of '81 were full-time homemakers, and of these, most expected to return to the labor force after their children were grown. The majority of women were combining careers and/or marriage and/or motherhood. Many of the wives spoke of the concessions they had made to their husbands' careers at the expense of their own. For example: "I was offered an excellent promotion in a small company in Chicago, but turned it down to relocate with my spouse." "I was transferred to Boston. I turned it down to remain in Washington, D.C., with my husband." "I quit a job to move to New York for 2 years so my husband could go to business school. Then I quit another job to move back to California."[48] Although flexibility of this sort is probably necessary for couples to stay together, it is usually the wives who make the sacrifices, ending up with diminished salaries and lesser careers than their partners.

For the most part, the Stanford graduates were struggling with the same problems that dual-earner couples are facing throughout the nation at every level of society: how to manage job and home and children in a society still geared, in many ways, to the notion that every breadwinner has a stay-at-home wife. (Think of package deliveries, home repairs, and children's illnesses and medical appointments.) The effects of dual-earner stress on working couples has become grist for the mill of myriad journalists, psychologists, and moralists in forums of every sort. Along this line, a column on family and work titled "Couples share suggestions for how to cope" (*San Francisco Chronicle*, January 16, 2000) summed up the letters of 150 readers who complained of toxic job spill into their personal lives. Long stable marriages crashed or almost crashed under the stress of unrealistic demands that managers placed on workers or that workers placed on themselves. Tips from the letter writers included the benefits of couples' therapy, church attendance, and family vacations. Conscious efforts to order priorities and to put the marriage at the top of the list were helpful to some of the couples. In an overscheduled world, scheduling time together may, paradoxically, be one way of salvaging a marriage.

Employers, be they large or small businesses, academic institutions, or government agencies, have only begun to address the needs of the two-paycheck family. Shared jobs and flextime are still very rare, and part-time work, when available, often marginalizes the person who chooses that option. Maternal leave is short and unpaid, even with the Family and Medical Leave Act of 1993, which requires companies with over fifty employees to grant up to twelve weeks of job-protected leave per year for family and medical reasons. These include the birth and care of a newborn child, the placement for adoption or foster care of a child, and the care of an immediate family member (spouse, child, or parent) with a serious health condition.

In this respect, we are far behind certain European nations, for example, Sweden, which offers an eleven-month *paid* leave for working mothers or fathers after the birth of a baby, and Denmark, with a year and a half, twelve months of which are fully paid. England has only thirteen weeks of parental leave, though the wife of the current prime minister—Cherie Blair, a prominent employment rights lawyer and four-time mother—put the subject of parental leave squarely at the heart of national politics when she pressured her husband (unsuccessfully) to take time off following the birth of their last child. Most European countries also have some kind of subsidized day care centers (*crèches*), following the French system inaugurated more than a half century ago. Neither the United States nor Japan, the two leading industrial nations in the world, provides paid childcare leave or affordable childcare services to meet the demand.[49] American mothers are often obliged to string together vacation, sick and parental allowances to get a proper maternity leave of twelve weeks, and, when they return to work, they usually have to spend an onerous part of their income on childcare services.

One hopeful American sign may be seen in the after-school programs that are springing up throughout the nation for children needing care from 3 P.M. to 6 P.M. Sponsored by coalitions of businesses, foundations, and the federal government, these offer a variety of learning experiences, ranging from music and math to cooking and construction. With 78 percent of mothers of school-age children now in the workforce, these programs are a godsend for working parents.

American wives and mothers, most of whom work inside and outside the home, are constantly improvising and juggling to provide adequate day care and schooling for their children, comfortable housing, wholesome meals, decent clothing, weekly entertainment, and summertime vacations. Little wonder that they complain and that some return, when economically feasible, to full-time homemaking.

Yet, as Stephanie Coontz argues in *The Way We Really Are,* wives and mothers will continue to work outside the home for more than financial reasons. Most women enjoy the satisfactions offered by their jobs. "They consistently tell interviewers they like the social respect, self-esteem, and friendship networks they gain from the job, despite the stress they may face finding acceptable childcare and negotiating household chores with their husbands." In support of this position, Coontz points to a 1995 Harris survey reporting that less than a third of working women would stay at home, if money were no object.[50]

There are several reasons married women like to work. In the first place, they do not want to be economically dependent on their husbands. They have absorbed the lessons of early feminists—Charlotte Perkins Gilman and Simone de Beauvoir, among others—arguing that women will always be the second sex as long as they depend on men for support. Some remember their own mothers asking their husbands for allowances and having little say in how the family income was spent. Many feel that earning an income puts them on an equal footing with their husbands, as expressed by one dual-career wife in the following manner: "I'm in the relationship because I want to be, not because somebody's taking care of me. . . . I feel like I don't have to say, 'Well, you're bringing in the money that's putting food on the table, that's keeping me alive.' I'm putting in money, too." [51]

Most women understand intuitively the theory of "bargaining power" outlined by gender theorists Strober and Chan. Put succinctly, "the more resources, particularly economic resources, a spouse brings to a marriage, the greater is his or her bargaining power."[52] Bargaining power affects the decisions couples make about almost everything, from the advancement of one partner's career over the other's to the division of household tasks. This hard-nosed, economic view of spousal relations is by no means the exclusive purview of academic theory. Even women's magazines have become more forthright about the clout a wife commands when she, too, brings home a paycheck. Clinical psychologist Judith Sills, writing in that bastion of domesticity *Family Circle* (March 7, 2000), states bluntly, "The power balance in a marriage changes when one person either stops or starts earning money. . . . Power automatically accrues to the one who earns the money."

Some wives and husbands keep their income in separate accounts. With divorce an eventuality for half of all marriages, both parties feel they must be cautious in money matters, just in case. Even women in secure marriages, who would like to take time off when they have young children, are afraid of losing both salary and seniority, because, if they divorced, they would find themselves in dire financial straits.[53]

Social Security also penalizes the person who takes time off from work. One CPA wife and mother, who stayed at home when her children were little, accurately observed: "For every quarter a mother stays home to take care of her kids, she gets zero on her Social Security. And all those zeros will be averaged into her final payment. . . . I froth at the mouth every time I get my statement from Social Security. Every zero year is factored in."[54]

A second, and in my opinion, equally important reason why married women choose to work is that they do not want to be confined to the perimeters of the home. They do not want to operate within the cagelike frame of traditional domesticity. Greater education for women has meant that their horizons extend far beyond the kitchen, the parlor, and the garden. Once again, we must remember that higher education for women is a relatively recent phenomenon. The American women's colleges and most coed universities were a late-nineteenth-century creation admitting only a very small percentage of females, mostly from the upper and middle classes. As late as 1950, there were three male students granted a BA for every female college graduate.[55] Today, females receive educations comparable to males— 55 percent of BAs, over 50 percent of law and medical degrees, and 45 percent of PhDs. Like the men in their college courses, they expect to use their minds for the rest of their lives. Paid employment can present a challenge to one's intelligence, as well as to one's interpersonal skills. It allows a person the opportunity to interact with others in the workplace, and sometimes even to make a difference in their lives.

I have no illusions about the nature of work in general. It does not always challenge the intellect, and rarely allows for innovation and imagination. It can produce stress and pain and damage to private life. Yet I cannot imagine the world of the immediate future without it. Wives, like husbands, look to the work world for satisfactions that few can find within themselves or within the four walls of their houses. Most husbands today assume that their wives will have a commitment outside the home, and many husbands are credited with being their wives' "strongest supporters." In addition, many husbands count on their wives to share the economic burdens of supporting a family.

Of course, there are some women who refuse this scenario, some wives who prefer to be the domestic anchor for their husbands and children. They find satisfaction in caring for their children, driving them to and from school, attending their soccer and baseball games, cooking, cleaning, washing and ironing, gardening, sewing, shopping, and taking care of a parent or sick relative. Theoretically, housewives, especially those with the means to pay for a maid or a team of house-cleaners, should have more time than employed women to read, answer E-mail, surf the Internet, look at television, play tennis, do yoga, go to the gym, take hikes, practice the piano, listen to music, paint, entertain, write letters or creative literature, do volunteer work, meet with friends, and follow their own rhythms. But few full-time homemakers, especially those with children, think of their lives as leisurely. Obligations to home, family, and the community always seem to expand into the hours one tries to sequester for oneself, perhaps because homemaking is, by nature, always open to the unpre-dictable—a sick child, a broken washing machine, storm damage to the roof. Moreover, without the extra income of a second wage earner, housewives often have to sacrifice material rewards in order to stay at home. For some women, being available to their children when they are small is reward enough. The life of a housewife (or house husband) can be fulfilling if it is freely chosen, if the other spouse's income is adequate, or if the wife has sufficient assets of her own. A relatively small percentage of married women today are economically able to choose this life.

With the increased longevity of women, the child-raising period takes up a relatively short part of the life span. If a woman waits until her late twenties to have a child, as many do, and lives until she is eighty, as statistics say she will, she will spend only a third of her life in the active phase of mothering. Before and after her child-rearing years, there are long stretches of time for paid employment or sustained vol-unteer work. Most wives, even those who take time off when their chil-dren are young, work for economic reasons, and many wives, even those who do not have to, work because they want to.

Every societal revolution has a conservative reaction that eventually forces it to retreat partially, if not wholly, from acquired ground. The backlash symbolized by the election of President Ronald Reagan in 1980 and invoked in the battle cry "family values" undid some of the victories claimed by the sexual and feminist revolutions. During the eighties, abortion rights began to be curtailed. ERA was all but buried. Androgyny gave way to a renewed femininity featuring sexy underwear, breast implants, and push-up bras. Expensive weddings with brides in elaborate white gowns came back into fashion. Women's paid employment came under attack, with wives accused of undermining their husbands, and mothers indicted for sacrificing their children on the altar of professional success. The popular press remained skeptical over women's ability to have both a successful marriage and a successful career, and castigated the working woman who wanted to "have it all."[56]

Documenting the backlash in 1992, author Susan Faludi exploded some of the antifeminist myths that had proliferated during the eighties.[57] Magazines and newspapers eager to discredit women's gains exploited questionable research, such as the 1986 Harvard-Yale marriage study announcing that unwed women over thirty had very little likelihood of ever marrying at all, or sociologist Lenore Weitzman's 1985 finding that divorced women had a 73 percent drop in their standard of living a year after divorce. Subsequent research proved both of these findings to be greatly exaggerated. The gloom-and-doom picture of liberated women promulgated by the media and the glowing pictures of mothers who had chosen to give up demanding careers in favor of domesticity were clearly intended to stop the clock and send women scurrying back to the safety of home.

Yet, according to historian Ruth Rosen's assessment, "By the end of the 20th century, feminist ideas had burrowed too deeply into our culture for any resistance or politics to root them out."[58] Even those who lamented the excesses of the sexual and feminist revolutions were not about to ask their daughters or sweethearts to remain virgins until marriage or to retreat full-time to the kitchen once they had become wives. Increasingly, men sizing up prospective spouses expected them to carry their weight in both the bedroom and the boardroom.

One sign of the times is that the old jokes about nagging, frigid, dumb, unattractive wives have run their course. Remember comedian Henny Youngman's repertoire of wife jokes? "Take my wife, please!" "My wife has a black belt in shopping." "She got a mudpack and looked great for two days. Then the mud fell off." "I've been in love with the same woman for forty-nine years. If my wife ever finds out, she'll kill me." Wives are no longer the targets of such easy ridicule coming from husbands confident of their superiority. If anything, jokes about husbands have become more numerous, as in the following examples currently circulating on E-mail:

"I think—therefore I'm single." Attributed to Lizz Winstead.

"I never married because there was no need. I have three pets at home which answer the same purpose as a husband. I have a dog which growls every morning, a parrot which swears all afternoon and a cat that comes home late at night." Attributed to Marie Corelli.

"Behind every successful man is a surprised woman." Attributed to Maryon Pearson.

In the vein of the last witticism, here is a joke that was frequently repeated in 1999. "Hillary and Bill Clinton drive into a gas station. The man at the pump is particularly warm toward the First Lady, and when they drive away, she tells her husband that he had been one of her first boyfriends. Bill says smugly: 'Aren't you glad you married me instead of a gas station attendant?' To which she replies, 'If I had married him, he'd be the president.' "

INTIMATIONS OF THE NEW WIFE

The story of Hillary and Bill Clinton played out on the national stage some of the ambiguities inherent in the role of the new wife. Like 1990s soap operas, theirs was a dramatic saga of dual-career ambitions, marriage, infidelity, forgiveness, and love. In 1992, America was not ready for Hillary Rodham Clinton. After Nancy Reagan and Barbara Bush, women who had incarnated the traditional wife par excellence, a lawyer first lady on a par with her husband was just too threatening for much of the American public. They viewed her political activities with suspicion and felt vindicated when her health care plan went down to defeat. During Clinton's first term in office, Hillary was constantly changing her tactics and her hairdo so as to meet public approval. But whatever she did, there were numerous Americans who made no secret of the revulsion they felt for her.

All of this changed, of course, when she became an injured wife. As the gross details of President Clinton's marital infidelity with Monica Lewinsky became daily pap for the media, and Hillary maintained her dignity in spite of everything, her popularity with the American people soared. She became the woman who "stood by her man," a wife with whom other American women could identify. The damage to Clinton's reputation did not spill over similarly to his spouse. She emerged from their sensational story with a determination to pursue her own career, even at the expense of abandoning the role of first lady during her husband's last year in office. As I write these pages, she has just been elected to the United States Senate. Is the American public now ready for wives who are as well educated, assertive, and as ambitious as Hillary Rodham Clinton?

Fundamental aspects of the new wife can be observed in those reliable standards, the women's magazines. At the start of the new millennium, they focus on homemaking, recipes, diet, health, work, children, love, and sex. The most venerable of these magazines known as "the seven sisters" (*Ladies' Home Journal, Redbook, McCall's, Good Housekeeping, Family Circle, Woman's Day,* and *Better Homes and Gardens*), originally oriented toward traditional wives with children, have been obliged to move with the times. Today, they are claiming the sexually explicit content that used to be the exclusive purview of magazines intended for single women (e.g., *Glamour, Cosmopolitan,* and *Mademoiselle*).

"101 Ways to Sex Up Your Marriage," in the January 2000 *Ladies' Home Journal,* assumes that spouses occasionally need to bring "more sizzle" into the bedroom, and that it's the wife's responsibility to make this happen. The February *Redbook* presents "Your 39 Most Embarrassing Sex Questions" in graphic detail, as well as an insightful piece titled "What Happy Couples Know about Marriages That Last." *More,* the magazine for older women put out by *Ladies' Home Journal,* offers a surprisingly frank and relatively guilt-free article titled "I Am the Other Woman," confessing the trials and tribulations of an anonymous woman in love with a married man.

Even financial matters have to be sexy. An article titled "Creating Financial Intimacy: A Couple's Guide to Getting Rich" (January 2000

Good Housekeeping) insinuates sex into the process of buying stock. It reads:

> *Consider buying a stock for your beloved. It's surprising how sexy (yes, sexy) such a gift can be. . . . Sneak off to a financial seminar together one evening instead of to a movie; sit in the back, dress up, and wear your best perfume. Scan the newstand for a financial magazine that features an article reflecting your family's situation, and share it during a quiet moment alone. All powerful and positive acts, acts that will help you and your money grow, and you and your husband grow closer.*

While the sexed-up prose is downright silly, the article does point to the central nexus of sex and money in the maintenance of a marriage. It argues convincingly that shared responsibility for money matters makes for a powerful bond between spouses. Whereas men once had total control over families finances, today, in more egalitarian marriages, both sex and money are often considered joint ventures capable of drawing spouses more closely together—that is, if they don't drive them further apart. It's not surprising that the year 2000 began with paeans in the popular press to both sources of empowerment for wives, with sexual performance hyped far beyond any other wifely virtue. Kinsey's midcentury belief that good sex is indispensable to enduring unions has by now become an American cliché, and, like most clichés, one that tends to obscure competing truths. While sexual satisfaction is generally recognized as a sensitive index of marital happiness, especially in the early years, there are undoubtedly some good marriages with bad or minimal sex, and some bad marriages with great sex.[59]

And what of love, that romantic feeling that gained primacy in the early nineteenth century and that has been claiming special status ever since? In the past, at least among middle- and upper-class couples, love was supposed to precede sex, indeed, to make sex possible. Today it is usually the other way around. Young people engage in sex with several partners, then "fall in love" with one of them. Subsequently some combination of sexual desire and romantic love impels the couple to vow to stay together forever. But sex and romance do not, in and of themselves, cement a relationship, at least not for a lifetime. Common interests, values, and goals, mutual respect and moral commitment, may, in the long run, prove as valuable as sex, love, and money in the preservation of a union.

Young women today, marrying on average around twenty-five, often have at least some college education and work experience behind them when they become wives. They enter into marriage on a relatively equal footing with their husbands, and expect to maintain this parity for the rest of their lives. The old ideal of companionate marriage has been reformulated under such new labels as egalitarian marriage, equal partnership, and marital equality.

Unfortunately, married life today is not yet truly equal. According to a 1997 research study, which follows the lead of sociologist Jessie Bernard in *The Future of Marriage* (1972), "his" marriage continues to be better than "hers."[60] The data on marital satisfaction, garnered from surveys, interviews, and personal assessments, indicate that husbands have a more positive view of marriage than their wives, and that wives fall behind husbands on numerous measures of marital satisfaction. One consistent finding is that single men do *worse* than married men on almost all measures of mental health (e.g., suicide, depression, nervous breakdown), whereas single women do *better* than married women on these same measures.[61] All agree that wives experience greater stress than husbands from their career/family obligations, and that women put more time into caring for children, aged parents, and sick relatives.

When couples divorce, it is almost always the ex-wife who loses out financially. According to the latest statistics, divorce produces a 27 percent decline in women's standard of living and 10 percent increase in that of men.[62] This represents an almost 40 percent gap between what ex-wives and what ex-husbands experience financially in the aftermath of a divorce. Part of this difference is attributable to the fact that mothers, in the great majority of cases, are granted custody of the children. Even when the mother is awarded child support, it is frequently insufficient and not always forthcoming. Another factor is the lower earning power of women on the whole—75 percent of what men earn. Many women are still segregated in low-paying jobs and hindered in advancement by home and childcare responsibilities, as well as by the sacrifices they have made promoting their husbands' careers rather than their own.

In addition to the disadvantageous financial consequences of divorce for many women and their children, the emotional distress is often deep and long-lasting. While no-fault divorce, first instituted in California in 1970 and subsequently adopted in most of the United States, was intended to remove the blame and acrimony from prolonged adversarial litigation, today's divorces are still often as bitter as those of the past. Divorce continues to be a major family disruption with prolonged consequences for the spouses, their offspring, and extended kin.

Here is how Susan Straight, an articulate ex-wife and mother of three school-aged children, described the devastation that divorce brought into her life, a devastation she shared with her best friend, who had been widowed.

> *My best friend on the street, Jeannine, whose four kids had baby-sat mine and played with them, lost her husband, too. He was killed in a car accident. Jeannine and I were both thirty-five that year. We couldn't believe we had to do this alone. Seven kids. Old houses with flickering electrical wires and flooding basements and overgrown hedges and missing shingles. Jeannine was in her last year of nursing school. I was working. We were stunned.*
>
> *. . . Some nights we were both mad. She'd met her husband at fourteen, like me. After we talked, I would lie in bed, my body aching, my hands raw from dishes and floors and branches and baby shampoo, thinking that when I got married, I always assumed I'd work hard, have kids and a house and some fun. . . .*
>
> *And when my husband first left, I thought, So I work a little harder. But now, the realization has set in, piled high and crackling as the mulberry leaves falling from those spear straight branches one more year; I have to do all of this forever. Fix the vacuum cleaner, kill the spiders, correct the spelling and make the math flash cards and pay for preschool and trim the tree. Trim the tree.*
>
> *Now, sometimes, I feel like a burro. A small frame, feet hard as hooves, back sagging a little. Now the edges of my life are a bit ragged, and things don't always get done as they should.*[63]

Susan Straight's story is, unfortunately, writ over and over again in the lives of myriad American mothers whose husbands have left them, or who have themselves chosen to leave an unhappy marriage, or who never had a husband in the first place. In her words, she and the other ex-wives have no "backup," and backup is "what marriage is really about." So if she and her children look "slightly askew," she asks us not to blame her. "When you see us, don't shake your heads and think, How irresponsible. Responsible is all I'm good at anymore."

In serial marriages, the husband often "marries down" in terms of age and is far more likely to start a new family. The ex-wife who remarries has a selection of males usually her own age or older, but fewer candidates to choose from, since there are more older women than older men. For the same reasons, widows remarry less frequently than widowers. Another difference between older men and older women lies in the ability to reproduce. After menopause, a woman is unable to become pregnant (without technological intervention), in contrast to men, who usually can go on reproducing in their fifties, sixties, and beyond. Whether this is advisable, given the father's probable death when his children are still young, the ability to reproduce at any age does confer a fundamental existential advantage to men.

At the same time, females have certain advantages over males. They live approximately seven years longer. They have the amazing possibility of carrying babies within their bodies and of establishing a unique connection to their offspring through pregnancy and lactation. They are probably more flexible than men in terms of sexual orientation, moving more easily between heterosexual and same-sex relations (though not everyone will see this as an advantage). They more frequently establish close bonds of friendship with other women that are sources of deep pleasure and ongoing support, whereas men, in general, have fewer intimate friends.

One thing many women have learned during the past twenty to thirty years is that wifehood is not one's only option. With women no longer economically dependent on men, they do not have to marry for the mere sake of survival. Business and professional women tend to defer marriage during early adulthood and sometimes do not marry at all. Susan Faludi's assertion that "the more women are paid, the less eager they are to marry" should not surprise us.[64] And even more than marriage per se, motherhood has become problematic for working women, given the "mommy gap" in wages between mothers and non-mothers. While the hourly wages of women without children are roughly 90 percent of men's, the comparable figure for women with children is 70 percent.[65] Thus women concerned about their present and future economic well-being are obliged to consider the effects of both marriage and motherhood on their working lives.

In the case of black women, the "marriage-market" theory advanced by sociologist Henry Walker attributes their low incidence of marriage to their new earning power, which is now roughly the same as that of black men. Perhaps even more important, black women have a smaller pool of economically viable black men to choose from, as compared to white women in relation to white men, since black men are more likely to have been killed, more likely to be incarcerated, and more likely to be unemployed than white men.[66]

Not surprisingly, careers loom larger than ever for women of all races, with many companies and institutions providing a kind of ersatz "family." Many people now look to their jobs for close interpersonal relations and for a sense of meaning they have not found either in their families or in their communities. Indeed, this growing job orientation is beginning to cause concern to many societal observers, who believe the workplace is replacing the home as the center of American life.

Another issue of concern is the "merging" of home life and work life that often occurs when people work out of their homes. Now that computers have made it possible for both men and women to earn substantial incomes without leaving the house, there is the danger that paid work will cannibalize the time needed for quality family life. While this may present a problem for some workaholics, it can also be a boon for parents needing flexible schedules for childcare. In some ways we may be returning to a preindustrial mode, when artisans, professionals, and shopkeepers did indeed work out of their homes, with children always in the wings or underfoot.

Alternatives to marriage come in numerous forms. The number of Americans living alone (a quarter of all households) has never been higher. The number of men and women living together without marrying has also reached a record high, with heterosexual couples often taking years to decide whether they will or will not become husband and wife. Same-sex couples cohabitate without the legal and economic benefits that a marriage license confers, although many are taking advantage of the "domestic partnerships" offered by numerous cities, states, and institutions. In the future, Vermont-style "civil unions" will probably serve the needs not only of gay couples, but also of heterosexuals opting for an intermediary step between cohabitation and marriage.

Similarly, childlessness is no longer seen as a curse for adult females. The proportion of childless women aged forty to forty-four was 19 percent in 1998 (up from 10 percent in 1980), and many of these women are childless by choice, according to some demographers.[67] At the same time, single parenting is on the ascendency, without the stigma of past eras. Unmarried girls and women who become pregnant accidentally often decide to bear and raise the child, rather than have an abortion or give the baby up for adoption. Some unmarried women, especially those around forty, are now choosing to be mothers without intending to marry the baby's father. All of these girls and women take on a formidable challenge when they raise a child on their own: at present, their children are much more likely to be brought up in poverty than children in two-parent families.

Some single mothers manage to extend the family network by living with relatives or friends. In black communities, where single mothers greatly outnumber married mothers, children often grow up in female households headed by a mother or grandmother. Private and government programs to bring fathers back into the picture may, in time, reverse this trend somewhat, but it is unlikely that the nuclear family consisting of a married couple and their children, which peaked numerically for blacks in 1950 and for whites in 1960, will return to its former hegemonic position in American society.[68]

What, then, can a woman today anticipate, or at at least hope, when she becomes a wife? Surely she hopes that her marriage will be among the 50 percent that adheres to a lifelong script. Despite the well-known statistics on divorce, people usually marry with the belief that *their* marriage is "for keeps"—86 percent, according to a survey conducted by the *New York Times Magazine* (May 7, 2000). And most women still hope to become mothers. In fact, motherhood has remained central to most women's core conception of self and may even have "supplanted marriage as a source of romantic fantasy for many young single women," in the judgment of Peggy Orenstein, the astute author of *School Girls* and *Flux*.[69]

The new wife will not be able to count on children to keep the marriage intact, as in the past when people often did stay together "for the children." In fact, children are known to bring conflict into a marriage, especially when they are very young and again in adolescence. Those spouses who make it past the stress-filled child-rearing years are likely to experience a bonus in later life. Older couples often enjoy a special bond based on their shared history—a level of intimacy paid for in past tears and joys. In the words of Mark Twain: "No man or woman really knows what perfect love is until they have been married a quarter of a century."[70]

When one vows at the onset of a marriage to live together "for better, for worse," one anticipates little of the "for worse" scenario. Yet heartache, tragedy, sickness, and death are invariably a part of marriage, especially in the later years. Then one is particularly grateful for the support and love of a lifelong partner—someone who remembers you as you once were and who continues to care for you as you are now. To be the intimate witness of another person's life is a privilege one can fully appreciate only with time. To have weathered the storms of early and middle marriage—the turmoil of children, the unfaithfulness of one or both spouses, the death of one's parents, the adult struggles of one's own children—can create an irreplaceable attachment to the person who has shared that history with you.

What I have referred to as "unfaithfulness" can, of course, make it impossible for a couple to go on as before. Many marriages do come to an end when one of the spouses has an affair. But many don't. Many continue to think of their marital union as the "essential" relationship, even while they engage in an extramarital affair. Since young people today have the opportunity to make love to more than one potential partner before they marry and since they tend to marry at a supposedly mature age, they *should* be ready to settle down to a monogamous union when they exchange vows. Yet, as we know, the "shoulds" sometimes falter in the face of unexpected passion. Even when one is seriously committed to one's spouse, temptations do arise, and married women as well as married men are more likely today than in the past to give in to those temptations. This does not necessarily lead to divorce, or even permanent bitterness, though it often creates turmoil and suffering. When a husband or wife has an affair, it is usually for a cluster of reasons, of which sex per se is only a part. The affair can act as a catalyst that forces the spouses to look more closely at their own relationship, to renegotiate the terms of their union, and to rededicate themselves to one another.

The present statistics on lifelong marriages being what they are, I do not envy today's young women the pain that will come from divorce, the hardships they will endure as single parents, the poverty in which many will live. But I do believe in their expanded possibilities, which are greater now than ever before and which contrast dramatically to the more circumscribed lives most married women accepted in the past and still experience today in many parts of the world. Above all, I wish them the courage to persevere toward that ideal of equality in marriage that has been in the making for several centuries.

Wives, spouses, partners, companions, and lovers all wish to be confirmed by their chosen mates and to share a profound, mutual connection. Such a union demands commitment and recommitment. Ironically, we may come to think of marriage as a vocation requiring the kind of devotion that was once expected only of celibate monks and nuns. To be a wife today when there are few prescriptions or proscriptions is a truly creative endeavor. It is no longer sufficient to "think back through our mothers," in the words of Virginia Woolf; we must project ahead into the future and ask ourselves what kind of marital legacy we want to leave for our daughters and sons.

While the traditional wife who submerged her identity into that of her husband may no longer represent a viable model for most women, Americans are not giving up on wifehood. Instead, they are straining to create more perfect unions on the basis of their new status as co-earners and their husbands' fledgling status as co-homemakers. I suspect that the death of the "little woman" will not be grieved by the multitude, even if society must endure severe birth pangs in producing the new wife.

NOTES

ONE

1. Translations from Genesis are from Robert Alter, *Genesis: Translation and Commentary* (New York and London: W. W. Norton, 1996). Other biblical citations are from the King James version.

2. E. Amado Levi-Valensi, "Marriage et couple: l'avènement du couple," *Encyclopaedia Universalis* (Paris: Encyclopaedia Universalis France, c. 1968, 1974–75 printing), vol. 10, p. 520.

3. Pamela Norris, *Eve: A Biography* (New York: New York University Press, 1999), pp. 58–61.

4. Frank Alvarez-Pereyre and Florence Heymann, "The Desire for Transcendence: the Hebrew Family Model and Jewish Family Practices," *A History of the Family*, ed. André Burguière et al.; trans. Sarah Hanbury Tenison, Rosemary Morris, and Andrew Wilson, (Oxford: Polity Press, 1996), vol. 1, p. 175.

5. As Robert Alter points out, when the nonagenarian Sarah "laughed" at the birth of Isaac, she was rejoicing, but also wondering if others might also be laughing *at* her. Alter, *Genesis*, p. 97.

6. For medieval manuscripts with illustrations of these two punishments, see the thirteenth-century "Traité de Droit" from Agen, reproduced in David Nicolle, *The Hamlyn History of Medieval Life* (London: Hamlyn, 1997), p. 116; and the 1348 "Zwickenauer Stadtrechtbuch" from the Stadtarchiv Zwichau, reproduced in Erika Uitz, *The Legend of Good Women: Medieval Women in Towns and Cities,* trans. Sheila Marnie (Mount Kisco, New York: Moyer Bell Limited, 1988), p. 122.

7. *Women's Lives in Medieval Europe: A Sourcebook,* ed. Emilie Amt (New York and London: Routledge, 1993), pp. 67–68.

8. See the discussion of this subject in Bernadette J. Brooten, *Love Between Women: Early Christian Responses to Female Homeroticism* (Chicago and London: University of Chicago Press, 1996), p. 62. For another interpretation, see Peter J. Gomes, *The Good Book: Reading the Bible with Mind and Heart* (New York: William Morrow and Company, 1996), p. 153.

9. The essential books on homosexuality in the ancient world are: John Boswell, *Christianity, Social Tolerance, and Homosexuality: Gay People in Western Europe from the Beginning of the Christian Era to the Fourteenth Century* (Chicago: University of Chicago

Press, 1980); John Boswell, *The Marriage of Likeness: Same-Sex Unions in Pre-Modern Europe* (London: HarperCollins, 1995); and Brooten, *Love Between Women.*

10. Isaiah M. Gafni, "The Institution of Marriage in Rabbinic Times," *The Jewish Family,* ed. David Kraemer (New York and Oxford: Oxford University Press, 1989), pp. 13–30.

11. Norris, *Eve,* pp. 75–77.

12. James A. Brundage, *Sex, Law and Marriage in the Middle Ages* (Aldershot, Hampshire, Great Britain: Variorum, 1993), chapters 1 and 2.

13. Homer, *The Odyssey,* trans. E. V. Rieu (Harmondsworth, Middlesex: Penguin Books, 1966), pp. 345–346. In this instance, the Rieu translation works better for the purpose of citation than the version by Robert Fagles (New York: Penguin, 1996), pp. 461–466.

14. Eva Cantarell, *Pandora's Daughters,* trans. Maureen B. Fant (Baltimore and London: Johns Hopkins University Press, 1987), p. 25.

15. Ralph Sealey, *Women and Law in Classical Greece* (Chapel Hill and London: University of North Carolina Press, 1990), p. 14.

16. Nancy Demand, *Birth, Death, and Motherhood in Classical Greece* (Baltimore and London: The Johns Hopkins University Press, 1994), p. 2.

17. Ibid. pp. 14–15.

18. Homer, *The Iliad,* trans. Robert Fagles, 18: 573–579 (New York: Viking Penguin, 1990), p. 483.

19. Cantarell, *Pandora's Daughters,* pp. 48–49.

20. Lysias's speech "On the Slaying of Eratosthenes" (Oxford ed.), sections 23–26, as cited and discussed in Elizabeth Wayland Barber, *Women's Work: The First 20,000 Years* (New York and London: Norton, 1994), pp. 273–277. See also Sabine Melchior-Bonnet and Aude de Tocqueville, *Histoire de l'Adultère* (Paris: Editions de la Martinière, 1999), pp. 10–20.

21. Plato, *The Symposium,* trans. Robin Waterfield (Oxford and New York: Oxford University Press, 1994), p. 28.

22. Cantarell, *Pandora's Daughters,* pp. 82–83.

23. Bruce S. Thornton, *Eros: The Myth of Ancient Greek Sexuality* (Boulder Colorado: Westview Press, 1997), p. 100.

24. Jane McIntosh Snyder, *Lesbian Desire in the Lyrics of Sappho* (New York: Columbia University Press, 1997), p. 8.

25. See D. C. Moses, "Livy's Lucretia and the Validity of Coerced Consent in Roman Law," *Consent and Coercion to Sex and Marriage in Ancient and Medieval Societies,* ed. A. E. Laiou, (Washington, D.C., Dumbarton, Oaks Research Library and Collection, 1993), pp. 39–81.

26. Pliny, *Letters and Panegyricus* (Cambridge, Massachusetts: Harvard University Press, Loeb Classics, 1969), vol. 1, pp. 43–47.

27. Susan Treggiari, *Roman Marriage: "Iusti Coniuges" from the Time of Cicero to the Time of Ulpian* (Oxford: Clarendon Press, 1991), pp. 159–160. This is the essential work on Roman marriage, and I have drawn heavily from it.

28. Ovid, *Amores,* trans. Grant Showerman (Cambridge, Mass., and London: Harvard University Press and William Heinemann, Ltd., 1977), p. 381.

29. *The Latin Poets,* ed. Francis R. B. Godolphin (New York: The Modern Library, 1949), pp. 23–31.

30. Thomas Wiedemann, *Adults and Children in the Roman Empire* (London: Routledge, 1989), p. 86.

31. *Plutarch's Lives,* trans. John Dryden (New York: The Modern Library, 195?), p. 1065.

32. *Women's Lives in Medieval Europe: A Sourcebook,* ed. Emilie Amt (New York and London: Routledge, 1993), pp. 34–35.

33. Pliny, *Letters and Panegyricus,* vol. 1, pp. 469–471.

34. Plutarch, "Advice on Marriage," *Selected Essays and Dialogues* (Oxford and New York: Oxford University Press, 1993), p. 286.

35. *Plutarch's Lives,* p. 774.

36. Gordon Williams, "Representations of Roman Women in Literature," *I Claudia: Women in Ancient Rome,* ed. Diana Kleiner and Susan Matheson (New Haven: Yale University Art Gallery, 1996), pp. 132–133.

37. Marilyn Yalom, *A History of the Breast* (New York: Knopf, 1997), pp. 25–26.

38. Aline Rousselle, "The Family under the Roman Empire: Signs and Gestures," *A History of the Family,* ed. Burguière, Klapisch-Zuber, Selen, and Zonabend, vol. 1, p. 275.

39. Mary Hamer, *Signs of Cleopatra: History, Politics, Representation* (London and New York: Routledge, 1993), p. 9.

40. This and the following citations concerning Antony and Cleopatra are from *Plutarch's Lives,* pp. 1137, 1148, 1152.

41. J. P. V. D. Balsdon, *Roman Women: Their History and Habits* (London: The Bodley Head, 1962), p. 68.

42. Klaus Fitschen, "Courtly Portraits of Women in the Era of the Adoptive Emperors (98–180) and Their Reception in Roman Society," *I Claudia,* ed. Kleiner and Matheson, p. 53.

43. Pliny, *Letters and Panegyricus,* vol. 1, pp. 403, 411.

44. Jean-Noël Robert, *Eros Romain: Sexe et morale dans l'ancienne Rome* (Paris: Hachette Littératures, 1998), pp. 135–37, and *Women's Lives in Medieval Europe,* ed. Amt, pp. 29–31.

45. Treggiari, *Roman Marriage,* pp. 231–241.

46. Boswell, *The Marriage of Likeness,* p. 65.

47. Seutonius, *The Twelve Caesars,* trans. Robert Graves (Harmondsworth, Middlesex, England: Penguin Books, 1972), p. 223.

48. Juvenal, *The Satires,* trans. Niall Rudd, (Oxford: Clarendon Press, 1991), Satire 2, lines 135–138, p. 13.

49. Juvenal, *The Satires,* Satire 6, lines 34–36, p. 38.

50. Brooten, *Love between Women,* p. 29.

51. Citations are from Plutarch, *Eroticus,* in *Selected Essays and Dialogues* (Oxford and New York: Oxford University Press, 1993), pp. 249–250, 279, and 281.

52. Juvenal, *The Satires,* p. 46.

TWO

1. For traditional ways of presenting medieval women's history, see "Introduction" to *Female Power in the Middle Ages,* ed. Karen Glente and Lise Winther-Jensen (Copenhagen: C. A. Reitzel, 1989).

2. See Christopher N. L. Brooke, *The Medieval Idea of Marriage* (Oxford: Oxford University Press, 1989); Alan Macfarlane, *Marriage and Love in England: Modes of Reproduction 1300–1840* (Oxford: Basil Blackwell, 1986); Roderick Phillips, *Putting Asunder: A History of Divorce in Western Society* (Cambridge, New York, New Rochelle, Melbourne, Sydney: Cambridge University Press, 1988), pp. 26–27; and Frances and Joseph Gies, *Marriage and the Family in the Middle Ages* (New York: Harper and Row, 1987).

3. This is the position of medievalist Jo Ann McNamara, "Victims of Progress," in *Female Power in the Middle Ages,* ed. Glente and Winther-Jensen, p. 29.

4. This and the following from Shulamith Shahar, *The Fourth Estate: A History of Women in the Middle Ages,* trans. Chaya Galai (London and New York: Methuen, 1983), pp. 89–90.

5. Cited by Barbara A. Hanawalt, *The Ties That Bound: Peasant Families in Medieval England* (New York and Oxford: Oxford University Press, 1986), p. 208.

6. Olwen Hufton, *The Prospect Before Her: A History of Women in Western Europe,* vol. 1, 1500–1800 (New York: Alfred A. Knopf, 1996), p. 70.

7. Werner Rösener, *Peasants in the Middle Ages,* trans. Alexander Stützer (Cambridge, England: Polity Press, 1992), p. 179.

8. Martha Saxton, "Foreword," to Erika Uitz, *The Legend of Good Women: Medieval Women in Towns and Cities,* trans. Sheila Marnie (Mount Kisco, New York: 1990), p. 9.

9. *Women's Lives in Medieval Europe: A Sourcebook,* ed. Emilie Amt (New York and London: Routledge, 1993), pp. 140–142.

10. Incident recounted by Georges Duby, *Mâle Moyen Âge: De l'amour et autres essais* (Paris: Flammarion, 1990), pp. 29–30.

11. *Women's Lives,* ed. Amt, p. 66.

12. The following citations are from the York manual, found in *Surtees Society Publications* 63 no. 24, as cited by George Elliott Howard, *A History of Matrimonial Institutions* (Chicago: The University of Chicago Press, 1904), vol. 1, pp. 304–307.

13. Samuel N. Rosenberg, "The Medieval Hebrew-French Wedding Song," *Shofar,* fall 1992, vol. 11, no. 1, pp. 26–28. I am grateful to Professor Rosenberg for calling this song to my attention.

14. This discussion is indebted to two famous essays by Georges Duby, "Le mariage dans la société du haut Moyen Age" and "L'amour en France au XIIe siècle," in Duby, *Mâle Moyen Âge,* especially pp. 40–42. See also J.-L. Flandrin, *Un temps pour embrasser. Aux origines de la morale sexualle occidental (VIe–XIe siècle)* (Paris: Le Seuil, 1983).

15. *Women's Lives,* ed. Amt, p. 23.

16. Reproduced in Shahar, *The Fourth Estate,* image 15.

17. Brigitte Cazelles, "Saints' Lives," in *A New History of French Literature,* ed. Denis Hollier (Cambridge, Massachusetts: Harvard University Press, 1994), pp. 13–18.

18. The latest modern French translator of their letters states, unequivocally, that Héloïse and Abelard did indeed exist and that the basic facts of their lives were "corroborated by their contemporaries," but since the oldest manuscripts date from the mid-thirteenth century—that is, a hundred years after the events—it is impossible to know to what extent the manuscripts that have come down to us correspond to the original documents. *Héloïse et Abélard, Lettres et vies,* trans. Yves Ferroul (Paris: GF-Flammarion, 1996), pp. 30–31. My English translations are from this edition.

19. Denis de Rougemont, *Love in the Western World* (New York: Pantheon, 1956). Originally published as *L'Amour et l'Occident* (Paris: Plon, 1946).

20. Chrétien de Troyes, *Lancelot ou le Chevalier de la Charrette,* ed. Mireille Demaules, trans. Daniel Poirion, (Paris: Gallimard, 1996), pp. 127–128.

21. Shahar, *The Fourth Estate,* p. 163.

22. *The Key to Love (La Clef d'Amors),* in *The Comedy of Eros: Medieval French Guides to the Art of Love,* trans. Norman R. Shapiro (Urbana and Chicago: University of Illinois Press, 1977), p. 36.

23. *The Key to Love,* in *The Comedy of Eros,* p. 16.

24. Guiart, *The Art of Love (L'Art d'Amors),* in *The Comedy of Eros,* p. 50.

25. Richard de Fournival, *Advice on Love (Consaus d'Amours),* in *The Comedy of Eros,* p. 104.

26. Robert de Fournival, *Advice on Love,* in *The Comedy of Eros,* p. 116.

27. Robert de Blois, *Advice to Ladies (Le Chastoiement des Dames),* in *The Comedy of Eros,* p. 76.

28. Ibid., p. 68.

29. Ria Lemaire, "The Semiotics of Private and Public Matrimonial Systems and their Discourse," in *Female Power,* ed. Glente and Winther-Jensen, pp. 77–104.

30. Ibid., p. 81.

31. Ibid., p. 86.

32. *Chansons des Trouvères,* ed. Samuel N. Rosenberg and Hans Tischler, with the collaboration of Marie-Geneviève Grossel (Paris: Livre de Poche, 1995), pp. 80–81.

33. Shulamith Shahar, "Cultural Attitudes and Strategies of Oppression: Medieval Motherhood," in *Female Power,* ed. Glente and Winther-Jensen, pp. 44–45.

34. Merry E. Wiesner, *Women and Gender in Early Modern Europe* (Cambridge: Cambridge University Press, 1993), pp. 51–52.

35. *Women's Lives,* ed. Amt, p. 97.

36. See Marilyn Yalom, *A History of the Breast* (New York: Knopf, 1997), p. 37.

37. *Women's Writing in Middle English,* ed. Alexandra Barratt (London and New York: Longman, 1992), p. 35.

38. Erika Uitz, *The Legend of Good Women* (Mount Kisco, New York: Moyer Bell Limited, 1990), pp. 71–72.

39. Uitz's book is a mine of information about burgher women's work on the continent. See also *Women's Lives,* ed. Amt, pp. 194–214.

40. Hufton, *The Prospect,* p. 64.

41. *Women's Lives,* ed. Amt, p. 208.

42. Ibid., p. 108.

43. Pearl Hogrefe, *Tudor Women: Commoners and Queens* (Ames: Iowa State University Press, 1975), p. xii; and *Private Life in the Fifteenth Century: Illustrated Letters of the Paston Family,* ed. Roger Virgoe (New York: Weidenfeld and Nicolson, 1989), p. 139.

44. *Le Mesnagier de Paris* (Paris: Livre de Poche, 1993), p. 25.

45. Chaucer, *Canterbury Tales,* ed. A. Kent and Constance Hieatt (New York: Bantam Books, 1964), pp. 187, 189, 219.

46. *The Book of Margery Kempe* (Harmondsworth, Middlesex: Penguin Books, 1985). This and the following citations from pp. 42–47, 57–58, and 60.

47. Their stories are beautifully told by Carol Lee Flinders in *Enduring Grace: Living Portraits of Seven Women Mystics* (San Francisco: HarperSanFrancisco, 1993).

48. *Christine's Vision,* part III, as quoted by Andrea Hopkins, in *Most Wise and Valiant Ladies* (New York: Welcome Rain, Distributed by Stewart, Tabori & Chang, 1997), p. 112.

49. *Christine de Pisan's Ballades, Rondeaux, and Virelais,* ed. Kenneth Varty (Leicester: Leicester University Press, 1965), pp. 3 and 5, my translations. See *The Writings of Christine de Pizan,* ed. Charity Cannon Willard (New York: Persea Books, 1994), for English translations of Pisan's poems.

50. Boccaccio, *Decameron,* VII, 5.

51. Beatrice Gottlieb, *The Family in the Western World from the Black Death to the Industrial Age* (New York and Oxford: Oxford University Press, 1993), p. 76.

52. Charles de la Roncière, "Tuscan Notables on the Eve of the Renaissance," in *A History of Private Life: Revelations of the Medieval World,* ed. Georges Duby, trans. Arthur Goldhammer (Cambridge, Mass., and London: The Belknap Press of Harvard University Press, 1988), vol. 2, p. 293.

53. Gottlieb *The Family,* p. 74.

54. Christiane Klapisch-Zuber, "The Griselda Complex" in *Women, Family, and Ritual in Renaissance Italy,* trans. Lydia Cochrane (Chicago and London: The University of Chicago Press, 1985), p. 214; and David Herlihy and Christian Klapisch-Zuber, *Tuscans and their Families: A Study of the Florentine Catasto of 1427* (New Haven and London: Yale University Press, 1985), pp. 223–226.

55. Stanley Chajnacki, "The Power of Love: Wives and Husbands in Late Medieval Venice," in *Women and Power in the Middle Ages,* ed. Mary Erler and Maryanne Kowalski (Athens and London: University of Georgia Press, 1988), p. 126–148.

56. James S. Grubb, *Provincial Families of the Renaissance: Private and Public Life in the Veneto* (Baltimore and London: The Johns Hopkins University Press, 1996), pp. 20–21.

57. Gene Brucker, *Giovanni and Lusanna: Love and Marriage in Renaissance Florence* (Berkeley and Los Angeles: University of California Press, 1986). Brucker's account of the story of Giovanni and Lusanna is of such particular interest, and only available to us in his edition, that I have paraphrased it extensively in the following pages.

58. *The Jew in the Medieval World: A Sourcebook,* ed. Jacob R. Marcus (Cincinnati: The Union American Hebrew Congregation, 1938), reprinted in *Women's Lives in Medieval Europe,* ed. Amt, pp. 293–296.

59. Gottlieb, *The Family,* p. 130. For Italy, see David Herlihy and Christian Klapisch-Zuber, *Tuscans,* pp. 83–84.

60. Diane G. Scillia, "Israel van Meckenem's Marriage à la Mode: The Alltagsleben," in *New Images of Medieval Women: Essays Toward a Cultural Anthropology,* ed. Edelgard E. DuBruck (Lewiston, New York: The Edwin Mellen Press, 1989), figures 8 and 9.

THREE

1. Martin Luther, "An Open Letter to the Christian Nobility," in *Three Treatises* (Philadelphia: The Fortress Press, 1960), pp. 68–69.

2. Martin Luther, "The Babylonian Captivity of the Church," in *Three Treatises,* p. 235.

3. Martin Luther, *Sämmtliche Werke* (Erlangen and Frankfurt: 1826–57), vol. 20, p. 84, as cited by Merry E. Wiesner, *Women and Gender in Early Modern Europe* (Cambridge, England: Cambridge University Press, 1993), p. 9.

4. *Dr. Martin Luther's Small Catechism* (Saint Louis: Concordia Publishing House, 1971), pp. 28 and 72.

5. Edith Simon, *Luther Alive: Martin Luther and the Making of the Reformation* (Garden City, New York: Doubleday & Company, 1968), p. 327.

6. Roland Bainton, *Women of the Reformation in Germany and Italy* (Minneapolis, Minnesota: Augsburg Publishing House, 1971), p. 27.

7. *Schachzabelbuch,* Codex poet., 1467. Würtembergische Landesbibliothek, Stuttgart. Reproduced in Erika Uitz, *The Legend of Good Women,* p. 143.

8. Bainton, *Women,* p. 36, citing Luther's *Tischreden.*

9. Bainton, *Women,* p. 82.

10. Ibid., pp. 87–88.

11. Ibid., p. 88.

12. Ibid., p. 91.

13. Eric Jose Carlson, *Marriage and the English Reformation* (Oxford, England, and Cambridge, Massachusetts: Blackwell, 1994), p. 42.

14. Lawrence Stone, *The Family, Sex and Marriage in England, 1500–1800* (London: Weidenfeld & Nicolson, 1977), p. 135.

15. Anthony Fletcher, "The Protestant Idea of Marriage in Early Modern England," in *Religion, Culture and Society in Early Modern Britain* (Cambridge, England: Cambridge University Press, 1994), p. 173.

16. Ibid., p. 167.

17. William Gouge, *Domestical Duties* (London: 1622), Epistle Dedicatory, as cited by Fletcher, "The Protestant Idea," p. 168.

18. William Gouge, *Domestical Duties,* as cited by N. H. Keeble, ed., *The Cultural Identity of Seventeenth-Century Woman* (London and New York: Routledge, 1994), p. 155.

19. Michael MacDonald, *Mystical Bedlam: Madness, Anxiety, and Healing in Seventeenth-Century England* (Cambridge, England: Cambridge University Press, 1981), pp. 100–101.

20. William Gouge, *Domestical Duties,* as cited by Anthony Fletcher, *Gender, Sex and Subordination in England 1500–1800* (New Haven and London: Yale University Press, 1995), p. 113.

21. Carlson, *Marriage,* p. 114.

22. On the late marriage of the English, see Peter Laslett, *The World We Have Lost* (New York: Charles Scribner's Sons, 1971), pp. 84–85, and Richard Smith's calculations from 1550–1599, as cited by Carlson, *Marriage,* p. 106. On the English nonmarried, see Alan Macfarlane, *Marriage and Love in England: Modes of Reproduction 1300–1840* (Oxford: Basil Blackwell, 1986), p. 8 and following.

23. Pearl Hogrefe, *Tudor Women: Commoners and Queens* (Ames: Iowa State University Press, 1975), p. 18.

24. John R. Gillis, *For Better, for Worse: British Marriages, 1600 to the Present* (New York and Oxford: Oxford University Press, 1985), pp. 45–46.

25. Merry E. Wiesner, *Women and Gender in Early Modern Europe* (Cambridge, England: Cambridge University Press, 1993), p. 49.

26. Gillis, *For Better,* p. 43.

27. Ibid., p. 63. See chapter 2 (pp. 55–83) for a mine of information about wedding practices.

28. Hogrefe, *Tudor Women,* p. 20, citing John Stockwood, author of *A Bartholomew Fairing for Parents* (1589).

29. Thos Becon, *Workes* (1560), as cited by Macfarlane, *Marriage and Love,* p. 135.

30. H. Smith, *A Preparative to Marriage* (London: 1591), p. 26, as cited by Fletcher, *Gender, Sex, and Subordination,* p. 106.

31. Macfarlane, *Marriage and Love,* pp. 124–125, citing Montesquieu, *The Spirit of the Laws* (1975), vol. 2, p. 6, and Engels, *Origin of the Family* (1902), p. 88.

32. Fletcher, *Gender, Sex, and Subordination,* p. 155.

33. See, for example, *Halfe a dozen good wives: all for a penny* (London, 1635?) in *The Roxburgh ballads,* ed. W. Chappell and J. W. Ebsworth, 9 vols. (London and Hertford, 1869–99), vol. 1, p. 451. Reproduced in *Women, Crime and the Courts in Early Modern England,* ed. Jenny Kermode and Garthine Walker (London: UCL Press, 1994), plate 5.

34. Martin Ingram, " 'Scolding Women Cucked or Washed': A Crisis in Gender Relations in Early Modern England?" *Women, Crime, and the Courts,* ed. Kermode and Walker, pp. 48–80.

35. MacDonald, *Mystical Bedlam,* p. 98.

36. Laura Gowing, "Language, Power and the Law: Women's Slander Litigation in Early Modern London" in *Women, Crime and the Courts,* ed. Kermode and Walker, pp. 29, 34–35.

37. Carlson, *Marriage,* p. 147.

38. William Whateley, *A Bride Bush* (1623), as cited in Keeble, *The Cultural Identity,* p. 150.

39. MacDonald, *Mystical Bedlam,* p. 40.

40. William Whateley, *The Bride Bush* (Amsterdam: Thetrum Orbis Terrarum, 1623; Norwood, New Jersey: W. J. Johnson, 1975), as cited by Fletcher, "The Protestant Idea," p. 177.

41. Gouge, *Domestical Duties,* p. 361, as cited by Fletcher, *Gender, Sex, and Subordination,* p. 114.

42. "The Bridegroomes Comming," in *The Complete Poetry and Selected Prose of John Donne* (New York: Modern Library, 1952), p. 181.

43. The information on the Thynne family letters derives from Fletcher, *Gender, Sex and Subordination,* pp. 154–157, based on A D. Wall, *Two Elizabethan Women: Correspondence of Joan and Maria Thynne 1575–1611* (Wiltshire Record Society, vol. 38, 1983).

44. Biographical information from *The Englishwoman's Diary,* ed. Harriet Blodgett (London: Fourth Estate, 1992), p. 17. Blodgett reproduces excerpts from the *Diary of Lady Margaret Hoby,* ed. Dorothy Meads (London: Routledge and Sons, 1930).

45. Rosamond Rosenmeier, *Anne Bradstreet Revisited* (Boston: Twayne Publishers, 1991), p. 16, citing Dod (1612). Rosenmeier provides a perceptive introduction to Bradstreet's life and work.

46. Rosenmeier, *Anne Bradstreet,* p. 73.

47. *The Complete Works of Anne Bradstreet,* ed. Joseph R. McElrath, Jr., and Allan P. Robb (Boston: Twayne Publishers, 1981), p. 216.

48. Ibid.

49. Ibid.

50. Lyle Koehler, *A Search for Power: The "Weaker Sex" in Seventeenth-Century New England* (Urbana, Chicago, London: University of Illinois Press, 1980), pp. 56–57.

51. Elizabeth Wade White, *Anne Bradstreet: The Tenth Muse* (New York: Oxford University Press, 1971), p. 4. This is the essential biography of Bradstreet.

52. *The Complete Works of Anne Bradstreet,* p. 200.

53. Nancy Woloch, *Women and the American Experience* (New York: Knopf, 1984), p. 23.

54. *The Complete Works of Anne Bradstreet,* pp. 179–180.

55. Ibid., p. 180.

56. Ibid., p. 181.

57. Ibid., pp. 182–183.

58. Woloch, *Women and the American Experience,* pp. 41–42.

59. White, *Anne Bradstreet,* pp. 172–173.

60. *The Complete Works of Anne Bradstreet,* pp. 7–8.

61. Koehler, *A Search,* p. 41.

62. Laurel Thatcher Ulrich, *Good Wives: Image and Reality in the Lives of Women in Northern New England 1650–1750* (New York: Vintage Books, 1991), p. 218, citing *Winthrop Papers,* Part 3N, MHS Collections, 5th Ser., I, 104–105.

63. See White, *Anne Bradstreet,* pp. 226–250, for this period in Bradstreet's life.

64. Ibid., p. 255.

65. Thomas Parker, *The Coppy of a Letter Written . . . to His Sister* (London, 1650), p. 13. Cited by Edmund S. Morgan, *The Puritan Family* (New York: Harper & Row, 1966), p. 44.

66. Koehler, *A Search,* p. 54.

67. Morgan, *The Puritan Family,* p. 87.

68. *The Complete Works of Anne Bradstreet,* p. 167.

69. Ulrich, *Good Wives,* pp. 111–112.

70. Edmund S. Morgan, "The Puritans and Sex," *The New England Quarterly* 15 (1942), p. 602; Julia Cherry Spruill, *Women's Life and Work in the Southern Colonies* (Chapel Hill: The University of North Carolina Press, 1938), pp. 314–320; Edmund Morgan, *The Puritan Family,* p. 41.

71. John D'Emilio and Estelle B. Freedman, *Intimate Matters: A History of Sexuality in America* (Chicago and London: The University of Chicago Press, 1997), p. 28.

72. Elizabeth Anticaglia, *Twelve American Women* (Chicago: Nelson Hall Co., 1975), pp. 8–9.

73. *Antinomianism in the Colony of Massachusetts Bay,* ed. Charles F. Adams, p. 329 (Boston, 1894), cited by Morgan, *The Puritan Family,* p. 19.

74. Melville Cobbledick, "The Status of Women in Puritan New England, 1630–1660: A Demographic Study," Ph.D. diss., Yale University, 1936. University Microfilms, Ann Arbor Michigan, p. 67.

75. Ibid., p. 78.

76. Woloch, *Women and the American Experience,* p. 30.

77. White, *Anne Bradstreet,* p. 132.

78. Morgan, "The Puritans and Sex," p. 600.

79. Spruill, *Women's Life and Work,* pp. 321–322.

80. Ulrich, *Good Wives,* pp. 19–20.

81. Ibid., p. 23.

82. Woloch, *Women and the American Experience,* p. 22.

83. Koehler, *A Search,* p. 124.

84. Woloch, *Women and the American Experience,* p. 18.

85. Ibid., p. 19, and H. R. McIlwaine, "The Maids Who Came to Virginia in 1620 and 1621 for Husbands," *The Reviewer* 1 (April 1, 1921), pp. 109–110.

86. Spruill, *Women's Life and Work,* pp. 8–9, and Carol Birkin, *First Generations: Women in Colonial America* (New York: Hill and Wang, 1996), p. 6.

87. George Alsop, "Character of the Province of Maryland," in *Narratives of Early Maryland,* ed. Clayton C. Hall (New York: Charles Scribner's Sons: 1910), p. 358.

88. Spruill, *Women's Life and Work,* p. 15.

89. This and the following case from Roger Thompson, *Women in Stuart England and America: A Comparative Study* (London and Boston: Routledge & Kegan Paul, 1974), pp. 36–37.

90. Anne Firor Scott and Suzanne Lebsock, *Virginia Women: The First Two Hundred Years* (Williamsburg, Virginia: The Colonial Williamsburg Foundation, 1988), p. 16.

91. Suzanne Lebsock, *Virginia Women 1600–1945* (Richmond: Virginia State Library, 1987), p. 28.

92. Robert E. T. Roberts, "Black-White Intermarriage in the United States," in *Inside the Mixed Marriage: Accounts of Changing Attitudes, Patterns, and Perceptions of Cross-Cultural and Interracial Marriage,* ed. Walton R. Johnson and D. Michael Warren (Lanham, New York, and London: University Press of America, 1994), p. 25.

93. Robert J. Sickels, *Race, Marriage and the Law* (Albuquerque: University of New Mexico Press, 1972), p. 64.

94. Lebsock, *Virginia Women,* p. 29.

95. Thompson, *Women in Stuart England and America,* p. 43.

96. D'Emilio and Freedman, *Intimate Matters,* p. 36.

97. Roberts, "Black-White Intermarriage," in *Inside the Mixed Marriage,* ed. Johnson and Warren, p. 28.

98. H. R. McIlwaine, "The Maids," p. 111.

99. Edmund S. Morgan, "The Puritans and Sex," p. 592.

100. Morgan, *The Puritan Family,* p. 47.

101. Gillis, *For Better,* p. 14.

FOUR

1. Jean-Jacques Rousseau, *Emile* (London: J. M. Dent & Sons, Ltd., 1943), Book V. While it has become fashionable to see Rousseau as the enemy of women, one must not forget his sympathetic portrayals of Julie in *La Nouvelle Héloïse* and of Madame Warens in his *Confessions.* Like many great thinkers and writers, Rousseau was a mass of contradictions.

2. Dr. James Fordyce, *The Character and Conduct of the Female Sex* (London: T. Cadell, 1776), p. 40.

3. Mary Beth Norton, *Liberty's Daughters: The Revolutionary Experience of American Women, 1750–1800* (Boston and Toronto: Little, Brown and Company, 1980), pp. 117–124.

4. John Ogden, *The Female Guide; or, Thoughts on the Education of That Sex, accomodated to the State of Society, Manners, and Government in the United States* (Concord, New Hampshire, 1793, pp. 39–41), cited by Linda K. Kerber, *Women of the Republic: Intellect and Ideology in Revolutionary America* (Chapel Hill: University of North Carolina Press, 1980) p. 252.

5. Norton, *Liberty's Daughters,* p. 21.

6. Julia Cherry Spruill, *Women's Life and Work in the Southern Colonies* (Chapel Hill: University of North Carolina Press, 1938), p. 66.

7. Ibid., p. 109.

8. Ibid., p. 179.

9. *Maryland Journal,* January 20, 1774, cited in Spruill, *Women's Life and Work,* p. 180.

10. *South Carolina Gazette,* July 12, 1770, cited in Spruill, *Women's Life and Work,* p. 182.

11. Edith B. Gelles, *"First Thoughts": Life and Letters of Abigail Adams* (New York: Twayne Publishers, 1998), p. 3. See also Gelles, *Portia: The World of Abigail Adams* (Bloomington: Indiana University Press, 1992).

12. *The Book of Abigail and John: Selected Letters of the Adams Family 1762–1784,* ed. L. H. Butterfield, Marc Friedlaender and Mary-Jo Kline (Cambridge, Massachusetts, and London: Harvard University Press, 1975), p. 121.

13. Ibid., p. 121.

14. Ibid., p. 123.

15. Gelles, *First Thoughts,* p. 15.

16. Ibid., p. 171.

17. Ibid., p. 172.

18. Woloch, *Women and the American Experience,* p. 85.

19. Cited by Pattie Cowell, *Women Poets in Pre-Revolutionary America, 1650–1775, An Anthology* (Troy, New York: The Whitston Publishing Company, 1981), p. 55.

20. Norton, *Liberty's Daughters,* p. 171.

21. Ibid., p. 177. This section relies heavily on Norton, pp. 170–194.

22. See Alfred F. Young, "The Women of Boston: 'Persons of Consequence' in the Making of the American Revolution, 1765–76," *Women and Politics in the Age of the Democratic Revolution,* ed. Harriet B. Applewhite and Darline G. Levy (Ann Arbor: the University of Michigan Press, 1990), especially pp. 193–207.

23. Ibid., p. 196.

24. Carol Berkin, *First Generations: Women in Colonial America* (New York: Hill and Wang, 1996), p. 167.

25. Norton, *Liberty's Daughters,* p. 176.

26. *Sklavin oder Bürgerin? Französische Revolution und Neue Weiblichkeit 1760–1830,* ed. Viktoria Schmidt-Linsenhoff (Frankfort: Historisches Museum Frankfurt, Jonas Verlag, 1989), p. 125.

27. Karen Offen, *European Feminisms, 1700–1950* (Stanford: Stanford University Press, 2000), pp. 27–68. See also *Women, the Family, and Freedom: The Debate in Documents,* ed. Susan Groag Bell and Karen M. Offen, vol. 1, 1750–1880 (Stanford: Stanford University Press, 1983), pp. 97–109.

28. Karen Offen, "Was Mary Wollstonecraft a Feminist? A Contextual Re-reading of *A Vindication of the Rights of Woman,* 1792–1992," in *Quilting a New Canon: Stitching Women's Words,* ed. Uma Parameswaran (Toronto: Sister Vision, Black Women and Women of Colour Press, 1996), p. 16.

29. Marilyn Yalom, *Blood Sisters: the French Revolution in Women's Memory* (New York: Basic Books, 1993), p. 93. A fuller account of the life of Madame Roland can be found in pp. 75–96.

30. Mme Roland, *Mémoires de Mme Roland,* ed. Paul de Roux (Paris: Mercure de France, 1986), p. 63. All translations from this work are my own.

31. Ibid., p. 65.

32. Ibid., pp. 93, 155.

33. C. A. Dauban, *Etude sur Madame Roland et son temps* (Paris: Henri Plon, 1864), p. CL.

34. Elisabeth Le Bas, "Manuscrit de Mme Le Bas," in *Autour de Robespierre, Le Conventionnel Le Bas,* ed. Stefant-Paul (pseudonym of Paul Coutant) (Paris: Flammarion, 1901), p. 127. This and the following quotations from Mme Le Bas are reproduced in Yalom, *Blood Sisters,* chapter 7.

35. Marie-Victoire de La Villirouët, *Une femme avocat, épisodes de la Révolution à Lamballe et à Paris. Mémoires de la comtesse de La Villirouët, née de Lambilly,* ed. Comte de Bellevue (Paris: J. Poisson, 1902), p. 33.

36. Madame de Ménerville, *Souvenirs d'Émigration* (Paris: P. Roger, 1934), p. 170.

37. Kerber, *Women of the Republic,* pp. 119–120.

38. Mary Wollstonecraft, *A Vindication of the Rights of Woman* (London: J. Johnson, 1792); ed. Miriam Kramnick (Harmondsworth, England: Penguin Books, 1975), p. 270.

39. Linda Kerber first used the term "republican mother" in her landmark article "The Republican Mother: Women and the Enlightenment—An American Perspective," *American Quarterly* 28 (Summer 1796), pp. 107–205.

40. Linda S. Popofsky and Marianne B. Sheldon, "French and American Women in the Age of Democratic Revolution, 1770–1815: A Comparative Perspective," in *History of European Ideas,* "Women in European Culture and Society" issue, 1987, p. 601.

41. Elke Harten and Hans-Christian Harten, *Femmes, Culture, et Révolution* (Paris: des femmes, 1989), pp. 561–562.

42. Edith Gelles, "Revisiting and Revising the Republican Mother," unpublished paper.

43. The term "regression in the service of the ego," to which I have added the word "male," will be familiar to readers of twentieth-century psychiatric literature.

FIVE

1. Theo Gift citation from "Little Woman," *Cassells Magazine,* 1873, vol. 7 (new series), p. 240. Cited by Judith Rowbotham, *Good Girls Make Good Wives* (Oxford: Basil Blackwell Ltd, 1989), p. 11.

2. Eliza Holman citation from *The American Slave: A Composite Autobiography,* ed. George P. Rawick, (Westport, Connecticut: Greenwood Press, 1972), vol. 4, part 2, p. 150.

3. Eliza (Chaplin) Nelson Letters 1819–1869. Essex Institute Library. Salem, Massachusetts. Cited by Mirra Bank, *Anonymous Was a Woman* (New York: St. Martin's Press, 1979), p. 50.

4. See especially Edward Shorter, *The Making of the Modern Family* (New York: Basic Books, 1975), and Carl Degler, *At Odds: Women and the Family in America from the Revolution to the Present* (New York and Oxford: Oxford University Press, 1981). How Victorian marriage continued throughout the century to be, on the one hand, both romantic and companionate and, on the other, an economic and social contract is the subject of Kate Washington's essay "The Thing Bartered: Love, Economics, and the Victorian Couple," in *Inside the American Couple,* ed. Marilyn Yalom and Laura Carstensen (Berkeley: University of California Press, forthcoming.)

5. Penny Kane, *Victorian Families in Fact and Fiction* (New York: St. Martin's Press, 1995), pp. 98–99.

6. Katherine Moore, *Victorian Wives* (New York: St. Martin's Press, 1974), pp. 57–58. Pamela Neville-Sington, *Fanny Trollope: The Life and Adventures of a Clever Woman* (London: Viking, 1997), pp. 32–33. John Gregory's advice from the 1770s was still relevant: "A woman, in this country, may easily prevent the first impressions of love, and every motive of prudence and delicacy should make her guard her heart against them, till such time as she has received the most convincing proofs of the attachment of a man of such merit, as will justify a reciprocal regard." John Gregory, *A Father's Legacy to His Daughters* (Chambersburg, Pennsylvania. Printed by Dover & Harper, for M. Carey, Philadelphia, 1796 [London: 1774]).

7. This and the following two citations from Lotte and Joseph Hamburger, *Troubled Lives: John and Sarah Austin* (Toronto, Buffalo, London: University of Toronto Press, 1985), pp. 12, 13, and 23.

8. Françoise Basch, *Relative Creatures: Victorian Women in Society and the Novel*, trans. Anthony Rudolf, (New York: Schocken, 1974), p. 26.

9. Greg and Ruskin citations from Basch, *Relative Creatures*, pp. 5 and 6.

10. William Acton, *The Functions and Disorders of the Reproductive Organs in Youth, in Adult Age, and in Advanced Life* [London: John Churchill, 1857], as cited from 1897 Philadelphia edition in *Victorian Women: A Documentary Account of Women's Lives in Nineteenth-Century England, France, and the United States*, ed. Erna Hellerstein, Leslie Hume, Karen Offen, Estelle Freedman, Barbara Gelpi, and Marilyn Yalom (Stanford: Stanford University Press, 1981), p. 178.

11. Auguste Debay, *Hygiène et physiologie du mariage* (Paris: E. Dentu, 1849), p. 138.

12. Charlotte Brontë, Letter to Ellen Nussey, 12 March 1839, cited by Patricia Beer, *Reader, I Married Him* (London and Basingstoke: The Macmillan Press Ltd, 1974), p. 6.

13. Cited by Neville-Sington, *Fanny Trollope*, p. 45.

14. *Not in God's Image: Women in History from the Greeks to the Victorians*, ed. Julia O'Faolain and Lauro Martines (New York, Hagerstown, San Francisco, London: Harper & Row Publishers, 1973), p. 318.

15. *Victorian Women*, ed. Hellerstein et al., p. 258. Much information in this chapter derives from the Victorian Women project at the Stanford Center for Research on Women, funded by the National Endowment for the Humanities, and which I directed from 1977 to 1981.

16. The Hon. Mrs. Norton, *A Letter to the Queen on Lord Chancellor Cranworth's Marriage and Divorce Bill* (London: Longman, Brown, Green and Longmans, 1855), pp. 9–11.

17. Lee Holcombe, "Victorian Wives and Property: Reform of the Married Women's Property Law, 1857–1882," in *A Widening Sphere: Changing Roles of Victorian Women*, ed. Martha Vicinus (Bloomington and London: Indiana University Press, 1977), p. 19.

18. *Victorian Women*, ed. Hellerstein et al., p. 260.

19. Lee Holcombe, "Victorian Wives and Property," in *A Widening Sphere*, ed. Vicinus, p. 15.

20. *Women, the Family, and Freedom: The Debate in Documents*, ed. Susan Groag Bell and Karen M. Offen (Stanford: Stanford University Press, 1983), vol. 1, 1750–1880, p. 253.

21. *The Elizabeth Cady Stanton–Susan B. Anthony Reader: Correspondence, Writings, Speeches*, ed. Ellen DuBois (Boston: Northeastern University Press, 1992), pp. 55–56.

22. Hendrik Hartog, *Man and Wife in America: A History* (Cambridge, Massachusetts: Harvard University Press, 2000), pp. 287–295.

23. Frances Trollope, *Domestic Manners of the Americans* (Oxford and New York: Oxford University Press, 1984 [1831]), p. 98.

24. J. S. Buckingham, *The Slave States of America* (London: Fisher, Son, & Co., 1842), vol. 1, p. 127.

25. Ibid., p. 231.

26. Letter from Mrs. Vivia A. B. Henderson, *Woman's Journal,* November 19, 1898, p. 375, cited by Barbara Ehrenreich and Deirdre English, *For Her Own Good: 150 Years of the Experts' Advice to Women* (Garden City, New York: Anchor Press/Doubleday, 1978), p. 150.

27. Cited by Katherine Moore, *Victorian Wives* (New York: St. Martin's Press, 1974), p. xxv.

28. Sara Grimké, *Letters on the Equality of the Sexes* (Boston: I. Knapp, 1838), p. 51.

29. George W. Burnap, *The Sphere and Duties of Woman* (Baltimore: John Murphy, 1848), pp. 145–46. See also Frances B. Cogan, *All American Girl: The Ideal of Real Womanhood in Mid-Nineteenth-Century America* (Athens and London: The University of Georgia Press), p. 79.

30. *Victorian Women,* ed. Hellerstein et al., pp. 15–17.

31. Burnap, *The Sphere,* pp. 45–46. For an understanding of the domestic ideology enveloping nineteenth-century American women, see Glenna Matthews, *"Just a Housewife": The Rise and Fall of Domesticity in America* (New York and Oxford: Oxford University Press, 1987), especially chapters 1 and 2. Also Nancy M. Theriot, *Mothers and Daughters in Nineteenth-Century America: The Biosocial Construction of Femininity* (Lexington: The University Press of Kentucky, 1996), and Ruth H. Bloch, "American Feminine Ideals in Transition: The Rise of the Model Mother, 1785–1815," *Feminist Studies,* 4 (1978): 101–125.

32. Elizabeth Cady Stanton, *Eighty Years and More: Reminiscences 1815–1897* (New York: Schocken Books, 1971 [1898]). All citations are from this edition.

33. Ellen M. Plante, *Women at Home in Victorian America: A Social History* (New York: Facts on File, Inc.), 1997, p. 23.

34. Harvey Green, *The Light of the Home: An Intimate View of the Lives of Women in Victorian America* (New York: Pantheon Books, 1983), p. 43.

35. Caroll Smith-Rosenberg, *Disorderly Conduct: Visions of Gender in America* (New York: Knopf, 1985), pp. 53–76.

36. Elizabeth Cady Stanton, *Solitude of Self, An Address delivered before the United States Congressional Committee on the Judiciary, Monday, January 18, 1892,* National American Woman Suffrage Association Series (Microfilm. New Haven, Conn., Research Publications, 1977. History of women, Reel 935, no. 7967), pp. 3–20.

37. George Fitzhugh, *Sociology for the South* (Richmond: Morris, 1854), pp. 214, 217.

38. Citations from Marli F. Weiner, *Mistresses and Slaves: Plantation Women in South Carolina, 1830–80* (Urbana and Chicago: University of Illinois Press, 1998), pp. 73, 66.

39. Virginia Cary, *Letters on Female Character, Addressed to a Young Lady, on the Death of Her Mother* (Richmond: 1828), p. 149. Cited by Suzanne Lebsock, *Virginia Women 1600–1945* (Richmond : Virginia State Library, 1987), p. 63.

40. Quotations from Eleanor Miot Boatwright, *Status of Women in Georgia, 1783–1860* (Brooklyn, New York: Carlson Publishing, Inc., 1994), pp. 24 and 53.

41. Boatwright, *Status,* p. 27, citing the Seventh and Eighth U.S. Census (1850 and 1860).

42. Boatwright, *Status,* p. 33.

43. Citations from *Tokens of Affection: The Letters of a Planter's Daughter in the Old South,* ed. Carol Bleser (Athens, Georgia, and London: The University of Georgia Press, 1996), pp. 110–111, 120, 131.

44. Boatwright, *Status,* p. 88.

45. Ibid., p. 36, citing Augusta *Georgia Constitutionalist,* February 25, 1841, citing *Batesville [Arkansas] News.*

46. Sarah Anderson diary, May 6, 1827, cited by Jan Lewis, *The Pursuit of Happiness: Family and Values in Jefferson's Virginia* (Cambridge, England: Cambridge University Press, 1984), p. 198.

47. Anne Firor Scott, *The Southern Lady: From Pedestal to Politics 1830–1930* (Chicago and London: The University of Chicago Press, 1970), pp. 27–28.

48. Weiner, *Mistress, and Slaves*; Eugene D. Genovese, "Life in the Big House," in *A Heritage of Her Own,* ed. Nancy Cott and Elizabeth Pleck (New York: Simon and Schuster, 1979), pp. 290–297; and Genovese, *Roll, Jordan, Role: The World the Slaves Made* (New York: Vintage Books, 1974).

49. Weiner, *Mistresses and Slaves,* p. 32.

50. Harriet Jacobs (Linda Brent, pseud.), *Incidents in the Life of a Slave Girl* (Boston: Published for the Author, 1861), p. 20.

51. Weiner, *Mistresses and Slaves,* pp. 35–36.

52. *The American Slave,* ed. George P. Rawick (Westport, Conn.: Greenwood Publishing Co., 1972), vol. 5, part 3, p. 83.

53. *The American Slave,* ed. Rawick, vol. 5, part 3, p. 77.

54. Scott, *The Southern Lady,* pp. 38–39.

55. Janet Farrell Brodie, *Contraception and Abortion in Nineteenth-Century America* (Ithaca and London: Cornell University Press, 1994), p. 2.

56. Weiner, *Mistresses and Slaves,* p. 22.

57. *The American Slave,* ed. Rawick, vol. 4, part 2, p. 163.

58. Ibid., p. 42.

59. Ibid., vol. 5, part 3, p. 191.

60. Ibid., part 4, pp. 176–178.

61. Weiner, *Mistresses and Slaves,* p. 85.

62. Ibid., p. 81.

63. *The American Slave,* ed. Rawick, vol. 4, part 2, pp. 104–105.

64. Eugene D. Genovese, *Roll, Jordan, Roll,* pp. 477–478.

65. Degler, *At Odds,* p. 114.

66. *The American Slave,* ed. Rawick, vol. 4, part 1, p. 63.

67. Ibid., p. 79.

68. Ibid., vol. 4, part 2, p. 288.

69. Ibid., p. 136.

70. Ibid., vol. 5, part 3, p. 244.

71. Ibid., vol. 4, part 1, p. 207.

72. Ibid., vol. 4, part 2, p. 17 and p. 194.

73. Ibid., vol. 5, part 3, p. 258.

74. Herbert G. Gutman, *The Black Family in Slavery and Freedom, 1750–1925* (New York: Vintage Books), p. 51.

75. Herbert G. Gutman, "Marital and Sexual Norms among Slave Women," in *A Heritage of Her Own,* ed. Cott and Pleck, p. 301.

76. Genovese, *Roll, Jordan, Roll,* p. 467.

77. *In Joy and in Sorrow: Women, Family, and Marriage in the Victorian South, 1830–1900,* ed. Carol Bleser (New York: Oxford University Press, 1991), p. 108.

78. *The American Slave*, ed. Rawick, vol. 4, part 1, p. 77.

79. Ibid., p. 107.

80. Ibid., p. 86.

81. Ibid., vol. 5, part 3, pp. 191–192.

82. Ibid., vol. 4, part 1, p. 224.

83. Ibid., vol. 4, part 2, p. 205.

84. *Weevils in the Wheat: Interviews with Virginia Ex-Slaves,* ed. Charles L. Perdue, Jr., Thomas E. Barden, and Robert K. Phillips (Bloomington, Ind.: University of Indiana Press, 1980), pp. 48–49. Cited by Lebsock, *Virginia Women,* p. 75.

85. Weiner, *Mistresses and Slaves,* p. 75.

86. Harriet Jacobs, *Incidents in the Life of a Slave Girl,* p. 53.

87. *The American Slave,* ed. Rawick, vol. 5, part 4, p. 167.

88. Ibid., vol. 4, part 2, p. 164.

89. Frances Anne Kemble, *Journal of a Residence on a Georgian Plantation in 1838–1839* (New York: Alfred A. Knopf, 1961), pp. 132–133, 136, 137, 140.

90. Citations found in Boatwright, *Status,* p. 55.

91. Scott, *The Southern Lady,* chapter 3, pp. 46–79. See also Lebsock, *Virginia Women,* pp. 76–77.

92. Buckingham, *Slave States,* vol. 1, pp. 140–141.

93. Citations from Scott, *The Southern Lady,* p. 40.

94. *The American Slave,* ed. Rawick, vol. 4, part 1, p. 69.

95. Ibid., vol. 5, part 4, p. 222.

SIX

1. Julie Roy Jeffrey, *Frontier Women: The Trans-Missippi West, 1840–1880* (New York: Hill and Wang, 1979), and Glenda Riley, *The Female Frontier: A Comparative View of Women on the Prairie and the Plains* (Lawrence, Kansas: University of Kansas, 1988), are two studies that have added considerably to our knowledge of trans-Mississippi women between 1840 and 1890. Jeffrey moves from the agricultural frontier located in the Far West between the 1840s and the 1880s, then to the mining frontier that opened with the California Gold Rush in 1849, and then to the urban frontier. Riley focusses on the prairie states of Iowa, Missouri, Illinois, Minnesota, and Indiana, and the plains states of Kansas, the Dakotas, Nebraska, Oklahoma, and parts of Colorado, Texas, Wyoming, and Montana. Joanna L. Stratton, *Pioneer Women: Voices from the Kansas Frontier* (New York: Simon and Schuster, 1981), focuses exclusively on Kansas. Stratton had the unbelievable good fortune of finding in her grandmother's attic the personal memoirs of 800 Kansas women—a treasure trove initiated by her great-grandmother, who had come to Kansas in 1884. Other useful sources are Lillian Schlissel, *Women's Diaries of the Westward Journey* (New York: Schocken, 1982) and Kenneth L. Holmes, ed. *Covered Wagon Women: Diaries from the Western Trails, 1840–90,* 11 volumes (Glendale, CA: Arthur H. Clark Company, 1983–93).

2. Charles Marc Bost, *Les derniers puritains: pionniers d'Amérique, 1851–1920* (Paris: Hachette, 1977).

3. Cited by Riley, *The Female Frontier,* p. 48.

4. Ibid., p. 31.

5. Ibid., p. 46.

6. Cited by Stratton, *Pioneer Women*, p. 55.

7. Mary Jane Hayden, *Pioneer Days* (San Jose, California: Murgotten's 1915), as cited by Cathy Luchetti, *"I Do!" Courtship, Love and Marriage on the American Frontier* (New York: Crown Trade Paperbacks, 1996), pp. 215–216.

8. Cited by Stratton, *Pioneer Women*, p. 44.

9. Cited by Susan Butruille, *Women's Voices from the Oregon Trail* (Boise, Idaho: Tamarack Books, 1993), p. 49.

10. Riley, *The Female Frontier*, p. 49. Cf. Jeffrey, *Frontier Women*, p. 57.

11. Bost, *Les derniers puritains*, p. 181. My translation.

12. *Mollie: The Journal of Mollie Dorsey Sanford in Nebraska and Colorado Territories, 1857–1866* (Lincoln: University of Nebraska Press, 1959), pp. 145–146.

13. Fred Lockley, *Conversations with Pioneer Women* (Eugene, Oregon: Rainy Day Press, 1993), pp. 98–99.

14. Luchetti, *"I Do!,"* pp. 170–172.

15. Susan Armitage, "Women's Literature and the American Frontier: A New Perspective on the Frontier Myth," *Women, Women Writers, and the West*, ed. L. L. Lee and Merrill Lewis (Troy, New York: The Whitston Publishing Company, 1980), pp. 5–13.

16. Sarah Winnemucca Hopkins, *Life among the Piutes; their wrongs and claims*, ed. Mrs. Horace Mann (Boston: For Sale by Cupples Upham and Co., G. P. Putnam's Sons, New York, and by the author, 1883). A short biography of Sarah Winnemucca is found in Elinor Rickey, *Eminent Women of the West* (Berkeley: Howell-North Books, 1975), pp. 125–151.

17. This and the following paragraphs based on Luchetti, *"I Do!,"* pp. 257–262.

18. Andrew Garcia, *Tough Trip Through Paradise,* ed. Bennet Stein (New York: Houghton Mifflin, 1967).

19. Johnny Faragher and Christine Stansell, "Women and their Families on the Overland Trail to California and Oregon, 1842–1867," in *A Heritage of Her Own: Toward a New Social History of American Women,* ed. Nancy Cott and Elizabeth Pleck (New York: Simon and Schuster, 1979), p. 246.

20. The following is based on Ruth Karr McKee, *Mary Richardson Walker: Her Book* (Caldwell, Idaho: The Caxton Printers, Ltd., 1945).

21. Luchetti, *"I Do!,"* p. 184.

22. "Original Diary of Kitturah Penton (Mrs. George) Belknap" as quoted in Susan Butruille, *Women's Voices,* p. 53 and following.

23. "Notes by the Wayside en Route to Oregon," by Lydia A. Rudd. Typescript in the collection of Lilly Library, Indiana University, Bloomington, Indiana.

24. Lockley, *Conversations,* pp. 42–44.

25. *Mollie: The Journal of Mollie Dorsey Sanford,* pp. xxx.

26. Mary Ballou, " 'I Hear the Hogs in My Kitchen': A Woman's View of the Gold Rush," in *Let Them Speak for Themselves:Women in the American West 1849–1900,* ed. Christiane Fischer (Hamden, Connecticut: Archon Books, 1977), pp. 42–46.

27. Rachel Haskell, "A Literate Woman in the Mines: the Diary of Rachel Haskell," in *Let Them Speak,* ed. Fischer, pp. 58–72.

28. James Henry Gleason, *Beloved Sister: The Letters of James Henry Gleason, 1841–1859* (Glendale, CA: The Arthur H. Clark Co., 1978).

29. Genaro Padilla, " 'Yo Sola Aprendi': Mexican Women's Personal Narratives from

Nineteenth-Century California," in *Revealing Lives: Autobiography, Biography, and Gender,* ed. Susan Groag Bell and Marilyn Yalom (Albany: SUNY Press, 1990), p. 123.

30. Luchetti, "*I Do!*," pp. 284–285.

31. Mary Bywater Cross, *Treasures in the Trunk: Quilts of the Oregon Trail* (Nashville Tennessee: Rutledge Hill Press, 1993), pp. 123–124.

32. Stanley Snow Ivins, "Notes on Mormon Polygamy," *Western Humanities Review* 10 (1956), pp. 229–239, and James E. Smith and Philip R. Kunz, "Polygyny and Fertility in Nineteenth-Century America," *Population Studies* 30 (1976), pp. 465–480.

33. Jeffrey, *Frontier Women,* pp. 166 and 172.

34. Ibid., p. 165.

35. Mary Ann Hafen, "Memories of a handcart Pioneer, with some account of frontier life in Utah and Nevada," in *Let Them Speak,* ed. Fischer, pp. 101–108.

36. Annie Clark Tanner, *A Mormon Mother: An Autobiography* (Salt Lake City: University of Utah Press, 1969), p. 116.

37. Lawrence Foster, "Polygamy and the Frontier: Mormon Women in Early Utah," *History of Women in the United States,* ed. Nancy Cott (Munich, London, New York, and Paris: K. G. Saur, 1992), vol. 2, p. 269.

38. Jeffrey, *Frontier Women,* p. 170.

39. Foster, "Polygamy," in *History of Women,* ed. Cott, pp. 279–80.

40. Hanna Crosby, *Sketch of the Life of Hannah A. Crosby,* from the Historical Records Survey and the Federal Writers project of the Utah Works Administration, 1935–39, as cited by Luchetti, "*I Do!*," pp. 187–188.

41. John Faragher, *Women and Men on the Overland Trail* (New Haven and London: Yale University Press, 1979), chapter 3.

42. Helen M. Carpenter, "A Trip Across the Plains in an Ox Wagon, 1857" (manuscript diary, Huntington Library), pp. 27–28, as cited by Faragher and Stansell, "Women and Their Families on the Overland Trail," in *A Heritage of Her Own,* ed. Cott and Pleck, p. 254.

43. Faragher and Stansell, "Women and Their Families on the Overland Trail," in *A Heritage of Her Own,* ed. Cott and Pleck, p. 255.

44. Bethenia Owens-Adair, *Dr. Owens-Adair: Some of Her Life Experiences* (Portland, Oregon: Mann & Beach, 1906), pp. 24–27.

45. Cited by Stratton, *Pioneer Women,* p. 58.

46. Hendrik Hartog, *Man and Wife in America: A History* (Cambridge, Massachusetts: Harvard University Press, 2000), p. 87.

47. Owens-Adair, *Dr. Owens-Adair,* pp. 52, 53.

SEVEN

1. This and the following citation from Henrick Ibsen, *A Doll's House and Other Plays* (Baltimore, Maryland: Penguin Books, 1967), trans. Peter Watts, pp. 228 and 334, note 11.

2. Margareta R. Matovic, *Stockholmsakenskap: Familjebildning och partnerval i Stockholm 1850–1890* (Stockholm: LiberFörlags, 1984), English summary pp. 364–377.) Matovic estimates that 42 percent of couples announcing the banns of matrimony between 1860 and 1890 were cohabiting, and around 11 percent legalized their premarital children when they married (p. 375).

3. Leo XIII, *Rerum Novarum,* 15 May 1891, excerpted in *Women, the Family, and*

Freedom, ed. Susan Groag Bell and Karen Offen (Stanford: Stanford University Press, 1983), vol 2, p. 95.

4. The term was first used by Sarah Grand in "The New Aspect of the Woman Question" in *North America Review,* vol. 158 (1894), p. xxx, reproduced in *The Late Victorian Marriage Question,* ed. Ann Heilmann (London: Routledge, 1998), vol. 2, pp. 271–276. I am indebted to Heilmann for having made this and so much other material on the Woman Question easily available in the five-volume Routledge/Thoemmes Press collection.

5. Dedication page to *Is Marriage a Failure?,* ed. Harry A. Quilter (London: Swan Sonnenschein & Co, 1888). Facsimile copy (New York: Garland, 1984).

6. Susan Turk Charles and Laura L. Carstensen, "Marriage in Old Age," in *Inside the American Couple,* ed. Marilyn Yalom and Laura L. Carstensen (Berkeley: University of California Press, forthcoming).

7. John Lucas, *The Literature of Change: Studies in the 19th Century Provincial Novel* (Hassocks, England: Harvester Press, 1977).

8. George Gissing, *The Odd Women* [1893], (New York: W. W. Norton, 1977), p. 87.

9. Ibid., p. 180.

10. Eliza Lynn Linton, "The Wild Women as Politicians," *Nineteenth Century,* vol. 30 (1891), pp. 79–88. Linton's three "Wild Women" articles are reproduced in Heilmann, *The Late Victorian Marriage Question,* at the end of vol. 1.

11. Abba Goold Woolson, ed., *Dress Reform* (New York: Arno Press, 1974 [1874]), p. 134.

12. Lillian Faderman, *Surpassing the Love of Men: Romantic Friendship and Love between Women from the Renaissance to the Present* (New York: William Morrow and Company, Inc. 1981), p. 190. See also Faderman, *To Believe in Women: What Lesbians Have Done for America—A History* (Boston and New York: Houghton Mifflin Company, 1999).

13. The following is based on Virginia Jeans Laas, *Love and Power in the Nineteenth Century: The Marriage of Violet Blair* (Fayetteville: The University of Arkansas Press, 1998).

14. See Sondra R. Herman, "Loving Courtship or the Marriage Market: The Ideal and Its Critics, 1871–1911," in *History of Women in the United States,* ed. Nancy Cott (Munich, London, New York, Paris: K. G. Saur: 1992), vol. 2, pp. 298–315.

15. Carl Degler, "Introduction," to Charlotte Perkins Gilman, *Women and Economics* (New York, Hagerstown, San Francisco, London: Harper & Row, 1966), p. xxv.

16. Charlotte Perkins Gilman, *The Home: Its Work and Influence* (Urbana: University of Illinois Press, 1972 [1902]), p. 277.

17. Gilman, *Women and Economics,* pp. 13–15.

18. Ibid., p. 157.

19. Ibid., p. 242.

20. Gilman, "All the World to Her," *Independent,* July 9, 1903, p. 1616.

21. See discussion of relation of mental breakdown to maternity in Marilyn Yalom, *Maternity, Mortality, and the Literature of Madness* (University Park and London: Pennsylvania State University Press, 1985).

22. Carl Degler, *At Odds: Women and the Family in America from the Revolution to the Present* (New York: Oxford University Press, 1981), pp. 409–410.

EIGHT

1. William Acton, *The Functions and Disorders of the Reproductive Organs in Childhood, Youth, Adult Age, and Advanced Life Considered in Their Physiological, Social, and Moral Relations* (3rd Am. ed.; Philadelphia, 1871), p. 164, as cited in *Victorian Women,* ed. Hellerstein et al., p. 178. See also John S. Haller, Jr., and Robin M. Haller, *The Physician and Sexuality in Victorian America* (Urbana, Chicago, London: University of Illinois Press, 1974), pp. 97–102; and Carl Degler, *At Odds* (New York: Oxford University Press, 1981), pp. 253–259.

2. Elizabeth Edson Evans, *The Abuse of Maternity* (Philadelphia: J. B. Lippincott & Co., 1875), pp. 118–119.

3. Compare George H. Napheys, *The Transmission of Life. Counsels on the Nature and Hygiene* (Philadelphia, 1871), with *The Physical Life of Woman: Advice to the Maiden, Wife and Mother* (Toronto: Rose Publishing Co., 1880, 3rd Canadian ed.), p. 76.

4. Edward B. Foote, *Plain Home Talk* (New York: Murray Hill Publishing Co., 1891), p. 631.

5. Quoted in Haller and Haller, *The Physician,* pp. 132–133.

6. *The Mosher Survey,* ed. James Mahood and Kristine Wenburg (New York: Arno, 1980). For summary, see Julia A. Ericksen, *Kiss and Tell: Surveying Sex in the Twentieth Century* (Cambridge, Massachusetts and London: Harvard University Press, 1999), pp. 28–30.

7. Carl Degler, "Introduction," *The Mosher Survey,* ed. Mahood and Wenburg, p. xiii.

8. Janet Farrell Brodie, *Contraception and Abortion in Nineteenth-Century America* (Ithaca and London: Cornell University Press, 1994), p. 185.

9. Norman Himes, *Medical History of Contraception* (Baltimore: The Williams & Wilkins Company, 1936), pp. 276–278.

10. Brodie, *Contraception,* pp. 216–219.

11. John D'Emilio and Estelle Freedman, *Intimate Matters: A History of Sexuality in America* (Chicago and London: The University of Chicago Press, 1997), citing Foote to Gilder, Dec. 21, 1876, Mary Hallock Foote Papers, Special Collections, Green Library, Stanford University.

12. D'Emilio and Freedman, citing Elizabeth Hampsten, *Read This Only to Yourself: The Private Writings of Mid-Western Women, 1880–1910* (Bloomington: Indiana University Press, 1982), p. 104.

13. This is the opinion of Peter Gay, *The Bourgeois Experience: Victoria to Freud* (New York and Oxford: Oxford University Press, 1984), p. 258, as well as Brodie, D'Emilio and Freedman, and other historians of nineteenth-century sexuality.

14. Napheys, *Physical Life,* p. 91, and W. R. D. Blackwood, "The Prevention of Conception," *Medical and Surgical Reporter* 59 (1888), p. 396, as cited by Haller and Haller, *The Physician,* p. 123.

15. Eliza B. Duffey, *What Women Should Know: A Woman's Book About Women* (Philadelphia: J. M. Stoddart & Co., 1873), pp. 131–133. Reprinted by Arno Press, 1974.

16. Leslie J. Reagan, *When Abortion Was a Crime: Women, Medicine, and Law in the United States, 1867–1973* (Berkeley, Los Angeles, London: University of California Press, 1997), p. 8.

17. James C. Mohr, *Abortion in America: The Origins and Evolution of National Policy, 1800–1900* (New York: Oxford University Press, 1978), p. 6 and following.

18. Brodie, *Contraception,* p. 255.

19. Mohr, *Abortion,* p. 86.

20. Lawrence J. Friedman, *Crime and Punishment in American History* (New York: Basic Books, 1993), pp. 229–230.

21. Cited by Mohr, *Abortion,* p. 88.

22. Brodie, *Contraception,* p. 268.

23. Reagan, *When Abortion,* pp. 46–61.

24. Ibid., chapter 1, "An Open Secret."

25. Ibid., p. 20.

26. The discussion of Margaret Sanger and the birth control movement is based primarily on Ellen Chesler, *Woman of Valor: Margaret Sanger and the Birth Control Movement in America* (New York: Simon and Schuster, 1992).

27. D'Emilio and Freedman, *Intimate Matters,* p. 172.

28. Kate Chopin, *The Awakening* (New York: Avon Books, 1972), p. 16.

29. See Bram Dijkstra, *Evil Sisters* (New York: Knopf, 1996).

30. Katherine B. Davis, *Factors in the Sex Life of Twenty-two Hundred Women* (New York: Harper & Brothers, 1929).

31. Dr. G. V. Hamilton, *A Research in Marriage* (New York: Albert and Charles Boni, 1929).

32. Millard S. Everett, Ph.D., *The Hygiene of Marriage: A Detailed Consideration of Sex and Marriage* (New York: The Vanguard Press, 1932).

33. William Chafe, *The Paradox of Change: American Women in the 20th Century* (New York and Oxford: Oxford University Press, 1991), pp. 115–116.

34. D'Emilio and Freedman, *Intimate Matters,* p. 246.

35. Dr. Fred J. Taussig, "Abortion in Relation to Fetal and Maternal Welfare," *The American Journal of Obstetrics and Gynecology,* November and December 1931.

36. This paragraph and the following are based on Leslie J. Reagan, *When Abortion Was a Crime,* pp. 135–136.

37. For a discussion of early spokesmen for abortion, see Reagan, *When Abortion,* pp. 139–140.

38. Ibid., p. 151.

39. Ibid., p. 159.

NINE

1. Evelyn W. Guthrie, "Home Is Where You Hang Your Hat," unpublished manuscript in the Hoover Archives, Stanford University.

2. These and the following statistics are from William Chafe, *The Paradox of Change: American Women in the 20th Century* (New York and Oxford: Oxford University Press, 1991), pp. 130–131.

3. Finnegan Alford-Cooper, *For Keeps: Marriages That Last a Lifetime* (Armonk, New York, and London: M. E. Sharpe, 1998), p. 4.

4. Leila J. Rupp, *Mobilizing Women for War: German and American Propaganda, 1939–1945* (Princeton, New Jersey: Princeton University Press, 1978), pp. 141–142.

5. Rupp, *Mobilizing Women,* p. 138.

6. Chafe, *The Paradox,* p. 131.

7. Karen Anderson, *Wartime Women: Sex Roles, Family Relations, and the Status of Women During World War II* (Westport, Connecticut, and London: Greenwood Press, 1981), p. 5.

8. International Labour Office, *The War and Women's Employment: the Experience of the United Kingdom and the United States* (Montreal: ILO, 1946), p. 234.

9. William M. Tuttle, Jr., *"Daddy's Gone to War": The Second World War in the Lives of America's Children* (New York and Oxford: Oxford University Press, 1993), chapter 5.

10. Tuttle, *"Daddy's Gone to War,"* p. 84, and Chafe, *The Paradox,* pp. 144–145.

11. International Labour Office, *The War,* p. 279.

12. *Since You Went Away: World War II Letters from American Women on the Home Front,* ed. Judy Barrett Litoff and David C. Smith (New York and Oxford: Oxford University Press, 1991), p. 105.

13. Tuttle, *"Daddy's Gone to War,"* pp. 70–71.

14. Ibid., pp. 60–63.

15. Cited by Anderson, *Wartime Women,* p. 29.

16. Glenna Matthews, *"Just a Housewife": The Rise and Fall of Domesticity in America* (New York and Oxford: Oxford University Press, 1987), p. 267. See also Anderson, *Wartime Women,* pp. 7–9.

17. Alford-Cooper, *For Keeps,* p. 111.

18. Amy Kesselman, *Fleeting Opportunities: Women Shipyard Workers in Portland and Vancouver during World War II and Reconversion* (Albany: State University of New York Press, 1990), p. 29.

19. Kesselman, *Fleeting Opportunities,* pp. 1–2, 28.

20. Virginia Snow Wilkinson, "From Housewife to Shipfitter," *Harper's,* September, 1943, pp. 328–337.

21. Kesselman, *Fleeting Opportunities,* p. 6.

22. Mary Martha Thomas, *Riveting and Rationing in Dixie* (Tuscaloosa and London: University of Alabama Press, 1987), p. 43.

23. *Since You Went Away,* ed. Litoff and Smith, p. 147.

24. Kesselman, *Fleeting Opportunities,* pp. 42–43.

25. Anderson, *Wartime Women,* p. 37.

26. Thomas, *Riveting,* p. 6, and chapter 3.

27. Ibid., p. 60.

28. Anderson, *Wartime Women,* pp. 28–29.

29. Ibid., pp. 32–33.

30. Ibid., p. 34.

31. Gertrude Morris's story is told in Olga Gruhzit-Hoyt, *They Also Served: American Women in World War II* (New York: A Birch Lane Press Book, Carol Publishing Group, 1995), pp. 77–80.

32. *Since You Went Away,* ed. Litoff and Smith, p. 163.

33. Dorothy Barnes's story in Gruhzit-Hoyt, *They Also Served,* pp. 109–114.

34. *Dear Boys: World War II Letters from a Woman Back Home,* ed. Judy Barnett Litoff and David C. Smith (Jackson and London: University Press of Mississippi, 1991), p. 155.

35. Tuttle, *"Daddy's Gone to War,"* pp. 24–25.

36. *The Good Housekeeping Cookbook* (New York and Toronto: Farrar & Rinehart, Inc., 1942), preface.

37. Priscilla Robertson and Hawley Jones, "Housekeeping after the War," *Harper's Magazine,* April 1994, p. 430.

38. Tuttle, "*Daddy's Gone to War,*" pp. 65–66.

39. Natsuki Aruga, "Continuity during Change in World War II: Berkeley, California, as Seen through the Eyes of Children," Ph.D. dissertation, Stanford University, May 1996, p. 181.

40. Margaret Culkin Banning, *Women in Defense* (New York: Duell, Sloan and Pearce, 1942), pp. 142–146.

41. Banning, *Women in Defense,* p. 177.

42. *Since You Went Away,* ed. Litoff and Smith, p. 101.

43. Maybelle Hargrove, "Diary of a Volunteer Red Corps Worker in Dibble General Hospital, World War II," in the Papers of Mrs. Edsall Ford, in the Hoover Archives, Stanford University.

44. Elfrieda Berthiaume Shukert and Barbara Smith Subetta, *War Brides of World War II* (Novato, CA: Presidio Press, 1988), pp.1–2.

45. Alford-Cooper, *For Keeps,* p. 47.

46. Ibid., p. 46.

47. Steven Mintz and Susan Kellogg, *Domestic Revolutions* (New York: Free Press, 1988), p. 171.

48. Alford-Cooper, *For Keeps,* p. 108.

49. Ibid., p. 109.

50. Nell Giles, "What About the Women," *Ladies' Home Journal,* June 1944, pp. 22–23. Cited by Rupp, *Mobilizing Women,* p. 161.

51. Cited by Glenna Matthews, "*Just a Housewife,*" p. 208.

52. Ibid., p. 210.

53. William Chafe, *The Paradox,* pp. 175–176.

TEN

1. For information on cohabitation, see Pamela J. Smock's study from the Institute for Social Research at the University of Michigan, as reported by the *New York Times,* D8, February 15, 2000. For statistics on out-of-wedlock births, see Amara Bachu, "Trends in Marital Status of U.S. Women at First Birth: 1930 to 1994," U.S. Bureau of the Census, Population Division Working Paper No. 20, March, 1998. Between 1990 and 1994, 86 percent of African-American mothers, 55 percent of Hispanic women, and 46 percent of white women either conceived or gave birth without the benefits of holy matrimony. Forty-one percent of these women were not married at the time of their first baby's birth.

2. Alfred Kinsey, Wardell Pomeroy, and Clyde Martin, *Sexual Behavior in the Human Male* (Philadelphia and London: W. B. Saunders, 1948), and Alfred Kinsey, Wardell Pomeroy, Clyde Martin, and Paul Gebhard, *Sexual Behavior in the Human Female* (New York: W. B. Saunders, 1953).

3. Kinsey et al., *Sexual Behavior in the Human Female,* Pocket Book Edition, 1965, p. 358.

4. Ibid., p. 286.

5. Ibid., p. 364.

6. Ibid., pp. 11–12.

7. Millicent McIntosh, Ph.D., "I am concerned . . . ," in *An Analysis of the Kinsey*

Reports on Sexual Behavior in the Human Male and Female, ed. Donald Geddes (New York: Dutton, 1954), pp. 140–141.

8. Emily Mudd, Ph.D., "Implications for Marriage and Sexual Adjustment," in ibid., p. 137.

9. Stephanie Coontz, *The Way We Never Were* (New York: Basic Books, 1992), p. 26.

10. Talcott Parsons, "Age and Sex in the Social Structure of the United States," in *Essays in Sociological Theory* (Glencoe, Illinois: Free Press, 1949), p. 223.

11. Marilyn Yalom, *A History of the Breast* (New York: Knopf, 1997), p. 141.

12. Susan M. Hartmann, *The Home Front and Beyond: American Women in the 1940s* (Boston: Twayne Publishers, 1982), pp. 174–175.

13. Eugenia Kaledin, *Mothers and More: American Women in the 1950s* (Boston: Twayne Publishers, 1984), p. 27.

14. Assata Shakur, *Assata* (Chicago: Lawrence Hill Books, 1987), p. 37, as cited by Ruth Rosen, *The World Split Open: How the Modern Women's Movement Changed America* (New York: Viking, 2000), p. 44.

15. Hartmann, *The Home Front,* p. 168.

16. Letter to Martha Bernays, November 15, 1883, in *The Letters of Sigmund Freud* (New York: Basic Books, 1975), p. 28.

17. John Bowlby, *Maternal Care and Mental Health* (Geneva: World Health Organization, 1951).

18. Marilyn Yalom, *Maternity, Mortality, and the Literature of Madness* (University Park and London: Pennsylvania State University Press, 1985), chapter 2.

19. Joseph C. Reingold, M.D., Ph.D., *The Fear of Being a Woman: A Theory of Maternal Destructiveness* (New York and London: Grune & Stratton, 1964), pp. 421–422.

20. Toni Carabillo, Judith Meuli, June Bundy Csida, *Feminist Chronicles 1953–1993* (Los Angeles: Women's Graphics, 1993), p. 39.

21. Coontz, *The Way We Never Were,* pp. 35–37.

22. Ibid., p. 37.

23. Mirra Komarovsky, *Blue-Collar Marriage* (New Haven: Vintage, 1962), p. 49.

24. Chafe, *The Paradox,* p. 188.

25. Finnegan Alford-Cooper, *For Keeps: Marriages That Last a Lifetime* (Armonk, New York, and London: M. E. Sharpe, 1998), p. 113.

26. Alford-Cooper, *For Keeps,* pp. 113–114.

27. Robert O. Blood and Donald Wolfe, *Husbands and Wives* (Glencoe, Illinois: The Free Press, 1960).

28. See Glenna Matthews, *"Just a Housewife": The Rise and Fall of Domesticity in America* (New York and Oxford: Oxford University Press, 1987).

29. Studs Terkel, *Working: People Talk About What They Do All Day and How They Feel About What They Do* (New York: Pantheon Books, 1974), p. 301.

30. Carabillo, Meuli, Csida, *Feminist Chronicles,* p. 48.

31. Ibid., p. 50.

32. Cartoon reproduced in *Newsweek,* December 20, 1999, p. 72.

33. Kingsley Davis, "Wives and Work: A Theory of the Sex-Role Revolution and Its Consequences," in *Feminism, Children, and the New Families,* ed. Sanford M. Dornbusch and Myra H. Strober (New York: Guilford Publications, Inc., 1988), p. 68; and Myra H. Strober and Agnes Miling Kaneko Chan, *The Road Winds Uphill All the Way: Gender*

Work and Family in the United States and Japan (Cambridge, Massachusetts, and London: MIT Press, 1999), p. xiv.

34. Chafe, *The Paradox,* p. 212.

35. This section is indebted to Rosen, *The World Split Open,* pp. 152–155.

36. William H. Masters and Virginia E. Johnson, *Human Sexual Response* (Boston: Little, Brown, 1966), and Masters and Johnson, *Human Sexual Inadequacy* (Boston: Little, Brown, 1970).

37. Marilyn Yalom, Wenda Brewster, and Suzanne Estler (1981), "Women of the Fifties: Their Past Sexual Experiences and Current Sexual Attitudes in the Context of Mother/Daughter Relationships," *Sex Roles: A Journal of Research* 7 (9), pp. 877–888. See also Marilyn Yalom, Suzanne Estler, and Wenda Brewster (1982), "Changes in Female Sexuality: A Study of Mother/Daughter Communication and Generational Differences." *Psychology of Women Quarterly* 7 (2), pp. 141–154.

38. Linda Wolfe, *Women and Sex in the 80s: The Cosmo Report* (Toronto, New York, London, Sydney: Bantam Books, 1982).

39. Myra H. Strober, "Two-Earner Families," and Davis, "Wives and Work," in *Feminism,* ed. Dornbusch and Strober, pp. 161 and 68.

40. Rhona Rapoport and Robert Rapoport, "The Dual Career Family," *Human Relations* 22, 1969, pp. 3–30. See also *Dual-Career Couples,* ed. Fran Pepitone-Rockwell (Beverly Hills and London: Sage Publications, 1980), pp. 14–15.

41. See appendix to Arlie Hochschild, *The Second Shift: Working Parents and the Revolution at Home* (New York: Avon, 1989), pp. 271–278.

42. Dana Vannoy-Hiller and William W. Philliber, *Equal Partners: Successful Women in Marriage* (Newbury Park, London, New Delhi: Sage Publications, 1989), p. 107.

43. Frances K. Goldschneider and Linda J. Waite, *New Families, No Families?* (Berkeley: University of California Press, 1991), p. 129.

44. Strober and Chan, *The Road,* p. 205.

45. Ruthellen Josselson, *Revising Herself: The Story of Women's Identity from College to Midlife* (New York and Oxford: Oxford University Press, 1996), pp. 200–202.

46. Strober and Chan, *The Road,* pp. 94 and 103.

47. Ibid., pp. 98–99.

48. Ibid., p. 101.

49. Ibid., p. 222.

50. Stephanie Coontz, *The Way We Really Are* (New York: Basic Books, 1997), p. 58.

51. Rosanna Hertz, *More Equal than Others: Women and Men in Dual-Career Marriages* (Berkeley, Los Angeles, London: University of California Press), 1986, p. 101.

52. Strober and Chan, *The Road,* p. 87.

53. David Elkind, *Ties That Stress: The New Family Imbalance* (Cambridge, Massachusetts, and London: Cambridge University Press, 1994), p. 51.

54. *Wellesley,* Winter 2000, p. 25.

55. Cynthia Fuchs Epstein, *Woman's Place: Options and Limits in Professional Careers* (Berkeley, Los Angeles, London: University of California Press, 1971), p. 57.

56. Vannoy-Hiller and Philliber, *Equal Partners,* pp. 16–17.

57. Susan Faludi, *Backlash: the Undeclared War Against American Women* (New York: Crown Publishers, Inc., 1992).

58. Rosen, *The World Split Open,* p. xv.

59. See, for example, Komarovsky, *Blue-Collar Marriage,* pp. 94–111.

60. Janice M. Steil, *Marital Equality: Its Relationship to the Well-Being of Husbands and Wives* (Thousand Oaks, London, New Delhi: Sage Publications, 1997), p. xix. See also differences in his and her appraisals of marriage in Alford-Cooper, *For Keeps,* p. 107.

61. Faludi, *Backlash,* pp. 17, 36–37.

62. Richard R. Peterson, "A Re-Evaluation of the Economic Consequences of Divorce," *American Sociological Review,* Vol. 61, No. 3, June 1996, pp. 528–536.

63. Susan Straight, "One Drip at a Time," in *Mothers Who Think: Tales of Real-Live Parenthood,* ed. Camille Peri and Kate Moses (New York: Villard Books, 1999), pp. 50, 51, 55. For a sensitive appraisal of divorce in America, see Barbara Defoe Whitehead, *The Divorce Culture: Rethinking Our Commitments to Marriage and Family* (New York: Vintage Books, 1998).

64. Faludi, *Backlash,* p. 16.

65. *Boston Globe,* May 13, 2000, A19, citing the work of economist Jane Waldfogel of Columbia University.

66. Henry A. Walker, "Black-White Differences in Marriage and Family Patterns," in *Feminism,* ed. Dornbusch and Strober, pp. 87–112.

67. Margaret L. Usdansky, "Numbers Show Families Growing Closer as They Pull Apart," *New York Times,* March 8, 2000, D10.

68. Walker, "Black-White Differences," in *Feminism,* ed. Dornbusch and Strober, pp. 92–93.

69. Peggy Orenstein, *Flux: Women on Sex, Work, Kids, Love, and Life in a Half-Changed World* (New York: Doubleday, 2000), p. 39.

70. This paragraph draws from Susan Turk Charles and Laura L. Carstensen, "Marriage in Old Age," in *Inside the American Couple,* ed. Marilyn Yalom and Laura Carstensen (Berkeley: University of California Press, forthcoming).

CREDITS AND PERMISSIONS

PHOTOGRAPHIC CREDITS

Adam and Eve by Lucas Cranach, the Elder. Norton Simon Art Foundation, Pasadena, California.

Italian Ketubah, 1752. Musée de l'Art et de l'Histoire Judaïque, Paris. Photo RMN.

Grave Stela, circa 400 B.C.E. J. Paul Getty Museum, Los Angeles.

Wall painting from Pompei, before 79 C.E. Museo Archeologico Nazionale, Naples.

Fragment of the Roman sarcophagus of M. Cornelius Status. Louvre, Paris.

Da Costa Book of Hours, the month of April, 1515. Pierpoint Morgan Library, New York.

Liber Feudorum Maior, Donación de Bernat Ató a Gausfred III. Late twelfth century. Archivo Corona Aragón, Barcelona.

Marriage of Saint Godelieve, central panel. Master of the Saint Godelieve Legend, fourth quarter of the fifteenth century. Metropolitan Museum of Art, New York, John Stewart Kennedy Fund, 12.79.

Jewish wedding ring. Fourteenth-century Alsace (Colmar). Musée du Moyen Age, Cluny, on loan to the Musée de l'Art et de l'Histoire Judaïque, Paris. Photo RMN.

Page from "Der Jungfrauspiegel," Rheinisches Landesmuseum, Bonn.

Italian game board, circa 1410. Courtesy of the Fogg Museum, Harvard University Art Museums, Henry W. Bliss Fund, 1925:8.

Israhel van Meckenem, *The Organ Player and his Wife*, circa 1495–1503. National Gallery of Art, Washington, D. C.

Katharina von Bora by Lucas Cranach the Elder. Nationalmuseum med Prins Eugens Waldemarsudde, Stockholm.

Wife accompanying husband for a tooth extraction. Pen drawing from a chess manual, 1467. Württembergische Landesbibliothek, Stuttgart. Reproduced from Erika Uitz, *The Legend of Good Women*, Mount Kisco, NY: Moyer Bell Ltd.

Wives of Henry VIII. British engraving, 1796. Fine Arts Museums of San Francisco, Achenbach Foundation for Graphic Arts, 1963.30.21327.

A New Yeare's Gift for Shrewes by Thomas Cecil, circa 1625–1640. British Museum, London.

American oak cradle. 1625–1675. Metropolitan Museum of Art, Gift of Mrs. Russell Sage, 1909.

Pocahontas. Engraving by Simon van de Passe, 1616. National Portrait Gallery, Washington, D. C.

Abigail Adams. Pastel portrait by Benjamin Blyth, circa 1766. Courtesy of the Massachusetts Historical Society.

Portrait of Chief Justice and Mrs. Oliver Ellsworth by Ralph Earl (1751–1801). Wadsworth Atheneum, Hartford. Gift of the Ellsworth Heirs.

Lavoisier and his Wife by Jacques Louis David. Metropolitan Museum of Art, New York.

"Declaration of the rights of man and citizen." Engraving by Niquet le Jeune, 1789. Musée Carnavalet, Paris.

The Long Engagement by Arthur Hughes, 1859. Birmingham City Museums and Art Gallery.

Elizabeth Cady Stanton and daughter. Photo courtesy of Elizabeth Cady Stanton Trust.

"Purity," *Godey's Lady's Book*, July 1850. Courtesy of Department of Special Collections, Stanford University Libraries.

Marriage certificate, Currier lithograph, 1848. Fine Arts Museums of San Francisco, Achenbach Foundation for Graphic Arts, Gift of Anne Hoopes in memory of Edgar M. Hoopes III, 1989.1.106.

Elderly black couple. Photo by Frances Benjamin Johnston, 1899. Library of Congress, Washington, D. C. From the American History CD-Rom.

Gold rush cartoon signed Manning, published by Park Row, New York, circa 1849. California Historical Society, San Francisco, FN-28824.

"Home and the Homeless," *Godey's Lady's Book*, May, 1859. Courtesy of Department of Special Collections, Stanford University Libraries.

Spanish colonial family, circa 1800. Mission San Diego de Alcala Museum. Copyright Kathleen Cohen.

Mary Carpenter Pickering Bell Quilt, circa 1855. Smithsonian Institution, Washington, D. C.

Charles Wilson Adams and Maria Abagail Henry Adams. Daguerreotype. California Historical Society, San Francisco, FN-25741.

Modern Marriage—*Moderne Ehe*, 1900. Photo Irenco Robert Bier AB, Stockholm.

"The Age of Iron," Currier and Ives lithograph, 1869. Library of Congress, Washington, D. C.

Daughters of the American Revolution, April 19, 1903. Photo by Frances Benjamin Johnston. Library of Congress, Washington, D. C. From the American History CD-Rom.

"Domestic Sewing Machine," circa 1882. Lithograph signed W. J. Morgan & Company, Cleveland. Library of Congress, Washington, D. C.

Depression couple. Photo by Walker Evans, 1935. Library of Congress, Washington, D. C. From the American History CD-Rom.

Contraceptive caps, circa 1925. Wellcome Medical Library, London.

"Should Your Wife Take a War Job?" World War II poster. Hoover Institution, Stanford University.

Palmolive soap advertisement, World War II.

Home canning poster, World War II. Hoover Institution, Stanford University.

Japanese "war bride," February 10, 1951. Library of Congress, Washington, D. C.

Fifties June bride. Private collection.

Gibson Ultra 600 Electric Range. Quantity Postcards, San Francisco.
ERA YES. Kate Palmer, 1982. By permission of the cartoonist.
New parents with twin girls. Photo Reid Yalom, 2000.

TEXT CREDITS

"Dear Abby" column by Abigail Van Buren. Copyright 1998 Universal Press Syndicate. Reprinted with permission. All rights reserved.

Norman R. Shapiro, *The Comedy of Eros*, 2nd edition (Urbana and Chicago: University of Illinois Press, 1997).

The Book of Margery Kempe, translated by B. A. Windeatt (Penguin Classics, 1965), copyright B. A. Windeatt, 1965.

Gene Bruckner, *Giovanni and Lusanna: Love and Marriage in Renaissance Florence* (Berkeley, California: University of California Press, 1986). Permission granted by the Regents of the University of California and the University of California Press.

Elizabeth Cady Stanton, *Eighty Years and More: Reminiscences 1815–1897* (New York: Schocken Books, 1971 [1898]).

The American Slave, ed. George P. Rawick (Westport, Connecticut: Greenwood Publishing Group, Inc., 1972), vols. 4 and 5.

Mollie Sanford, *Mollie: The Journal of Mollie Dorsey Sanford* (Lincoln, Nebraska: University of Nebraska Press, 1959).

James Henry Gleason, *Beloved Sister: The Letters of James Henry Gleason, 1841–1859* (Glendale, CA: The Arthur H. Clark Co., 1978).

Susan G. Butruille, *Women's Voices from the Oregon Trail* (Boise, Idaho: Tamarack Books, 1995).

Lydia A. Rudd, "Notes by the Wayside en Route to Oregon," Lilly Library, Indiana University, Bloomington, IN.

The Late-Victorian Marriage Question, ed. Ann Heilmann (London: Routledge/Thoemmes Press, 1998), 5 vols.

Victoria Jeans Laas, *Love and Power in the Nineteenth Century: The Marriage of Violet Blair* (Fayetteville: The University of Arkansas Press, 1998).

Mrs. Maybell Hargrove, Unpublished diary, in Mrs. Edsel P. Ford Collection, Hoover Institution Archives, Stanford University.

Dear Boys: World War II Letters from a Woman Back Home, ed. Judy Barnett Litoff and Davie C. Smith (Jackson and London: University Press of Mississippi, 1991).

Since You Went Away: World War II Letters from American Women on the Home Front, 1991, edited by Judy Barnett Litoff and David C. Smith. Used by permission of Oxford University Press, Inc.

Linda Wolfe, *Women and Sex in the 80s: The Cosmo Report* (New York: Arbor House, 1981). (Bantam paperback, 1982.)

INDEX

Abbott, Mrs. Lyman, 286–87
Abelard, 60–65, 69
Abimelech, King, 7
abortion, 302–4
   Depression era America,
      314–16
   Roe v. Wade, 373
Abraham, 7–8
abuse, 23, 111
   in Colonial America, 148
   in the late twentieth
      century, 363–64
   legal permission for, 46
   in medieval Europe,
      45–47
   runaway wives, 150–51
   See also rape
Abuse of Maternity (Evans),
   295
Acton, William, 182, 204–5
Adam, 1, **2**, 3, 58
Adam and Eve (Cranach, the
   elder),**2**
Adams, Abigail, 151–56,
   152, 158
Adams, Betsy, 158
Adams, Charles Wilson, 251,
   252,**254**
Adams, John, 151–56, 158
Adams, Maria Abagail Henry,
   251–52, **254**
Adams, Samuel, 158
adultery
   in ancient Greece, 22–23
   in Biblical times, 12
   Christianity and, 12–13
   in medieval Europe,
      65–66, 91–92
   in Puritan New England,
      134–35
   in Roman times, 31–32
   in Tudor and Stuart
      England, 120–21
   unfaithfulness, 399–400
advertising and a wife's
   image, 359, **360**, 361

advice (and conduct)
   literature
   in the antebellum South,
      204
   in Colonial America, 148
   in the late twentieth
      century, 358
   in medieval Europe, 67–68
   in Tudor and Stuart
      England, 110–11, 122
   in the Victorian era, 180,
      181–83,195
   women's magazines, 286,
      364, 372, 392–93
   See also literature and
      women
Advice on Love (Fournival), 68
Advice to Ladies (Bolis), 68
Aeschylus, 19
affection, displays of, 32–33
African Americans
   antimiscegenation laws,
      142, 144, 193
   black women and the
      marriage market, 397
   Depression era abortions,
      314
   and marriage, 142, 144,
      224
   and World War II, 330,
      331–33, 343
   See also slavery
Agamemnon, 10, 19
Age of Iron (Currier and Ives),
   266, 267–68
Albert, Prince, 183
Alexander III, Pope, 52
Alltagsleben (Van Meckenem),
   95
America
   antebellum South, 203–25
   Colonial period, 146–51
   Depression era couple, **312**
   early history, women's
      position in, 140–41
   marital laws, 189–91

Puritan New England,
      126–45
   the Revolutionary War,
      158–61
   Western frontier, 226–62
   the Woman Question in,
      280–93
   women in the population,
      141–42, 144–45
   World War II, 317–51
   Victorian era, 191–203
American Association of
   College Women, 344
American Birth Control
   League, 313
*American Journal of Obstetrics
   and Gynecology*
   (Taussig), 314
American Medical
   Association, 303
American Red Cross, 344–45,
   345–48
Amores (Ovid), 28
Amsdorf, Dr., 102
Anderson, Sarah, 208
Angelo of Foligno, 80
Anna Karenina (Tolstoy), 277
antebellum South, 203–25
   antimiscegenation laws,
      142, 144, 193
   slavery, 192, 208, 210,
      210–14, 214–23
   slavery, opposition to,
      223
   women, expectations of,
      205–6
   women, population of,
      205
Anthony, Mark, 30, 35–37
Anthony, Susan B., 190, 194,
   195
"Antinomian controversy,"
   135–36
Antoinette, Marie, 165
Antonio, 88
Apollodorus, 22

Aristophanes, 20, 24
Aristotle, 22, 24
Arnolfini and His Wife (van
    Eyck), 94
Arnoud, 52
Artemis, 21
Ashmore, Ruth, 286
Ashton, James, 299
Asini, Fra Felice, 89
Astrolabe, 62
Augustine, Saint, 15, 57
Augustus (Octavius), 30, 31,
    35, 36, 37–38
Austen, Jane, 180, 183
Austin, John, 178–80
Austin, Sarah Taylor, 178–80,
    181
Awakening, The (Chopin),
    308

Baby and Child Care (Spock),
    358
Ballou, Mary, 246–52
Balzac, Honoré de, 276
Bancroft, Mrs. Hubert Howe,
    257
Barton, Clara, 344
Bashkirtseff, Marie, 265
Bazaar-Book of Decorum, 199
Beauvoir, Simone de,
    362–63, 369, 387
Beecher, Catherine, 195
Beethoven, Ludwig van, 174
Beeton, Mrs., 181, 183
"Before the birth of one of her
    Children" (Bradstreet),
    129–30
Belknap, George, 238
Belknap, Jessie (son), 238
Belknap, Kitturah (Kit)
    Penton, 238
Bell, John Bruce, 251
Bell, Virginia, 216
Bell Jar, The (Plath), 361
Bendy, Edgar, 224
Bening, Simon, 48
Bernard, Jessie, 394
Berry, Fanny, 220
betrothal
    ancient Greece, 21
    Roman times, 27
Better Homes and Gardens,
    323, 363
Beverley, Charlotte, 219
biblical times, 1–16
    Abraham and Sarah, 7–8
    Adam and Eve, 1, **2**, 3, 58
    Elkanah and Hannah, 6–7

Jacob and Rachel, 8–9
Job, 10
    Mary and Joseph, 11
bicycles and women's
    liberation,
    285–86
bigamy, 89–91
birth control, 70, 297, 305–7
    in the antebellum South,
    212
    condoms, 300
    diaphragms, 300
    Margaret Sanger, 304–6
    rhythm method, 307
    See also abortion;
        contraception
bisexuality, 22. *Ses also*
    lesbianism;
    homosexuality
Bjørnson, Bjønstjerne, 265
Blackstone, William, 185
Blackwell, Antoinette Brown,
    175
Blackwood, W. R. D., 301
Blair, Sarah Harrison, 142
Blinn, Odelia, 304
Bloomer, Amelia Jenks, 198
Blyth, Benjamin, 152
Boatwright, Eleanor Miot, 205
Boccaccio, 83
Bodichon, Barbara Leigh
    Smith, 187, 189
Bolis, Robert de, 68
Book of Household Management
    (Beeton), 181
Book of Margery Kempe, The,
    77–81
Book of Nature (Ashton), 299
*Book of the Knight of La Tour-
    Landry, The,* 76
Bora, Katherina von, 98,
    100–5, **101**
Bost, Sophie, 226, 230
Bost, Theodore, 226, 230
Boston Evening Post, 159
Boston Women's Health
    Collective, 372
Boswell, John, 40
Bowlby, John, 361
Bracton, Henry de, 46
Bradstreet, Anne, 126–34,
    145
Bradstreet, Samuel (son), 132
Bradstreet, Simon (husband),
    126
Bradstreet, Simon (son), 128,
    132
Brasher, Helena Kortwright,
    161

breast-feeding, 128–29
Bremer, Frederika, 264, 265
Bride's Bush, A (Whateley),
    122
"Bridegroomes Comming,
    The" (Donne), 122
Bridget of Sweden, Saint, 80
*Brief Summary in Plain
    Language, of the Most
    Important Laws
    concerning Women, A*
    (Bodichon), 187
Brontë, Charlotte, 184
Browning, Elizabeth, 187
Brucker, Gene, 87
Bryan, Maria, 206–7
Buckingham, J. S., 191
Bumpas, Fanny Moore Webb,
    223
Burnap, George, 194
Burras, Anne, 141
Burton, Richard, 358
Butler, Pierce Butler, 221,
    222
Butzer, Elisabeth, 106–7
Butzer, Nathanael, 106–7

Caesar, Julius, 35
Caesarion, 35
Caird, Mona, 268–70, 276
Calpurnia, 38–39
Calvin, John, 133
Comfort, Alex, 372
Canterbury Tales (Chaucer),
    45, 53, 75
Cantwell, John, 151
Cantwell, Sarah, 151
Capellanus, Andreas, 67
Capito, Wolfgang Fabricius,
    106
Carlson, Eric, 111
Carter, Cato, 217
Cary, Virginia Randolph, 204
Casti Conubii (Pius X), 307
Castel, Etienne de, 81
Catherine of Aragon, 108
Catholicism
    and birth control, 307, 370
    church weddings, 52–55,
        53
    and clerical marriage,
        58–60
    monasticism, 15
    See also Protestantism
Caton, Mrs. W. B., 228
Catullus, 29, 31
Cawnt, Elizabeth, 113
Cell newspaper, 305

Center for Research on Women (Institute for Research on Women and Gender), 374
Chafe, William, 322, 351
Champagne, Marie de, 67
Chan, Agnes, 384, 387
Charles I, 127
Charles V, 81
chastity
  in medieval Europe, 79–80
  in Roman times, 25, 27
Châtelet, Madame du, 162
Chaucer, Geoffrey, 45, 53, 75
chess, religious opposition to, 69–70
Chicago Times, 303, 304
Child, Lydia Maria, 183, 212
childbirth (and care)
  in the antebellum South, 212–14
  barrenness, 128
  breast-feeding, 128–29
  in Colonial America, 150
  cradle, **129**
  death and, 129–30, 136–37
  infant packs, 382–83, **382**
  in the late twentieth century, 353–54, 358, 367, 389–90
  longevity of women and, 389–90
  in medieval Europe, 70–73, **72**
  out of wedlock, 177
  single mothers, 398
  in the Victorian era, 199
  on the Western frontier, 230, 256
  in World War II, 338
childlessness, 398
Chopin, Kate, 308
Chrétien de Troyes, 66
Christianity
  and adultery, 12–13
  banns, 53–53
  conceptions of marriage, 14–15
  hierarchy of womanhood, 58, **59**, 60
  See also Catholicism; Protestantism
Christina of Markyate, 51
Christine de Pizan, 81–82
Chrysostome, Saint John, 57
Church of England, 108
Cicero, 31

City of Women, The (Christine de Pizan), 81
Clark, Anne, 220
Cleopatra, 35–37
Clinton, Bill, 167, 391–92
Clinton, Hillary Rodham, 167, 391–92
clitorodectomy, 41–42
Clodia, 31
Clytemnestra, 10
Cochrane, Cecilia Maria, 186
Cohen Falcon, Hakkym ben Jehiel, 92–93
Collet, Camilla, 264
Collins, Frances, 304
Collins, William, 150–51
Commentaries on the Laws of England (Blackstone), 185
Common Sense Book of Baby Care (Spock), 358
Comstock, Anthony, 300, 305
condoms, 300
Condorcet, Madame, 162
Condorcet, Marquis de, 165
"Conservative Woman, The" (Ashmore), 286
contraception, 70, 297–98, 298–301
  cervical caps, **314**
  in Depression era America, 313–14
  diaphragms, 300, 301
  oral contraception, 363
  in Roman times, 30
  See also abortions; birth control; suppositories
Coontz, Stephanie, 363, 386
Cornelia, 33, 34
Cornelia Tyche, 39
Cosmo Report, 375–79
Cosmopolitan magazine, 375
Cotton, John, 136, 144–45
Council of Trent, 46
couples, artistic depictions of, 94–95, **96**
courtship and engagement
  in the antebellum South, 206–7, 208
  bride's quilts, 208, 251, **253**
  The Long Engagement (Hughes), **179**
  in medieval Europe, 51
  in Native Americans, 233–34
  in Roman times, 28

in Tudor England, 112–14
in Victorian England, 178–80
Cranach, Lucas, the elder, 2, 101
Cranmer, Archbishop, 107
Crosby, Hannah, 258
Cross, Marie Bywater, 251
Crow, Polly, 329

"Daddy's Gone to War" (Tuttle), 323
Daily Telegraph
  letters to, 268, 270–75
Danton, Georges, 166
Dati, Gregorio, 84
Daughters of the American Revolution, **284**, 343
Daumier, Honoré, 383
David, Jacques Louis, 162, **163**
Davis, Hugh, 144
Davis, Katherine Bement, 309–10
Day, Doris, 358
"Dear Boys" column (Somerville), 336–38
Debay, Auguste, 182
"Declaration of the Rights of Women and the Female Citizen" (de Gouges), 164
Degler, Carl, 216, 297
D'Emilio, John, 301, 313
d'Épinay, Madame, 162
Detrick, Carrie Lassell, 227–28
Dialects of Sex (Firestone), 371
Diana (slave), 220
diaphragms, 300
Dick-Read, Grantly, 358
Dickens, Charles, 180
Dickerman, Elizabeth, 138
Dickinson, Emily, 134, 175
Dickson, Rosa, 326–27
distaff and spindle, 29
divorce
  after World War II, 350
  in ancient Greece, 22, 23
  in Biblical times, 4–6
  and the Jewish culture, 92–93
  in the late twentieth century, 353–54, 395–96, 399
  and the Mormons, 257

divorce (*continued*)
    in Puritan New England,
        135
    in Roman times, 30–31
    serial marriages, 396–97
    in the Victorian era,
        186–87, 187–88, 286
Dixon, Helen, 121
Dod, John, 126
Doll's House (Ibsen), 263–64
Donne, John, 122
"Donors Engelbrechts and his
    wife" (painting), 94
Dorothea of Montau, 80–81
Doryphorus, 40
dowries
    in Biblical times, 4, 5
    in medieval Europe, 47,
        50–52, 82–88
    in the late Victorian era,
        265
Ducis, Jean François, 162, 164
ducking stools, 205
Dudley, Dorothy, 127,
    133–34
Dudley, Mary Winthrop, 138
Dudley, Thomas, 127, 134
Duffey, Eliza, 301
Duplay, Elisabeth, 167–68

Earl, Ralph, **157**
Easton, Elizabeth, 111
Eck, Mrs., 351
Edmondston, Catherine, 204
education (of women), 172
    in the antebellum South,
        204
    in late twentieth century,
        388
    in medieval Europe, 73
    in Puritan New England,
        131–32
    in Stuart England, 126
    in Victorian era, 195, 285
    on the Western frontier,
        259–60, 261–62
*Eighty Years and More:
    Reminiscences
    1815–1897* (Stanton),
    196
Eisenhower, Mamie, 363
Elkanah, 6–7
Ellis, Havelock, 306, 308
Ellis, Sarah Stickney, 182,
    183
Ellsworth, Oliver and Mrs.,
    157
Émile (Rousseau), 147

Emma (Austen), 183
employment
    in medieval Europe,
        73–74
    in postwar waives,
        348–51
    Rosie the Riveter, 322
    shipbuilding wives,
        326–30
    at the turn-of-the-century,
        292–93
    in Victorian America,
        288–91
    volunteerism as, 342–48,
        365–66
    in World War II, 317–20,
        320–26
    See also housework
employment (work
    revolution), 380–91
    dual-earner couples,
        380–81, 385–87
    househusbands, 381–83
    husbands, working
        mother's effects on, 384
    the marriage market,
        396–97
    maternal leave, 385–86
    opposition, 390–91
    women, longevity of,
        389–90
    women, lower earning
        power of, 389–90
engagement. *See* courtship
    and engagement
England
    marital laws, 185–89
    Married Women's Property
        Act, 188–89, 227
    New Woman in, 268–70
    Tudor and Stuart period,
        108–25
    the Victorian era, 177–85
Equal Rights Amendment
    (ERA), 363, 370–71,
    371, 390
"Equality of Persons"
    (Donne), 122
Eratosthenes, 23
Eroticus (Plutarch), 42
Euphiletos, 23
*European Feminism,
    1700–1950* (Offen), 164
Evans, Elizabeth, 295
Eve, 1, **2**, 58
    as the "bad" wife, 18, 182
    as an improvement, 3
    and the "taint" of sexuality,
        15

Eve (Norris), 14
Everett, Millard, 311

*Factors in the Sex Lives of
    Twenty two Hundred
    Women* (Davis), 309
Faludi, Susan, 390
Family and Medical Leave
    Act of 1993, 385–86
Family Circle, 387
Faragher, John, 260
Father Knows Best, 358–59
*Father's Legacy to his Daughter,
    A* (Gregory), 148
Fear of Flying (Jong), 372
Federation of Women's Clubs,
    344
Felicie, Jacoba, 74
Fellows, Elvina Apperson,
    240–41
Female Eunuch (Greer), 372
female sexuality
    early Christian teachers
        and, 15
    in the Victorian era,
        294–98
    See also abortion; birth
        control
Feminine Mystique, The
    (Friedan), 201, 369
feminism (and the feminist
    movement), 190
    Age of Enlightenment and,
        164–65
    and Eve, 3
    opposition to, 266–68,
        357, 370, 390–91
    Seneca Falls Declaration,
        190, 202
    suffrage, 193–94
    support of, 265–66
    in the Victorian era, 189,
        265–66
    literature, 372–73
Fidelio (Beethoven), 174
Fields, Annie, 280
Fifteen Joys of Marriage, 76
Firestone, Shulamith, 371
Fitzhugh, George, 203–4
Flaubert, Gustave, 276–77
Flint, Mrs. (slave owner),
    220–21
Floyd, Major, 206–7
Flux (Orenstein), 399
Foote, Edward B., 295,
    300
Foote, Mary Hallock, 301
Forrest, Mistress, 141

Forrest, Thomas, 141
4–H Clubs, 344
Fournival, Richard de, 68
France
    Civil Code of 1804, 172
    "Declaration of the Right of
        Man and the Citizen,"
        164, **173**
    the Revolution, 161–71
    women under the
        Republic, 171–74
Frederick, Elektor, 102
Frederick II, 12, 52
Freedman, Estelle, 301, 313
Freud, Sigmund, 308, 361
Friedan, Betty, 201, 369
Friedman, Lawrence M.,
    303
"From Housewife to Ship-
    fitter" (Wilkinson),
    327
Frontrunner magazine, 291
*Fruits of Philosophy; or, The
    Private Companion of
    Young Married People*
    (Knowlton), 299
Fulbert, 61–62, 62, 63
Fulvia, 35
Future of Marriage, The
    (Bernard), 394

Gabber, Josephine, 315
Gallop, Hannah, 132
Galloway, Grace Growden,
    161
Garcia, Andrew, 235
Gaskell, Elizabeth, 187
Gelles, Edith, 151, 153, 173
Generation of Vipers (Wylie),
    362
"Geneva Bible," 133
Gift, Theo, 175
Gilder, Helena, 301
Giles, Nell, 350–51
Gillis, John, 145
Gilman, Charlotte Perkins,
    288–91, 291–93,
    387
Gilman, George Houghton,
    291
Giovanni, 88–92
Gissing, George, 277–79
Glatz, Kaspar, 102
Gleason, Catarina Watson,
    250–51
Gleason, James Henry,
    250–51
Godelieve, Saint, **53**

*Godlie Forme of Household
    Government: For the
    Ordering of Private
    Families, according to the
    direction of God's Word, A*
    (Dod), 97, 126
Godey's Lady's Book, 195, **209**,
    248
"Goodbye and Good Luck"
    (Paley), 352
Good Housekeeping Cookbook,
    339
Good Housekeeping magazine,
    286, 393
Good Wives (Ulrich), 138
Gouge, William, 110–11
Gouges, Olympe de, 164
Graeme, Elizabeth, 160–61
Graeme, Henry, 160–61
Grand, Sarah, 276
Grandchamp, Sophie, 165
Greek times, 16–25
    Agamemnon and
        Clytemnestra, 10, 19
    Jason and Medea, 19
    Odysseus and Penelope,
        16–19
    Oedipus and Jocasta, 19
Greer, Germaine, 372
Greg, W. R., 182
Gregory, John, 148
Griffitts, Hannah, 158
Grimké, Sarah, 194
Guinevere, 66
Guthrie, Evelyn, 317–20, 344
Gutman, Herbert, 218

Hafen, John, 255
Hafen, Mary Ann, 255–56
Hagar, 7
Hale, Sarah Josepha, 195,
    209
Hall, Radclyffe, 308
Hamilton, Cicely, 292
Hamilton, Gilbert, 309–10
handfasting, 112–13
Hannah, 6–7
Hardy, Thomas, 277
Hargrove, Maybelle, 346
Harper's Magazine, 342, 348
Harris, John, 138
Hartog, Hendrik, 191
Haskell, Ella (daughter), 247
Haskell, Rachell, 247–49
Hawkins, Jane, 128
Hayden, Mary Jane, 228
Haywire, Joan, 123
Helen of Troy, 18

Héloïse, 60–65, 69, 91
Hemingway, Ernest, 16, 362
Henderson, David, 217
Henry VIII, 108
Hepburn, Katharine, 358
Hera, 16, 21
Higgins, Michael, 304
Hill, Master (slave owner),
    217
History of Rome (Livy), 25
Hite Report, 373
Hobby, Oveta Culp, 334
Hoby, Margaret Dakins,
    124–25
Hoby, Thomas, 124, 125
Hollick, Frederick, 299
Holman, Eliza, 175
Homemakers' Clubs, 344
Homer, 16, 21–22, 29
homosexuality
    in ancient Greece, 23–24
    in Biblical times, 13
    marriage alternatives, 398
    in Roman times, 40–41
Hopkins, Anne Yale, 131
Hopkins, Edward, 131
Hopkins, Sarah
    Winnemucca, 233
Horney, Karen, 361
househusbands, 381–83
housework (and chores), **48**
    in antebellum South, 208,
        210, 210–12
    in Colonial America,
        148–50
    domestic life, **248**
    in the late twentieth
        Century, 364–69
    in medieval Europe, 74
    on the Oregon Trail,
        238–39
    philanthropy, 181
    in Puritan New England,
        137–38, 138–40
    servants, 137–38
    in the Victorian era, 181,
        183, 192, 288–91
    on the Western frontier,
        229–30, 256–57,
        259–60
    during World War II, 324,
        336–38, 339–43
    See also employment
Hubbard, Robert, 113
Hughes, Arthur, 179
Human Comedy (Balzac), 276
Huntingdon, Countless, 124
Husbands and Wives (study),
    366–67

Hutchinson, Anne, 135–36
Hygiene of Marriage, The
(Everett), 311
"Hymn to Aphrodite"
(Sappho), 24–25

I Love Lucy, 359
Ibsen, Henrik, 263–64, 265
Iliad (Homer), 21–22
"In Praise of Marriage"
(Christine de Pizan),
81
*Incidents in the Life of a Slave
Girl* (Child), 212
Indiana (Sand), 276
Intimate Matters
(D'Emilio/Freedman),
301
Isaac, 7, 8
Ishmael, 7
Iseut, 65–66

Jacob, 8–9
Jacobs, Harriet, 212, 220
James I, 126, 127
Jane Eyre (Brontë), 184
Janin, Albert, 282–83,
284–85
Janin, Violet Blair, 281–85
Jason, 19
Jerome, Saint, 15, 57, 58
Jesus, 98
and adultery, 12
and homosexuality, 13
on marriage, 12, 15
Jewett, Sarah Orne, 280
Job, 10
Jocasta, 19
John Birch Society, 370
Johns, Auntie Thomas,
220
Johnson, Lyndon, 369
Johnston, Frances Benjamin,
224, 284
Jong, Erica, 372
Jordan, Cecily, 142
Joseph, 11, 16
Josselson, Ruthellen, 384
Jovinian, 57
Joy of Sex (Comfort), 372
Judah, Gershom ben, 55
Judaism
conceptions of marriage,
13–14
and divorce, 92–93
husband living with the
bride's family, 84–85

Ketubah (marriage
contract), 4, **5**, 84
marriage ceremony, 55–56
and polygamy, 3–4, 7
wedding ring, **57**
Jude the Obscure (Hardy), 277
Julia (daughter of Augustus),
31
Julia (wife of Pompey), 31
Julia Secundina, 39
Julian of Norwich, 81
Jungfrauspiegel, Der, 58
Junior League, 344
Juvenal, 40–41, 41

Kay, Ellen, 265
Keayne, Benjamin, 134–35
Keayne, Sarah, 134–35
Keller, Ludwig, 105
Kelly, Frances, 188
Kelly, James, 188
Kemble, Fanny, 221–22
Kempe, Margery, 70, 77–81
Kennedy, Robert, 370
Kerber, Linda, 172
Kesselman, Amy, 330
Ketubah (marriage contract),
4, **5**
Killpack, Marjorie Reid,
344–45
King, Martin Luther, Jr., 369,
370
King, Nancy, 217
Kinsey, Alfred, 310–11, 355
Kinsey report, 355–57, 393
Knowlton, Charles, 299
Komarovsky, Mirra, 364
Koehler, Lyle, 140

La Bas, Philippe, 167–68
Laban, 8, 9
Ladies' Association, 160
Ladies' Home Journal, 286,
288, 350–51, 364,
392–93
Laius, 19
Lambilly, Marie-Victoire de,
169–70
Lancelot, 66
Lancelot (Chrétien), 66
Lass, Virginia, 281–85
latchkey children, 323
Lavoisier, Antoine Laurent,
162, **163**, 164
Lavoisier, Marie Anne
Pierrette Paulze, 162,
163, 164

Lawrence, D. H., 372
Leah, 8, 9
Leigh, Frances Butler, 218
Lemaire, Ria, 69
Leo IX, Pope, 58
Leo XIII, Pope, 266
Lepidus, 35
lesbianism, 308
in ancient Greece, 24
in Biblical times, 13
Boston marriages, 280
marriage alternatives, 398
in Roman times, 41–42
in Victorian America, 280
"Letter to Artists: Especially
Women Artists, A"
(Merritt), 280
"Letter to her Husband, A"
(Bradstreet), 130
*Letter to the Queen on Lord
Chancellor Cranworth's
Marriage and Divorce Bill*
(Norton), 187
*Letters on the Equability of the
Sexes* (Grimké), 194
Letters to Mothers (Sigourney),
183
Lex Julia, 31–32
Life magazine, 351
*Life and Adventures of a Clever
Woman, The* (F.
Trollope), 185
Life of Saint Alexius, 58
Linton, Eliza Lynn, 276,
279
Lippe-Weissenfeld, William,
283–84
literature and women
Anne Bradstreet, 129–31,
133–34
classical Greek, 19–20
late twentieth century,
361–64, 369
medieval European, 45,
53, 75–77
the new sexuality, 308–9
Tudor and Stuart English,
115–20
twentieth-century, 16
Victorian era, 180,
183–85, 276–79
and the Woman Question,
263–64
women's magazines, 286,
364, 372, 392–93
See also advice literature;
misogyny
"Little Woman" (Gift), 175
Livia, 38

Living of Charlotte Perkins Gilman, The (Gilman), 292
Livy, 25
London Times, 180
love, 394
  primacy in marriage arrangements, 111, 175–76
  See also romantic love
Luce, Clare Booth, 370
Lucretia, 25
Lusanna, 88–92
Luther, Martin, 98–105, 269
Lysias, 23
Lysistrata (Aristophanes), 20

McCall's magazine, 317, 364, 370
McIntosh, Millicent, 357
McKean, Sally, 160
Madame Bovary (Flaubert), 276–77
Malthus, Robert, 299
Man & Wife in America (Hartog), 191
Man in the Gray Flannel Suit, The (Wilson), 362
Marat, Jean Paul, 166
Marietta, 90
marital laws
  in America, 189–91
  in England, 185–89
  Married Women's Property Act, 188–89, 227
  property rights of wives, 190–91, 264
  Stockholm marriages, 265
Mark of Cornwall, 65
Marks, Jeannette, 280
Marlowe, Christopher, 18
marriage
  alternatives, 398
  childlessness, 398
  single mothers, 398
"Marriage" (Caird), 268–70
  letters responding to, 268, 270–75
Marriage as a Trade (Hamilton), 292
marriage ceremony
  in ancient Greece, 21–22
  in the antebellum South, 208
  banns, 53–53
  Marriage Certificate (Currier lithograph), 210

in the Jewish community, 55–56
June bride, **353**
medieval Europe, 52–55, **53**
Native American, 233–34, 235–36
Prayer Book of 1552, 108–9, 113
Puritans and, 114–15
in Roman times, 28–29, 40
same-sex unions, 40–42
as a sacrament, 46, 108
in Tudor England, 114
wedding veils, 208
on the Western frontier, 243–44, 246–52, 260–61
marriage contract
  in ancient Greece, 21
  in Biblical times, 4, **5**
  in medieval Europe, 47–49, 49–51, 51–52, 84
  in Roman times, 26–27, 30
Martial, 41
Martineau, Harriet, 187
Marvin, Maria, 117, 123
Mary, 11, 16
  as the "good" wife, 18
Mary of Oignies, 80
Master of Frankfurt, 94
Masters and Johnson, 373
Maugeret, Marie, 265
Mayor of Casterbridge, The (Hardy), 277
Medea, 19
medical and health issues
  clitorodectomy, 41–42
  in the late twentieth century, 372–73
  in medieval Europe, 72–73
  mental illness, 121, 361–62
medieval Europe, 45–96
  Christian hierarchy of womanhood, 58, **59**, 60
  Christine de Pizan, 81–82
  couples, artistic depictions of, 94–95, **96**
  Héloïse and Abelard, 60–65, 69, 91
  Lancelot and Guinevere, 66
  legal and religious considerations, 45–60
  Lusanna and Giovanni, 88–92
  Margery Kempe, 70, 77–81, 125

property considerations, 49–51, **50**
romantic love, the birth of, 65–70
Tristan and Iseut, 65–66
Melvin, Charles, 334
Melvin, Alvira Vahlenkamp, 334
Mémoires de deux jeunes mariées (Balzac), 276
Ménerville, Elisa Fougeret de, 170–71
Mensinga, Wilhelm Peter, 300
Merritt, Anne Lea, 280
Mesnagier de Paris, Le, 75–76
Metellus, 31
Metsys, Quentin, 94–95
midwives, 74, 230
Mill, Harriet Taylor, 189
Mill, John Stuart, 189, 268, 361
Miller, Henry, 372
Millett, Kate, 372
misogyny, 15, 42
  and the Age of Enlightenment, 147–48, 164
  Christian theologians and, 58, 59
  in medieval Europe, 75–77
  in the Victorian era, 182
  women's "natural inferiority," 148
Mitchell, S. Weir, 291
"Modern Marriage," 266–67, **267**
monasticism, 15
Money Lender and His Wife, The (Metsys), 94–95
Monroe, Marilyn, 358
Moral Questions Affecting Married Life (Pius XII), 307
Morgan, Edmund, 145
Morris, Gertrude, 333–34
Morris, Mrs. Robert, 160
Mosher, Allettie, 301
Mosher, Clelia, 296; 309, 311
Mother's Book , The (Child), 183
Mott, Lucretia, 190
Mr. Mom, 383
Mrs. Doubtfire, 383
Ms. magazine, 372
Mudd, Emily, 357

Napheys, George H., 295, 301

Napier, Robert, 111, 121
Napoleon, 171, 172
National Council of Catholic Women, 344
National Council of Jewish Women, 344
National Council of Negro Women, 344
National Federation of Business and Professional Women, 343
National Housing Agency, 342–43
National Organization for Women (NOW), 369–70
Native Americans
  marriage, 142, 144, 233–34
  marriage (interracial), 235–36, 249–50
  missionaries and, 237–38
Nero, 40
New Yeare's Gift for Shrewes, A (Cecil), **119**
New York Times, 383
Nietzsche, Friedrich, 266
Norris, Pamela, 14
Norton, Caroline Sheridan, 186–87
Norton, George, 186
Norton, Mary Beth, 148, 158
Nucci, Andrea, 88

Octavia (Antony's wife), 36, 37
Octavia (Nero's wife), 40
Odd Women, The (Gissing), 277–79
Odom, Major (slave owner), 220
Odysseus, 16, 18–19
Odyssey (Homer), 16
Oecolampadius, 105–6
Oedipus, 19
Offen, Karen, 164
"Open Letter to the Christian Nobility of the German Nation" (Luther), 98–99
Orenstein, Peggy, 399
Ouida, 276
Our Bodies, Ourselves, 372
Our Mutual Friend (Dickens), 180
Ovid, 28
Owens-Adair, Bethenia, 260, 261–62
Ozzie and Harriet, 359

Paley, Grace, 352
Parker, Thomas, 133
Parsons, Talcott, 357
patriarchy
  Christianity and, 14–15
  in medieval Europe, 84
  in Roman times, 26–27
  in Tudor and Stuart England, 114–15
  during the late Victorian era, **266,** 266–68, **267**
Paul, Saint, 98, 135
  on homosexuality, 13
  on marriage, 15, 110
  on the subjugation of wives, 14–15
Pearson, Maryon, 391
Penelope, 16–19
Peninnah, 7
Pericles, 20
Peter, Saint, 98
Phyllis, Aunt (slave), 220
Pickering, Mary Carpenter, 251
Pico de Avila, Maria Inocent, 249
Pitcher, Mollie, 322
Pius X, Pope, 307
Pius XII, Pope, 307
Pivot of Civilization, The (Sanger), 306
Place, Francis, 299
Planned Parenthood, 316
Plath, Sylvia, 361
Plato, 24
Pliny the Younger, 27, 32, 38–39
Plummer, Beatrice, 139
Plutarch, 24, 31, 33, 36, 37, 42
Pocahontas, 142, **143**
political involvement of women
  American Revolutionary War, 158–61
  Civil Rights Act, 369
  French Revolution, 161–71
  late twentieth century, 363
  Victorian England, 279
polygamy, 55, 235
  in Biblical times, 3–4, 7
  Mormon plural marriages, 252–58
  See also bigamy
Pooley, Greville, 142
Pompey, 30, 33, 34
Poppaea, 40

popular media and a wife's image, 458–59, **360,** 361
population of women
  in America, 141–42, 144–45, 205
  in Victorian England, 277–78
Porter, Lavinia, 259–60
Powers, Betty, 214, 219–20
Powhatan, 142
Prayer Book of 1552, 108–9, 113
"Prelude on the Babylonian Captivity" (Luther), 98–99
prenuptial agreements, 139
Pride and Prejudice (Austen), 183
"Prologue, The" (Bradstreet), 131
property, wives considered as, 4, 42–44, 46
  in medieval Europe, 47–49
prostitution, 299
Protestantism
  and birth control, 306–7
  clerical marriage, 98
  Germany and the Reformation, 98–108
  Martin Luther, 98–105
  Puritan New England, 126–45
  Tudor and Stuart England, 108–25
  See also Catholicism
Proverbs, on the ideal wife, 10–11
Purcell, Anne, 304
Purgatory of Married Men, The, 77
Puritans
  and adultery, 120–21
  "Antinomian controversy," 135–36
  and divorce, 135
  marital practices, 114–15
  in New England, 126–45
  separation of sexes, 131
  and women in church, 135, 136

Quintus, 31

Rachel, 8–9
rape, 25
  ritual enactment of, 29

slavery, sexual exploitation
of, 219–21
See also spousal abuse
Rawlins, Stephan, 111
Reagan, Leslie J., 304,
315–16
Reagan, Nancy, 392
Reagan, Ronald, 390
Rebekah, 8
Redbook magazine, 359, 364,
374, 393
Reed, Esther, 160
Research in Marriage, A
(Hamilton), 309
responsibilities of wives
in Roman times, 33–35
Reynolds, Debbie, 358
Reynolds, Mary, 217
*Rhythm of Sterility and Fertility
in Women, The,* 307
Rich, Adrienne, 134
Richards, Franklin D., 257
Richards, Jane Snyder, 257
Riveting and Rationing in Dixie
(Thomas), 331
Robespierre, Maximilien,
166, 167, 168, 169
Roland, Marie-Jeanne
(Manon) Phlipon, 162,
165–67
Rolfe, John, 142
Roman times, 25–42
Anthony and Cleopatra,
35–37
Augustus and Livia, 37–38
fidelity to dead spouse,
39–40
illustrations of, **26,** 34
Pliny the Younger and
Calpurnia, 38–39
political, 33–34, 35
same-sex unions, 40–42
romantic love
the birth of, 65–70,
175–76
late twentieth century, 394
medieval songs, 68–69
See also love
Romeo and Juliet
(Shakespeare), 117–18
Roosevelt, Eleanor, 363
Rosen, Ruth, 390
Rosenberg, Samuel, 55–56
Rosenblatt, Wilbrandis,
105–7
Roth, Philip, 16
Roussel, Nelly, 265
Roussel, Jean-Jacques, 147,
164

Rudd, Lydia A., 239–40
Rufus (slave), 214–15
Ruga, Spurius Carvilius, 30
Rupp, Leila J., 322
Rush, Julia Stockton, 160
Ruskin, John, 182
Russell, Rosalind, 358

Sachsenspiegel, 46
San Francisco Chronicle, 385
Sanford, Byron N., 241, 243,
244–46
Sanford, Mollie Dorsey, 231,
241–46
Sand, George, 276
Sanger, Margaret, 304–6, 313
Sappho, 24–25
Sarah, 7–8
Sartre, Jean-Paul, 362
Savannah Telegraph, 223
School Girls (Orenstein), 399
Schoolcraft, Marie Howard,
204
Schreiner, Olive, 265–66,
276
Schwabenspiegel, 46
Scott, Anne Firor, 222–23
Scribonia, 37
Second Sex, The (Beauvoir),
362, 369
Secundus, Julius, 39
Seneca Falls Convention,
190, 202
Seneca the Younger, 38, 41
Ser Luca, 84
servants, 137–38
sexual harassment of, 138
*Several Poems Compiled with
Great Variety of Wit and
Learning* (Bradstreet),
133
Sexual Politics (Millett), 372
sexual relations
the new sexuality, 308–13
premarital sex, 352–53
and procreation, 297–98
post-betrothal activities,
113–14
as a solemn duty, 56–57
as vice, 299–300
sexual revolution
(1950–2000), 355–79
literature, 201, 362–63,
369, 373–73
opposition to, 357, 370
oral contraception, 363
political involvement, 363,
369–70

popular media and
advertising, 458–59,
360, 361
premarital sex, 352–53
psychiatry and, 361–62
reports and studies,
355–57 373, 374,
375–79
Roe v. Wade, 373
women's magazines and,
392–93
Shakespeare, William, 115–20
Shaw, George Bernard, 266
Shepherd, Virginia Hayes ,
220
Shewmake, Susan Cornwall,
223
"Short Happy Life of Francis
Macomber, The"
(Hemingway), 362
Showings (Julian of Norwich),
81
Sigourney, Lydia, 183
Sills, Judith, 387
single mothers, 398
slavery, 192, 208, 210,
210–14, 214–23
American Freedmen's
Inquiry Commission,
218
antimiscegenation laws,
142, 144, 193
opposition to, 223
separation of families,
221–22
sexual exploitation of,
219–21
slave marriages, 142, 144,
175, 215–18, 223–24
World Anti-Slavery
Convention, 197, 198
Small Catechism (Luther), 99
Smith, Gerritt, 197
Smith, William, 154
"Solitude of Self, The"
(Stanton), 202
Somerville, Mrs. Keith
Frazier, 336–38
Sophocles, 19
Soranus, 41
Southern Lady, The (Scott),
222–23
SPARS (U.S. Coast Guard),
333
Spock, Benjamin, 358
Sporus, 40
Spotswood, Alexander, 144
spousal abuse, 23, 111
in Colonial America, 148

spousal abuse (*continued*)
in the late twentieth
century, 363–64
legal permission for, 46
in medieval Europe, 45–47
runaway wives, 150–51
See also rape
Spragg, Eleanor, 142
Staël, Madame de, 172
Stanford study, 384–85, 387
Stansell, Christine, 260
Stanton, Elizabeth Cady, 190,
194, 195–203, **202**,
207, 306
Stanton, Henry B., 197,
199–200, 202
Statilia Messallina, 40
Steinem, Gloria, 372
Stephens, Dorothy Barnes,
335–36
Stephens, James R., 335–36
Stetson, Charles Walter, 291
Stetson, Katherine, 291
Stockholm marriages, 265
Stone, Lucy, 175, 194
Storer, Horatio, 303
"Story of My Misfortunes,
The" (Abelard), 60
Straight, Susan, 395–96
Strecker, Edward, 362
Strindberg, August, 266
Strober, Myra, 384, 387
Subjection of Women, The
(Mill), 189
Suetonius, 40
suffrage. *See under* feminism
Sukie (slave), 220
suppositories, 30

Tacitus, 33, 38
Talmud and Eve, 3
Taming of the Shrew, The
(Shakespeare), 118–20
Tanner, Annie Clark, 257
Tarquinius, Sextus, 25
Taussig, Fred J., 314
Taylor, Elizabeth, 358
Telemachus, 18
Tenth Muse, The (Bradstreet),
132–33
Terentia, 31
Terkel, Studs, 368
Tertullian, 15
Tess of the d'Urbervilles
(Hardy), 277
Theory of the Leisure Class
(Veblen), 288
Thomas, Gertrude, 204

Thomas, Mary, 331
Thompson, Berenice, 326
Thompson, Clara, 361
Three Men and a Baby, 383
Thynne, John, 123
Thynne, Thomas, 117, 123
Tiberius, 38
"To my Dear and Loving
Husband" (Bradstreet),
130
Tolstoy, Leo, 266, 277
tooth extraction, **104**
Treatise on Domestic Economy
(Beecher), 195
Treatise on Love (Capellanus),
67
Treen, Catherine, 150–51
Tristan, 65–66
Trollope, Anthony (son),
177
Trollope, Frances, 177–78,
185, 191
Trollope, Thomas, 177–78
Trotula, 72–73
Turia, 39
Tuttle, William, 323
Twain, Mark, 399
Tyler, Elaine, 338

Uitz, Erika, 73
Ulrich, Laurel, 138, 141
unfaithfulness, 399–400
Updike, John, 16

Valerius Maximus, 38
van Adrichem, Symon, 94
van de Passe, Simon, 143
van Du vendoorde, Lysbeth,
94
van Eyck, Jan, 94
Van Meckenem, Israhel, 95
Veblen, Thorstein, 288
venereal disease, 299
Vermigli, 107
vice, suppression of,
299–300
Victoria, Queen, 183, 208
*Vindication of the Rights of
Women* (Wollstonecraft),
153, 172, 194
von Suttner, Bertha, 266

WACS (Women's Army
Corps)/WAAC (Women's
Auxiliary Army Corps),
333–34, 334–35

WAFS (Women's Auxiliary
Ferry Squadron), 333
Walker, Elkanah, 236
Walker, Henry, 397
Walker, Mary Richardson,
236
Ward, Mrs. Humphry, 276
Warner, Dr. (abortionist), 304
Washington, George, 156
Washington, Martha, 160
Watson, Henry, 212
Watson, Sophia, 211–12
Way We Never Were, The
(Coonitz), 363
Way We Really Are, The
(Coontz), 387
Wayne, Anthony, 158
WAVES (Women Accepted
for Voluntary Service of
the U.S. Navy), 333,
335–36
wedding ring, **57**, 84
weddings
in ancient Greece, 21–22
in the antebellum South,
208
banns, 53–53
Marriage Certificate
(Currier lithograph), **210**
in the Jewish community,
55–56
June bride, **353**
medieval Europe, 52–55,
53
Native American, 233–34,
235–36
Prayer Book of 1552,
108–9, 113
Puritans and, 114–15
in Roman times, 28–29, 40
same-sex unions, 40–42
as a sacrament, 46, 108
in Tudor England, 114
wedding veils, 208
on the Western frontier,
243–44, 246–52,
260–61
wedding contracts
in ancient Greece, 21
in Biblical times, 4, **5**
in medieval Europe, 47–49,
49–51, 51–52, 84
in Roman times, 26–27, 30
Weiner, Marli, 211
Weitzman, Lenore, 390
Well of Loneliness, The (Hall),
308
Wells, H. G., 306
Wendy, Minerva, 223

Chapter 13

"A time to love, and a time to hate. . . ."

If there is something you would so like to do . . . make it a dream and make it come true. . . . Believe that it will with all of your heart . . . believe in it fully right from the start. . . . Feel the success of it, keep it in view . . . make it an intricate real part of you . . . never let doubt interfere anywhere . . . breathe life into it, think about it and care . . . what happens, you know, is all up to you. . . . If you love it enough, your dream will come true!

Every thinking person knows it is easier to love someone and to accept him with a warmer and more natural feeling when this can be spontaneous rather than something expected or demanded.

Making someone feel it is his duty to love, or demanding attention, will surely narrow the chances of anything worthwhile ever developing on its own. So much of the happiness of life is an invitation not a command, a leading and not a pushing.

No one loves us because they ought to, or because our position in life or family demands it, but because we have attracted it to us by our ability to love rightly. Love has been called the bond of perfection and certainly this is the only bond that can endure. For it is every man's urge to be free to express what he chooses to express, and he will be free if only in his thoughts.

*

We like to think others are the reason we live. It is a wonderful thing to love and be loved. We are inspired by such love to rise above ourselves higher than we thought possible. It gives us reason to rise in the morning, makes us more ready to face the activities of the day, and helps us step more easily over the obstacles. If we become disillusioned about that love, we cannot call it bad.

Love is a channel and if that channel breaks down we cannot be right in falling back to be less than we know we can be. It is then that we should be grateful for the smallest part of that love and know what we have accomplished through it was by and for ourselves. We cannot attach ourselves to another person and make him responsible for us. We are responsible to ourselves, and no one else has the power to make or break us. We merely accept another's love as a gift, but the responsibility is our own.

To receive, one must first give as it has been anonymously written:

Love is the filling from one's own another's cup;
Love is the daily laying down and taking up;
A choosing of the stony path through each new day
That other feet may tread with ease a smoother way.
Love is not blind, but looks abroad through other eyes;
And asks not, "Must I give?" but "May I sacrifice?"
Love hides its grief, that other hearts and lips may sing;
And burdened walks, that other lives may wing.
Hast thou a love like this within thy soul?
'Twill crown the life with blessings when thou dost reach the goal.

*

It was Emerson who said never to lose an opportunity to see something beautiful for beauty is God's handwriting.

We sometimes lose touch with beauty for the mere lack of it in our own hearts. We become so saturated with the grotesque and the unnatural that we allow true beauty to flow away from us until everything becomes dark and unsightly.

Beauty is that quiet something that may be only a feeling,

but it is so right that no one can mistake its source. Beauty can be the scent and sight of orange blossoms in the moist, late evening air, or tender thought and concern for the smallest of life's creatures. It can be the first rays of morning sunlight that lovingly touch the new green leaves of spring, or the brush of human fingers in acknowledgment of something deeper and better than the mundane. Beauty is joy in the laughing face of a child, or soft understanding in a mother's face. Beauty is that which transcends time and space and circumstance, for true beauty is love. And true love is God in action.

*

Hate breaks man away from his power to reason. Every thing worthwhile is forgotten and only a white fury is directed at someone or something.

Hate is an emotion to which the normal person has given little thought. It becomes a word to express a strong dislike, but hate as a strong and passionate dislike is reserved for those persons and those things that are outside the normal person's comprehension. And it is right that he should not waste himself feeling hatred.

If there be anything to hate, it should be the oppression of mankind, the force of ignorance and stupidity, the laxity of standing up for what is right and good, and the imposition of person against person. To stand back and pretend these things do not matter is morally wrong and unforgivable. Most people who cause these things hate themselves first, and could care less what price they have to pay since the main part of them has already been destroyed. To protect them only to allow them the same privilege of imposing their hate again and again on the innocent should in itself be hated. If anyone must give any part of his emotions over to hate, let it be for these things.

*

How could you be anything but good . . . when you have so instilled in me . . . this freedom, this ability to feel the joy . . . of just being me without fear and prejudice and lack-luster.

What are you but the greatest friend . . . who would say nothing but good to me . . . to lift me past the dark levels I have known . . . and have given me new vision of both my inner self and the world about me. . . . What can I say of you except that I know no greater joy than thinking of you with love . . . though I may not see you ever again . . . you have given me so much more than most whom I have always known . . . so now that life is new and dear . . . shall I not do as much and pass along to others the right to live and learn . . . and know that there are such as you?

*

The greatest debt we owe to other people is love. How many times in the space of a few seconds have others given us the little something that changed our thinking and changed our lives.

Suppose the man whistling gala tunes was aware that he lifted someone's spirits, or that in the darkest mood and fit of depression someone said something positive and changed a pattern of wrong thinking to one of success.

Someone's thoughtful consideration makes us feel more needed and suddenly we too have our places in the world. And someone asks our help and we know we have something worthy of giving.

But most of all we owe to God. The cardinals' songs, the dappled pattern of sunlight on the walk, the delicate petals of the crocus, and the night song of the merry mimicker.

How great our gifts and even greater our debt of love.

*

Riches consist not in the extent of possessions, but in the ability to appreciate. How great our blessings and how small our appreciation.

The richest people in the world are those who can see the changes of the seasons, the faces of those whom they love and more important, they can see past the doors of prejudice and hate and despair. They are rich because they can breathe deeply the fragrance of flowers, but also peace. They can feel the cool and the heat and the tender touch of a hand, but also the touch of souls.

For these blessed few, food, both spiritual and material, is fully appreciated and enjoyed. Their hearing is tuned to the sounds and songs of the land, but never to sarcasm or cynicism.

The ultimate is love, for to be truly loved is to be truly rich.

Chapter 14

"A time of war, and a time of peace. . . ."

Whether I am walking in the rain . . . or trudging in the snow . . . I know the pressure of your hand . . . to help me as I go . . . along life's path though tired my soul . . . I know I must be true . . . the purpose and the reason for . . . the love I know for you. . . . To lift my chin and steadfast be . . . to keep a clear, dry eye. . . . To know that never in the world . . . would you ever make me cry . . . will keep me prayerfully with you . . . though you be far away. . . . My heart is happy just to know . . . you're coming back one day.

Has there ever been a righteous, just, or holy war? There have been wars that were believed necessary, but can we call them holy?

There are too many impaired personalities involved to call war a thing of spiritual wholeness. The only holiness in any conflict is the unimpaired innocence of those who are involved by requirement or caught in circumstance. The Greek poet Sophocles, over four hundred years before Christ stated wisely: "War loves to seek its victims in the young." And anything that seeks to victimize our young is not worthy of adoration.

If man must fight to feel like a man, he has missed the whole essence and beauty of true manhood, whether it is in the world conflicts, the world of commerce, or in the world of the personal man. The theory of dictatorship, "listen to me and I will create for you a Utopia," has been the bad seed planted in the first mind that started the first war. Sadly, that seed has multiplied and led millions upon millions to go and fight the enemy for reasons they have only been told about, while all about them are the real and terrible enemies —ignorance, disease, superstition, and prejudice.

The wisdom and warm humanity of Winston Churchill was revealed in his expressed thoughts that human tragedy lies

113

in the fact that after all the exertions and sacrifices of millions of people and of the victories for whatever the purpose, righteous cause or peace or security, we still have not found the true meaning of peace and face even greater perils than those we have overcome.

The greatest perils we face lie within man himself. A lasting national stability is dependent entirely upon the individual. Here is where wars begin, with the constant condemnation of leadership, with lack of respect for authority, for family and friends, and secretly for self, until the ultimate is open conflict. When man cannot live with himself, neither can he live with others. His only hope is to change. And resistance to change seems inherent. He is one in armies of people resisting change. Yet, change for the better is the only hope, changes that can take unfamiliar threads from this seeming chaotic contemporary philosophy and weave them into something of lasting value. To love freedom and to love our own does not mean we must hate and make war to keep them. We, who have gone so far past the point of turning back, must instead change our destiny to peace by changing our human patterns.

A time for war? Yes, there is a time for anything we want to strive after. As Greek philosopher Pythagoras wrote, "It is only necessary to make war with five things: with the maladies of the body, the ignorances of the mind, with the passions of the body, with the seditions of the city, and the discords of families." When we overcome these, we shall have overcome the need, or a time, for wars.

*

If I owe no man anything, If I do not step on his toes, infringe on his property, or cause him grief, am I free to do as I please, regardless of what it is?

The philosophy that anyone can live high and handsome

as long as he does not hurt anyone else is ignorant of who "anyone" is. No matter how much he avoids hurting other persons, he forgets that within him is the real self, not the one who puts up fronts, rationalizes the wrongs, and justifies every action, but the one that he trespasses against every time he side-steps justice.

In achieving happiness any man must first be on friendly terms with himself. Nearly eight hundred years ago, Saint Bernard wrote, "Nothing can work me damage except me, and I am the real sufferer by my own fault."

If a man is unhappy with himself, he infringes on the rights of other people by having nothing of himself to contribute to society. He cannot live alone because his house is divided against itself, and a house divided is a house at war.

And yet, how many of us have purchased peace with personal sacrifices. It is said that every time someone does a wrong, someone sacrifices. It seems sometimes the innocent must pay because the guilty will not accept the responsibility. Peace at any price is unreasonable and standing straight with such a burden is impossible. Sooner or later the responsibility must go home to roost and it is the responsibility of the innocent to stand away and allow the guilty room to put down their feet. It is often peace purchased with pain for we do not even leave regret without a little hurt. Can we forget? Forgive perhaps?

Remember the *Rubáiyát* of Omar Khayyam:

> The Moving Finger writes; and, having writ,
> Moves on: nor all your Piety nor Wit
> Shall lure it back to cancel half a line,
> Nor all your tears wash out a word of it.

Perhaps we cannot forget our wars in their entireties, but with forgiveness we can live in peace.

*

There have always been anxious ages, times when it seemed life could not possibly continue as it was. Since the first record of events there seems to have been more passion than compassion, more giving than receiving, more fear than hope.

There is little use in man's denying his anxiety when it shows so plainly in the way he drives his car, the manner in which he blasts out at other people, blaming them and accusing everyone of being the cause of his trouble.

The fault for all anxiety lies at the center of the one who finds trouble everywhere. This is a fact that mankind does not want to admit, but there are natural laws of attraction and repulsion that he sets into motion by his attitude, whether it is faith-filled or adamant.

Peace must have its beginning place, and it will never be in the midst of fiery anxiety where people are only willing to give what is demanded or whose continual search for wrong seems more important than finding right.

Peace will begin where it is believed possible. It will begin with peaceful persons who believe in good.

To some, peace is nonexistent and life will always be a fight, a continual struggle for a foothold. Hardships and the necessities of life build into such persons a will of iron. They remember too well the times when grit was the only thing that held together body, soul, and spirit. There was born a sort of pride that in the face of impossible odds a fight had taken place and strength of effort, determination, and fortitude had won. Suddenly, the fight itself becomes the important thing, and it represents a trophy testifying that anything less than a struggle is an insult to a fighting spirit.

It is suddenly compulsory that everyone, particularly the young, who know little of the kind of difficulties their elders have experienced, realize how hard and fierce and desperate the fight has been to produce a world of ease for them. And yet in these present days of anxiety, has there been a concentrated effort to give the young the moral and spiritual stamina they need to live with their affluence? They have an even greater need for strength and courage to battle a psychological and emotional war. Perhaps they have been provided only trophies of their elders' physical labors and hardships and a form religion without joy.

Where is the moral and religious link between generation and generation in these times of anxiety? It can be heartbreaking to have tradition tread upon, but even more to those with whom it began. Each generation must have the liberty to follow tradition or to make its own. Whatever son acquires from father cannot be lightly transferred or pushed, but breathed and sensed and loved through with nothing of indebtedness. Dependency and demands create rebellion where "honor thy father and mother" and "provoke not thy children" are overlooked or forgotten. Fulfillment in every generation must come through its own efforts.

There is great consolation in this present day to know that such liberty to seek demands life and cannot be trampled into nothingness. Daniel Webster said it this way, "If the true spark of religious and civil liberty be kindled, it will burn. Human agency cannot extinguish it. Like the earth's central fire, it may be smothered for a time; the ocean may overwhelm it; mountains may press it down; but its inherent and unconquerable force will heave both the ocean and the land, and at some time or another, in some place or another, the volcano will break out and flame to heaven."

There have always been anxious ages, but this one can be less so if generation can say to generation, "What we have done has been for us. It has been our best and has given us reason and purpose and some happiness. We hope it will be for your benefit also, but we only ask that you do what you can, be the best you can in this age, which neither of us yet knows how to handle. Try to make it something with which you can live, something you can reflect to your heirs in hopes it will make their age one of supreme peace."

*

Most human problems begin because everyone is trying to say the same thing but in a different way. The average person dislikes anything that looks or sounds different from the way he would have expressed it. Can he possibly say anything is less true because it is not said in the way he likes to hear it?

There is an unequaled joy in finding a kindred soul who thinks and believes and acts in a well-known way, but if there were never differences in human beings where would there be growth? Is it not the differences and variety that stimulates deep thinking, self-knowledge, and the desire to stretch the mind?

Strong and beautiful friendships are born because of differences in background and teaching. Basic truths and good and love serve as the foundation for an opportunity to learn even more, and for the excellent opportunity to create a permanent peace.

*

It is very quiet here among the stars . . . except for their singing I hear only the beat of my own heart . . . and I know from these heights . . . from this level of seeing and feeling . . . how foolish I have been to allow myself to hear anything but the music of the heart and soul . . . for in my lifetime of living on a lower level . . . where one has to take evil into account . . . I heard the voice of the dark and morbid . . . I listened and I contributed to the voice of woe . . . I was bent on telling my own troubles . . . and determined

that others should know of my worst conditions . . . that I added to the world's peacelessness and loveless condition . . . and gave off an aura that would attract no more than madness . . . but in rising above those voices I can hear something different . . . and I can look down on my emotions and down on the paths I have been following . . . and I can see how foolish it was to pass my time . . . believing that I could drag to me love in its greatest and most holy sense . . . for no matter what I say, or how beautifully . . . if I have not love . . . I am only talking loudly.

Though I know all the mysteries of life and I am exalted for my knowledge . . . and have not love . . . I am nothing.

If I give everything I have to someone else . . . even if I give my very being to be martyred . . . and I have not love . . . then I am nothing.

I have come to know that love can suffer a long time . . . and it can still be kind and gentle . . . it can only give of itself, never thinking of being envious or resentful . . . for there is sufficient love for every person.

Love is not a proud thing given only to me . . . so that I can point to it as if it were my private accomplishment . . . but it is the highest, the kindest, most gentle, respectful, and giving emotion . . . ever to be experienced . . . it has no need to shout, for its presence is like a garden of flowers I cannot see . . . but their beneficent influence diffuses itself throughout my soul.

I must enjoy again and again the knowledge that love has no need to seek its own . . . that which is mine will come to me . . . in so much greater degree . . . in so much more beauty . . . in so much more holiness than I could ever seek on my own . . . and in the joy of it . . . there is always forgiveness so that regret has no place to gain entrance.

Because love is not continually seeking to find things wrong . . . it is not easily provoked . . . and so it is lasting and forever beautiful . . . no matter where there is great oratory, prophecies, or knowledge . . . they shall all go before this love fails . . .

Here on the heights I am first to catch the sun's rays and last to reflect the rosy glow . . . Now knowing this, how shall I live . . . but with great joy and patience . . . because I am loved, I am something . . . I am grateful!

✻

This is the age of questioning. Young and old want to know the reason of things. Why haven't the teachings of the church and our beliefs in a higher power delivered us from war, poverty, and unhappiness in general? What is the meaning of all the rebellion in nearly every phase of life, in areas we thought to be unchangeable? Why is the world running scared, fearfully guarding every minute possession and eyeing every neighbor as a threat?

We were not created alike, we were not expected to respond in the same manner. Regardless of how fallible those who claim to live by faith seem to be, we cannot blame the Creator for the weakness in that response. There must be a willingness to try, a strength and peace within each individual, before there can be peace around the world.

If we cannot get along with the person next to us, how do we expect others to be different? Who are we to blame except ourselves for our inability to shoulder our share of the responsibility? If peace is possible, let it begin with us—as individuals.

Chapter 15

"He hath made every thing beautiful in its time. . . ."

I shall remember the happy things. I shall remember the special persons, the peaceful, tranquil times. I shall live each moment with some joy, seeing the best in everyone, finding fulfillment in the bird's song, the flowers, the raindrops.

The world responds to me as I say "hello" to it, friendly or cheerless, it is mine to mold second by second.

Regardless of how the past has been, this moment, this day is mine to live. It contains all the ingredients I need to be happy, if only quietly and thoughtfully within myself. That, after all, is part of the reward for thinking, speaking, and remembering only the joys of the past and present.

Since I must walk daily with memories, how much better they be the good ones rather than those best forgotten.

Wrote Henry Ware, American divine, "The shaping of our own life is our own work. It is a thing of beauty, or a thing of shame, as we ourselves make it."

✻

There seems to be a time for every thing . . . a creative time when we begin to build something new . . . a time of order when we put every thing in its right place . . . a time of sadness when laughing is at one end and crying at the other . . .

playing Yo-yo with the emotions. . . . There is a time when the pendulum of faith swings very high and in its full swing also finds the lows . . . there is a time when amiability and agreement are light and easy . . . and a time when there is no neutral ground on which to work . . . a time for sheer happiness so that nothing is accomplished except on dancing feet . . . and a time when the spirit is so submerged in the God everywhere present, that a lack of courage would be impossible.

Life has so much more beauty than unpleasantness that we cannot ignore the comet's tail . . . the meteor flashing across a star-studded sky . . . a cool breeze carrying the fragrance of honeysuckle . . . the early dawn misty pink and golden . . . a sweet sleep full of quiet breathing and happy dreams . . . the sun's golden tanning . . . the salt air's tangy breath . . . and every man's faith that takes him nearer his God and love.

We cannot forget the opportunity, the time of challenge . . . the moment of truth, the discovery of a new self we have not known . . . the fear that can melt away with a little courage . . . the aching with love for the hurt of someone else . . . the miracle of a baby . . . a rippling brook, the singing trees. . . . There is a purpose to every thing under heaven . . . for He has made every thing beautiful in its time.

❋

"A thing of beauty is a joy forever; its loveliness increases; it will never pass into nothingness; but still will keep a bower quiet for us, and a sleep full of sweet dreams, and health, and quiet breathing." These beautiful words are from John Keats's *Endymion*. The healing power of peaceful rest.

If only in these nervous times we could go to that place of beauty. If only we could put down every responsibility and turn for a few moments to the loveliness that increases.

What is beauty? Is it grace? Charm? Fair of face? Or is it something even better, something unseen but felt? Perhaps it is the soul of man.

Beauty is that which everyone expects to find in tangible things and only finds the search to be endless. In its true essence it is all that we love and hold sacred, the true meaning behind all meanings, the love behind all loves, and the deep spiritual mystique hidden in man where he seldom thinks to look for it. It is that which makes everything beautiful in its time.

✳

The sky is a woman, changeable and ever-changing. She can wear the smooth, sun-washed face of gentle smiles and suddenly lift her black brows in a stormy rage, split the heavily charged atmosphere with sharp tongues of lightning, and loose torrents of tears without regard for the innocent. But for her changeable ways she possesses the profound and basic constancy that has guided man by her stars, warmed him with sunlight, refreshed him with raindrops, and romanced him with moonlight. Her personality varies with the season, the day, the hour, and the moment to correspond with her most extraordinary display of colorful gowns and dazzling array of jewels. No man has ever learned the depths of her infinite soul and no man has been allowed to follow all the secret channels of her heart. They can only study and surmise, probe and make guesses that later may be proved wrong. Her airways support the great wings of the golden eagle and the gigantic superjets in their long flights. Space capsules orbit the earth through her vacuum but no one possesses her and no one questions her position.

Morning so often finds her still half asleep, still adorned with her jewels from the night before. Then she comes forth quickly in her blue morning coat and rose-tinted cheeks to

127

touch the earth with dew-laden kisses and to rejoice with a chorus of bird song. Man loses when he sleeps past this magic hour, when he could let his spirit soar to touch the first rays of the morning sun, for it is in the freeing of his spirit that he is eventually free in all other ways. Not anything physical or material can bind him when his spirit flies straight up to those infinite, fathomless depths.

The midday sun washes the sky to palest blue so that even the wings of the highflying gull, once tinted the green of the sea, are lost from vision. It is impossible to face such brilliance with the naked eye, but the sun's influence is felt everywhere. Life-giving rays tan and heal man's body. The seeds he plants are sprouted and drawn through the earth's crust to productivity. As the earth makes its annual revolution around the sun, all the varying degrees of heat and cold are felt in her ethereal atmosphere. There was no human to witness this beginning, but the Creator is the Master Artist making a journey through space too marvelous to comprehend.

The evening sky, like embers upon the hearth, sets strange shadows across the land. Tints of amethyst and sapphire are tinged with gold and streaked with the deep red of the rainbow. Swift flights of birds and wandering thistledown are silhouetted for a brief moment. And suddenly there is nothing left of the day but the faint rose-colored fabric of content. The day is done. It is twilight time. Like early morning it is a delightful mixture of night and day, except in reverse. Instead of the bright bird voices, now they murmur and cheep in their good-night ceremonies. And there is one still too full of joy to contain it all. He sings out, sounding as out of place in the quiet as laughing aloud in the chapel.

Overhead the evening star boldly adorns the breast of the sky, and one by one the fabulous curve of her cheek gathers the fiery stones. In a mood of frivolity she flings them across the heavens, leaving flames and vapor trailing behind. The round, jolly face of the moon moves up in the eastern sky, silvering the edges of a stray white cloud and paling the stars with the exception of the brightest. Their bewitchment and beauty have inspired poets from Homer and the author of Job down to Tennyson. Men of fancy have compared them to fireflies, dewdrops, and diamonds.

There is so much mystery and beauty in our Lady's unfathomable depths. The first simple shepherds tending their flocks in the meadows named the stars that guided them. One perfect star, splendid in its brilliance and purpose, led Wise Men to a new beginning.

This cerulean lady is an ever-changing Masterpiece. She, indeed, is a timeless beauty.

✻

Come with me through the snow-filled woods and feel their quiet peacefulness reach into your very soul. Here in the serenity of this trackless forest there is communion with life in its deepest sense. There is a contrast between the bright flash of the redbird's wings and the soft furry blending of cottontails with the snow. An even greater contrast lies between the quiet air where breath hangs in a misty vapor and the moving, thriving life beneath the blanket of white where nature is already preparing for another season.

Above our heads the trees interlock their ice-covered branches forming a gossamer pattern as intricate as the spider's web. The air is so crystal clear that the tinkling of a cowbell carries across from the woodland barnyard. The skaters on the pond and the sleds along the slope have rhythm and movement in keeping with the long, silent strains of sound heard, but unheard. To stand breathlessly, still relates to the timelessness, the seeming weightlessness of a thousand diamonds caught in space.

Is this forever? There are no visible signs of change. There

129

is nothing to promise that these woods will ever give birth to new life. Truly every thing is beautiful in its time, but every thing must continuously have a new season in which to be beautiful, a breaking up to rebuild. Even in the beauty and healing solitude of these beautiful woods, we must know that this too shall pass. It will pass in the orderly procession of nature that it might come again, not as a cold, barren waste, but as a magical mystical winter wonderland that breathes silently and majestically with pulsating life and purpose.

❋

To every thing a season, a purpose for every thing under heaven. All of life has a reason. Each part of our lives has a purpose. A time of birth, a time of growth, a time of maturity, a time of death. In between each purposeful and significant division, lies all the hurts, all the tears, all the smiles, all loves that make us the persons we are. Even regrets have a purpose, if only to realize how good it is to have raised our sights again.

The poetry and simplicity of the Indian's life is so expressed;

A time to sing
A time to sigh
A time to laugh
A time to cry
A time to live
A time to die

A time to let go the old so that newness of mind and spirit can come in. For He has made every thing beautiful in whatever stage it is in.

130

2

BE EASY

Any parent will tell you that there are easy babies and there are hard babies. Easy babies eat anything you feed them, take long naps, make nice cooing noises, never fuss, and sleep through the night. Hard babies cry and demand and fret and barf and never, ever sleep. The hard baby is miserable and she makes *you* miserable and you just can't wait for her to go to kindergarten so you can mix yourself a giant Long Island iced tea and catch up on all those *Us Weekly* magazines she's been keeping you from.

I've got news for you. Most of the people you work with can ignore that you're a hard baby when the good times are rolling. You can gripe and snipe and bellyache all you want as long as you get your work done on time and don't steal money from the till. But when times are not so good and your boss is looking for heavy stuff to throw overboard, you're going to see a lot of hard babies—what I call high-maintenance employees—floating in the water, waving their little pink slips. Now *that* would really make you cry.

Being easy to work with is critical to bulletproofing your job. And not just easy today, the day you happen to hear a rumor about department cutbacks, but easy all the time, as in easy to work with, easy to talk to, easy to be with, and, most of all, *not* hard. Hard employees are a pain in the ass, always making noise and trouble and more work for everyone else. In the end, they don't contribute as much as they cost, so **when your boss has to choose between the easy guy and the hard guy, he will pick the easy guy.**

15. QUIT COMPLAINING

Look, the squeaky wheel may get the grease, but it's probably also going to get fired. It really is that simple. So quit complaining.

Who, you? Yeah, you, the one who's bellyaching that the office is too cold or that you can't work the phone system or that there are no gluten-free bagels served at the weekly staff meeting or that the soap in the ladies room is giving you hives. First of all, *no one* wants to hear about your hives. And second, if most of what you have to say every day comes off as whiny background elevator Muzak, you have bigger problems than those hives, believe me.

Does your commute suck? Too bad. Are you behind on your TPSs? Too bad. Is your cubicle too small? Don't want to hear it. It doesn't matter if you're a company all-star, complaining will bring you down.

Complaining about anything at work should be a last resort, a

TRUE STORY

Roberta was a midlevel manager in a small communications company. She was known to be extremely skilled at her job but also to be a regular fusspot about various conditions around the office that she considered to be of environmental concern. She was particularly agitated by the existence of overhead fluorescent lighting and complained regularly to her boss and at general staff meetings about how bad the light was for everyone. Her colleagues just ignored her until she began switching off the overhead lights nearest her workspace and using a desk lamp instead. This made her feel better but pretty much left her colleagues in the dark. The next item on her office activist agenda was the egregious use of nonorganic products by the cleaning service. When she dashed off a memo about it to the CEO, her boss made a mental note to meet with her about her annoying green "issues." But there was no need to. Two weeks later, he got word from Corporate that he'd have to cut 4 percent of his staff, and without a second thought, Roberta's name went to the top of his list.

yellow flag you throw on the field just before you call the EPA about the cancer-causing asbestos you're inhaling through the air duct over your desk. That's because to your boss or your coworkers, there's no difference between you sending peevish e-mails to HR about your less-than-ergonomic chair and blowing the whistle to the feds on your Fortune 100 company—it's all a pain in the ass, and it makes things worse for everyone.

If you have a *real* issue that needs resolving—say, a mysterious deduction that keeps appearing on your pay stub—then resolve it without complaining. Present your problem to the appropriate person as a well-informed matter of fact, not a complaint. Pro-

ASK YOURSELF:

▶ Am I being emotional, confrontational, or petty when I complain?

▶ Am I complaining about something in the past?

▶ Am I complaining about something that has a solution?

▶ Do I know what my manager should do before I present him with a problem?

▶ Will my manager look good as a result of resolving my problem?

vide any and all backup information or other assistance to help the other person solve your problem. If you know exactly how the problem can be solved, spell it out. If you make it easy—and pleasant—for people to help you, they're generally inclined to do so. In many of these cases, those friends you've strategically cultivated around the company can come in mighty handy.

Your extraneous gripes also contribute on a larger scale to a general culture of complaining in your workplace that is a plague on morale. And the minute your superiors have an excuse (ahem, downsizing) to get rid of the plague, they will.

The chronic complainer is like a cat that takes a swipe at you every time you walk by; at first you ignore it, then you avoid it, then you give the little kitty away. Terminated! So next time you want to complain about the temperature in the office, put on a sweater and shut up.

▶▶▶ *Resist the urge to gripe and moan.*
▶▶▶ *Find ways to resolve your issues without complaining.*

16. WATCH YOUR MOUTH

You know what? Your mother was right. If you can't say some-thing nice, don't say anything at all. This is doubly true at work and triply true when the job climate is dicey. Someone who doesn't know enough to temper his words when interacting with his colleagues isn't worth hanging on to when hard person-nel choices are being made. In fact, managers are often relieved at the chance to unload unpleasant creeps and blame it on layoffs.

Bullying, ridicule, derision, condescension, and sarcasm have no place at work. No matter how incompetent or stupid or dull you think a coworker might be, pointing it out to him, whether in private or in front of others, is inappropriate and wrong. This kind of behavior will peg you as neon-nuclear toxic, and I guar-antee that your colleagues will avoid you and your managers will look for a way to separate you from the herd.

Unfortunately, most people who fall into this category are un-aware of what reprehensible boors they are. If you answer "yes" to any of the questions below (bad news), your job isn't even close to being bulletproof and (good news) you're an excellent candidate for Jungian deconstruction.

▶ Have you ever made someone at work cry?
▶ Has anyone ever quit his job after an exchange with you?
▶ Do you regularly curse or use harsh words in conversation with coworkers?
▶ Do you consider yourself the only competent person in your office, including your boss, his boss, and the CEO?
▶ Do people confront you with problems or criticism in pairs or groups (safety in numbers) rather than one-on-one?

JUST SO YOU KNOW

By now in your work life you must have experienced at least one occasion where the tone or content of an e-mail you sent or received caused an unintended rift between you and the person on the other end. E-mail is a wonder, and people communicate more and better because of it, no doubt. But the fact that it lacks the nuances of face-to-face communication can give an innocent message the effect of a Molotov cocktail. That's why I try to keep e-mail friendly—smileys and LOLs abound, in my case—but I don't try to be funny or convey anger. There are too many ways for that to go wrong, and it's completely unnecessary. That's also why I make a point of using my BlackBerry to receive messages only and to answer messages when I'm back at my office using my computer. If the message I need to send isn't "See you in front of the restaurant at 7:30," it's safer to compose a literate, measured, effective response at my desk.

Even if you're not the office Godzilla, dropping F-bombs all over the place, you may still have problems. People who regularly aim garden-variety disses, joking insults, trash-talking banter, and left-handed compliments at their coworkers come off over the long term as smart alecks and punks—not feared so much as barely tolerated, and certainly not a sentimental favorite come pink slip season. Grandstanders and loud-mouthed braggarts are equally vulnerable.

So how can you make sure your mouth doesn't get you into a world of trouble at work?

▶ Choose your words carefully. Don't use negative or disparaging terms in conversation with colleagues—or *about* colleagues when speaking with your boss. Lead with a positive remark, even